ALWD

COMPANION

ASPEN PUBLISHERS

A L W D

C O M P A N I O N

A CITATION PRACTICE BOOK

Association of Legal Writing Directors
and
Coleen M. Barger
University of Arkansas at Little Rock
William H. Bowen School of Law

Brooke J. Bowman
Stetson University
College of Law

Wolters Kluwer

Law & Business

AUSTIN   BOSTON   CHICAGO   NEW YORK   THE NETHERLANDS

Aspen Publishers
Attn: Permissions Department
76 Ninth Avenue, 7th Floor
New York, NY 10011-5201

To contact Customer Care, e-mail customer.service@aspenpublishers.com,
call 1-800-234-1660, fax 1-800-901-9075, or mail correspondence to:

Aspen Publishers
Attn: Order Department
PO Box 990
Frederick, MD 21705

Printed in the United States of America.

1 2 3 4 5 6 7 8 9 0

ISBN 978-0-7355-8929-2

Library of Congress Cataloging-in-Publication Data

ALWD companion : a citation practice book / Association of Legal Writing
Directors and Coleen M. Barger.
    p. cm.
  Includes bibliographical references and index.
  ISBN 978-0-7355-8929-2
  1. Citation of legal authorities—United States. 2. Annotations and citations
(Law)—United States. I. Barger, Coleen M., 1951- II. Association of Legal
Writing Directors.

  KF245.A454 2010
  808'.027—dc22

                              2010026836

About Wolters Kluwer Law & Business

Wolters Kluwer Law & Business is a leading provider of research information and workflow solutions in key specialty areas. The strengths of the individual brands of Aspen Publishers, CCH, Kluwer Law International and Loislaw are aligned within Wolters Kluwer Law & Business to provide comprehensive, in-depth solutions and expert-authored content for the legal, professional and education markets.

CCH was founded in 1913 and has served more than four generations of business professionals and their clients. The CCH products in the Wolters Kluwer Law & Business group are highly regarded electronic and print resources for legal, securities, antitrust and trade regulation, government contracting, banking, pension, payroll, employment and labor, and healthcare reimbursement and compliance professionals.

Aspen Publishers is a leading information provider for attorneys, business professionals and law students. Written by preeminent authorities, Aspen products offer analytical and practical information in a range of specialty practice areas from securities law and intellectual property to mergers and acquisitions and pension/benefits. Aspen's trusted legal education resources provide professors and students with high-quality, up-to-date and effective resources for successful instruction and study in all areas of the law.

Kluwer Law International supplies the global business community with comprehensive English-language international legal information. Legal practitioners, corporate counsel and business executives around the world rely on the Kluwer Law International journals, loose-leafs, books and electronic products for authoritative information in many areas of international legal practice.

Loislaw is a premier provider of digitized legal content to small law firm practitioners of various specializations. Loislaw provides attorneys with the ability to quickly and efficiently find the necessary legal information they need, when and where they need it, by facilitating access to primary law as well as state-specific law, records, forms and treatises.

Wolters Kluwer Law & Business, a unit of Wolters Kluwer, is headquartered in New York and Riverwoods, Illinois. Wolters Kluwer is a leading multinational publisher and information services company.

Summary

# of Contents

CONTENTS

PART 2   CITING SPECIFIC SOURCES OF PRIMARY LAW

PART 3   **CITING SECONDARY SOURCES AND PRACTICE MATERIALS**

CHAPTER 9. BOOKS, TREATISES, AND LOOSELEAFS   199

CHAPTER 10. LEGAL PERIODICALS   229

PART 4   ALTERNATE FORMATS

About
the Authors

The Association of Legal Writing Directors is a learned society for professors who coordinate legal writing instruction in legal education. ALWD members teach at nearly all American law schools. ALWD is headquartered at the University of Michigan Law School, 625 South State Street, Ann Arbor, MI 48109-1215.

Coleen M. Barger is Professor of Law at the University of Arkansas at Little Rock William H. Bowen School of Law, where she has taught legal writing, legal research, and appellate advocacy courses since 1992. She is a co-founder and Developments Editor of the *Journal of Appellate Practice and Process*, a faculty-edited law journal that has followed *ALWD Citation Manual* format since 2000. Professor Barger is also the author of *Arkansas Legal Research* (Carolina Academic Press 2007) and a co-editor of *Legal Writing Prof Blog*, http://lawprofessors.typepad.com/legalwriting/. She has served on the boards of both the Association of Legal Writing Directors and the Legal Writing Institute.

Brooke J. Bowman is Professor of Legal Skills at Stetson University College of Law, where she teaches Research and Writing I and II, Advanced Legal Research, and Legal Drafting classes and Polishing for Professionals workshop, as well as serving as a Moot Court advisor and coordinating the Scholarly Writing Series. In addition to her J.D. degree, Professor Bowman holds a master's degree in Library and Information Science. She just completed a second term as the Managing Editor for *Legal Writing: The Journal of the Legal Writing Institute* and is starting a term as the journal's Assistant Editor in Chief.

ACKNOWLEDGMENTS

We thank the ALWD officers and directors who envisioned this project, invited us to join it, and gave unwavering support to our efforts—in particular Terrill Pollman, Judith Stinson, and Mary Beth Beazley.

Special thanks go to Dean Darby Dickerson of Stetson University College of Law, not only for the *ALWD Citation Manual* itself, but also for her generosity and willingness to answer our questions.

Coleen thanks the faculty and Dean John DiPippa of the UALR Bowen School of Law for the law school's generous financial and collegial support. Brooke thanks Stetson University College of Law for providing support and resources to complete this project.

We are also grateful for the enthusiasm and support of our friends at Aspen Publishers, including Carol McGeehan, George Serafin, John Chatelaine, Barbara Roth, and Troy Froebe. And we are especially indebted to an outstanding group of legal writing and research teachers, the anonymous reviewers who read our first drafts and offered detailed and helpful feedback, ideas, and encouragement.

Thanks go to Professors David Cleveland, Lawrence M. Friedman, and Suzanne Rowe, the text of whose writings formed the basis for a number of the exercises in the *Companion*, and to Professor Kristin Gerdy, editor in chief of *Legal Writing: The Journal of the Legal Writing Institute*, for use of a portion of the Table of Contents from a recent volume of *Legal Writing*. We also thank our LRW colleagues across the nation for their publications that provided a wealth of resources to use when compiling the exercises in the chapters on secondary sources.

We would also like to acknowledge and thank the following publishers who granted permission to reproduce the following materials for this book:

The American Law Institute for section 2.09 of the Model Penal Code and section 520, comment (e) from the *Restatement (Second) of Torts*.

LexisNexis, a division of Reed Elsevier Inc., for captions and titles from the following LEXIS databases: Cal. AG LEXIS; Conn. App. LEXIS; Ga. App. LEXIS; Me. LEXIS; Mont. LEXIS; N.D. LEXIS; Ohio App. LEXIS; Pa. LEXIS; Tex. LEXIS; U.S. LEXIS; U.S. App. LEXIS; U.S. Dist. LEXIS; Va. App. LEXIS; Wyo. LEXIS; selected excerpts from Nevada Revised Statutes Annotated on LexisNexis, and symbols and selected results from Shepard's.

Thomson Reuters for case captions/titles from Westlaw or West Reporters, selected excerpts from West's Smith-Hurd Illinois Compiled Statutes Annotated, Michigan Compiled Laws Annotated, and the Code of Federal Regulations on Westlaw, and selected excerpts of cases and KeyCite results from Westlaw or West Reporters, selected excerpts from West Digests, and selected excerpts from American Law Reports 3d and American Law Reports Federal 2d.

INTRODUCTION

When you were a college student, you probably learned to use citations in preparing papers and bibliographies, demonstrating to your professors that you had done the necessary amount of research that the assignment demanded, and giving credit to those authors whose ideas and language you borrowed or quoted. Depending on the discipline you were studying, your papers likely followed MLA (Modern Language Association),[1] APA (American Psychological Association),[2] Turabian,[3] or another standard citation style. Whatever the citation style the discipline follows, it develops a kind of shorthand or code that its practitioners recognize and emulate when they cite the sources upon which their writing relies.

It should come as no surprise, then, to learn that the legal community has its own expectations and conventions for citing sources used in legal documents. What you may not realize, however, is the amount of information a legal citation conveys to its reader, nor may you appreciate the inherent skepticism that legal readers bring to their professional reading, due in no small measure to the adversarial nature of the American legal system.

Just as they did in your undergraduate writing, citations in your legal writing reflect the extent of your research; they also demonstrate your careful work to avoid plagiarism by providing attribution to the work of others. But as Part 1, Section A of the *ALWD Citation Manual* explains, citations perform other important functions in legal writing. Citations tell readers where they may locate the cited sources, whether in print or electronic formats; they contain important clues for assessing how authoritative those sources are; and they indicate the level of support the sources provide for an author's propositions.

Being careful to construct your citations correctly will pay off in many ways. For one thing, the office memoranda and briefs you write as a beginning law student may earn higher grades, insofar as those grades reflect an assessment of citation format. Furthermore, as you progress in your legal education, you will discover that mastery of legal citation format is one of the high expectations for students engaged in scholarly writing, such as seminar papers or case notes, or in law review editing. And as you begin your legal career, working as a law clerk or new associate, you will find that supervising attorneys and judges will be more inclined to trust, and be persuaded by, the research and reasoning of those whose attention to detail in citations reflects the writer's mastery of citation rules.

The *ALWD Companion* will assist you not only in learning the building blocks for citing the most common sources used in legal writing, but also in mastering many of the more

---

[1] *MLA Handbook for Writers of Research Papers* (7th ed., Modern Lang. Assn. 2009).
[2] *Publication Manual of the American Psychological Association* (6th ed., Am. Psychol. Assn. 2009).
[3] Kate L. Turabian, *A Manual for Writers of Term Papers, Theses, and Dissertations* (Wayne C. Booth et al. eds., 7th ed., U. Chi. Press 2007).

sophisticated citation practices of legal writing. Although the *Manual* contains excellent explanations of the citation components for each source, it does not provide a way for you to learn and practice citation skills. That is the purpose of the *Companion*.

The exercises in this book progress from basic to intermediate to expert levels. The exercises cover primary sources, including federal and state constitutions, statutes, cases, and administrative law. They also cover commonly used secondary sources, with heavy emphasis on law reviews and treatises; procedural and court rules; and court documents. All exercises are designed to present you with citations in context. They are drawn from a variety of print and online sources of the law and legal commentary (e.g., captions in print reporters, LexisNexis, and Westlaw; West digests; annotations; judicial opinions; law review articles).

Exercises at the basic level, primarily presented as multiple-choice questions, help you learn the fundamental components of the most common legal sources. Intermediate- and expert-level exercises emphasize use of the *Manual* as a reference work for locating rules and examples for less commonly used sources such as state and federal legislation; ethics and attorney general opinions; executive orders; looseleafs; interviews; recordings; scholarly working papers; Web sites; and email. Exercises at the intermediate level develop your experience with these sources, through multiple-choice and short-answer exercises. At the expert level, you will construct citations on your own. The book also provides capstone exercises for you to assess your mastery of fundamental citation skills, and to the extent practicable, they have been set in the context of written documents. In other words, you will work with citations within the kinds of documents that lawyers typically produce.

Each exercise begins with references to particular rules or other relevant sections of the *Manual*. Read these rules or sections prior to beginning each exercise, and consult them as you work through the exercise. By regularly consulting the *Manual* as you do the exercises, you will become familiar with its contents and its helpful examples. That familiarity will be an important asset to you as you begin to construct citations in your own legal writing.

ALWD

COMPANION

THE WAY CITATIONS WORK

Part 1 provides exercises covering the fundamental components of legal citations, from identifying legal citations and the type of information presented in the citations, to working with the rules in the *ALWD Citation Manual* that are applicable to all citations, to incorporating citations within a document, to providing citations for and formatting quotations. As you work through the exercises in Part 1, you will be introduced to many of the helpful features of the *ALWD Citation Manual* and some of the rules that are used with all citations.

CHAPTER 1

BUILDING CITATIONS

What is a legal citation?
What purposes do legal citations serve?
What are the general attributes or characteristics of legal citations?

As you begin to learn about legal citations, these are just three of the questions you will ask. The goal of this chapter is not only to answer these three questions, but also to build a bridge between the citations you learned about and used in your undergraduate papers and the citations you will learn about and use in your legal documents.

Let's start with the first question on the list: **What is a legal citation?** The answer to this will help you understand the purposes for legal citation and the different attributes or characteristics of legal citations. Generally, a legal citation is a reference

> to a specific legal authority or other source. A legal citation contains various words, abbreviations, and numbers presented in a specific format that allows a reader to locate the cited material.[1]

Basically, a citation is a location code. It helps the reader find the source illustrated by the citation, and it also helps the reader find the referenced information *within* the source.

As we discussed in the Introduction to this *Companion*, you have been exposed to citations at some point in your undergraduate career. But actually, your exposure to citations probably occurred long before that—before you learned about the MLA, APA, Turabian, or other citation style. For example, you have provided citations to your mother for years when you answered a question with the comment, "Because my mother said so." Or while reading a newspaper article, if you read a statement such as, "According to a Gallup poll, 60% of

---

[1] ALWD & Darby Dickerson, *ALWD Citation Manual* 3 (4th ed., Aspen Publishers 2010).

Americans feel that . . . ." Whether you were aware of it at the time or not, you were reading a citation to a Gallup poll. Consider this example:

- "Nearly 10.7 million households had negative equity in their homes in the third quarter, according to First American CoreLogic, a real-estate information company based in Santa Ana, Calif."[2]

This example includes a citation as well. The author is citing the First American CoreLogic.

Comparing these three examples with the citations you provided in papers you wrote in undergrad, you probably remember providing much more information in your citations. For example, when we look at the endnotes from an article published in the *Journal of Forensic and Legal Medicine*,[3] we can see how much more information the citations provide.

What type of additional information does the reader need? Let's examine the endnote citations in the box. Endnote 1 displays several types of information, such as the names of the authors of an article— Choudhry NK, Fletcher RH, and Soumerai SB—and its title, *Systematic Review: The Relationship between Clinical Experience and Quality of Health Care.*

The information that follows is a little more difficult to decipher because it consists of an abbreviation and a series of numbers; basically, the information is

> 1. Choudhry NK, Fletcher RH, Soumerai SB. Systematic review: the relationship between clinical experience and quality of health care. *Am Int Med* 2005; 142:260–73.
> 2. Sutherland K, Leatherman S. Does certification improve medical standards? *BMJ* 2006;333:439–41.
> 3. MORI attitudes to medical regulation and revalidation of doctors DOH; 2005.

presented as a "code." Each discipline has its own citation style or "code," and one of the goals of this *Companion* is to assist you in learning the legal citation "code." Even though the "codes" vary among disciplines, much of the information that is provided in the citation "code" is common sense, once you learn the different types of information that you should expect to see.

Even without knowing the particular code used in these citations, we can guess what type of information is provided next in endnote 1's citation. After the title is an abbreviation, *Ann Int Med*. We can guess that the abbreviation *Ann Int Med* is an abbreviation for a medical journal. It is! The medical journal is the *Annals of Internal Medicine*. After the journal abbreviation, the next piece of information is "2005." That information is easily recognizable; it is the year the article was published. And the final information in the citation is 142:260–73. We can guess the numbers 260–73 are the pages of the journal on which the article will be found. And the number 142? That is the volume number of the journal.

As explained in Part 1, Section A of the *ALWD Citation Manual*, most citations contain the following information: the author, title of the source, page numbers, a publisher, and the date of publication. Do not worry if you were not able to identify the different pieces of information that appeared in the endnotes in the text box provided above. This skill will come with practice. The goal is that even though these citations contain more information than the simple examples introduced initially, you expected to find certain types of information in the citation—like the author(s), title, page numbers, etc.

---

[2] Ruth Simon & James R. Hagerty, *1 in 4 Borrowers under Water*, 254 Wall St. J. A1 (Nov. 24, 2009).
[3] P.G. Green, *The Challenge of Recertification*, 16 J. Forensic & Leg. Med. 48, 50 (2009).

American Bar Association
Commission on Law and Aging &
American Psychological Associa-
tion (2005). *Assessment of older
adults with diminished capacity:
A handbook for lawyers.*
Washington, DC. American Bar
Association and American
Psychological Association.

ABA Commn. on L. & Aging &
Am. Psychol. Assn., *Assessment of
Older Adults with Diminished
Capacity: A Handbook for
Lawyers* 5 (ABA & Am. Psychol.
Assn. 2005).

The primary difference between the citations that you used in undergrad and legal citations is the way the information is presented. The same types of information are generally included in both citation styles, but the presentation of the information is different. Let's compare two citation styles shown in the box. The citations are for the same source, but the first citation is in APA style and the second citation is in *ALWD Manual* style.

The same type of information is presented in both citations, such as the author (American Bar Association Commission on Law and Aging and the American Psychological Association), the title (*Assessment of Older Adults with Diminished Capacity: A Handbook for Lawyers*), the publisher (the American Bar Association and the American Psychological Association), and the year of publication (2005). But each discipline has its own "code" or format for the citation. The information is presented in a certain way and presented in a certain order. The "codes" are different.

The codes or citations contain the information that is needed to help the reader find the source in the library or online. Yes, the reader could probably find a source such as a book given only the book's author or title, but one of the goals of citation is that the citation provides *sufficient* information to lead the reader to the book referred to in the citation and only to that book. In addition, you will also want to include a "pinpoint reference"—the location of the specific information within the book. Why provide a pinpoint reference? You don't want the reader to read an entire book (or an entire law review article, case, etc.) to find the information that is "referenced" in the citation. The goal of the citation is to lead the reader directly to the specific source *and* the specific information discussed *within* that source.

Let's discuss the second question from the beginning of this chapter: **What purposes do citations serve?** The primary purpose of citation is to provide proper attribution, i.e., crediting the creator of the ideas and his or her expression with authorship. Proper attribution is the *only* way to prevent plagiarism, and it is an attorney's ethical responsibility to provide proper attribution. Plagiarism is defined as "the practice of taking someone else's work or ideas and passing them off as one's own."[4] How does citation prevent plagiarism? When determining whether a citation is needed in a particular instance, ask yourself two questions: (1) Where did the information come from? (2) Whose words are you using?

In reference to the first question, if the information came from a particular source or group of sources, you need a citation. The citation tells the reader that the information was not your own original thought and where the information can be found. You will find that given the nature of the law, there are a lot of citations in legal documents.

In reference to the second question—whose words are you using?—if you are paraphrasing the information you found in a particular source, you just need a citation. However, if you are quoting the language of the source, you must indicate that the language is "borrowed" or "copied." Do this by putting the language of the source in quotation marks (or for a longer quotation, presenting the language in a block quotation).

Besides preventing plagiarism, citations serve a number of other purposes. By looking at a citation, the reader can tell the weight and persuasiveness of the source, the type and degree of support the source provides to the writer's proposition, the currency of the source, and the validity of the source. First, the weight and persuasiveness of the source: By looking at the

---

[4] *The New Oxford American Dictionary* 1304 (Elizabeth J. Jewel & Frank Abate eds., Oxford U. Press 2001).

citation, a reader can learn whether the source is a primary source (or the law—constitutions, statutes, cases, and administrative regulations) or a secondary source (a source that is not the law, but provides interpretation, explanation, or commentary on the law, such as a law review article). In addition, a reader can learn whether the primary authority is binding (for example, the constitution, statutes, and regulations in force in a particular jurisdiction are binding on the courts within that jurisdiction, and decisions from higher courts are binding on the lower courts in that jursisdiction) or persuasive (for example, cases from another jurisdiction or from lower court within the same jurisdiction). No secondary source is binding.

Let's look at an example of how citations serve a weight and persuasiveness function. Suppose that you are writing an appellate brief to Florida's Second District Court of Appeal (an intermediate appellate court in the state court system), and you have composed the string citation shown in the box. (A string citation is one in which more than one source supports a particular proposition.) You can determine the weight and persuasiveness of the sources from reviewing the information in the citation.

> *Pinellas Park v. Brown*, 604 So. 2d 1222, 1224 (Fla. 1992); *see generally* J. Douglas Drushal, *Consumer Protection and Higher Education—Student Suits Against Schools*, 37 Ohio St. L.J. 608, 615 (1976).

The first citation is to a case, a primary source. A reader knows whether this case is binding or persuasive by looking at the abbreviation for the court that decided the case. This information can be found in the parenthetical at the end of the full citation. In this instance, the abbreviation is "Fla.," which represents the Florida Supreme Court. The Florida Supreme Court is the highest court in the Florida court system; therefore, this case is binding because the appellate brief is being written for an intermediate appellate court, which is a court lower than the Florida Supreme Court. And the second citation is to a law review article (the reader can tell from looking at the abbreviation, Ohio St. L.J., which is the "code" for the *Ohio State Law Journal*). Secondary sources are always persuasive.

Another purpose for citations is to indicate the type and degree of support the cited source gives the stated proposition. Signals provide that type of information. Rule 44.3 sets out many different types of signals—*see, accord, see also, cf., see generally*, for example. Place a signal before the citation when it does not directly support the proposition discussed. (If there is no signal before a citation, the citation directly supports the proposition.) The phrase "*see generally*" in front of the citation to the law review article in the citation above is an example of a signal.

The reader can also see the currency of the sources by looking at the dates of publication. For example, the case was decided sixteen years after the law review article was published. And the reader can determine the validity of the sources from looking at the citation. For example, if the case citation includes subsequent history with terms such as *overruled* or *vacated*, the reader should question the validity of the case, given what has happened after the case was decided.

And finally, let's address the third question from the beginning of this chapter: **What are the general attributes or characteristics of legal citations?** Legal citations have several common attributes or characteristics.[5] Four significant characteristics are *code, uniqueness, tradition,* and *readability*:

- **Code**:[6] Each citation style has a "code" for each source. The code provides all the information in a concise manner, as demonstrated by the use of abbreviations in the examples above. Each piece of information in a citation serves a specific purpose, and each citation as a whole provides all the necessary information for the reader to find the source.

---

[5] Paul Axel-Lute, *Legal Citation Form: Theory and Practice*, 75 L. Libr. J. 148 (1982).
[6] *Id.* at 148–149.

- **Uniqueness:**[7] As discussed earlier, each discipline has its own citation style, but within a discipline's citation style, the codes for the different sources are unique. For example, the citation to a law review article is different from the citation to a case; the codes for the two sources are not identical. There are some common features to the different codes within a particular discipline, but the presentation of the information for that particular source is unique to that source, which helps the reader differentiate between the citation codes for different sources.
- **Tradition:**[8] The unique characteristics of legal citations have a long history. In the law, the citation format that you will become familiar with has been around for a long time, and the general types of information—author, title, pinpoint reference, publisher, and year of publication—have not really changed.
- **Readability:**[9] Legal readers expect citations to contain certain information. This information is presented in a certain order and in a certain format. This is one of the fundamental goals of this *Companion*—to assist you in learning, first, how to identify and read legal citations, and second, to understand the types of information a citation contains.

The goals of the exercises that follow are to (1) assist you in identifying citations and the different purposes that citations serve; and (2) introduce you to the *Manual* and its helpful features.

EXERCISE SET 1-A

ALL LEVELS: IDENTIFYING LEGAL CITATIONS

Instructions: The purpose of this exercise is to help you identify legal citations. Two selections are provided below. The first selection is from a case,[10] and the second selection is from a law review article.[11] Review the two selections and identify citations by underlining, circling, or highlighting them. The citations in these two selections will be used in completing Exercise Set 1-B.

Selection 1:

One of the limited exceptions to the warrant requirement and, indeed, to the requirement of probable cause, is voluntary consent to the search. *Schneckloth v. Bustamonte*, 412 U.S. 218, 219, 222 (1973); *People v. Singleteary*, 324 N.E.2d 103, 105 (N.Y. 1974); *People v. Carter*, 283 N.E.2d 746, 746–747 (N.Y. 1972); *People v. Pelow*, 247 N.E.2d 150, 151 (N.Y. 1969); *Loria*, 179 N.E.2d at 482; *cf. People v. Lane*, 179 N.E.2d 339, 340 (N.Y. 1961). In the instant case, the People concede that the legality of the search of the Gonzalez apartments turns entirely upon the validity of either of the Gonzalez[es]' consents. (Indeed, the agents by obtaining and relying on the signed consents indicated unequivocally that they recognized the doubtfulness of a right to a rummage search without a warrant. *Cf. Clements*, 339 N.E.2d at 172. Of course, the People also recognize that theirs is the heavy burden of proving the voluntariness of the purported consents. *See Bumper v. N.C.*, 391 U.S. 543, 548–549 (1968); *People v. Kuhn*, 306 N.E.2d 777, 780 (N.Y. 1973); *Whitehurst*, 254 N.E.2d at 906; *Jackson*, 360 N.Y.S.2d at 518; *Stepps*, 296 N.Y.S.2d at 731.

---

[7] *Id.* at 148.
[8] *Id.* at 149.
[9] *Id.*
[10] *People v. Gonzalez*, 347 N.E.2d 575, 579–580 (N.Y. 1976) (We have edited the citations within this exercise.).
[11] Suzanne E. Rowe, *Reasonable Accommodations for Unreasonable Requests: The Americans with Disabilities Act in Legal Writing Courses*, 12 Leg. Writing 3 (2006).

Selection 2:[12]

---

4   *The Journal of the Legal Writing Institute*   [Vol. 12

with learning disabilities.[4] If these students receive accommodations that do more than level the playing field,[5] they may graduate without developing essential skills in legal analysis, organization, writing, research, oral communication, and citation, and will be, as a result, unable to practice law successfully.[6]

By enacting the ADA,[7] Congress recognized that millions of persons[8] have physical and mental disabilities[9] and society's his-

---

[4] Regulations promulgated under the ADA refer to "specific learning disabilities" as impairments that may need accommodation. *See e.g.* 28 C.F.R. § 35.104 (2006). For background on law students with learning disabilities, see Susan Johanne Adams, *Leveling the Floor: Classroom Accommodations for Law Students with Disabilities*, 48 J. Leg. Educ. 273 (1998); Lisa Eichhorn, *Reasonable Accommodations and Awkward Compromises: Issues Concerning Learning Disabled Students and Professional Schools in the Law School Context*, 26 J.L. & Educ. 31 (1997); Tracey I. Levy, *Legal Obligations and Workplace Implications for Institutions of Higher Education Accommodating Learning Disabled Students*, 30 J.L. & Educ. 85 (2001); and M. Kay Runyan & Joseph F. Smith, Jr., *Identifying and Accommodating Learning Disabled Law School Students*, 41 J. Leg. Educ. 317 (1991). For a useful summary of key cases, *see* Richard E. Kaye, *What Constitutes Reasonable Accommodation under Federal Statutes Protecting Rights of Disabled Individual, as Regards Educational Program or School Rules as Applied to Learning Disabled Student*, 166 A.L.R. Fed. 503 (2000). For an overview of ADA issues in higher education law, see Laura F. Rothstein, *Disability Issues in Legal Education: A Symposium*, 41 J. Leg. Educ. 301 (1991).

[5] An assistant dean with visual disabilities stated that members of the disabled community favor strict application of the ADA. They want the ADA only to level the playing field for those with true disabilities, enabling them to be evaluated and to succeed on the same basis as all others. *See* Ludwick at AALS, *supra* n. 2; *see also* G.R. Overton, *Accommodation of Disabled Persons*, B. Examr. 6, 8 (Feb. 1991) (stating that "few disabled persons will seek an advantage by requesting more than they need"); *but see* Eichhorn, *supra* n. 4, at 36 (quoting a dean who suggested that students who are "'more desperate than they are disabled'" may take advantage of the broad definition of learning disabilities to seek excessive accommodations).

[6] *See* ABA Sec. Leg. Educ. & Admis. to B., *Legal Education and Professional Development: An Educational Continuum, Report of the Task Force on Law Schools and the Profession: Narrowing the Gap* (ABA 1992) [hereinafter *MacCrate Report*] (listing fundamental skills of lawyers, including written and oral communication); Bryant G. Garth & Joanne Martin, *Law Schools and the Construction of Competence*, 43 J. Leg. Educ. 469 (1993). The Garth and Martin article analyzes the results of a survey of hiring partners in Chicago and new associates in Chicago, Springfield, and smaller Missouri communities. The survey showed that written and oral communication skills were the most important, ranking above legal analysis and reasoning. Garth & Martin, *supra* n. 6, at 474.

[7] The Act was effective as of July 26, 1992. Pub. L. No. 101-336, 104 Stat. 327 (1990).

[8] The Act is not limited to United States citizens. *See* 42 U.S.C. § 12111(4) (providing non-exclusive definition for "employee" as an "individual employed by an employer"); *see also Torrico v. Intl. Bus. Machs. Corp.*, 213 F. Supp. 2d 390, 403 (S.D.N.Y. 2002) (stating "an employer cannot evade the application of the antidiscrimination laws to U.S.-based non-citizen employees by sending them to temporary duty outside the United States").

---

[12] This is just part of one page of a law review article. Do not worry that the selection starts with an incomplete sentence. Focus on the citations in the selection.

EXERCISE SET 1-B

ALL LEVELS: IDENTIFYING OTHER PURPOSES

Before beginning Exercise Set 1-B All Levels, review the following and keep the *Manual* at hand as you work through the exercise:

• Part A, "Purpose and Use of Citations," in the Introductory Material, page 3

Instructions: Using the selections in Exercise Set 1-A above and the citations you identified in those selections, answer the following questions.

1-B.1. Look at the citations you identified in selection 1 in Exercise Set 1-A. What type of authority is referred to in the citations?

a. Primary authority
b. Secondary authority
c. Both primary and secondary authority

1-B.2. Look at the citations you identified in selection 2 in Exercise Set 1-A. The sources listed here are just a few of the sources referred to in the footnotes. Identify the type of authority each source represents by circling "primary" or "secondary."

1-B.2.a. C.F.R. (or the Code of Federal Regulations)
Primary   Secondary

1-B.2.b. J. Leg. Educ. (or the *Journal of Legal Education*)
Primary   Secondary

1-B.2.c. A.L.R. Fed. (or the American Law Reports, Federal Series)
Primary   Secondary

1-B.2.d. U.S.C. (or the United States Code)
Primary   Secondary

1-B.2.e. F. Supp. 2d (or the Federal Supplement, Second Series)
Primary   Secondary

1-B.3. Look at the citations you identified in selection 2 in Exercise Set 1-A. Not all the sources referenced in the citations directly support the propositions in the text of the article. Which of the following signals are used in selection 2? Mark all that apply.

a. *see generally*
b. *cf.*
c. *but see*
d. *contra*

1-B.4. Look at the citations you identified in selection 2 in Exercise Set 1-A. In footnote 4, the author cites the C.F.R. (Code of Federal Regulations, a primary source). In what year was the regulation published?

    a. 2000
    b. 2001
    c. 2002
    d. 2006

1-B.5. Look at the citations you identified in selection 2 in Exercise Set 1-A. In what year was the oldest secondary source published?

    a. 1990
    b. 1991
    c. 1992
    d. 1993

EXERCISE SET 1-C

ALL LEVELS: *ALWD CITATION MANUAL*—A HELPFUL REFERENCE TOOL

Before beginning Exercise Set 1-C All Levels, review the following and keep the *Manual* at hand as you work through the exercises:

• Part B, "How to Use This Book," in the Introductory Material, pages 4–7

To complete the exercises, you may also need to refer to the following:

• *Manual*'s Table of Contents
• *Manual*'s Index

Instructions: In using the Table of Contents and the Index to answer the questions, you will be introduced to a number of helpful features in the *Manual*, including the Fast Formats ("which provide[ ] sample citations for the commonly cited materials within that category" or rule governing the major sources[13]) and the Sidebars (which "provide additional information on various concepts, caveats about common mistakes, and tips for citing particular sources"[14]).

1-C.1. Turn to the Table of Contents. Which part of the *Manual* contains the rules for citing primary sources in print?

    a. Part 1
    b. Part 2
    c. Part 3
    d. Part 4

---

[13] ALWD & Dickerson, *supra* n. 1, at 5–6.
[14] *Id.* at 6.

1-C.2. According to the Table of Contents, which part of the *Manual* contains the rules for citing secondary authority in print?

    a. Part 2
    b. Part 3
    c. Part 4
    d. Part 5

1-C.3. According to the Table of Contents, which part of the *Manual* contains the rules for formatting quotations?

    a. Part 3
    b. Part 4
    c. Part 5
    d. Part 6

1-C.4. In the selection from the law review article in Exercise Set 1-A above, a number of the citations were from a journal abbreviated J. Leg. Educ., but there were also citations to a journal abbreviated J.L. & Educ. Using the Index, choose the appendix that will help you determine what the abbreviation J.L. & Educ. stands for.

    a. Appendix 5
    b. Appendix 4
    c. Appendix 2
    d. Appendix 1

1-C.5. When you cite a case, your citation must include an abbreviation for the court that decided it. Using the Index, choose the appendix that lists the court abbreviations for all the state and federal courts.

    a. Appendix 1
    b. Appendix 2
    c. Appendix 3
    d. Appendix 4

1-C.6. In the selection from the law review article in Exercise Set 1-A above, a case citation in one of the footnotes used the reporter abbreviation "F. Supp. 2d." Using the Index, choose the chart that contains a list of the common reporter abbreviations.

    a. Chart 12.1
    b. Chart 12.2
    c. Chart 24.1
    d. Chart 26.1

1-C.7. A helpful secondary source for providing a general overview on a topic is a legal encyclopedia. Using the Index, choose the chart that contains a list of encyclopedia abbreviations.

    a. Chart 12.1
    b. Chart 12.2
    c. Chart 24.1
    d. Chart 26.1

1-C.8. This chapter discusses the importance of not only providing information about the source generally, but also indicating where within the source the specific information can be found ("pinpoint pages"). According to the Index, which of the Sidebars listed below discusses the importance of using pinpoint citations?

a. Sidebar 3.1
b. Sidebar 5.1
c. Sidebar 5.2
d. Sidebar 6.1

1-C.9. Cases are one of the first primary sources you learn about in law school. On what page of the *Manual* will you find the Fast Formats for cases?

a. Page 69
b. Page 119
c. Page 123
d. Page 139

1-C.10. Another helpful source is a legal dictionary. On what page of the *Manual* will you find the Fast Formats for dictionaries?

a. Page 222
b. Page 237
c. Page 254
d. Page 257

CHAPTER 2

USING CITATIONS IN CONTEXT

Legal writing makes liberal use of citations. Not only do legal writers refer to sources for every statement they use, they sometimes also refer to multiple authorities for a single proposition. Lawyers are accustomed to seeing citations, and they adjust their reading style to accommodate their citation needs. Lawyers slow down to read a citation carefully when they need the information it contains, and they skip over a citation when they are not interested in its content. To make the reader's job a little easier, legal writers are careful to position citations to be helpful and to create the fewest hurdles to a reader's understanding. This is what section A of this chapter discusses—the frequency and placement of citations within legal documents.

Section B covers another purpose of citations that was discussed in Chapter 1—the type and degree of support a citation provides. In order to indicate the type and degree of support, you will place signals in front of citations. Section C continues the discussion about the frequency of citation and adds a related concept, string citations. Specifically, section C covers the order in which the citations should appear. And section D discusses a concept primarily related to signals—explanatory parentheticals.

A. FREQUENCY AND PLACEMENT

As you draft your first legal documents, think about the following questions:

- How often do I need citations?
- How many sources do I need to refer to in a citation?

You will ask these questions because you have probably noticed how many citations are included in the cases you are reading. The number of citations in legal documents is much higher than the number of citations appearing in non-legal documents. Non-legal documents generally do not contain many citations.

In order to answer those two questions, let's look at Rule 43.2:

> Place a citation immediately after each sentence, or part of a sentence, that contains a statement of legal principle, a reference to or description of a legal authority, an idea, a thought, or an expression borrowed from another source.

This rule explains why there are so many citations in legal documents. Legal arguments are built on existing principles of law. Let's apply Rule 43.2 to a simple sentence to see how this works. Suppose you write the following sentence in your document:

> In order for there to be a contract, there must be an offer, acceptance, and consideration.

This is a statement of legal principle, so we know from Rule 43.2 that there needs to be a citation. But where? It all depends upon where you found the statement. If you found the statement in a single case, you only need a citation to that case at the end of the sentence.

> In order for there to be a contract, there must be an offer, acceptance, and consideration. **Citation.**

When you place a citation on its own following the text it supports, you have placed it into what is known as a "citation sentence," as explained in Rule 43.1(a). But you could have placed the full citation at the beginning of the sentence. For example,

> As stated in *citation*, in order for there to be a contract, there must be an offer, acceptance, and consideration.

A citation that is integrated into the text of the sentence is known as an "embedded citation," as explained in Rule 43.1(c). Because the embedded citation contains all the necessary information, no additional citation is needed at the end of the sentence. There are two important aspects of embedded citations to keep in mind. First, the case name in an embedded case citation uses almost no abbreviations. Only a few select abbreviations are allowed in embedded case citations, as explained in Rule 2.3. Second, because an embedded citation is grammatically part of the sentence (usually as part of a prepositional phrase), it makes the sentence longer and harder to read. Even if the reader does not presently need the citation information, he or she cannot easily skip an embedded citation.

One way to make an embedded citation to a case somewhat easier to read is to use only the case name in the text and to place the remainder of the citation in a citation sentence. Such citations are sometimes referred to as "split citations," and they are commonly used in short citations. For example,

> As stated in *Smith v. Jones*, in order for there to be a contract, there must be an offer, acceptance, and consideration. 123 So. 3d 268, 270 (Fla. 2015).

Up until this point, we have been assuming that support for the entire sentence came from one source. But what if part of the sentence came from one case and part came from a different case? For example, you found the information about an offer in case A, and you found the information about acceptance and consideration in case B. Where should you put the citation? You should follow Rule 43.1(b), putting each citation *immediately after* the word or phrase it supports and setting each citation off with commas, in what is known as a "citation clause." In this example, the citation to case A should be placed in a citation clause after the word "offer," and the citation to case B should be placed in a citation clause after the word "consideration," as shown below.

In order for there to be a contract, there must be an offer, *citation A*, acceptance, and consideration, *citation B*.

In law review articles and books, the citations are placed in footnotes or endnotes. The footnote or endnote number immediately follows the sentence or part of the sentence supported by the citation. Table 2.1 below uses boldface type to illustrate the placement of citations in citation sentences, citation clauses, embedded citations, split citations, and footnotes.

TABLE 2.1
PLACEMENT OF CITATIONS

Citation sentence	While a lawyer may delegate certain tasks to his assistants, as supervising attorney, she has the ultimate responsibility for the nonlawyer's compliance with applicable provisions of the Model Rules. **Mays v. Neal, 938 S.W.2d 830, 835 (Ark. 1997).**
Citation clauses	Although the court says it prefers to "read the rules as they are written," **Sturdivant v. Sturdivant, 241 S.W.3d 740, 743 (Ark. 2006),** it views disqualification as "a drastic measure that should only be imposed when the circumstances clearly require it," **Burnette v. Morgan, 794 S.W.2d 145, 148 (Ark. 1990).**
Embedded citation	In **Mays v. Neal, 938 S.W.2d 830, 835 (Ark. 1997),** the court reminded attorneys that they have "the ultimate responsibility for the nonlawyer's compliance" with ethical rules.
Split citation	In **Sturdivant v. Sturdivant,** the attorney's disqualification was required because she represented a client with "interests materially adverse to those of her prospective client." **241 S.W.3d 740, 746 (Ark. 2006).**
Footnote citations	While a lawyer may delegate certain tasks to his assistants, as supervising attorney, she has the ultimate responsibility for the nonlawyer's compliance with applicable provisions of the Model Rules.[1] Although the court says it prefers to "read the rules as they are written,"[2] it views disqualification as "a drastic measure that should only be imposed when the circumstances clearly require it."[3] [1]Mays v. Neal, 938 S.W.2d 830, 835 (Ark. 1997). [2]*Sturdivant v. Sturdivant,* 241 S.W.3d 740, 743 (Ark. 2006). [3]*Burnette v. Morgan,* 794 S.W.2d 145, 148 (Ark. 1990).

The exercises in this section help you understand how many citations legal documents actually contain. In fact, if you are not sure whether a citation is needed, it is better to err on the side of providing the citation.

EXERCISE SET 2-A

ALL LEVELS: FREQUENCY AND PLACEMENT

Before beginning Exercise Set 2-A All Levels, review the following and keep the *Manual* at hand as you work through the exercises:

- Rule 43.1, Placement Options
- Rule 43.2, Frequency of Citation

2-A.1. Identify the form of citation placement:

An egregious breach of social norms may qualify as a serious invasion of privacy. *Four Navy Seals v. Associated Press*, 413 F. Supp. 2d 1136, 1143 (S.D. Cal. 2005).

a. Citation sentence
b. Embedded citation
c. Split citation
d. Citation clause

2-A.2. Identify the form of citation placement:

Furthermore, in *Schlesinger v. Merrill Lynch, Pierce, Fenner & Smith*, 567 N.E.2d 912, 916 (Mass. 1991), the court discussed how a person may relinquish a privacy right by placing herself in contexts where her expectation of privacy is reduced.

a. Citation sentence
b. Embedded citation
c. Split citation
d. Citation clause

2-A.3. Identify the form of citation placement:

An egregious breach of social norms may qualify as a serious invasion of privacy, *Four Navy Seals v. Associated Press*, 413 F. Supp. 2d 1136, 1143 (S.D. Cal. 2005), and a person may relinquish a privacy right by placing herself in contexts where her expectation of privacy is reduced, *Schlesinger v. Merrill Lynch, Pierce, Fenner & Smith*, 567 N.E.2d 912, 916 (Mass. 1991).

a. Citation sentence
b. Embedded citation
c. Split citation
d. Citation clause

2-A.4. Identify the form of citation placement:

In *Four Navy Seals v. Associated Press*, the court stated that an egregious breach of social norms may qualify as a serious invasion of privacy. 413 F. Supp. 2d 1136, 1143 (S.D. Cal. 2005).

a. Citation sentence
b. Embedded citation
c. Split citation
d. Citation clause

2-A.5. Determine whether a citation sentence is needed after the following sentence:

The court held that the punishment was reasonable in light of the circumstances and affirmed summary judgment in favor of the defendant.

a. Yes, a citation sentence is needed.
b. No, a citation sentence is not needed.

2-A.6. Determine whether a citation sentence is needed after the following sentence:

The United States Supreme Court stated that courts should respect the disciplinary choices teachers and administrators "reasonable believe to be necessary for [the child's] proper control, training, and education."

a. Yes, a citation sentence is needed.
b. No, a citation sentence is not needed.

2-A.7. Determine whether a citation sentence is needed after the following sentence:

According to Florida Statutes § 741.30(1)(a), any family or household member who has been a victim of domestic violence or has a fear that he or she is "in imminent damage of becoming the victim of" domestic violence has standing to seek an injunction for protection.

a. Yes, a citation sentence is needed.
b. No, a citation sentence is not needed.

2-A.8.   Is the case name, *Rey v. Perez-Gurri*, sufficient information for the citation?

> In *Rey v. Perez-Gurri*, the petitioner alleged her husband made numerous threats and assaults against her throughout their marriage including pointing a gun at her, attempting to hit her with the car, and threatening her life.

a. Yes. No more citation information is needed.
b. No. An embedded citation or a split citation is needed.

2-A.9.   The following passage comes from an inter-office, predictive memorandum that discusses whether the client, a husband, can seek an injunction for protection from his wife. Determine whether citations are needed in the designated places. For each question, check the **Yes** or **No** blank to indicate whether a citation is needed in that location.

> Any family or household member who has been a victim of domestic violence or has a reasonable fear that he or she is "in imminent danger of becoming the victim of" domestic violence has standing to seek an injunction for protection. [**2-A.9.a.**] Before granting an injunction, the court will have to determine that the husband believes he is in "imminent" danger, [**2-A.9.b.**] and his fear of domestic violence is "reasonable." [**2-A.9.c.**] When deciding how much of a threat the husband's wife presents, the court will consider the current allegations and the aggressor's "behavior within the context of the relationship and its history." [**2-A.9.d.**]
> The petitioner for a domestic violence injunction does not have to prove she had already been victimized, but she must show a "reasonable cause to believe that she is *about to become* a victim of domestic violence." [**2-A.9.e.**] In *Rey*, [**2-A.9.f.**] the petitioner alleged her husband made numerous threats and assaults against her throughout their marriage including pointing a gun at her, attempting to hit her with the car, and threatening her life. The husband denied her allegations but admitted to a past drug problem. [**2-A.9.g.**] The trial court found the wife failed to prove her husband had the ability to carry out his threats and denied the petition. [**2-A.9.h.**] The appellate court reversed the trial court's decision and granted a permanent injunction because of his ability, opportunity, and willingness to use violence against his wife. [**2-A.9.i.**] The court looked to a case in which the husband was found to not have the ability to carry out his threats because he was committed to a mental hospital. [**2-A.9.j.**] In contrast, the husband in *Rey* had visitation rights with the couple's children, was known to have owned a gun, and had shown ability and willingness to use guns to threaten his wife "in an aggressive manner" in the past. [**2-A.9.k.**]

2-A.10.   The following passage comes from a memorandum of law written in support of a motion for summary judgment. The movants (a high school, a high school teacher, and the principal) dispute the allegations made by a student that he was deprived his substantive due process rights guaranteed by the Fourteenth Amendment. Determine whether citations are needed in the designated places. For each question, check the **Yes** or **No** blank to indicate whether a citation is needed in that location.

A. The Application of Corporal Punishment Was Reasonably Necessary

> Punishment must be "shocking to the conscience" for courts to abandon deference to school administrators in determining appropriate disciplinary policy for maintaining order in schools. [**2-A.10.a.**] In *Wise v. Pea Ridge School District*, [**2-A.10.b.**] the plaintiff was one of several students who played dodge ball despite being told twice to discontinue the game. Because

the students ignored the verbal warnings, they each received two swats with a wooden paddle. [**2-A.10.c.**] The court reasoned that the use of corporal punishment was reasonable because the earlier reprimands "failed to deter" the students' behavior, and in light of the circumstances, the court affirmed summary judgment for the defendant. [**2-A.10.d.**]

* * *

In this case, corporal punishment was necessary to maintain an environment conducive to learning. [**2-A.10.e.**] Unlike *Meyer*, in which a teacher struck the student with no clear pedagogical or disciplinary purpose, here, force was applied for the clear disciplinary purpose of restoring the learning environment that the student disrupted. [**2-A.10.f.**] Unlike *Meyer*, in which the circumstances and the teacher's testimony revealed an uncertain objective in administering force, here, force was applied in response to the student's failure to abide by earlier warnings. [**2-A.10.g.**]

B. SIGNALS: PROVIDING TYPE AND DEGREE OF SUPPORT

In addition to providing the needed reference and quotation information, citations also serve the purpose of indicating the type and degree of support the cited sources provide, and this is done with the use of signals. When the citation does not directly support the proposition, a "signal" must be provided. Rule 44.3 lists the five categories of signals and defines each one: support (*see, accord, see also,* and *cf.*); comparison (*compare . . . with*); contradiction (*contra, but see,* and *but cf.*); background (*see generally*); and example (*e.g.*).

   Whether you use a signal depends solely on how you are using the sources that you are referring to in the citation; consequently, you have leeway with how you use signals, given the sources that you have found and the way the sources relate to each other. The exercises in this section help you understand the basic rules regarding signals.

EXERCISE SET 2-B

ALL LEVELS: SIGNALS: PROVIDING TYPE AND DEGREE OF SUPPORT

Before beginning Exercise Set 2-B Basic Level, review the following and keep the *Manual* at hand as you work through the exercises:

- Rule 44.1, Purpose of Signals
- Rule 44.2, Use of Signals
- Rule 44.3, Categories of Signals

2-B.1.   This question has two parts. Both parts refer to the following sentence:

> Materially adverse changes in employment include "hiring, firing, failing to promote, reassignment with significantly different responsibilities, or a decision causing a significant change in benefits." *Id.* at 798.

2-B.1.a. Is a signal needed before the citation?

a. Yes, a signal is needed.
b. No, a signal is not needed.

2-B.1.b. Briefly explain your answer to 2-B.1.a., and provide the applicable rule.

2-B.2. This question has two parts. Both parts refer to the following sentence:

> The United States Supreme Court held that Title IX is enforceable through an implied private right of action for monetary damages. *Franklin*, 503 U.S. at 76.

2-B.2.a. Is a signal needed before the citation?

a. Yes, a signal is needed.
b. No, a signal is not needed.

2-B.2.b. Briefly explain your answer to question 2-B.2.a., and provide the applicable rule.

2-B.3. This question has two parts. Both parts refer to the following sentence:

> Many cases have stated that there is a fundamental constitutional right to a fair and impartial trial afforded to any litigant in our judicial system, and in order to promote and foster public trust and confidence in our system, there must not only be actual judicial impartiality, but also the appearance of impartiality. *Jordan*, 49 F.3d at 155.

2-B.3.a. Is a signal needed before the citation?

a. Yes, a signal is needed.
b. No, a signal is not needed.

2-B.3.b. Briefly explain your answer to question 2-B.3.a., and provide the applicable rule.

2-B.4. Many cases support the proposition, but you want to refer to only two or three of them. Identify which signal is appropriate.

a. *See*
b. *See also*
c. *See generally*
d. *E.g.*

2-B.5. The portion of the case that supports the proposition is in dicta. Identify which signal is appropriate.

a. *See*
b. *See also*
c. *But see*
d. *Cf.*

2-B.6. The client's case is in Illinois, and you have referred to the applicable Illinois law; however, you would also like to refer to a similar Texas statute on point. (The signal is needed in front of the Texas statute.) Identify which signal is appropriate.

    a. *Compare . . . with*
    b. *See also*
    c. *Accord*
    d. *See generally*

2-B.7. Circuit courts of appeal have reached different conclusions on an issue (a situation known as a "circuit split"), and you want to refer to cases on both sides of the issue. Identify which signal is appropriate.

    a. *See generally*
    b. *Compare . . . with*
    c. *E.g.*
    d. *See also*

2-B.8. There is a case on point, but you only want to refer to the case as helpful background information. Identify which signal is appropriate.

    a. *See generally*
    b. *See also*
    c. *Cf.*
    d. *E.g.*

2-B.9. You are writing an inter-office memorandum about an accident involving a Segway Human Transporter. The single case that supports the proposition does so through analogy, because it involves a snowmobile accident. Which signal should you use in this situation?

2-B.10. For the same memorandum referenced above, another case contradicts the proposition, also through analogy, because it involves a jet ski. Which signal should you use in this situation?

C. ORDER OF CITATIONS

At times, you may wish to refer to multiple sources to support a particular proposition. Combining multiple sources in a single citation is known as "string citation." While string citations are more commonly used in law review articles or other scholarly works, you will occasionally need to use a string citation in a legal memorandum or brief. The number of sources you cite for a particular proposition depends upon the factors identified in Rule 43.3, including the type of document you are writing, its audience, the number of relevant authorities to the legal issues being considered, and "how well established or contested the stated proposition is."

When more than one source supports a particular proposition, use Rule 45 to put the citations in the proper order within the string citation. The logic of the order presented in Rule 45 is based on hierarchy: primary sources come before secondary sources; federal sources come before state sources; higher courts come before lower courts; and if two cases are from the same court, the more recent case comes first. This hierarchy is also seen in Appendix 1.

The basic-level questions provide a general overview of ordering sources, and the intermediate-level questions cover working with specific sources. The expert-level questions further test the specifics of Rule 45, but also add signals with the citations.

EXERCISE SET 2-C

BASIC LEVEL: ORDER OF CITATIONS

Before beginning Exercise Set 2-C Basic Level, review the following and keep the *Manual* at hand as you work through the exercises:

- Rule 45.1, Applicability
- Rule 45.3, General Ordering Rules

To complete the exercises, you may also need to refer to the following:

- Appendix 1, Primary Sources by Jurisdiction

2-C.1. Two sources directly support the proposition, a secondary source and a primary source. Which source should be first in the citation?

a. Secondary source
b. Primary source

2-C.2. Two sources directly support the proposition, a federal primary source and a state primary source. Which source should be first in the citation?

a. Federal primary source
b. State primary source

2-C.3. Two sources directly support the proposition; one is from the highest court in a state and the other is from a lower court in the same state. Which source should be first in the citation?

a. Lower state court
b. Highest state court

2-C.4. Two cases directly support the proposition; both are from the same federal appellate court, the Eleventh Circuit. One case is published in 2003 and the other case is published in 2005. Which case should be first in the citation?

a. The case published in 2005.
b. The case published in 2003.

2-C.5. Two state cases directly support the proposition; one was decided by the Florida Supreme Court (the highest court in the state), and the other case was decided by the Arkansas Court of Appeals (the intermediate appellate court). Which case should be first in the citation?

a. The Florida Supreme Court case
b. The Arkansas Court of Appeals case

EXERCISE SET 2-C

INTERMEDIATE LEVEL: ORDER OF CITATIONS

Before beginning Exercise Set 2-C Intermediate Level, review the following and keep the *Manual* at hand while you work through the exercises:

• Rule 45.1, Applicability
• Rule 45.4, Specific Order of Authorities

To complete the exercises, you may also need to refer to the following:

• Appendix 1, Primary Sources by Jurisdiction

2-C.6. The following cases appear in a single citation sentence, and all directly support the proposition. Select the answer that has the sources in the correct order.

Source 1:   *Murphy v. Boston Herald, Inc.*, 865 N.E. 2d 746 (Mass. 2007).
Source 2:   *Clancy v. Town of Mashpee*, 21 Mass. L. Rptr. 722 (Mass. Super. 2006).
Source 3:   *Reilly v. Associated Press*, 797 N.E.2d 1204 (Mass. App. 2003).
Source 4:   *Nelson v. Salem St. College*, 845 N.E.2d 338 (Mass. 2006).
Source 5:   *Cefalu v. Globe Newsp. Co.*, 391 N.E.2d 935 (Mass. App. 1979).

a. 5, 3, 4, 3, 1
b. 1, 2, 4, 3, 5
c. 1, 4, 3, 5, 2
d. 1, 4, 2, 3, 5

2-C.7. The following sources appear in a single citation sentence, and all directly support the proposition. Select the answer that has the sources in the correct order.

Source 1:   17 U.S.C. § 101 (2006).
Source 2:   *UMG Recordings, Inc. v. MP3.Com, Inc.*, 92 F. Supp. 2d 349, 352 (S.D.N.Y. 2000).
Source 3:   *Campbell v. Acuff-Rose Music, Inc.*, 510 U.S. 569, 575 (1994).
Source 4:   *Am. Geophysical Union v. Texaco, Inc.*, 60 F.3d 913, 917 (2d Cir. 1995).
Source 5:   *Kelly v. Arriba Soft Corp.*, 336 F.3d 811, 814 (9th Cir. 2003).

a. 3, 4, 5, 2, 1
b. 3, 5, 4, 2, 1
c. 1, 3, 5, 4, 2
d. 1, 3, 4, 5, 2

2-C.8.   The following sources appear in a single citation sentence, and all directly support the proposition. Select the answer that has the sources in the correct order.

Source 1:   *Dasey v. Anderson,* 304 F.3d 148 (1st Cir. 2002).
Source 2:   *Clancy v. Town of Mashpee,* 21 Mass. L. Rptr. 722 (Mass. Super. 2006).
Source 3:   *Reilly v. Associated Press,* 797 N.E.2d 1204 (Mass. App. 2003).
Source 4:   *Nelson v. Salem St. College,* 845 N.E.2d 338 (Mass. 2006).
Source 5:   Mass. Gen. Laws ch. 214, § 1B (2008).
Source 6:   *Albright v. Morton,* 321 F. Supp. 2d 130 (D. Mass. 2004).

a. 5, 1, 6, 4, 3, 2
b. 5, 4, 6, 2, 4, 1
c. 5, 4, 3, 2, 1, 6
d. 5, 1, 4, 3, 2, 6

EXERCISE SET 2-C

EXPERT LEVEL: ORDER OF CITATIONS

Before beginning Exercise Set 2-C Expert Level, review the following, and keep the *Manual* at hand as you work through the exercises:

• Rule 44.6, Placement and Typeface of Signals
• Rule 44.8, Order of Signals and Punctuation between Different Signals
• Rule 45.2, Punctuation between Citations
• Rule 45.4, Specific Order of Authorities

2-C.9.   Suppose the two cases that you want to refer to support a particular proposition and both cases support the proposition implicitly. Which of the following string citations is correct?

a. *See Johnson v. Yellow Freight Sys., Inc.,* 734 F.2d 1304, 1309 (8th Cir. 1984); *see Plummer v. W. Intl. Hotels Co.,* 656 F.2d 502, 505 (9th Cir. 1981).
b. *See Plummer v. W. Intl. Hotels Co.,* 656 F.2d 502, 505 (9th Cir. 1981); *see Johnson v. Yellow Freight Sys., Inc.,* 734 F.2d 1304, 1309 (8th Cir. 1984).
c. *See Johnson v. Yellow Freight Sys., Inc.,* 734 F.2d 1304, 1309 (8th Cir. 1984); *Plummer v. W. Intl. Hotels Co.,* 656 F.2d 502, 505 (9th Cir. 1981).
d. *See Plummer v. W. Intl. Hotels Co.,* 656 F.2d 502, 505 (9th Cir. 1981); *Johnson v. Yellow Freight Sys., Inc.,* 734 F.2d 1304, 1309 (8th Cir. 1984).

2-C.10.   Number the following sources in the order they should appear in a string citation.

a. *See Grutter v. Bollinger,* 539 U.S. 309, 343 (2003).
b. Preston C. Green, III, *Racial Balancing Provisions and Charter Schools: Are Charter Schools Out on a Constitutional Limb?* 2001 BYU Educ. & L.J. 65, 67.
c. *See generally* Joe Nathan, *Charter Schools: Creating Hope and Opportunity for American Education* (Jossey-Bass Publishers 1996).
d. *Compare* 20 U.S.C. § 8061 (1994) *with* 20 U.S.C.A. § 6301 (West 2003).
e. *Beaufort Co. Bd. of Educ. v. Lighthouse Charter Sch. Comm.,* 516 S.E.2d 655, 660 (S.C. 1999).
f. Fla. Stat. Ann. § 1002.33(7) (West Supp. 2005).

2-C.11. You are drafting a citation sentence that must contain the following sources with the appropriate signals. Draft one citation sentence, or string citation, given the information provided below.

- Two cases come to different outcomes on the same issue:
  - ○ *Plummer v. W. Intl. Hotels Co.*, 656 F.2d 502, 504–505 (9th Cir. 1981).
  - ○ *Johnson v. Yellow Freight Sys., Inc.*, 734 F.2d 1304, 1309 (8th Cir. 1984).

- This source supports the proposition implicitly. *Cortes v. Maxus Exploration Co.*, 758 F. Supp. 1182, 1184–1185 (S.D. Tex. 1991).
- This source contradicts the stated proposition. *Spruill v. Winner Ford of Dover, Ltd.*, 175 F.R.D. 194, 198 (D. Del. 1997).
- This source is just one example of the many authorities that discuss the proposition. *Paolitto v. John Brown E. & C., Inc.*, 151 F.3d 60, 65 (2d Cir. 1998).

2-C.12. For your first draft, you wrote the string citation below. Rewrite it for your final draft by putting the sources in the correct order and correcting, if necessary, typeface and punctuation.

> U.S. Const. amend. XIV, § 1. Jack Greenburg, *Diversity, the University, and the World Outside*, 103 Colum. L. Rev. 1610, 1615 (2003). But See *Grutter v. Bollinger*, 539 U.S. 306, 326 (2003). See *Fullilove v. Klutznick*, 448 U.S. 448, 459 (1980). See *Adarand Constructors, Inc. v. Pena*, 515 U.S. 200, 227 (1995).

D. EXPLANATORY PARENTHETICALS

According to Rule 46.1, "[a]n explanatory parenthetical is a device that can help readers understand the significance of a cited authority." Explanatory parentheticals are used primarily in citations in treatises, law review articles, and other scholarly works, but they can be found in legal memoranda and court documents in three instances:

- when certain signals precede a citation;
- when you need only a short description of the source to explain its importance; or
- when you want to describe the relationship between two sources.

Crafting explanatory parentheticals is more of an art than a science, but here are several tips to help you with the exercises below:

- An explanatory parenthetical follows the source that it is describing.
- An explanatory parenthetical may follow a full citation, a short-form citation, or *id.*
- An explanatory parenthetical may be constructed as a sentence fragment, a full sentence, or even a quotation. Typically, the explanatory parenthetical contains a sentence fragment that starts with a gerund (an –ing word, such as holding, explaining, quoting, distinguishing, stating).
- Insert one space between the end of the citation and the opening parenthesis of the explanatory parenthetical, and end the citation with a period after the closing parenthesis.

EXERCISE SET 2-D

ALL LEVELS: EXPLANATORY PARENTHETICALS

Before beginning Exercise Set 2-D All Levels, review the following and keep the *Manual* at hand as you work through the exercises:

- Rule 44.4, Signals and Explanatory Parentheticals
- Rule 46.0, Explanatory Parentheticals and Related Authority
- Sidebar 46.1, Using Explanatory Parentheticals Effectively

2-D.1. You want to quote from source A, and source A contains an internal quotation from source B. Draft the explanatory parenthetical that follows source A.

      Source A: *Olson v. Lambert*, 60 P.3d 554, 556 (Or. App. 2002).
      Source B: *Gortmaker*, 655 P.2d at 588.

2-D.2. Suppose you want to add emphasis to the quotation in question 2-D.1. Where should the (emphasis added) parenthetical go?

a. After the citation for source A, but before the explanatory parenthetical.
b. In the explanatory parenthetical, after the citation for source B.
c. At the end of the citation for source A, after the explanatory parenthetical.

2-D.3. Correct the punctuation in the following explanatory parenthetical.

      Fla. Stat. § 1002.33(3)(a) (2009) ("An application for a new charter school may be made by an individual, teachers, parents, a group of individuals, a municipality, or a legal entity organized under the laws of this state").

2-D.4. You would like to refer to source A, adding an explanatory parenthetical to explain that source A interprets source B. Draft the explanatory parenthetical that follows source A.

      Source A: *State v. Hash*, 528 P.2d 482 (Or. App. 1978).
      Source B: Or. Rev. Stat. § 164.055(b) (1978).

2-D.5. This question has three parts. Each question asks where to place the explanatory parenthetical in the full citation provided below—in position A, B, or C. Hint: Read all three explanatory parentheticals before answering the questions.

      Forest Grove Sch. Dist. v. T.A., 640 F. Supp. 2d 1320 (D. Or. 2005) **A**, *rev'd*, 523 F.3d 1078 (9th Cir. 2008) **B**, *aff'd*, 129 S. Ct. 2484 (2009) **C**.

2-D.5.a. Where should you place the following parenthetical?

(reversing the district court's decision because T.A. may recover reimbursement under 20 U.S.C. § 1415(i)(2)(c))

a. In position A
b. In position B
c. In position C

2-D.5.b. Where should you place the following parenthetical?

(discussing how the courts of appeals have reached inconsistent results on this issue)

a. In position A
b. In position B
c. In position C

2-D.5.c. Where should you place the following parenthetical?

(holding that T.A.'s parents could not receive tuition reimbursement under the IDEA)

a. In position A
b. In position B
c. In position C

2-D.6. Rewrite the following sentence to convert it to a sentence fragment starting with a gerund (an –ing word) for placement in an explanatory parenthetical.

The article summarizes the OCR letter rulings at two universities with regards to the students' due process rights and their mental health conditions.

2-D.7. You would like to refer to a case in which the judge listed seven cases (from both the United States Supreme Court and the United States Court of Appeals for the Seventh Circuit) and three cases from other jurisdictions. Draft an explanatory parenthetical that describes the fact that the judge provided the list of cases for the attorney. Present the information as a sentence fragment starting with a gerund (an –ing word).

2-D.8. You are writing an inter-office memorandum about the felon-in-possession-of-a-firearm statute in your jurisdiction, and you have one case in which the court determined the firearm was "readily capable" of use as a weapon because it could be reassembled in 15 to 20 minutes, at a cost of $25. A weapon is "readily capable" if it can be repaired within a reasonable time and at a reasonable cost. On your answer sheet, draft an explanatory parenthetical for this case. Present the information as a sentence fragment starting with a gerund (an –ing word).

CHAPTER

3

WORKING WITH RULES

APPLICABLE TO ALL CITATIONS

As we discussed in Chapter 1, citations are location codes; they provide the reader with sufficient information to find the source, whether it is available online or in print. The information in the citations is presented in a concise yet consistent manner. This chapter discusses the applicable rules that are used when formatting *all* citations, and we will revisit these rules throughout the *Companion.*

A. TYPEFACE

Citations typically employ two typefaces—(1) ordinary type and (2) *italics* (or its alternative, underlining). Determining which components of a citation should be presented in which typeface is pretty straightforward. The first subsection of each *ALWD Citation Manual* rule for a particular source lists all the components contained in that source's full citation. Any component that needs to be *italicized* (or if you prefer, underlined) is identified in the example. Whether you choose to italicize or underline, be consistent throughout your document. For example, if you choose to underline the appropriate components of a citation, then you must also underline things like signals, cross-references, phrases describing subsequent or prior history, short forms, and emphasis added to quotations. This choice also means you will use underlining instead of italics in *every* citation that calls for that typeface. To determine which words in the text of your document should be italicized, refer to Rule 1.8, which may in turn require you to consult the most current edition of *Black's Law Dictionary.*[1]

In addition to helping you learn about the typeface in citations, the exercises in this chapter also help you become even more familiar with the *Manual.* This is because while Rule 1.0 governs the typeface for citations, Rule 1.0 discusses typeface only generally. To determine which components of citations are italicized, consult the rule for the specific source you are citing.

EXERCISE SET 3-A

BASIC LEVEL: TYPEFACE

Before beginning Exercise Set 3-A Basic Level, review the following rule and keep the *Manual* at hand as you work through the exercises:

• Rule 1.0, Typeface for Citations

Instructions: Use the Table of Contents, Index, or Fast Format Locator to find the applicable rules and examples for specific sources. In the blanks on your answer sheet, write the rule number, including applicable subsection(s), for the full citation format, and identify the component(s) of the full citation that use the indicated typeface.

3-A.1. Identify the rule that you would use to format a citation to a case. Which component(s) of the citation should be presented in *italics*?

3-A.2. Identify the rule that you would use to format a citation to a federal statute currently in force. Which component(s) of the citation should be presented in *italics*?

3-A.3. Identify the rule that you would use to format a citation to a legal dictionary. Which component(s) of the citation should be presented in *italics*?

3-A.4. Identify the rule that you would use to format a citation to a law review article. Which component(s) of the citation should be presented in *italics*?

3-A.5. Identify the rule that you would use to format a citation to an American Law Reports (A.L.R.) annotation. Which component(s) of the citation should be presented in *italics*?

3-A.6. Identify the rule that you would use to format a citation to an encyclopedia entry. Which component(s) of the citation should be presented in *italics*?

3-A.7. Identify the rule that you would use to format a citation to a book. Which component(s) of the citation should be presented in *italics*?

---

[1] The ninth edition is the most current edition of *Black's Law Dictionary.* It was published in 2009.

3-A.8. Identify the rule that you would use to format a citation to a constitutional provision currently in force. Which component(s) of the citation should be presented in *italics*?

EXERCISE SET 3-A

INTERMEDIATE LEVEL: TYPEFACE

Before beginning Exercise Set 3-A Intermediate Level, review the following rule and keep the *Manual* at hand as you work through the exercises:

• Rule 1.0, Typeface for Citations

Instructions: Use the Table of Contents, Index, or Fast Format Locator to find the applicable rules and examples for specific sources. In the blanks on your answer sheet, write the rule number, including applicable subsection(s), for the full citation format, and circle the name of the appropriate typeface for the indicated component.

3-A.9. You would like to refer to a federal statute and include the name of the statute in the citation. Identify the rule that you would use to format the citation, and circle the correct typeface to use in representing the name of the statute.

3-A.10. You are writing a memorandum of law in support of a motion to dismiss. Identify the rule that you will use to cite the motion (a type of court document). Circle the correct typeface to use in representing the title of the motion.

3-A.11. You would like to use the phrase "res ipsa loquitur" in the text of an inter-office memorandum. Identify the rule that you would use to format the phrase, and circle the correct typeface to use in representing the phrase.

3-A.12. You would like to use the abbreviation "e.g." in the text of your legal document, rather than as a signal. Identify the rule that you would use to format the abbreviation, and circle the correct typeface to use in representing the abbreviation.

3-A.13. Identify the rule that you would use to refer to the subsequent history to a case. What typeface should be used for the subsequent history phrase?

3-A.14. You would like to use the word "arguendo" in the text of your legal document. Identify the rule that you would use to format the word, and circle the correct typeface to use in representing the word.

3-A.15. You would like to use the phrase "per curiam" in the text of your legal document. Identify the rule that you would use to format the phrase, and circle the correct typeface to use in representing the phrase.

EXERCISE SET 3-A

EXPERT LEVEL: TYPEFACE

Before beginning Exercise Set 3-A Expert Level, review the following and keep the *Manual* at hand as you work through the exercises:

• Rule 1.0, Typeface for Citations

3-A.16. Underline the words in the following title of a law review article that should be italicized.

> Caperton v. A.T. Massey Coal Co.: Due Process Limitations
> on the Appearance of Judicial Bias

3-A.17. Underline the words in the following title of a law review article that should be italicized.

> "A Failure to Act" from Brown v. Board of Education to Sheff v. O'Neill:
> The American Educational System Will Remain Segregated

3-A.18. Rewrite the sentence on your answer sheet, underlining the words that should be italicized.

> Dr. G. Robb Cooper and James Prescott wrote an article in which they state that "Brown's practical impact has been ambiguous at best." G. Robb Cooper & James Prescott, What Did Brown Do for You? Brown v. Board Fifty Years Later, 14 Pub. Interest L. Rptr. 231, 231 (2009).

B.   ABBREVIATIONS

One way to make citations more concise is to use abbreviations, as explained in Rule 2.2. Some citation components are always abbreviated (such as the names of reporters or names of courts in a case citation), whereas other components (such as the case name) may or may not be abbreviated. The *Manual* contains helpful charts and appendices to assist you with components that are always abbreviated. For example, the citation to a law review article includes an abbreviation for the name of the periodical that published the article, and Appendix 5 lists abbreviations for many of the legal periodicals. A green triangle in an abbreviation in a chart or appendix indicates a space.

Sometimes, the location of the citation determines whether abbreviations are permissible. For example, you may abbreviate words in a case name, if you so choose. However, if you place the case name in the text of the sentence instead of in a citation sentence, you should not abbreviate any words in the case name other than those listed in Rule 2.3.

Table 3.1 below summarizes the general rules regarding abbreviations and spacing. Consult charts and sidebars in specific source rules (such as Chart 12.1, Common Reporter Abbreviations, and Sidebar 13.1, Referring to Constitutions in Text), or use applicable appendices (e.g., Appendix 3 for general abbreviations, Appendix 5 for abbreviations for legal periodicals) to locate abbreviations. Pay close attention to the introductions to the applicable appendices. The introduction to Appendix 3 discusses how to create the plural of a word listed in the appendix; the introduction to Appendix 5 discusses how to create an abbreviation for a journal or law review that is not listed in that appendix.

TABLE 3.1

SPACING OF ABBREVIATIONS

Consecutive single capital letters
 	
Rule 2.2(a)
	If the abbreviation has consecutive single capital letters, there are no spaces between the letters. For example, in the abbreviation for Bar Journal,
	
	  Bar is abbreviated B.
	  Journal is abbreviated J.
	  Bar Journal is abbreviated B.J.
	
	The popular citation symbols—&, ¶, and §—are not considered single capital letters; therefore, a space is needed before and after these three symbols.
	
	An ordinal number is considered a single capital letter.
	
	For example, in the abbreviation for the *Pacific Reporter, Fourth Series.*
	  Pacific Reporter is abbreviated P.
	  Fourth is abbreviated 4th
	
	Because both abbreviations are single capital letters, the abbreviation is P.4th.

Single capital letters and longer abbreviations
 	
Rule 2.2(c)-(d)
	If the abbreviation contains a single capital letter and a longer abbreviation or a word that is not abbreviated, insert a space between the single capital letter and the longer abbreviation or unabbreviated word.
	
	For example, in the abbreviation for Federal Supplement
	  Federal is abbreviated F.
	  Supplement is abbreviated Supp.
	
	The abbreviation for Federal Supplement is F. Supp., with a space between the two abbreviations.

Guidance for abbreviating legal periodicals
 	
Rule 2.2(b)
Appendix 5
Appendix 3
	Look up periodical abbreviations in Appendix 5. If the periodical is not listed, create an abbreviation using any words in the periodical title that appear in Appendix 3.
	
	Many legal periodicals use abbreviations for institutions or geographic locations. Following Rule 2.2(b), you should separate "the institutional or geographical abbreviation from the other parts of the abbreviation."
	
	For example, suppose you need the abbreviation for the fictitious journal *Southern University Bar Journal.* Use Appendix 3 abbreviations, as shown.
	  Southern is abbreviated S.
	  University is abbreviated U.
	  Bar is abbreviated B.
	  Journal is abbreviated J.
	
	Even though the abbreviation uses single capitals, Rule 2.2(b) requires the institutional abbreviation, S.U., to be separated from the rest of the abbreviation. The correct abbreviation is therefore S.U. B.J.

One goal of these exercises is to familiarize you with the helpful charts and appendices in the *Manual* that assist you when writing abbreviations; another goal is to introduce you to the fundamental rules regarding abbreviations so that you use existing *Manual* abbreviations to create an abbreviation when it is not listed in one of the rules, charts, sidebars, or appendices.

EXERCISE SET 3-B

BASIC LEVEL: ABBREVIATIONS

Before beginning Exercise Set 3-B Basic Level, review the following and keep the *Manual* at hand as you work through the exercises:

- Rule 2.0, Abbreviations
- Appendix 1, Primary Sources by Jurisdiction
- Appendix 3, General Abbreviations
- Appendix 4, Court Abbreviations
- Appendix 5, Abbreviations for Legal Periodicals

Instructions: Use the Table of Contents, Index, or Fast Format Locator to find the applicable rules and examples for specific sources.

3-B.1. You find a case in the *United States Supreme Court Reports, Lawyers' Edition, Second Series*. Which of the following is the correct abbreviation for the reporter?

a. U.S.
b. S. Ct.
c. L. Ed.
d. L. Ed. 2d

3-B.2. You find a case in the *Federal Reporter, Third Series*. Which of the following is the correct abbreviation for the reporter?

a. F. 3d
b. F.3d
c. F.3rd
d. F. 3rd

3-B.3. What is the court abbreviation to use in a full citation to a case from the United States Court of Appeals for the Eleventh Circuit?

a. 11th Cir.
b. 11th Cir.
c. 11th Cir
d. 11 Cir.

3-B.4. What is the court abbreviation to use in a full citation to a case from the Georgia Supreme Court?

a. Ga. S. Ct.
b. Ga. Super.
c. Ga. App.
d. Ga.

3-B.5. You are citing a Massachusetts Superior Court case. What is the abbreviation for the reporter in which you found the case?

a. Mass.
b. Mass. App. Div.
c. Mass. L. Rptr.
d. Mass. Supp.

3-B.6. You are citing a statute from the *Arizona Revised Statutes Annotated*. What is the abbreviation for the *Arizona Revised Statutes Annotated*?

a. Ariz. Rev. Stat.
b. Ariz. Rev. Stat. Ann.
c. Ariz. Sess. Laws
d. Ariz. Rev. Stats. Ann.

3-B.7. You are citing a statute from the *United States Code Annotated*. What is the abbreviation for the *United States Code Annotated*?

a. U.S. Code Ann.
b. U.S.C. Ann.
c. U.S.C.A.
d. U.S.C.

3-B.8. The Law Student Division of the American Bar Association publishes a magazine titled *Student Lawyer*, and you would like to cite an article from that magazine. What is the abbreviation for *Student Lawyer*?

a. Student Lawyer
b. Stud. Law.
c. Stud. Lawyer
d. Student Law.

3-B.9. You would like to cite an article from the *Notre Dame Journal of Law, Ethics and Public Policy*. What is the abbreviation for that periodical?

a. Notre Dame J.L. Ethics & Pub. Policy
b. Notre Dame J.L. Ethics & Pub. Pol.
c. Notre Dame J.L. Ethics & Pub. Pol'y
d. ND J.L., Ethics & Pub. Policy

3-B.10. Which words in the following case name can be abbreviated? **Check all that apply.**

National Foundation v. Johnson Building

a. National
b. Foundation
c. Johnson
d. Building

EXERCISE SET 3-B

INTERMEDIATE LEVEL: ABBREVIATIONS

Before beginning Exercise Set 3-B Intermediate Level, review the following and keep the *Manual* at hand as you work through the exercises:

• Rule 2.0, Abbreviations
• Appendix 1, Primary Sources by Jurisdiction
• Appendix 3, General Abbreviations

Instructions: Use the Table of Contents, Index, or Fast Format Locator to find the applicable rules and examples for specific sources.

3-B.11. What is the abbreviation for the Alabama Constitution?

    a. Alabama Constitution
    b. Alabama Const.
    c. Ala. Constitution
    d. Ala. Const.

3-B.12. What is the abbreviation for the Federal Rules of Civil Procedure?

    a. Federal Rules of Civil Procedure
    b. Fed. Rs. Civ. P.
    c. Fed. R. Civ. P.
    d. F.R. Civ. P.

3-B.13. What is the abbreviation for *Regulations of Connecticut State Agencies*?

    a. Regs. Conn. St. Agencies
    b. Regs. Conn. Agencies
    c. Regs. Conn. St. Agen.
    d. Regs. Conn. Agen.

3-B.14. On your answer sheet, write the abbreviation for following case name.

Australia Party Limited v. Elizabeth Bay Development Service Systems

EXERCISE SET 3-B

EXPERT LEVEL: ABBREVIATIONS

Before beginning Exercise Set 3-B Expert Level, review the following and keep the *Manual* at hand as you work through the exercises:

- Rule 2.0, Abbreviations
- Appendix 3, General Abbreviations
- Appendix 5, Abbreviations for Legal Periodicals

Instructions: Use the Table of Contents, Index, or Fast Format Locator to find the applicable rules and examples for specific sources.

To form the plural of a word listed in Appendix 3, add "s" to the end of the abbreviation "unless the word listed indicates otherwise." If a periodical is not listed in Appendix 5, create its abbreviation by using Appendix 3, and if a geographic or institutional entity is part of its name, by following Rule 2.2(b).

3-B.15. On your answer sheet, write the abbreviation for the following case name.

Anthem Enterprises v. New York Regional Medical Centers

3-B.16. On your answer sheet, write the abbreviation for the following journal.

The Journal for Practicing Immigration Attorneys and Judges

3-B.17. On your answer sheet, write the correct format for the case name.

According to the United States Supreme Court in *Pioneer Inv. Serv. Co. v. Brunswick Associated LP*, the courts must take into account all relevant circumstances surrounding a party's omission. 507 U.S. 380, 395 (1993).

3-B.18. On your answer sheet, write the correct format for the case name.

In *Southwell v. S. Poverty L. Ctr.*, the court held that the publisher was not liable for actual malice when it published factually false statements that the publisher reasonably believed were true at the time of the publication. 949 F. Supp. 1303, 1309 (W.D. Mich. 1996).

3-B.19. On your answer sheet, write the abbreviation for the Texas Rules of Appellate Procedure.

3-B.20. On your answer sheet, write the abbreviation for a Senate Joint Resolution.

C. CAPITALIZATION

The capitalization rules in Rule 3.0 are used not only for the titles of sources, but are also used for the capitalization of headings, subheadings, and specific words used in legal documents.

There are some differences between the capitalization rules in the *Manual* and rules in other legal and non-legal style manuals, so it is important to become familiar with Rule 3.0.

Rule 3.0 has three parts. Rule 3.1 governs the capitalization of titles of sources. (This is the part of the rule that also applies to headings within a document.) Rule 3.2 provides general guidance for capitalization, and Rule 3.3 discusses the capitalization of specific words. These exercises will help you become familiar with all three parts of the rule.

EXERCISE SET 3-C

BASIC LEVEL: CAPITALIZATION

Before beginning Exercise Set 3-C Basic Level, review the following and keep the *Manual* at hand as you work through the exercises:

• Rule 3.1, Words in Titles
• Rule 3.3, Capitalizing Specific Words

Instructions: Double underline the first letter of each word that should be capitalized in each of the following titles.

For example: ALWD citation manual: a professional system of citation

3-C.1. Double underline the first letter of each word that should be capitalized in the following title:

appellate review of sentencing decisions

3-C.2. Double underline the first letter of each word that should be capitalized in the following title:

forum shopping through the federal rules of evidence

3-C.3. Double underline the first letter of each word that should be capitalized in the following title:

protecting the appropriations power: why congress should care about settlements at the department of justice

3-C.4. Double underline the first letter of each word that should be capitalized in the following title:

the lawyer's dilemma: to be or not to be a problem-solving negotiator

3-C.5. Double underline the first letter of each word that should be capitalized in the following title:

toward a fair use standard

3-C.6. Should the word "court" be capitalized in the following sentence?

The California Supreme **court** affirmed the lower court's decision.

a. Yes
b. No

3-C.7. Assuming that the word "court" refers to the United States Supreme Court, should the word "court" be capitalized in this sentence?

> The **court** denied certiorari, even though circuits were split on the issues.

a. Yes
b. No

EXERCISE SET 3-C

INTERMEDIATE LEVEL: CAPITALIZATION

Before beginning Exercise Set 3-C Intermediate Level, review the following and keep the *Manual* at hand as you work through the exercises:

- Rule 3.1, Words in Titles
- Rule 3.3, Capitalizing Specific Words

Instructions: Double underline the first letter of each word that should be capitalized in each of the following titles.

For example: ALWD citation manual: a professional system of citation

3-C.8. Double underline the first letter of each word that should be capitalized in the following title:

> fairly random: on compensating audited taxpayers

3-C.9. Double underline the first letter of each word that should be capitalized in the following title:

> form-based codes: measured success through both mandatory and optional implementation

3-C.10. Double underline the first letter of each word that should be capitalized in the following title:

> protecting the party girl: a new approach for evaluating intoxicated consent

3-C.11. Double underline the first letter of each word that should be capitalized in the following title:

> is this your bedroom?: reconsidering third-party consent searches under modern living arrangements

3-C.12. Double underline the first letter of each word that should be capitalized in the following title:

> one cheer for credit rating agencies: how the mark-to-mark accounting debate highlights the case for rating-dependent capital regulation

3-C.13. You are drafting an appellate brief to be submitted to the United States Court of Appeals for the Fifth Circuit. Should the word "court" be capitalized?

This **court** should affirm the lower court's holding because the judge should not be recused under 28 U.S.C. § 455(a)-(b)(1).

a. Yes
b. No

3-C.14. The sentence below appears in a case description in an inter-office memorandum. Should the word "defendant" be capitalized?

The court reasoned that the defendant had received a fair trial.

a. Yes
b. No

EXERCISE SET 3-C

EXPERT LEVEL: CAPITALIZATION

Before beginning Exercise Set 3-C Expert Level, review the following and keep the *Manual* at hand as you work through the exercises:

- Rule 1.0, Typeface
- Rule 3.0, Spelling and Capitalization

These exercises test your knowledge of both capitalization and typeface (sections A and C of this chapter).

3-C.15. Write the title, using the correct typeface (use underlining) and capitalization.

disputants' perceptions of dispute resolution procedures: an ex ante and ex post longitudinal empirical study

3-C.16. Write the title, using the correct typeface (use underlining) and capitalization.

when are public employees not really public employees? in the aftermath of garcetti v. ceballos

3-C.17. Write the title, using the correct typeface (use underlining) and capitalization.

raising the dead: an examination of in re kingsbury and maine's law regarding intestate succession and posthumous paternity testing.

3-C.18. Write the title, using the correct typeface (use underlining) and capitalization.

rev. rule 99-43: when to hold'em, when to fold'em, and when to book-down

D.   NUMBERS

When you present numbers that appear in citation sentences, citation clauses, or embedded citations, or numbers that appear in textual material, consult Rule 4.0. If the number appears in a citation (whether in a citation sentence or in an embedded citation), present the number as a numeral, unless you are citing a law review article or book that spells out the number in its title (e.g., *Thirteen Ways of Looking at a Lawsuit*).

It is the numbers that appear in the textual materials that require a little more practice, which the following exercises provide. Rule 4.2 covers everything from whether numbers should be designated as numbers or words, to how to present numbers with a dollar or percentage symbol, to how to present fractions. There is no expert level in this set of exercises.

EXERCISE SET 3-D

BASIC LEVEL: NUMBERS

Before beginning Exercise Set 3-D Basic Level, review the following and keep the *Manual* at hand as you work through the exercises:

• Rule 4.0, Numbers

3-D.1. Select the correct ordinal number to refer to a decision by the Twelfth District Court of Appeals.

    a. 12
    b. 12th
    c. 12th
    d. 12th.

3-D.2. Select the correct ordinal number to use to refer to a decision by the Second Circuit Court of Appeals.

    a. 2d
    b. 2nd
    c. 2d.
    d. 2th

3-D.3. Which sentence presents the date in the correct format?

    a. The appellate brief is due on Monday, November 30th, 2009.
    b. The appellate brief is due on Monday, November 30, 2009.

3-D.4. Correct the way the number appears in the following sentence.

    There are 2 cases in this jurisdiction that address this issue.

3-D.5. Correct the way the number appears in the following sentence.

    326 prospective jurors filled out questionnaires.

3-D.6. Correct the way the number appears in the following sentence.

At six thirty in the morning, the alarm rang.

3-D.7. Correct the way the numbers appear in the following sentence.

After the defendant robbed twenty-five jewelry stores over the past seven years, he was caught with over one hundred and thirty-two diamonds, forty-seven gold watches, and fifty-nine sets of cufflinks.

3-D.8. Correct the way the numbers appear in the following sentence.

The student must prove (I) she was subjected to sexual harassment, (II) she provided actual notice of the harassment to the school administrators, and (III) the administrator's response amounted to deliberate indifference.

EXERCISE SET 3-D

INTERMEDIATE LEVEL: NUMBERS

Before beginning Exercise Set 3-D Intermediate Level, review the following and keep the *Manual* at hand as you work through the exercises:

• Rule 4.0, Numbers

3-D.9. Correct the way the numbers appear in the following sentence.

The repairs took 3 to 4 minutes to complete and cost six dollars.

3-D.10. Correct the way the numbers appear in the following sentence.

Less than 2 decades old, the charter school movement has produced approximately 3400 charter schools enrolling nearly 1,000,000 students across the United States.

3-D.11. Correct the way the numbers appear in the following sentence.

Of the 300 cases the court has heard in the last 6 months, fourteen of the cases, or just over 25% or ¼, were decided in favor of the plaintiff.

E. PINPOINT REFERENCES

A number of rules—Rules 5.0 (Page and Location Numbers), 6.0 (Citing Sections and Paragraphs), 7.0 (Citing Footnotes and Endnotes), and 9.0 (Graphical Material, Appendices, and Other Subdivisions)—are helpful when you are providing a citation's pinpoint reference.

It is important not only to refer accurately to the source of the information—the case, the statute, the law review article, etc.—but also to provide a "pinpoint" reference, which gives the specific location of the information *within* the source. Pinpoint references are used whether you have paraphrased or quoted the information in text.

Sometimes the pinpoint reference is simply a page number or a span of pages; other times, the pinpoint reference is to a section and subsection. On occasion, both a section number and page number are available; in that case, use both (starting with the section number, followed by the page number). The importance of using pinpoint references cannot be emphasized enough. The accuracy of the pinpoint reference is so important that there is a sidebar addressing that topic, Sidebar 5.1.

It is rare that citations do not include pinpoint references. One example of a citation in which a pinpoint reference would not be needed is when the citation is referring to the entire source. Citing a source using the *"see generally"* signal indicates that the source is being used as helpful background information. Typically, the *entire* source provides helpful background information; therefore, a pinpoint reference is not necessary.

When you provide a pinpoint reference, be as specific as possible. For example, if you are citing a footnote in a case, the pinpoint reference not only gives the page of the case that the information is found on, but also includes the footnote number. If you are citing a statute's subsection, the pinpoint reference must include the section to which the subsection belongs.

The goals of the exercises below are to assist you in identifying the pinpoint reference in a citation and to familiarize you with two common pinpoint references—pages and subsections. There is no expert level in this set of exercises.

EXERCISE SET 3-E

BASIC LEVEL: PINPOINT REFERENCES

Before beginning Exercise Set 3-E Basic Level, review the following and keep the *Manual* at hand as you work through the exercises:

- Rule 5.0, Page and Location Numbers
- Rule 6.0, Citing Sections and Paragraphs

3-E.1. Identify the pinpoint reference in the following citation.

> *Byrd v. Lamari*, 846 So. 2d 334, 336 (Ala. 2003).

a. 846
b. 334
c. 336
d. 2d

3-E.2. Identify the pinpoint reference in the following citation.

> Carol Bast & Linda Samuels, *Plagiarism and Legal Scholarship in the Age of Information Sharing: The Need for Intellectual Honesty*, 57 Cath. U. L. Rev. 777, 780–782 (2008).

    a. 777
    b. 780–782
    c. 780
    d. 782

3-E.3. Identify the pinpoint reference in the following citation.

       28 U.S.C. § 455(a)-(b) (2006).

    a. 455
    b. 455(a)
    c. 455(b)
    d. 455(a)-(b)

3-E.4. **True or False:** If the case starts on page 1257 and the pinpoint page is also 1257, it is not necessary to repeat the pinpoint page.

    a. True
    b. False

3-E.5. The information is found on pages 106 to 116. Construct the pinpoint reference.

3-E.6. The information is found not only on pages 106 to 116, but also on 124 and 132. Construct the pinpoint reference.

EXERCISE SET 3-E

INTERMEDIATE LEVEL: PINPOINT REFERENCES

> Before beginning Exercise Set 3-E Intermediate Level, review the following and keep the *Manual* at hand as you work through the exercises:
>
> • Rule 5.0, Page and Location Numbers
> • Rule 6.0, Citing Sections and Paragraphs
> • Rule 7.0, Citing Footnotes and Endnotes

3-E.7. Look at only the pinpoint reference in the citation, and answer the following true/false question:

True or False: If the information you wanted to refer to is on page 113 of the law review article, the pinpoint reference in the citations is correct.

Sophie Sparrow, *Practicing Civility in the Legal Writing Course: Helping Law Students Learn Professionalism*, 13 Leg. Writing 113, 113 (2007).

    a. True
    b. False

3-E.8.   The document you are citing does not have page numbers, but it does have subsections.

> **True or False:** Even though the document does not have page numbers, number the pages so that you can use the page numbers as pinpoint references.

a. True
b. False

3-E.9.   The information is found not only on page 110, but also in section 15.2. Construct the pinpoint reference.

3-E.10. The information is found in sections 106 to 116. Construct the pinpoint reference.

3-E.11. You want to refer to section 1003.01 of the Florida Statutes, and the beginning of your citation is as follows: Fla. Stat. § 1003.01 (2009). But you also need to reference subdivisions (1), (9)(a), and (9)(d). Construct the pinpoint reference.

3-E.12. You want to refer to Sophie Sparrow's article (see the full citation below), but you would like to refer to footnotes 6 and 8 on page 115. Construct the pinpoint reference to go into the blank in the citation.

> Sophie Sparrow, *Practicing Civility in the Legal Writing Course: Helping Law Students Learn Professionalism*, 13 Leg. Writing 113, ___ (2007).

CHAPTER 4

USING QUOTATIONS

By necessity, by proclivity, and by delight, we all quote.[1]

As a competent and ethical legal writer, you should be not only careful to give attribution to all sources from which you borrow, but equally careful to indicate, via quotation, any specific language reproduced from such sources. When you quote, you should select only the most pertinent language from the cited source, mindful of its original context, and reproduce it accurately. Such care shows consideration for your readers; inexpertly edited quotations adversely affect your document's readability, and too much quotation dulls the reader's attention. Most important, your quotations will faithfully represent the source's original meaning.

Assuming you have found important language to quote from a source, you must decide how to present that quotation. Your first decision concerns how much to quote. Quotations are classified as **short** (fewer than fifty words or four lines of text) or **long** (at least fifty words or five lines of text). A quotation's length affects its format, the placement of its citation (in documents without footnotes), and often its punctuation. Your second decision affects the way you will fit the quotation into your text, including whether to weave the quotation into your own text or to present a freestanding quotation. Moreover, should you decide to edit a quotation, you will explicitly indicate any alterations or omissions, using square brackets, ellipsis points, or explanatory parentheticals to signal your changes.

Section A provides practice with format, placement, and punctuation of both short and long quotations, including handling quotations within quotations. In section B, you will practice editing quotations using brackets, ellipses, and parentheticals.

---

[1] Ralph Waldo Emerson, *Quotation and Originality*, in *Complete Works of Ralph Waldo Emerson* vol. 8, 178 (Edward Waldo Emerson ed., centenary ed., Houghton, Mifflin & Co. 1904) (available at http://books .google.com/books?id=eH_K1dqo_E0C&pg=PR17#v=onepage&q=&f=false). Emerson also wrote, "Next to the originator of a good sentence is the first quoter of it." *Id.* at 191. He has, however, often been credited with this observation as well: "I hate quotations. Tell me what you know."

A. FORMAT, PLACEMENT, AND PUNCTUATION

Use a quotation only when the language itself is worth attention (e.g., when your writing concerns the relevant words of a statute). It's your choice as the writer whether and how much to quote, and it's your job to integrate the quotation into your writing in a grammatical fashion.

Short Quotations

Consult Rule 47.4 when you use short quotations in your writing. Short quotations are easily woven into the text, and, when well chosen, can enliven your writing with memorable or key language from the quoted authority. Strive to quote the shortest possible excerpt from the original source, while preserving its meaning. Whether you are quoting a single word, a phrase, a clause, or a complete sentence, enclose a short quotation in **double quotation marks**, and cite the quotation's source.

When you quote an entire sentence without alteration, simply enclose it in double quotation marks, as shown in the first box at right.

When you quote less than a complete sentence (i.e., a word, phrase, or clause), ensure that the quotation grammatically and sensibly fits the textual sentence into which it is inserted. If the quotation does not easily fit the sentence, change the sentence or edit the quotation—or both. You may need to change the form of some words or add or delete words to make the quotation fit smoothly into your sentence's syntax, as shown in the second box.[2]

Be careful as you punctuate short quotations. Always place **commas and periods inside** the quotation marks, *even if* they are not present in the quotation's source. Do not insert a comma before the quotation unless (1) it would be needed even if you were not quoting, or (2) you are using an introductory phrase to attribute a direct quotation to its speaker or writer (e.g., he said, the court wrote, the rule states). It may help to imagine the quoted words floating in a cartoon bubble. Watch for verbs indicating speech or writing (e.g., ask, declare, exclaim, remark, say, state, write), as illustrated below, and insert a comma after the verb and before the quotation.

> "While commercial motivation and fair use can exist side by side, the court may consider whether the alleged infringing use was primarily for public benefit or for private commercial gain." **Citation**

> In assessing a claim of sexual harassment to be actionable, the court determines whether the conduct was "sufficiently severe or pervasive to alter the conditions of [the victim's] employment and create an abusive working environment." **Citation**

Federal Rule of Evidence 607 **states,** "The credibility of a witness may be attacked by any party, including the party calling the witness."

> The credibility of a witness may be attacked by any party, including the party calling the witness.

---

[2] Alterations and omissions are covered below in section B.

In a dissenting opinion, Justice Blackmun **wrote,** "The Constitution requires that criminal defendants be provided with a fair trial, not merely a 'good faith' try at a fair trial."

> The Constitution requires that criminal defendants be provided with a fair trial, not merely a "good faith" try at a fair trial.

Always place **colons and semi-colons outside** the quotation marks. A **question mark or an exclamation mark** may appear in **either place**: put it *inside* the quotation marks if it is part of the material being quoted; if not, place it *outside* the quotation marks. As you proofread your writing, check to be sure that every quotation has matching opening and closing marks.

Table 4.1 contrasts in **bold** an original source and a short quotation from that source, with its punctuation, to illustrate the foregoing rules.

TABLE 4.1

COMPARING PUNCTUATION IN ORIGINAL SOURCE AND QUOTATION

Original source	Quotation
To this end no man **can be a judge in his own case** and no man is **permitted to try cases where he has an interest in the outcome.**[3]	The Court recited the general rules that no one **"can be a judge in his own case,"** nor is anyone **"permitted to try cases where he has an interest in the outcome."**
The Court stated that content discrimination may be permissible if it **preserves the purposes of the limited forum,** but viewpoint discrimination is presumed impermissible **when directed against speech otherwise within the forum's limitation.**[4]	The ordinance's discrimination on the basis of the speech's content **"preserves the purposes of the limited forum";** such discrimination is not permissible, however, **"when directed against speech otherwise within the forum's limitation."**
At bottom, this matter requires that we decide one fundamental issue: **whether a reasonable, well-informed observer could question the Judge's impartiality.**[5]	In deciding the motion to recuse, did the Court consider **"whether a reasonable, well-informed observer could question the Judge's impartiality"**?
Why should we refuse to let state courts enforce apartheid in residential areas of our cities but let state courts enforce apartheid in restaurants? If a court decree is state action in one case, it is in the other. Property rights, so heavily underscored, are equally involved in each case.[6]	In his concurring opinion, Justice Douglas asked, **"Why should we refuse to let state courts enforce apartheid in residential areas of our cities but let state courts enforce apartheid in restaurants?"**

---

[3] *In re Murchison*, 349 U.S. 133, 136 (1955).
[4] *Pooh-Bah Enters., Inc. v. Co. of Cook*, 905 N.E.2d 781, 794 (Ill. 2009).
[5] *In re U.S.*, 572 F.3d 301, 310 (7th Cir. 2009).
[6] *Bell v. Md.*, 378 U.S. 226, 259 (1964) (Douglas, J., concurring).

You must also consider where to place the citation to a short quotation. In a **document without footnotes**, such as an inter-office memorandum or a brief, cite the source of a quotation in a *citation sentence* immediately following the sentence containing the quotation. A sentence in text may contain quotations from more than one source, or from more than one page, section, or other subdivision within the same source (i.e., from more than one pinpoint reference). In such cases, cite the source of each quotation in a citation clause following each quotation's closing quotation marks. If the source of the quotation is identifiable from other text in your sentence, however, such as an embedded citation, no additional citation is needed. Read Rules 43.2(a), 43.2(b), and 47.4(b), and study the examples in each.

In a **document with footnotes**, such as a law review article, place the footnote number immediately after the closing quotation mark, even if it is not at the end of the sentence in text. If a sentence in text contains more than one quoted phrase from the same pinpoint reference, however, you may either place a footnote reference after each quotation, or place a single footnote reference to the source at the end of the sentence in text. Read Rule 47.4(c), and study the examples. Table 4.2 demonstrates the placement of citations to short quotations.

TABLE 4.2

PLACEMENT OF CITATIONS TO SHORT QUOTATIONS

Documents without footnotes	Although experts may offer opinion testimony "[i]f scientific, technical, or other specialized knowledge will assist the trier of fact to understand the evidence or to determine a fact in issue," Fed. R. Evid. 702, they cannot "escape screening by the district court simply by stating that their conclusions were not reached by any particular method or technique," *Watkins v. Telsmith, Inc.,* 121 F.3d 984, 991 (5th Cir. 1997).
Documents with footnotes	Although experts may offer opinion testimony "[i]f scientific, technical, or other specialized knowledge will assist the trier of fact to understand the evidence or to determine a fact in issue,"[22] they cannot "escape screening by the district court simply by stating that their conclusions were not reached by any particular method or technique."[23] [22]Fed. R. Evid. 702. [23]*Watkins v. Telsmith, Inc.,* 121 F.3d 984, 991 (5th Cir. 1997).

Long Quotations, Poetry, and Epigraphs

Consult Rules 47.5 and 47.6 when you use long quotations, poetry, or epigraphs in your writing. An **epigraph** is a quotation used to introduce a work or a chapter. The Emerson quotation that begins this chapter is an epigraph.

Long quotations, poetry, and epigraphs are presented in **block format**, but they are *not* enclosed within quotation marks, as the following example demonstrates:

> Long quotations are easily spotted by their unique formatting, which makes them stand out on the page. Long quotations begin on a new line, and they are typically presented in left-justified, single-spaced lines,[7] inside a frame of white space. The frame is created by using one-tab or half-inch indentions on both the left and right margins.

Although it is possible to integrate a long quotation into your own sentence, most long quotations stand on their own. They are often preceded by an introductory sentence ending in a colon. Do not indent the first line of the block unless the quotation comes from the indented beginning of a paragraph in the original source. If you wish to quote multiple paragraphs, keep the original paragraph organization, but use block formatting for them all, and indent the first line of each paragraph.

The only time a long quotation is *not* placed in block format is when it is reproduced within a citation's explanatory parenthetical. Such quotations are instead treated like short quotations and enclosed in double quotation marks. An example is provided with Rule 47.5(b).

The citation to the source of the long quotation, poem, or epigraph should not be placed in the block itself because it is not part of the quotation. Only the actual quotation goes into the block, as the example in Rule 47.5(a) demonstrates. In **documents without footnotes**, place the citation on a new line at the left margin. In **documents with footnotes**, place the footnote number at the end of the block. Table 4.3 illustrates the placement of citations to long quotations.

TABLE 4.3

PLACEMENT OF CITATIONS TO LONG QUOTATIONS

Documents without footnotes	Even when they are advocates, good writers care about their readers. They look for ways to simplify their writing and to make the reading easier. One way is to use headings to mark the logical subdivisions of a text: The more complicated the document, the simpler and the more overt you should make the structure. The best way to do this is to use informative, easily accessible headings. Good headings and subheadings make a document much easier to follow. Not only do they serve as navigational aids for readers, but they'll also help you organize thoughts logically. Bryan A. Garner, *Garner on Language and Writing* 99 (ABA 2009). The organization should be tied to the logic of the analysis. But far too often, the organization reveals that the writer opted to "retrace the history of how [he] thought through an issue." Stephen V. Armstrong & Timothy P. Terrell, *Thinking Like a Writer* 29 (3d ed., Practising L. Inst. 2008).

---

[7] Some court rules require briefs to be double-spaced throughout, even if you are using long quotations. If your jurisdiction's court rules have such a requirement, follow it when you prepare briefs.

TABLE 4.3

(Continued)

Documents with footnotes	Even when they are advocates, good writers care about their readers. They look for ways to simplify their writing and to make the reading easier. One way is to use headings to mark the logical subdivisions of a text:

> The more complicated the document, the simpler and the more overt you should make the structure. The best way to do this is to use informative, easily accessible headings. Good headings and subheadings make a document much easier to follow. Not only do they serve as navigational aids for readers, but they'll also help you organize thoughts logically.[14]

> The organization should be tied to the logic of the analysis. But far too often, the organization reveals that the writer opted to "retrace the history of how [he] thought through an issue."[15]

[14]Bryan A. Garner, *Garner on Language and Writing* 99 (ABA 2009).
[15]*Stephen V. Armstrong & Timothy P. Terrell, Thinking Like a Writer* 29 (3d ed., Practising L. Inst. 2008).

Sources Quoting Other Sources

If a short quotation itself contains another quotation, the internal quotation is enclosed in **single quotation marks**. The citation should parenthetically indicate the internal quotation's source. Place the parenthetical immediately after the citation to the main quotation and before an explanatory parenthetical, if any. Begin the parenthetical with the gerund "quoting"; use ordinary roman type, not italics. See the example in the box, which puts the internal quotation in bold.

Do not rely on the format of the citation to the internal source as given in the source you are quoting. It may be obsolete, inaccurate, or incomplete. Look up the internal source yourself, and construct its citation according to applicable *ALWD Citation Manual* rules. If the internal citation itself has a parenthetical (e.g., a date parenthetical), watch the parentheses, and be sure you have closed both sets.

> The Court explained that the "enquiry focuses on whether the new work merely supersedes the objects of the original creation, or whether and to what extent it is **'transformative,'** altering the original with new expression, meaning, or message." *Campbell*, 510 U.S. at 579 (quoting Pierre N. Leval, *Toward a Fair Use Standard*, 103 Harv. L. Rev. 1105, 1111 (1990)).

An internal quotation within a block-format quotation is enclosed in **double quotation marks**, as shown in the example below. If the long quotation contains the citation to the internal quotation's source, it is customary to retain it as it appears in the original instead of citing it parenthetically. You may, however, correct any errors in the quoted citation, as long as you indicate your alterations (see more on this in section B below). For more examples of quotations within long and short quotations, see Rule 47.7.

> Determining proximate cause is ordinarily a function for the jury, not the court, as the Arkansas Supreme Court has previously noted:
>
> > Under the comparative fault statute, there must be a determination of proximate cause before any fault can be assessed against a claiming party. *Craig v. Traylor*, 323 Ark. 363, 915 S.W.2d 257 (1996). . . . Proximate cause is defined as **"that which in a natural and continuous sequence, unbroken by any efficient intervening cause, produces the injury, and without which the result would not have occurred."** *Id.* at 370, 915 S.W.2d at 260 (quoting *Williams v. Mozark Fire Extinguisher Co.*, 318 Ark. 792, 888 S.W.2d 303 (1994)).
>
> *Ouachita Wilderness Inst., Inc. v. Mergen*, 947 S.W.2d 780, 785 (Ark. 1997).

As the writer, you retain ultimate control over what and how much to quote. If you find it awkward or unwieldy to present a quotation that itself contains another quotation, you may prefer to go directly to the older quoted source and use it on its own. If that is not a feasible option, however, consider editing the quotation, following the guidelines set out below in section B.

You will find basic-level and intermediate-level exercises in Exercise Set 4-A. All expert-level questions for this chapter are placed in the capstone expert-level exercises in Exercise Set 4-B.

EXERCISE SET 4-A

BASIC LEVEL: FORMAT, PLACEMENT, AND PUNCTUATION

Before beginning Exercise Set 4-A Basic Level, review the following and keep the *Manual* at hand as you work through the exercises:

- Rule 43.0, Citation Placement and Use
- Rule 47.3, Relation to Text
- Rule 47.4, Short Quotations
- Rule 47.5, Longer Quotations
- Rule 47.7, Quotations within Quotations

4-A.1.   The quotation shown below is from *United States v. Vig*, 167 F.3d 443, 451 (8th Cir. 1999) (Arnold, J., dissenting). Which sentence correctly incorporates and punctuates the quotation?

> Is it significant that computer files can be made into tangible objects by printing, or is printing from files just like tearing pages from a book?

a. Arguing against the majority's interpretation of the statute, the dissent asked, "Is it significant that computer files can be made into tangible objects by printing, or is printing from files just like tearing pages from a book?"

b. Arguing against the majority's interpretation of the statute, the dissent asked, "Is it significant that computer files can be made into tangible objects by printing, or is printing from files just like tearing pages from a book"?

c. Arguing against the majority's interpretation of the statute, the dissent asked "Is it significant that computer files can be made into tangible objects by printing, or is printing from files just like tearing pages from a book."

d. Arguing against the majority's interpretation of the statute, the dissent asked if "it is significant that computer files can be made into tangible objects by printing, or is printing from files just like tearing pages from a book".

4-A.2. The quotation shown below is from *United States v. Cronic*, 466 U.S. 648, 656 (1984). Which sentence correctly and grammatically incorporates and punctuates the language **in bold**?

> The right to the effective assistance of counsel is thus the right of the accused to require the prosecution's case to survive **the crucible of meaningful adversarial testing**.

a. The right to counsel demands that the prosecution's evidence against the accused be subjected to, "the crucible of meaningful adversarial testing."

b. The right to counsel demands that the prosecution's evidence against the accused be subjected to, "the crucible of meaningful adversarial testing."

c. The right to counsel demands that the prosecution's evidence against the accused be subjected to "the crucible of meaningful adversarial testing."

d. The right to counsel demands that the prosecution's evidence against the accused be subjected to "the crucible of meaningful adversarial testing".

4-A.3. Which sentence correctly uses, punctuates, and places the citations for quotations from the language **in bold** in the two passages shown below?

> 42 U.S.C. § 12132 (2006):
>
> Subject to the provisions of this subchapter, no **qualified individual with a disability** shall, by reason of such disability, **be excluded from participation in or be denied the benefits of the services, programs, or activities of a public entity**, or be subjected to discrimination by any such entity.
>
> *Alexander v. Choate*, 469 U.S. 287, 301 (1985):
>
> The benefit itself, of course, cannot be defined in a way that effectively denies otherwise qualified handicapped individuals the **meaningful access** to which they are entitled; to assure meaningful access, reasonable accommodations in the grantee's program or benefit may have to be made.

a. A "qualified individual with a disability" cannot "be excluded from participation in or be denied the benefits of the services, programs, or activities of a public entity" on the basis of that disability, a protection that has been characterized as a guarantee of "meaningful access" to government benefits and programs. 42 U.S.C. § 12132 (2006); *Alexander v. Choate*, 469 U.S. 287, 301 (1985).

b. A "qualified individual with a disability" cannot "be excluded from participation in or be denied the benefits of the services, programs, or activities of a public entity" on the basis of that disability, 42 U.S.C. § 12132 (2006), a protection that has been characterized as a guarantee of "meaningful access" to government benefits and programs, *Alexander v. Choate*, 469 U.S. 287, 301 (1985).

c. A "qualified individual with a disability" 42 U.S.C. § 12132 (2006), cannot "be excluded from participation in or be denied the benefits of the services, programs, or activities of a public entity" 42 U.S.C. § 12132 (2006), on the basis of that disability, a protection that has been characterized as a guarantee of "meaningful access" to government benefits and programs. *Alexander v. Choate*, 469 U.S. 287, 301 (1985).

d. A "qualified individual with a disability" cannot "be excluded from participation in or be denied the benefits of the services, programs, or activities of a public entity" on the basis of that disability, a protection that has been characterized as a guarantee of "meaningful access" to government benefits and programs. *Alexander v. Choate*, 469 U.S. 287, 301 (1985); 42 U.S.C. § 12132 (2006).

4-A.4. The following passage appears in *Alexander v. Eeds*, 392 F.3d 138, 142 (5th Cir. 2004). You wish to quote the language **in bold** in your brief in support of a motion for summary judgment. Which of the following correctly quotes and cites the passage?

> Facts are material only if they could affect the lawsuit's outcome. *Anderson v. Liberty Lobby, Inc.*, 477 U.S. 242, 248, 106 S. Ct. 2505, 91 L. Ed. 2d 202 (1986). Any factual controversy will be resolved in the nonmovant's favor, **but only "when both parties have submitted evidence of contradictory facts."** *Olabisiomotosho v. City of Houston*, 185 F.3d 521, 525 (5th Cir. 1999).

    a. In deciding whether facts are material, the court must resolve controversies in favor of the nonmoving party, "but only when both parties have submitted evidence of contradictory facts." *Alexander v. Eeds*, 392 F.3d 138, 142 (5th Cir. 2004) (quoting *Olabisiomotosho v. City of Houston*, 185 F.3d 521, 525 (5th Cir. 1999)).

    b. In deciding whether facts are material, the court must resolve controversies in favor of the nonmoving party, "but only 'when both parties have submitted evidence of contradictory facts.'" *Alexander v. Eeds*, 392 F.3d 138, 142 (5th Cir. 2004) (quoting *Olabisiomotosho v. City of Houston*, 185 F.3d 521, 525 (5th Cir. 1999)).

    c. In deciding whether facts are material, the court must resolve controversies in favor of the nonmoving party, "but only 'when both parties have submitted evidence of contradictory facts.'" *Alexander v. Eeds*, 392 F.3d 138, 142 (5th Cir. 2004), *quoting Olabisiomotosho v. City of Houston*, 185 F.3d 521, 525 (5th Cir. 1999).

    d. In deciding whether facts are material, the court must resolve controversies in favor of the nonmoving party, "but only "when both parties have submitted evidence of contradictory facts." *Alexander v. Eeds*, 392 F.3d 138, 142 (5th Cir. 2004) (quoting *Olabisiomotosho v. City of Houston*, 185 F.3d 521, 525 (5th Cir. 1999).

4-A.5. The quotation shown below is from *Erickson v. Farmland Industries, Inc.*, 271 F.3d 718, 724 (8th Cir. 2001). Which sentence correctly and grammatically incorporates and punctuates the language **in bold**?

> The direct evidence required to shift the burden of proof is **evidence of conduct or statements by persons involved in making the employment decision directly manifesting a discriminatory attitude, of a sufficient quantum and gravity** that would allow the factfinder to conclude that attitude more likely than not was a motivating factor in the employment decision.

    a. Without "evidence of conduct or statements by persons involved in making the employment decision directly manifesting a discriminatory attitude, of a sufficient quantum and gravity", the burden of proof should not be shifted.

    b. When the plaintiff presented, "evidence of conduct or statements by persons involved in making the employment decision directly manifesting a discriminatory attitude, of a sufficient quantum and gravity" the burden of proof should have shifted.

    c. By presenting "evidence of conduct or statements by persons involved in making the employment decision directly manifesting a discriminatory attitude, of a sufficient quantum and gravity."

    d. The burden of proof shifted when the plaintiff presented "evidence of conduct or statements by persons involved in making the employment decision directly manifesting a discriminatory attitude, of a sufficient quantum and gravity" to convince a jury that his firing was the result of the supervisor's bias.

4-A.6.   You are writing a seminar paper on the constitutionality of the death penalty, and you wish to quote the passage shown below from the concurring opinion of Justice Brennan in *Furman v. Georgia*, 408 U.S. 238, 272 (1972). Which of the following correctly quotes and cites the passage?

> More than the presence of pain, however, is comprehended in the judgment that the extreme severity of a punishment makes it degrading to the dignity of human beings. The barbaric punishments condemned by history, "punishments which inflict torture, such as the rack, the thumbscrew, the iron boot, the stretching of limbs and the like," are, of course, "attended with acute pain and suffering." *O'Neil v. Vermont*, 144 U.S. 323, 339 (1892) (Field, J., dissenting).

a. As one justice wrote, "More than the presence of pain, however, is comprehended in the judgment that the extreme severity of a punishment makes it degrading to the dignity of human beings. The barbaric punishments condemned by history, 'punishments which inflict torture, such as the rack, the thumbscrew, the iron boot, the stretching of limbs and the like,' are, of course, 'attended with acute pain and suffering.' *O'Neil v. Vermont*, 144 U.S. 323, 339 (1892) (Field, J., dissenting)." *Furman v. Georgia*, 408 U.S. 238, 272 (1972) (Brennan, J., concurring).

b. As one justice wrote, "More than the presence of pain, however, is comprehended in the judgment that the extreme severity of a punishment makes it degrading to the dignity of human beings. The barbaric punishments condemned by history, "punishments which inflict torture, such as the rack, the thumbscrew, the iron boot, the stretching of limbs and the like," are, of course, "attended with acute pain and suffering." *Furman v. Georgia*, 408 U.S. 238, 272 (1972) (Brennan, J., concurring) (quoting *O'Neil v. Vermont*, 144 U.S. 323, 339 (1892) (Field, J., dissenting)).

c. As one justice wrote,

> More than the presence of pain, however, is comprehended in the judgment that the extreme severity of a punishment makes it degrading to the dignity of human beings. The barbaric punishments condemned by history, "punishments which inflict torture, such as the rack, the thumbscrew, the iron boot, the stretching of limbs and the like," are, of course, "attended with acute pain and suffering." *O'Neil v. Vermont*, 144 U.S. 323, 339 (1892) (Field, J., dissenting).

Furman v. Georgia, 408 U.S. 238, 272 (1972) (Brennan, J., concurring).

d. As one justice wrote,

> More than the presence of pain, however, is comprehended in the judgment that the extreme severity of a punishment makes it degrading to the dignity of human beings. The barbaric punishments condemned by history, 'punishments which inflict torture, such as the rack, the thumbscrew, the iron boot, the stretching of limbs and the like,' are, of course, 'attended with acute pain and suffering.'

Furman v. Georgia, 408 U.S. 238, 272 (1972) (quoting *O'Neil v. Vermont*, 144 U.S. 323, 339 (1892) (Field, J., dissenting)) (Brennan, J., concurring).

4-A.7. The quotation shown below is from Massachusetts General Laws Annotated chapter 111, section 156 (West 2003). Which sentence correctly and grammatically incorporates and punctuates the language **in bold**?

> No person shall in a city occupy or use a building for a livery stable, or a stable for taking or keeping horses and carriages for hire or to let, **within two hundred feet of a church or meeting house erected and used for the public worship of God**, without the written consent of the religious society or parish worshipping therein; but this section shall not prevent such occupation and use if authorized by law on May seventeenth, eighteen hundred and ninety-one, to the extent then authorized.

    a. If it keeps its horses and carriages, "within two hundred feet of a church or meeting house erected and used for the public worship of God" the defendant will be violating the statute.

    b. Unless it had been in the building since May 17, 1891, or had written consent of the religious society or parish worshipping in a "church or meeting house erected and used for the public worship of God", the defendant would not be allowed to keep horses and carriages within two hundred feet.

    c. The defendant cannot occupy or use the building, "within two hundred feet of a church or meeting house erected and used for the public worship of God," as a livery stable or stable for keeping horses and carriages.

    d. If the religious group does not consent in writing to its presence, the defendant's carriage-tour company will have to lease another site, due to a statute that prohibits keeping horses and carriages "within two hundred feet of a church or meeting house erected and used for the public worship of God."

4-A.8. The quotation shown below is from David R. Cleveland, *Overturning the Last Stone: The Final Step in Returning Precedential Status to All Opinions*, 10 J. App. Prac. & Process 61, 137 (2009). Which sentence correctly and grammatically incorporates and punctuates the language **in bold**?

> Some have argued that the practice of declaring certain (now most) decisions of the federal courts to be non-precedential is not a cause for alarm.[397] The better perspective, however, is that the practice **causes an even more insidious harm than cutting the courts free from precedent.** Allowing courts to choose at the time of opinion writing what decisions are and are not precedent allows them to deprive the common law of valuable precedents, **to make law good only for a single time and place, to treat similar cases dissimilarly, and to cause some issues to evade review.**[398]

    a. Professor Cleveland argues that the federal courts' practice with regard to designating which of their opinions are non-precedential, "causes an even more insidious harm than cutting the courts free from precedent," in part because it has the effect, "to make law good only for a single time and place, to treat similar cases dissimilarly, and to cause some issues to evade review."

    b. Professor Cleveland declares that allowing courts to stamp their decisions as non-precedential "causes an even more insidious harm than cutting the courts free from precedent," not just because it adversely affects the development of the common law, but also because it allows courts "to make law good only for a single time and place, to treat similar cases dissimilarly, and to cause some issues to evade review."

    c. The courts' common practice of designating most of their opinions as non-precedential, says Professor Cleveland, "causes an even more insidious harm than cutting the courts free from precedent" because it permits them 'to make law good only for a single time and place, to treat similar cases dissimilarly, and to cause some issues to evade review."

    d. Arguing that it is harmful to let federal courts decide on their own "to make law good only for a single time and place, to treat similar cases dissimilarly, and to cause some issues to evade review", Professor Cleveland views the practice of declaring some decisions as non-precedential "causes an even more insidious harm than cutting the courts free from precedent".

EXERCISE SET 4-A

INTERMEDIATE LEVEL: FORMAT, PLACEMENT, AND PUNCTUATION

> Before beginning Exercise Set 4-A Intermediate Level, review the following and keep the *Manual* at hand as you work through the exercises:
>
> - Rule 43.0, Citation Placement and Use
> - Rule 47.2, Accuracy
> - Rule 47.3, Relation to Text
>
> - Rule 47.4, Short Quotations
> - Rule 47.5, Longer Quotations
> - Rule 47.7, Quotations within Quotations

4-A.9.   The quotation below is from *Chevron U.S.A., Inc. v. Natural Resources Defense Council, Inc.*, 467 U.S. 837, 866 (1984). Which sentence not only correctly and grammatically incorporates and punctuates the entire quotation, but also correctly places its citation?

When a challenge to an agency construction of a statutory provision, fairly conceptualized, really centers on the wisdom of the agency's policy, rather than whether it is a reasonable choice within a gap left open by Congress, the challenge must fail. In such a case, federal judges—who have no constituency— have a duty to respect legitimate policy choices made by those who do.

---

a. Agreeing with the EPA's regulatory response, the majority explained that "When a challenge to an agency construction of a statutory provision, fairly conceptualized, really centers on the wisdom of the agency's policy, rather than whether it is a reasonable choice within a gap left open by Congress, the challenge must fail. In such a case, federal judges—who have no constituency—have a duty to respect legitimate policy choices made by those who do." *Chevron U.S.A., Inc. v. Nat. Resources Def. Council, Inc.*, 467 U.S. 837, 866 (1984).

b. As the Supreme Court has pointed out, when it comes to making policy, agencies are due a great deal of deference:

> When a challenge to an agency construction of a statutory provision, fairly conceptualized, really centers on the wisdom of the agency's policy, rather than whether it is a reasonable choice within a gap left open by Congress, the challenge must fail. In such a case, federal judges—who have no constituency—have a duty to respect legitimate policy choices made by those who do. *Chevron U.S.A., Inc. v. Nat. Resources Def. Council, Inc.*, 467 U.S. 837, 866 (1984).

c. The Court recognized Congress's power to delegate certain kinds of decision-making to federal agencies, without second-guessing by the courts:

> When a challenge to an agency construction of a statutory provision, fairly conceptualized, really centers on the wisdom of the agency's policy, rather than whether it is a reasonable choice within a gap left open by Congress, the challenge must fail. In such a case, federal judges—who have no constituency—have a duty to respect legitimate policy choices made by those who do.

> *Chevron U.S.A., Inc. v. Nat. Resources Def. Council, Inc.*, 467 U.S. 837, 866 (1984).

d. In explaining why it was reversing the circuit court, the Supreme Court stated, "When a challenge to an agency construction of a statutory provision, fairly conceptualized, really centers on the wisdom of the agency's policy, rather than whether it is a reasonable choice within a gap left open by Congress, the challenge must fail. In such a case, federal judges—who have no constituency—have a duty to respect legitimate policy choices made by those who do."

Chevron U.S.A., Inc. v. Nat. Resources Def. Council, Inc., 467 U.S. 837, 866 (1984).

4-A.10. The quotation below is from *Obert v. Saville*, 624 N.E.2d 928, 931 (Ill. App. 2d Dist. 1993) (citations omitted). Which sentence correctly and grammatically incorporates and punctuates language from the quotation?

> A reviewing court is entitled to have issues clearly defined with pertinent authority cited and cohesive arguments presented, and it is not a repository into which an appellant may foist the burden of argument and research; it is neither the function nor the obligation of this court to act as an advocate or search the record for error.

a. The court refused to consider the party's brief, stating that "A reviewing court is entitled to have issues clearly defined with pertinent authority cited and cohesive arguments presented".

b. The judge wrote "A reviewing court is entitled to have issues clearly defined with pertinent authority cited and cohesive arguments presented . . .".

c. Expressing its frustration with an inadequate brief, the court declared, "A reviewing court is entitled to have issues clearly defined with pertinent authority cited and cohesive arguments presented."

d. The case needed careful research and writing, "A reviewing court is entitled to have issues clearly defined with pertinent authority cited and cohesive arguments presented[.]"

4-A.11. Which sentence not only correctly and grammatically uses and punctuates the quotations from the two passages of Lawrence Friedman's book shown below, but also correctly places their citations?

> Lawrence M. Friedman, *A History of American Law* 573 (2d ed., Simon & Schuster, Inc. 1985):
>
> As of 1900, most states still *technically* recognized the possibility of a common-law crime. But some states had statutes that specifically abolished the concept. These statutes stated bluntly that all crimes were listed in the penal code, and nothing else was a crime.
>
> Lawrence M. Friedman, A History of American Law 582 (2d ed., Simon & Schuster, Inc. 1985):
>
> Over the years, the criminal codes, like the dollar, became markedly inflated. Traditional crimes—treason, murder, burglary, arson, and rape—stayed on the books; new crimes were constantly added.

a. Even though some state statutes claimed "that all crimes were listed in the penal code," with changing times, states "constantly added new crimes." Lawrence M. Friedman, *A History of American Law* 573, 582 (2d ed., Simon & Schuster, Inc. 1985).

b. Common-law crime was "specifically abolished" by some state statutes, Lawrence M. Friedman, *A History of American Law* 573 (2d ed., Simon & Schuster, Inc. 1985), and in order to enumerate all the possible offenses, "new crimes were constantly added," *id.* at 582.

c. Criminal codes had to "become markedly inflated" over the years, Lawrence M. Friedman, *A History of American Law* 582 (2d ed., Simon & Schuster, Inc. 1985), despite the claim of many early twentieth-century codes that "all crimes were listed in the penal code." *Id.* at 573.

d. By 1900, most states, "*technically* recognized the possibility of a common-law crime," Lawrence M. Friedman, *A History of American Law* 573, 582 (2d ed., Simon & Schuster, Inc. 1985), and while crimes such as, "treason, murder, burglary, arson, and rape stayed on the books, new crimes were constantly added," *id.*

4-A.12.   Which sentence not only correctly and grammatically uses and punctuates the quotations from the three passages shown below, but also correctly places their citations?

Federal Rule of Evidence 607:

The credibility of a witness may be attacked by any party, including the party calling the witness.

U.S. v. Carter, 973 F.2d 1509, 1513 (10th Cir. 1992):

Appellate courts are reluctant to find that a party called a witness for an improper purpose. The reason is simple. Evaluating the purpose of counsel's decision to call a witness is akin to pushing a string—neither is easy.

U.S. v. Webster, 734 F.2d 1191, 1192 (7th Cir. 1984):

But it would be an abuse of the rule, in a criminal case, for the prosecution to call a witness that it knew would not give it useful evidence, just so it could introduce hearsay evidence against the defendant in the hope that the jury would miss the subtle distinction between impeachment and substantive evidence—or, if it didn't miss it, would ignore it. The purpose would not be to impeach the witness but to put in hearsay as substantive evidence against the defendant, which Rule 607 does not contemplate or authorize.

---

a. While "any party, including the party calling the witness," is permitted to impeach a witness's credibility, and even though courts should be "reluctant to find that a party called a witness for an improper purpose," if the Government deliberately called a witness who had no personal knowledge of the defendant's statements, its "purpose would not be to impeach the witness but to put in hearsay as substantive evidence against the defendant, which Rule 607 does not contemplate or authorize." Fed. R. Evid. 607; *U.S. v. Carter*, 973 F.2d 1509, 1513 (10th Cir. 1992); *U.S. v. Webster*, 734 F.2d 1191, 1192 (7th Cir. 1984).

b. While "any party, including the party calling the witness" is permitted to impeach a witness's credibility, Fed. R. Evid. 607, and even though courts should be, "reluctant to find that a party called a witness for an improper purpose," *U.S. v. Carter*, 973 F.2d 1509, 1513 (10th Cir. 1992), if the Government deliberately called a witness who had no personal knowledge of the defendant's statements, its "purpose would not be to impeach the witness but to put in hearsay as substantive evidence against the defendant, which Rule 607 does not contemplate or authorize." *U.S. v. Webster*, 734 F.2d 1191, 1192 (7th Cir. 1984).

c. While "any party, including the party calling the witness," is permitted to impeach a witness's credibility, Fed. R. Evid. 607; and even though courts should be "reluctant to find that a party called a witness for an improper purpose," *U.S. v. Carter*, 973 F.2d 1509, 1513 (10th Cir. 1992); if the Government deliberately called a witness who had no personal knowledge of the defendant's statements, its "purpose would not be to impeach the witness but to put in hearsay as substantive evidence against the defendant, which Rule 607 does not contemplate or authorize;" *U.S. v. Webster*, 734 F.2d 1191, 1192 (7th Cir. 1984).

d. While "any party, including the party calling the witness" is permitted to impeach a witness's credibility, Fed. R. Evid. 607, and even though courts should be "reluctant to find that a party called a witness for an improper purpose," *U.S. v. Carter*, 973 F.2d 1509, 1513 (10th Cir. 1992), if the Government deliberately called a witness who had no personal knowledge of the defendant's statements, its "purpose would not be to impeach the witness but to put in hearsay as substantive evidence against the defendant, which Rule 607 does not contemplate or authorize," *U.S. v. Webster*, 734 F.2d 1191, 1192 (7th Cir. 1984).

EXERCISE SET 4-A

EXPERT LEVEL: FORMAT, PLACEMENT, AND PUNCTUATION

Before beginning Exercise Set 4-A Expert Level, review the following and keep the *Manual* at hand as you work through the exercises:

- Rule 43.0, Citation Placement and Use
- Rule 47.3, Relation to Text
- Rule 47.4, Short Quotations
- Rule 47.5, Longer Quotations
- Rule 47.7, Quotations within Quotations

The questions in this exercise set are based on a passage adapted from *Oregon v. Ice*, _____ U.S. _____, 129 S. Ct. 711, 717 (2009). Insert quotations of the **bold-face phrases** into the corresponding sentences below, using appropriate punctuation, where necessary, to keep the sentences grammatically correct.

Our application of *Apprendi's* rule [4-A.13] **must honor the "longstanding common-law practice"** in which the rule is rooted. *Cunningham*, 549 U.S. at 281. The rule's animating principle is [4-A.14] **the preservation of the jury's historic role as a bulwark between the State and the accused** at the trial for an alleged offense. *See Apprendi*, 530 U.S. at 477. Guided by that principle, our opinions make clear that [4-A.15] **the Sixth Amendment does not countenance legislative encroachment on the jury's traditional domain**. *See id.* at 497. We accordingly considered whether the finding of a particular fact was understood as within "the domain of the jury . . . by those who framed the Bill of Rights." *Harris v. U.S.*, 536 U.S. 545, 557 (2002) (plurality opinion). In undertaking this inquiry, we remain cognizant that [4-A.16] **administration of a discrete criminal justice system is among the basic sovereign prerogatives** States retain. *See e.g. Patterson v. N.Y.*, 432 U.S. 197, 201 (1977).

4-A.13. In deciding whether to apply the rule from *Apprendi* to the Oregon case, the Court determined that it _____ that is the foundation of the rule.

4-A.14. The opinion noted _____.

4-A.15. Even though _____, the Court had to give due weight to concerns for state sovereignty.

4-A.16. Thus, remembering that _____, the Court declined to extend *Apprendi*.

B. REPRODUCING QUOTED MATERIAL WITH ACCURACY

Accurate quotation demands careful proofreading. When you quote, compare what you have typed to the original text. It may help to read aloud or highlight the words on your computer screen or paper copy. Confirm and correct, if necessary, the way you have reproduced the original source's wording, spelling, capitalization, and punctuation. Pay attention to whether the original contains omissions, alterations, or words italicized for emphasis, and reproduce it as shown. You may prefer, however, to make changes to the original in order for it to fit your text and needs. You are permitted to make those changes, provided you clearly indicate what you have changed by using brackets, parentheticals, or ellipsis.

Alterations and Emphasis

To make a quotation fit the syntax of the sentence into which it is inserted, you may need to *alter* some of the words in the original or *add* words. For example, it may be necessary to change the tense of a verb, change the number of a noun or pronoun, convert a capital letter to lowercase (or vice versa), add punctuation, or add a preposition. Enclose your changes in square brackets, as shown in the following example.

> *Original*: Even when no client-lawyer relationship ensues, a lawyer who has had discussions with a prospective client shall not use or reveal information learned in the consultation, except as Rule 1.9 would permit with respect to information of a former client. N.Y. R. Prof. Conduct 1.18(b).

> *Quotation showing alterations*: Even if they ultimately do not develop a professional relationship with a person seeking legal representation, lawyers in New York "who ha[ve] had discussions with a prospective client" have the same obligations "not [to] use or reveal information learned in the consultation" that they have under Rule 1.9's requirements for former clients. N.Y. R. Prof. Conduct 1.18(b).

To *emphasize* certain words, italicize (or underline) the chosen words without enclosing them in brackets; then add a parenthetical to the citation that advises the reader that the emphasis was added. *See* Rule 1.7; Rule 48.5(a). If the original source italicizes words for emphasis, it is not necessary to indicate that emphasis in a parenthetical, although many writers elect to do so. The following example demonstrates how to indicate emphasis you have added.

> *Original*: Consider the possibility that the speech of government workers who serve as the voice or the face of the government potentially poses such grave threats to government expression to justify government's control of even their off-duty communications. Under this view, certain positions trigger such high public expectations that those employees could never escape their governmental role to speak purely as private citizens even when off the job.[8]

> *Quotation showing emphasis*: One scholar notes concern that certain public employees "who serve as the voice or the face of the government . . . pose[] such grave threats to government expression" that they can "never escape their governmental role to speak purely as private citizens *even when off the job.*" Helen Norton, *Constraining Public Employee Speech: Government's Control of Its Workers' Speech to Protect Its Own Expression*, 59 Duke L.J. 1, 50 (2009) (emphasis added).

---

[8] Helen Norton, *Constraining Public Employee Speech: Government's Control of Its Workers' Speech to Protect Its Own Expression*, 59 Duke L.J. 1, 50 (2009).

Omissions

Omissions are indicated in different ways, depending on what has been omitted and where. Indicate the omission of one or more *words* from the selected language of a quotation by using **ellipses**. Indicate the omission of one or more *letters* from a single word by using **empty brackets**. Indicate the omission of footnotes or citations by adding a **parenthetical** to the citation that describes the omission. The following examples demonstrate these three kinds of omission.

Example 1: Indicating omissions with ellipses

Original: Absent a claim of need to protect military, diplomatic, or sensitive national security secrets, we find it difficult to accept the argument that even the very important interest in confidentiality of Presidential communications is significantly diminished by production of such material for in camera inspection with all the protection that a district court will be obliged to provide.[9]

Quotation omitting words: Unless the President claims a "need to protect military, diplomatic, or sensitive national security secrets," the Court reasoned, it would be "difficult to accept the argument that . . . the . . . interest in confidentiality of Presidential communications is significantly diminished by production of such material for in camera inspection." *U.S. v. Nixon*, 418 U.S. 683, 706 (1974).

Example 2: Indicating omissions with ellipses and brackets

Original: Corporations, and any community chest, fund, or foundation, organized and operated exclusively for religious, charitable, scientific, testing for public safety, literary, or educational purposes, or to foster national or international amateur sports competition (but only if no part of its activities involve the provision of athletic facilities or equipment), or for the prevention of cruelty to children or animals, no part of the net earnings of which inures to the benefit of any private share-holder or individual, no substantial part of the activities of which is carrying on propaganda, or otherwise attempting, to influence legislation (except as otherwise provided in subsection (h)), and which does not participate in, or intervene in (including the publishing or distributing of statements), any political campaign on behalf of any candidate for public office.[10]

Quotation omitting words and letters: Petitioner argues that it is exempt from taxes because Petitioner is a nonpolitical "[c]orporation[] . . . organized and operated exclusively for . . . educational purposes" and because its youth lacrosse leagues "foster national or international amateur sports competition . . . ." 26 U.S.C. § 501(c)(3) (2006).

Example 3: Indicating omissions with parentheticals

Original: By allowing the open exchange of ideas and the voicing of criticisms of those in power, free speech protects the heart of the democratic process. *See, e.g.*, *Garrison v. Louisiana*, 379 U.S. 64, 74-75, 85 S. Ct. 209, 13 L. Ed. 2d 125 (1964) ("[S]peech concerning public affairs . . . is the essence of self-government."); *see generally* Alexander Meiklejohn, *Free Speech and Its Relation to Self-Government* 15-16, 24-27, 39 (1948) ("[Freedom of speech] is a deduction from the basic American agreement that public issues shall be decided by

---

[9] *U.S. v. Nixon*, 418 U.S. 683, 701 (1974) (footnotes omitted).
[10] 26 U.S.C. § 501(c)(3) (2006).

universal suffrage."). Without free speech our system of government might slip into tyranny by, and over, the ignorant.[11]

Quotation omitting citations: "By allowing the open exchange of ideas and the voicing of criticisms of those in power, free speech protects the heart of the democratic process. Without free speech our system of government might slip into tyranny by, and over, the ignorant." *Gordon v. Griffith*, 88 F. Supp. 2d 38, 41 (E.D.N.Y. 2000) (citations omitted).

 When you use the ellipsis to indicate an omission, be careful with the formatting. Indicate the ellipsis by inserting three spaced periods into the quotation in place of the missing words. Not only should you insert spaces between the points, but you should also have a space before and after the entire ellipsis (^.^.^.^). Think of the ellipsis as a *symbol* for omission; imagine it as *three dots in a box*. That way, you won't accidentally let ellipsis points straddle two lines of text, two on one line, and one by itself on the next. This image may also help you remember to *add a final period* when the ellipsis comes at the end of a sentence. The ellipsis indicates an omission, nothing more. If the sentence should end with a period, add the period *after* the ellipsis, followed immediately by the closing quotation marks.

Incorrect
"A claimant can collaterally attack an inadequately noticed administrative forfeiture by suing for equitable relief . . ."

Correct
"A claimant can collaterally attack an inadequately noticed administrative forfeiture by suing for equitable relief . . . ."

To indicate the omission of larger blocks of material (i.e., a paragraph or more), center the ellipsis on its own line and insert five to seven spaces between each ellipsis point. See the example in Rule 49.4(d).

You may not always need an ellipsis, however. If you're quoting no more than a word or phrase from a sentence, you don't need an ellipsis at all. And you don't need ellipsis points at the beginning of *any* quotation. Take a look at Rules 49.3(b), 49.3(c), and their examples. If you leave off the end of a quoted sentence that sounds complete despite the omission, use the ellipsis to signal that you've shortened the original, as nothing else will indicate to the reader that you've quoted less than the whole sentence. See the example in Rule 49.4(b).

Error Correction & [sic]

Sometimes an original source contains an error (e.g., a typographical or grammatical mistake, or an error of fact). If you don't want the reader to think that you were the one who erred, you may signal that the error is in the quotation's original source. Do so by inserting the word "[sic]" (Latin for "thus") in square brackets immediately following the error. Alternatively, you may elect to correct the error, substituting the correction in square brackets for the erroneous matter. Should you prefer to insert [sic], resist the temptation to use it in a mean-spirited fashion. Do not italicize [sic]. For additional guidance on using [sic], see the examples in Rule 48.6.

---

[11] *Gordon v. Griffith*, 88 F. Supp. 2d 38, 41 (E.D.N.Y. 2000).

EXERCISE SET 4-B

BASIC LEVEL: REPRODUCING QUOTED MATERIAL WITH ACCURACY

Before beginning Exercise Set 4-B Basic Level, review the following and keep the *Manual* at hand as you work through the exercises:

- Rule 1.7, Italics to Show Emphasis
- Rule 47.0, Quotations
- Rule 48.0, Altering Quoted Material
- Rule 49.0, Omissions within Quoted Material

4-B.1. The following sentence appeared in *Caban v. Mohammed*, 441 U.S. 380, 392 (1979). Which of the following correctly incorporates and punctuates the language **in bold**?

> In those cases where the father never has **come forward to participate in the rearing of his child, nothing in the Equal Protection Clause precludes the State from withholding from him the privilege of vetoing the adoption of that child.**

a. The Court made it clear that if the father had not 'come forward to participate in the rearing of his child, nothing in the Equal Protection Clause [would] preclude[ ] the State from withholding from him the privilege of vetoing the adoption of that child.'

b. The Court made it clear that if the father had not "come forward to participate in the rearing of his child, nothing in the Equal Protection Clause would preclude the State from withholding the privilege of vetoing the adoption of that child."

c. The Court made it clear that if the father had not "come forward to participate in the rearing of his child, nothing in the Equal Protection Clause [would have] preclude[d] the State from withholding from him the privilege of vetoing the adoption of that child."

d. The Court made it clear that if the father had not "come forward to participate in the rearing of his child, nothing in the Equal Protection Clause [would have] preclude[d] the State from withholding from him the privilege of vetoing the adoption of that child".

4-B.2. The following sentence appeared in *Wojewski v. Rapid City Regional Hospital, Inc.*, 450 F.3d 338, 345 (8th Cir. 2006). Which of the following correctly incorporates and punctuates the language **in bold**?

> **Given the similarity between Title I and the Rehabilitation Act**, absent authority to the contrary, we construe both to apply to an employee-employer relationship and decline appellant's invitation to extend coverage of the Rehabilitation Act to independent contractors.

a. The court refused to apply the Rehabilitation Act to independent contractors, "[g]iven the similarity between Title I and the Rehabilitation Act."

b. The court refused to apply the Rehabilitation Act to independent contractors, "Given the similarity between Title I and the Rehabilitation Act."

c. The court refused to apply the Rehabilitation Act to independent contractors, "[g]iven the similarity between Title I and the Rehabilitation Act".

d. The court refused to apply the Rehabilitation Act to independent contractors, "given the similarity between Title I and the Rehabilitation Act."

4-B.3. You represent a father who wants to prevent his ex-wife, who has custody of their child, from changing the child's last name. You found a relevant passage in *Mark v. Kahn*, 131 N.E.2d 758, 761–762 (Mass. 1956). You want to quote this passage (using block format) but **omit** the sentences **in bold**. Which of the following block-format quotations correctly does that?

> **It does not appear here that the plaintiff's children have ever consented to being called Kahn. However, in view of their ages their consent would not necessarily be decisive.** Until they reach an age when they are capable of making an intelligent choice in the matter of their name they ought not to have another name foisted upon them which they may later reject. **Prior to that time one in the plaintiff's position ought to have the right to be heard to prevent a change or use of a name different from that of their birth.** The bond between a father and his children in circumstances like the present is tenuous at best and if their name is changed that bond may be weakened if not destroyed.

a. Until they reach an age when they are capable of making an intelligent choice in the matter of their name they ought not to have another name foisted upon them which they may later reject. The bond between a father and his children in circumstances like the present is tenuous at best and if their name is changed that bond may be weakened if not destroyed.

b. . . . Until they reach an age when they are capable of making an intelligent choice in the matter of their name they ought not to have another name foisted upon them which they may later reject . . . The bond between a father and his children in circumstances like the present is tenuous at best and if their name is changed that bond may be weakened if not destroyed.

c. Until they reach an age when they are capable of making an intelligent choice in the matter of their name they ought not to have another name foisted upon them which they may later reject. . . . The bond between a father and his children in circumstances like the present is tenuous at best and if their name is changed that bond may be weakened if not destroyed.

d. Until they reach an age when they are capable of making an intelligent choice in the matter of their name they ought not to have another name foisted upon them which they may later reject. [Internal sentence omitted.] The bond between a father and his children in circumstances like the present is tenuous at best and if their name is changed that bond may be weakened if not destroyed.

4-B.4. Which sentence correctly quotes, punctuates, and cites its quotations from this passage in *Reed v. Marley*, 321 S.W.2d 193, 196 (Ark. 1959)?

> At the outset, it is well to point out that the moving party does not have an *absolute right* to the order requiring the examination. The rule itself (and likewise our statute), recites that the court in which the action is pending *may* order the physical or mental examination, and repeated decisions hold that the granting of the order lies within the sound discretion of the court. Bucher v. Krause, 7 Cir., 200 F.2d 576, Strasser v. Prudential Insurance Co. of America, D.C., 1 F.R.D. 125. While the rule has been liberally construed, "fishing expeditions" will not be allowed.

   a. The court not only observed that ". . . the moving party does not have an *absolute right* . . ." to a Rule 35 order, but it also emphasized that "fishing expeditions" will not be allowed." *Reed v. Marley*, 321 S.W.2d 193, 196 (Ark. 1959) (emphasis in original).

   b. The court not only observed that "the moving party does not have an *absolute right*" to a Rule 35 order, but it also emphasized that " 'fishing expeditions' will not be allowed." *Reed v. Marley*, 321 S.W.2d 193, 196 (Ark. 1959).

   c. The court not only observed that "the moving party does not have an *absolute right* ..." to a Rule 35 order, but it also emphasized that "fishing expeditions will not be allowed." *Reed v. Marley*, 321 S.W.2d 193, 196 (Ark. 1959) (emphasis added).

   d. The court not only observed that "[T]he moving party does not have an *absolute right*" to a Rule 35 order, but it also emphasized that "[F]ishing expeditions" will *not* be allowed". *Reed v. Marley*, 321 S.W.2d 193, 196 (Ark. 1959) (first emphasis in original, second emphasis added).

4-B.5. The following passage appeared in a law review article. It contains a typographical error in the last sentence ("than" instead of "then"). Which of the following quotations and citations correctly attributes the error to the original source?

> If the *Miranda* decision represents true constitutional interpretation, and all unwarned statements taken during custodial interrogation are "compelled" within the meaning of the Self-Incrimination Clause, the impeachment and "fruits" exceptions to *Miranda* should fall.[1] If it is not true constitutional interpretation, than the Court has no business reversing state criminal convictions for its violation.

   a. "If it is not true constitutional interpretation, then [sic] the Court has no business reversing state criminal convictions for its violation." Susan R. Klein, *Identifying and Reformulating Prophylactic Rules, Safe Harbors, and Incidental Rights in Constitutional Criminal Procedure,* 99 Mich. L. Rev. 1030, 1030–1031 (2001).

   b. "If it is not true constitutional interpretation, than the Court has no business reversing state criminal convictions for its violation." Susan R. Klein, *Identifying and Reformulating Prophylactic Rules, Safe Harbors, and Incidental Rights in Constitutional Criminal Procedure,* 99 Mich. L. Rev. 1030, 1030–1031 (2001) (sic).

   c. "If it is not true constitutional interpretation, than the Court has no business reversing state criminal convictions for its violation." Susan R. Klein, *Identifying and Reformulating Prophylactic Rules, Safe Harbors, and Incidental Rights in Constitutional Criminal Procedure,* 99 Mich. L. Rev. 1030, 1030–1031 (2001) [*sic*].

   d. "If it is not true constitutional interpretation, than [sic] the Court has no business reversing state criminal convictions for its violation." Susan R. Klein, *Identifying and Reformulating Prophylactic Rules, Safe Harbors, and Incidental Rights in Constitutional Criminal Procedure,* 99 Mich. L. Rev. 1030, 1030–1031 (2001).

EXERCISE SET 4-B

INTERMEDIATE LEVEL: REPRODUCING QUOTED MATERIAL WITH ACCURACY

Before beginning Exercise Set 4-B Intermediate Level, review the following and keep the *Manual* at hand as you work through the exercises:

- Rule 1.7, Italics to Show Emphasis
- Rule 47.0, Quotations
- Rule 48.0, Altering Quoted Material
- Rule 49.0, Omissions within Quoted Material

4-B.6. The following passage appeared in *Schlagenhauf v. Holder*, 379 U.S. 104, 118 (1964), describing the "in controversy" and "good cause" requirements of Rule 35 of the Federal Rules of Civil Procedure. Assume that you wish to quote from this passage and emphasize the language shown **in bold**, which was not emphasized in the original. Which sentence and citation correctly indicate that added emphasis?

> They are not met by mere conclusory allegations of the pleadings—nor by mere relevance to the case—but require an **affirmative showing** by the movant that each condition as to which the examination is sought is really and genuinely in controversy and that good cause exists for ordering each particular examination.

a. According to the Supreme Court, the "in controversy" and "good cause" requirements of Federal Rule of Civil Procedure 35 "require the moving party to make an **affirmative showing**" that the conditions to be examined really are "in controversy and that good cause exists" for the examination order. *Schlagenhauf v. Holder*, 379 U.S. 104, 118 (1964) (emphasis added).

b. Federal Rule of Civil Procedure 35 has been said to "require an *affirmative showing* by the movant that each condition as to which the examination is sought is really and genuinely in controversy and that good cause exists for ordering each particular examination." *Schlagenhauf v. Holder*, 379 U.S. 104, 118 (1964) (emphasis added).

c. The trial court should not order an examination unless the movant makes an "*affirmative showing*" that each condition is in genuine controversy and that good cause exists for the order (emphasis added). *Schlagenhauf v. Holder*, 379 U.S. 104, 118 (1964).

d. Federal Rule of Civil Procedure 35 "require[s] the moving party to make an ["affirmative showing"] . . . that each condition as to which the examination is sought is . . . in controversy and that good cause exists for ordering [the conditions to be examined]." *Schlagenhauf v. Holder*, 379 U.S. 104, 118 (1964) (emphasizing that the movant bears the burden of demonstrating compliance with the rule).

4-B.7.   You represent an employer in a sexual harassment case, and you're writing a brief in support of a motion for summary judgment. In the brief, you wish to use, but slightly modify, language from the following passage in *Baldwin v. Blue Cross/Blue Shield of Alabama*, 480 F.3d 1287, 1303–1304 (11th Cir. 2007). Which of the following sentences correctly incorporates that language?

> A threshold step in correcting harassment is to determine if any occurred, and that requires an investigation that is reasonable given the circumstances. The requirement of a reasonable investigation does not include a requirement that the employer credit uncorroborated statements the complainant makes if they are disputed by the alleged harasser. Nothing in the *Faragher-Ellerth* defense puts a thumb on either side of the scale in a he-said, she-said situation. The employer is not required to credit the statements on the she-said side absent circumstances indicating that it would be unreasonable not to do so.

   a. Investigating a complaint of harassment "does not require an employer to credit uncorroborated statements the complainant makes if they are disputed by the alleged harasser, [and] *Faragher-Ellerth* puts a thumb on either side of the scale in a he-said, she-said situation."

   b. The employer must first "determine if any [harassment] occurred, and that requires an investigation that is reasonable under the circumstances, [but] does not include a requirement that the employer credit uncorroborated statements" in dispute. The employer is not required to credit [the complainant's] statements . . . absent circumstances that it would be unreasonable not to do so."

   c. Conducting a reasonable investigation into harassment does not require an employer to give "credit [to] uncorroborated statements the complainant makes if they are disputed by the alleged harasser," unless "it would be unreasonable not to do so."

   d. An employer must first determine whether any "harassment" took place, requiring an investigation that is reasonable given the circumstances; it does not require that the employer credit uncorroborated statements the complainant makes if they are disputed by the alleged harasser. Nothing in the *Faragher-Ellerth* defense "puts a thumb on either side of the scale" in a he-said, she-said situation unless there are circumstances indicating that it would be unreasonable not to do so.

4-B.8.   The following passage appears in *McDade v. West*, 223 F.3d 1135, 1139 (9th Cir. 2000). Which of the following sentences correctly quotes, punctuates, and cites language from the passage?

Here, we face the novel question of whether a state employee who accesses confidential information through a government-owned computer database acts "under color of state law." To establish a prima facie case under 42 U.S.C. § 1983, McDade must demonstrate proof that (1) the action occurred "under color of law" and (2) the action resulted in a deprivation of a constitutional right or a federal statutory right. *Parratt v. Taylor*, 451 U.S. 527, 535, 101 S. Ct. 1908, 68 L. Ed. 2d 420 (1981), *overruled on other grounds by Daniels v. Williams*, 474 U.S. 327, 330–31, 106 S. Ct. 662, 88 L. Ed. 2d 662 (1986). The district court found that Ms. West was acting in the ambit of her personal pursuits rather than under color of law when she accessed the database to find McDade's location. Therefore, it found the element of color of law to be missing from the undisputed facts of this case.

---

a. The Ninth Circuit was "faced [with] the novel question of whether a state employee who accesses confidential information … through a government-owned computer database acts "under color of state law." *McDade v. West*, 223 F.3d 1135, 1139 (9th Cir. 2000) (citation omitted).

b. The court explained that 42 U.S.C. § 1983 requires proof that a state employee's actions taken "under color of state law . . ." resulted in deprivation of a person's constitutional right or federal statutory right. *McDade v. West*, 223 F.3d 1135, 1139 (9th Cir. 2000) (quoting *Parratt v. Taylor*, 451 U.S. 527, 535, 101 S. Ct. 1908, 68 L. Ed. 2d 420 (1981), *overruled on other grounds by Daniels v. Williams*, 474 U.S. 327, 330-31, 106 S. Ct. 662, 88 L. Ed. 2d 662 (1986)).

c. Title 42, section 1983 of the United States Code applies when a state employee's "action occurred 'under color of state law'" and "resulted in a deprivation of a constitutional right or federal statutory right." *McDade v. West*, 223 F.3d 1135, 1139 (9th Cir. 2000) (citation omitted).

d. The court had to "face the novel question of whether a state employee who accesses confidential information through a government-owned computer database acts 'under color of state law' and "the action resulted in a deprivation of a constitutional right or a federal statutory right. (quoting *Parratt v. Taylor*, 451 U.S. 527, 535, 101 S. Ct. 1908, 68 L. Ed. 2d 420 (1981))".

4-B.9. Which of the following sentences correctly quotes, punctuates, and cites language from the following passage in *Donahue v. Consolidated Rail Corp.*, 224 F.3d 226, 231 (3d Cir. 2000)?

In disability discrimination cases, courts must evaluate the significance of the risk that an employee would pose by considering four interrelated factors: the nature of the risk, the duration of the risk, the severity of the risk, and the probability that the potential harm will occur. *See, e.g., School Bd. of Nassau County v. Arline*, 480 U.S. 273, 288, 107 S. Ct. 1123, 94 L. Ed. 2d 307 (1987); *Nunes v. Wal-Mart Stores, Inc.*, 164 F.3d 1243, 1248 (9th Cir.1999) (a court should consider the *Arline* factors when considering whether an employer is justified in not hiring an employee on the grounds that he would endanger others); *EEOC v. Amego*, 110 F.3d at 145 (1st Cir. 1997) (same); *Estate of Mauro v. Borgess Med. Ctr.*, 137 F.3d 398, 402-03 (6th Cir. 1998) (same). If the threatened harm is grievous, of course, even a small risk may be "significant." As another court of appeals recently noted:

> [I]t is the potential gravity of the harm that imbues certain odds with significance. . . . [W]e are far more likely to consider walking a tightrope to pose a significant risk if the rope is fifty feet off the ground than if it is one foot off the ground. This is so even if the odds of losing our balance are the same however far we have to fall.

Onishea v. Hopper, 171 F.3d 1289, 1297 (11th Cir. 1999).

---

    a. "[E]ven a small risk may be 'significant ... '" if "... the potential gravity of the harm ... imbues certain odds with significance ..., [much as we] ... consider walking a tightrope to pose a significant risk if the rope is fifty feet off the ground," but not if it is just one foot high, even if the odds of falling are the same. *Donahue v. Consol. Rail Corp.*, 224 F.3d 226, 231 (3d Cir. 2000).

    b. The court must also assess the "probability that the potential harm will occur"; "even a small risk may be 'significant.'" *Donahue v. Consol. Rail Corp.*, 224 F.3d 226, 231 (3d Cir. 2000). For example, one would foresee a greater threat of harm in "walking a tightrope . . . if the rope is fifty feet off the ground than if it is one foot off the ground," even if the chance of falling were the same. *Id.* (quoting *Onishea v. Hopper*, 171 F.3d 1289, 1297 (11th Cir. 1999)).

    c. In its evaluation of "the probability that the potential harm will occur," the court must consider how serious a threat is posed by the harm, for "it is the potential gravity of the harm that imbues certain odds with significance.... [W]e are far more likely to consider walking a tightrope to pose a significant risk if the rope is fifty feet off the ground than if it is one foot off the ground. This is so even if the odds of losing our balance are the same however far we have to fall." *Donahue v. Consol. Rail Corp.*, 224 F.3d 226, 231 (3d Cir. 2000) (quoting *Onishea v. Hopper*, 171 F.3d 1289, 1297 (11th Cir. 1999)).

    d. Federal courts are rightly concerned about the dangers that hiring a disabled employee may pose to other employees: "If the threatened harm is grievous, of course, even a small risk may be "significant," because it is the "potential gravity of the harm that imbues certain odds with significance. . . ." *Onishea v. Hopper*, 171 F.3d 1289, 1297 (11th Cir. 1999)." *Donahue v. Consol. Rail Corp.*, 224 F.3d 226, 231 (3d Cir. 2000).

EXERCISE SET 4-B

EXPERT LEVEL: REPRODUCING QUOTED MATERIAL WITH ACCURACY

Before beginning Exercise Set 4-B Expert Level, review the following and keep the *Manual* at hand as you work through the exercises:

- Rule 43.0, Citation Placement and Use
- Rule 47.0, Quotations
- Rule 47.3, Relation to Text
- Rule 47.4, Short Quotations

- Rule 47.5, Longer Quotations
- Rule 47.7, Quotations within Quotations
- Rule 48.0, Altering Quoted Material
- Rule 49.0, Omissions within Quoted Material

4-B.10.   The box below displays a passage from *United States v. Ortiz*, 804 F.2d 1161, 1165 (10th Cir. 1986). Edit the text by (1) writing in corrections for any *errors or omissions* you find in the placement or use of quotation marks, ellipsis, or brackets in the writer's discussion of the case, and (2) drawing a caret ∧ and, in the spaces between the lines, adding citations for quotations in the passage where needed.

"Inducement" may be defined as government conduct which creates a substantial risk that an undisposed person or otherwise law-abiding citizen would commit the offense. This definition implicates the obvious question of whether the defendant was eager or reluctant to engage in the charged criminal conduct. Governmental inducement may take the form of "persuasion, fraudulent representations, threats, coercive tactics, harassment, promises of reward, or pleas based on need, sympathy, or friendship." *U.S. v. Burkley*, 591 F.2d 903, 913 n. 18 (D.C. Cir. 1978). Evidence that a government agent solicited, requested, or approached the defendant to engage in criminal conduct, standing alone, is insufficient to constitute inducement. *Id.* Inducement also will not be shown by evidence that the government agent initiated the contact with the defendant or proposed the crime. *U.S. v. Andrews*, 765 F.2d 1491, 1499 (11th Cir. 1985).

    The entrapment defense contemplates that an "undisposed person or otherwise law-abiding citizen" was induced to violate the criminal laws by the actions of government agents. Several forms of inducement exist, extending from simple persuasive tactics to more egregious kinds of conduct such as ". . . fraudulent representations, threats, coercive tactics, harassment, promises of reward, and pleas based on need, sympathy, or friendship." Another important consideration is whether the defendant seemed ". . . eager or reluctant to engage in the charged criminal conduct."

    A defendant raising the entrapment defense will not carry his burden of proof, however, if he merely provides evidence that a government agent solicited, requested, or approached him to engage in criminal conduct. By itself, such evidence is not strong enough to prove inducement. Nor can he prove inducement by merely presenting ". . . evidence that the government agent initiated the contact with the defendant or proposed the crime.

CITING SPECIFIC SOURCES

OF PRIMARY LAW

Part 2 provides exercises covering sources of primary law. Primary law is created by a constitution or by one of the three branches of government—legislative, judicial, or executive—at the national, state, or local levels. When you cite primary law, your most important job is to convey with accuracy information attesting to its origin, its location, and its currency.

Part 2 begins with the primary authorities most familiar to law-trained readers: reported cases, constitutions, statutory codes, newly enacted legislation (session laws and slip laws), and local ordinances. It then addresses two aspects of legislative law-making: bills in the making (pending legislation) and bills in the past (legislative history). Finally, Part 2 considers the wide-ranging materials promulgated by the executive branch of government, including regulatory materials created by administrative agencies and executive orders from a government's highest-ranking elected official.

CHAPTER

CASES

An accurate case citation not only supplies the necessary information for locating the case in print or online sources, but it also gives important clues about the case's origin, its authoritativeness, and its continued viability. This chapter gives you practice in working with each of the major case citation components and in using case citations in context. In section A, you will work with the rules for constructing the case-name component of the citation. In section B, you will practice constructing accurate reporter and page references. In section C, you will draft parenthetical phrases with court name abbreviations and appropriate dates. Section D covers the essential skill of appending relevant subsequent history to a case citation. Finally, in section E, you will gain valuable experience working with short-form citations to cases.

A. CASE NAMES

The first component in every case citation is the case name, derived from the names of the actual litigants in the case. Lawyers typically refer to cases by these case names. (You may already know several famous case names, such as *Roe v. Wade*, *Bush v. Gore*, or *Brown v. Board of Education*.) One of the conventions of legal citation is to shorten case names, not only to keep the citation's length more manageable, but also to create an easier form of reference to the case. To construct an accurate case name for a full citation, you must complete three tasks:

- First, you must determine the nature of the litigants by looking at the case's caption. Who are the parties in this case? They may be individuals or entities. They may be acting for themselves or acting on behalf of others.

- Second, you must determine which words to keep and which to omit from the party names in the case's caption.
- Finally, you should consider whether any of the words left in the case name may be abbreviated.

Determine the nature of the litigants by looking at the case's **caption**. Pay attention to *what kind* of party is involved: an individual? an organization? a union? a state? a city? a governmental official? a person acting on another's behalf? a red Mustang convertible? the Estate of Elvis Presley? This determination does not require a sophisticated understanding of civil procedure; all the clues are right there in the caption of the case. (In fact, you should never go beyond what's listed in the caption in constructing the case name portion of a citation.)

One way to shorten the case name is by omitting unneeded words. When individuals are parties, use just their surnames. Rule 12.2(d) provides guidance for citing the names of individuals. If the party is an organization, however, omit only duplicative business designations, not any other words in the organization's name, as explained in Rule 12.2(e). For example, a business named Jeffrey L. Miller & Son Consulting Co., Inc. would be shown as *Jeffrey L. Miller & Son Consulting Co.*

Consult Rule 12.2(c) when you are deciding which parties to use in the case name. You should shorten the case name by omitting additional parties that appear in the caption. It's not unusual to see several parties aligned on one side of the case. Citation rules do not ask us to choose one on the merits; we just take the first-listed party, whoever that is. If the caption displays a phrase such as "*et al.*" (and others) or "*et ux.*" (and spouse), you should omit that phrase, too.

A **relator** is not an additional party, but rather, as Rule 12.2(o) explains, a person or entity who acts on another's behalf, such as an adult representing the interests of a minor, a guardian representing an incapacitated individual, or the government acting on behalf of someone incarcerated. The citation identifies the relator and the party who cannot self-represent as a unit. Examine the caption to determine who is the relator and who is the party being represented. Put the relator's name first, followed by the italicized phrase "*ex rel.*" (on behalf of) and the name of the represented party. For example, the case name for the caption shown at right is *Stevens ex rel. Park View Corp. v. Richardson.*

> R.W. STEVENS, By and For the Benefit of PARK VIEW CORPORATION, an Alaska corporation, Appellant,
>
> v.
>
> F.M. RICHARDSON, Rose-Marie Richardson, Hector Guzman, and Providence Guzman, Appellees.
>
> No. S-1860.
>
> Supreme Court of Alaska.
>
> May 6, 1988.

Not all cases have adversarial parties. For example, a case may involve a single party's application to the court without notice to another party (an *ex parte* action) or a proceeding that concerns a legal status (an *in rem* action, such as an estate, an adoption, or a bankruptcy). Such cases often use procedural phrases as part of the case name. For example, the case name for the caption shown at right should be set out as *In re Breedlove.* For help in understanding and using procedural phrases, consult Rule 12.2(p), Procedural phrases in case names, and Sidebar 12.3, Explanation of Commonly Used Procedural Phrases.

> In the Matter of Meredith M. BREEDLOVE.
>
> No. 20091.
>
> Supreme Court of Appeals of West Virginia.
>
> Submitted Sept. 18, 1991.
>
> Decided Dec. 6, 1991.

Always omit from case names such things as articles and prepositions, superfluous business designations, portions of certain procedural phrases, and larger geographical references. *See* Rule 12.2(e)(5), (6) (additional geographical references, second business designations); Rule 12.2(f) (unions); Rule 12.2(i) (cities and municipalities); Rule 12.2(j) (additional geographical references); Rule 12.2(n) (additional geographical references).

According to Rule 12.2(e)(3), a writer "may" abbreviate words in the case name of a citation. Legal writing favors abbreviations because they cut a citation's length. Consult Appendix 3, General Abbreviations, for words in the names of *organizational* litigants, whether they are businesses, governmental agencies, or other entities. If you abbreviate any word in a case name, you must abbreviate *all* words in that case name that are in Appendix 3. But never abbreviate the name of an *individual*, even if it is identical to a word appearing in Appendix 3. And unless the citation refers by name to one of the fifty states in the United States, do not abbreviate a party name that consists of a *single word*.

When a case name is used in a **textual sentence**, however, do not abbreviate any words unless they are commonly used acronyms or certain business designations, as explained in Rules 2.3 and 12.2(e)(5). The exercises in this section (and in the rest of the chapter) assume that you have elected to abbreviate case names in citations.

EXERCISE SET 5-A

BASIC LEVEL: CASE NAMES

> Before beginning Exercise Set 5-A Basic Level, review the following and keep the *Manual* at hand as you work through the exercises:
>
> - Rule 12.2, Case Name
> - Sidebar 12.1, Distinguishing Case Names from Party Names
> - Sidebar 12.3, Explanation of Commonly Used Procedural Phrases
>
> To complete the exercises, you may also need to refer to the following:
>
> - Rule 1.1, Typeface Choices
> - Rule 2.2, Spacing for Abbreviations
> - Appendix 3, General Abbreviations

5-A.1. Wayne Curtis Poore sued his wife, Diann Poore, for divorce. The trial court dismissed the husband's complaint. He appealed. The name in the full caption of the case on appeal is "Wayne Curtis Poore v. Diann Poore." How should the case name appear in a full citation?

   a. *Poore v. Poore*
   b. *Wayne Poore v. Diann Poore*
   c. *Wayne Curtis Poore v. Diann Poore*
   d. *In re Poore*

must be underlined or italized

5-A.2. Your online research retrieves the following case decided by the Court of Appeals of Kansas. How should the case name appear in a full citation?

> In the Matter of the Marriage of Fusao TAKUSAGAWA, Appellee, and Mieko Takusagawa, Appellant.

a. *In re Takusagawa*
b. *In re Marriage of Takusagawa* — *Correct; used to show procedural.*
c. *In re Matter of Marriage of Takusagawa*
d. *In the Matter of the Marriage of Takusagawa and Takusagawa*

5-A.3. Using Westlaw, you find a case that displays the caption below. How should the case name appear in a full citation?

> United States Court of Appeals,
> Fifth Circuit.
> Russell J. HENDERSON; et al., Plaintiffs,
> Doreen Keeler; Planned Parenthood of Louisiana, Inc., Plaintiffs-Appellees,
> v.
> Richard STALDER, Etc.; et al., Defendants,
> Richard Stalder, Secretary, Department of Public Safety and Corrections;
> John Kennedy,
> State Treasurer, Defendants-Appellants.
> No. 03-30699.
> Dec. 21, 2005.

a. *Henderson v. Stalder*
b. *Henderson* ~~et al.~~ *v. Stalder* ~~et al.~~
c. *Henderson, Keeler, & Planned Parenthood of Louisiana, Inc. v. Stalder & Kennedy*
d. *Russell J. Henderson, Plaintiff v. Richard Stalder, Defendant*

5-A.4. Frank Mello sued the Sara Lee Corporation, claiming he had been wrongfully denied benefits from the company's pension plan. The trial court granted his motion for summary judgment; the company appealed. Examine the caption from the Federal Reporter. How should the case name appear in a full citation?

a. *Mello v. Lee*
b. *Mello v. Lee et al.*
c. *Mello v. Lee Corporation*
d. *Mello v. Sara Lee Corp.*

Should abbreviate when you can

> Frank C. MELLO, Plaintiff–Appellee,
> v.
> SARA LEE CORPORATION,
> et al., Defendants,
>
> Sara Lee Corporation; Sara Lee Corporation Consolidated Pension and Retirement Plan, Defendants–Appellants.
>
> No. 04–60814.
>
> United States Court of Appeals,
> Fifth Circuit.
>
> Nov. 22, 2005.

5-A.5. You are briefing an appeal to the Virginia Court of Appeals concerning a defendant's conditional guilty plea. Using LexisNexis, you find a case displaying the caption below. How should the case name appear in a full citation?

> TONY MELVIN WITCHER v. <u>COMMONWEALTH</u> OF VIRGINIA
> Record No. 0428-05-3
> COURT OF APPEALS OF VIRGINIA
> 47 Va. App. 273; 623 S.E.2d 432; 2005 Va. App. LEXIS 526
> December 28, 2005, Decided

a. *Witcher v. Com.*
b. *Witcher v. Commonwealth* ·
c. *Witcher v. State*
d. *Witcher v. Va.*

5-A.6. Your seminar paper deals with an issue of criminal anarchy. Using Westlaw, you find a case displaying the caption below. How should the case name appear in a full citation?

> Supreme Court of the United States.
> GITLOW
> v.
> PEOPLE OF THE STATE OF NEW YORK.
> No. 19.
> Reargued Nov. 23, 1923.
> Decided June 8, 1925.

a. *Gitlow v. People*
b. *Gitlow v. State*
c. *Gitlow v. N.Y.*
d. *Gitlow v. People of State of New York*

5-A.7. In researching a tax question, you find a case whose running head (from the top of the page in the Federal Reporter) and caption (at the beginning of the case itself) are shown at right. How should the case name appear in a full citation?

a. *Warda v. C.I.R.*
b. *Warda v. Commr.*
c. *Warda v. Commr. IRS*
d. *Warda v. Commr. of Internal Rev.*

> **WARDA v. C.I.R.**
> Cite as 15 F.3d 533 (6th Cir. 1994)

> Ethel M. WARDA, Petitioner–Appellant,
> v.
> COMMISSIONER OF INTERNAL
> REVENUE, Respondent–
> Appellee.
> No. 92–2344.
> United States Court of Appeals,
> Sixth Circuit.
> Argued Oct. 15, 1993.
> Decided Jan. 26, 1994.

5-A.8.　In an appeal involving the termination of parental rights, you wish to cite a case you found using Westlaw. The caption appears below. How should the case name appear in a full citation?

Court of Civil Appeals of Alabama.

J.W.M.

v.

CLEBURNE COUNTY DEPARTMENT OF HUMAN RESOURCES.

2060505.

Aug. 31, 2007.

a. *J. W. M. v. Cleburne County Department of Human Resources*
b. *J.W.M. v. Cleburne County Dept. of Human Resources*
c. *J.W.M. v. Cleburne Co. Dept. of Hum. Res.*
d. *J. v. Cleburne Co. Dept. of Hum. Res.*

5-A.9.　You are writing a paper about the First Amendment and its effect on new technology. In a law review article by John A. Humbach, *"Sexting" and the First Amendment*, 37 Hastings Const. L.Q. 433, 437 n. 21 (2010), you found a footnote referring to a case. The text of the footnote and the case caption are set out below. How should the case name appear in a full citation?

> 18 U.S.C. § 2257 (2006); *see* Connection Distrib. Co. v. Holder, 557 F.3d 321, 325 (6th Cir. 2009). The law and its registration requirements also apply to persons who take explicit pictures of persons over eighteen. *Id.* So sexting teens, who are legally adults, can also be felony sex offenders under this statute.

a. Connection Dist. Co. v. Holder
b. *Connection Distrib. Co. v. Holder*
c. *Connection Distribg. Co. v. Holder*
d. Connection Distrib. Co. v. Holder

> **CONNECTION DISTRIBUTING CO.;**
> **Rondee Kamins; Jane Doe; John**
> **Doe, Plaintiffs–Appellants,**
>
> v.
>
> **Eric H. HOLDER, Jr., Attorney**
> **General, Defendant–**
> **Appellee.**
>
> No. 06–3822.
>
> United States Court of Appeals,
> Sixth Circuit.
>
> Argued: Sept. 10, 2008.
>
> Decided and Filed: Feb. 20, 2009.

5-A.10.　You are writing a seminar paper on the topic of subrogation. In one section of the paper, you discuss contractual waiver of subrogation, and you cite a case from the Colorado Supreme Court, whose KeyCite result is shown below. How should the case name appear in a full citation?

➡ 3 KeyCited Citation:
Copper Mountain, Inc. v. Industrial Systems, Inc., 2009 WL 662072 (Colo. Mar 16, 2009) (NO. 08SC28)

a. *Copper Mountain, Inc. v. Industrial Systems, Inc.*
b. *Copper Mountain, Inc. v. Industrial Sys., Inc.*
c. *Copper Mt., Inc. v. Indus. Sys., Inc.*
d. *Copper Mt. v. Indus. Sys.*

EXERCISE SET 5-A

INTERMEDIATE LEVEL: CASE NAMES

Before beginning Exercise Set 5-A Intermediate Level, review the following and keep the *Manual* at hand as you work through the exercises:

• Rule 12.2, Case Name
• Sidebar 12.1, Distinguishing Case Names from Party Names
• Sidebar 12.2, Public Official Named as a Party
• Sidebar 12.3, Explanation of Commonly Used Procedural Phrases

To complete the exercises, you may also need to refer to the following:

• Rule 2.2, Spacing for Abbreviations
• Rule 2.3, Authorities Referred to in Textual Sentences
• Appendix 3, General Abbreviations

5-A.11. In writing a paper about civil forfeiture, you discuss a case from the United States Court of Appeals for the First Circuit. Examine its caption from the Federal Reporter. How should the case name appear in a full citation?

a. *United States of America v. One Parcel of Real Property with Buildings, Appurtenances and Improvements Known as 116 Emerson Street, Located in the City of Providence, Rhode Island*
b. *United States v. 1 Parcel of Real Prop.*
c. *U.S. v. One Parcel of Real Property*
d. *U.S. v. 116 Emerson St.*

> **UNITED STATES of America,**
> **Plaintiff, Appellant,**
>
> v.
>
> **ONE PARCEL OF REAL PROPERTY WITH BUILDINGS, APPURTENANCES AND IMPROVEMENTS KNOWN AS 116 EMERSON STREET, LOCATED IN the CITY OF PROVIDENCE, RHODE ISLAND, Defendant, Appellee.**
>
> No. 91–1019.
>
> United States Court of Appeals, First Circuit.
>
> Heard May 8, 1991.
> Decided Aug. 21, 1991.

5-A.12. You wish to cite the case shown in this Federal Reporter caption. How should the case name appear in a full citation?

a. *Jack Walters & Sons Corp. v. Morton Bldg., Inc.*
b. *Walters & Sons Corp. v. Morton Bldg., Inc.*
c. *Walters & Sons v. Morton Bldg.*
d. *Walters v. Morton*

> **JACK WALTERS & SONS CORP.,**
> **Plaintiff-Appellant,**
>
> v.
>
> **MORTON BUILDING, INC.,**
> **Defendant-Appellee.**

5-A.13. Your case note about labor law cites an interesting case from the United States Court of Appeals for the Second Circuit. Examine its caption from the Federal Reporter. How should the case name appear in a full citation?

a. *McLeod, Regl. Dir. 2d Region NLRB v. Chefs, Cooks, Pastry Cooks & Assistants, Loc. 89*

b. *McLeod v. Chefs, Cooks, Pastry Cooks & Assistants, Loc. 89*

c. *McLeod v. Chefs, Cooks, Pastry Cooks & Assistants, Loc. 89, Hotel & Restaurant Employees & Bartenders Intl. Union*

d. *McLeod v. Chefs*

> Ivan C. McLEOD, Regional Director of the Second Region of the National Labor Relations Board, for and on behalf of the National Labor Relations Board, Petitioner-Appellee,
>
> v.
>
> CHEFS, COOKS, PASTRY COOKS AND ASSISTANTS, LOCAL 89, HOTEL AND RESTAURANT EMPLOYEES AND BARTENDERS INTERNATIONAL UNION, AFL-CIO,
>
> and
>
> Dining Room Employees Union, Local 1, Hotel and Restaurant Employees and Bartenders International Union, AFL-CIO, Respondents-Appellants.
>
> No. 228, Docket 26507.
>
> United States Court of Appeals Second Circuit.
>
> Argued Jan. 11, 1961.
>
> Decided Feb. 8, 1961.

5-A.14. The Westlaw caption displayed below is from an appeal brought by Donna Medley on behalf of her ward, Chrissy F. How should the case name appear in a full citation?

> CHRISSY F., By her next friend and Guardian ad litem Donna MEDLEY, Plaintiff-Appellee,
>
> v.
>
> MISSISSIPPI DEPARTMENT OF PUBLIC WELFARE, et al., Defendants-Appellants.
>
> No. 90-1332
> United States Court of Appeals, Fifth Circuit.
> March 8, 1991.

a. *F. v. Miss. Dept. of Pub. Welfare*

b. *Medley v. Miss. Dept. of Pub. Welfare*

c. *Chrissy F. ex rel. Medley v. Miss. Dept. of Pub. Welfare*

d. *Medley ex rel. Chrissy F. v. Miss. Dept. of Pub. Welfare*

5-A.15. Researching Tennessee statutes of limitation in Westlaw, you find a case showing the following caption. Choose the correct form of the full case name to insert in the blank in this sentence in your brief.

Just as the plaintiff in _____ failed to do, the Plaintiffs failed to file their complaint before the statute of limitations expired on their claim.

The ESTATE OF Robyn BUTLER, et al.

v.

LAMPLIGHTER APARTMENTS, et al.

No. M2007-02508-COA-R3-CV.

June 24, 2008 Session.

Aug. 20, 2008.

a. *Estate of Butler v. Lamplighter Apartments*
b. *Estate of Butler v. Lamplighter Apts.*
c. *Est. of Butler v. Lamplighter Apts.*
d. *Butler et al. v. Lamplighter Apts. et al.*

[handwritten: While using citation in txt of document don't abbreviate.]

5-A.16. Write the case name you would use in a full citation to the case whose Westlaw caption is shown below.

United States District Court, M.D. Florida,

Orlando Division.

Ex parte Joseph CHAYOON.

No. 6:06-cv-1812-Orl-19JGG.

April 10, 2007.

5-A.17. In researching an issue of probable cause, you find a case involving a Portuguese woman arrested for passing a forged check. Using its caption from the Federal Reporter, write the full case name.

Ana Maria Caeiro PALHAVA DE VARELLA–CID, Plaintiff, Appellant,

v.

The BOSTON FIVE CENTS SAVINGS BANK, and George H. Coleman, Defendants, Appellees.

No. 85–1777.

United States Court of Appeals, First Circuit.

Argued Jan. 10, 1986.

Decided March 26, 1986.

5-A.18. Write the case name you would use in a full citation to the case whose caption is shown below.

United States Court of Appeals,

Seventh Circuit.

Alden Management Services, Inc., Plaintiff-Appellant,

v.

Elaine Chao, Secretary of Labor, Defendant-Appellee.

No. 07-3828.

Argued June 2, 2008.

Decided June 25, 2008.

5-A.19. Write the case name you would use in a full citation to the case whose Westlaw caption is shown below.

District Court of Appeal of Florida,
Second District.
Peninsular Properties Braden River, LLC, and Manatee River Corporation, Appellants,
v.
City of Bradenton, Florida, Appellee.
No. 2D06-5302.
Aug. 1, 2007.
Rehearing Denied Oct. 5, 2007.

5-A.20. Write the case name you would use in a full citation to the case whose Westlaw caption is shown below.

United States Court of Appeals,
First Circuit.
United States of America, Appellee,
v.
Rafael Yeje-Cabrera, Defendant, Appellant.
United States of America, Appellee,
v.
Wilfredo Pérez, Defendant, Appellant.
United States of America, Appellee/Cross-Appellant,
v.
William Olivero, a/k/a K, a/k/a Alejandro, Defendant, Appellant/Cross-Appellee.
Nos. 03-1329, 03-1510, 03-1874, 03-1969.
Heard Sept. 7, 2005.
Decided Nov. 2, 2005.

EXERCISE SET 5-A

EXPERT LEVEL: CASE NAMES

Before beginning Exercise Set 5-A Expert Level, review the following and keep the *Manual* at hand as you work through the exercises:

- Rule 12.2, Case Name
- Sidebar 12.1, Distinguishing Case Names from Party Names
- Sidebar 12.2, Public Official Named as a Party
- Sidebar 12.3, Explanation of Commonly Used Procedural Phrases

To complete the exercises, you may also need to refer to the following:

- Rule 1.1, Typeface Choices
- Rule 2.2, Spacing for Abbreviations
- Appendix 3, General Abbreviations

5-A.21. Write the case name you would use in a full citation to the case whose caption is shown at right.

U.S. v. **CERTAIN REAL PROPERTY AND PREMISES**
Cite as 954 F.2d 29 (2nd Cir. 1992)

UNITED STATES of America,
Plaintiff-Appellee,

v.

CERTAIN REAL PROPERTY AND PREMISES KNOWN AS 38 WHALERS COVE DRIVE, BABYLON, NEW YORK, Defendant, Edward J. Levin, Claimant-Appellant.

No. 981, Docket 90–6268.

United States Court of Appeals, Second Circuit.

Argued Feb. 14, 1991.
Decided Jan. 3, 1992.

5-A.22. Write the case name you would use in a full citation to the case whose Westlaw caption is shown below.

United States Court of Appeals,
Tenth Circuit.
In re Phillip L. Hilgers and Nanette Hilgers, Debtors,
D. Michael Case, Trustee, Plaintiff-Appellee,
v.
Phillip L. Hilgers; Nanette Hilgers; Phillip L. Hilgers, as Trustee of the
Laverne W.
Hilgers Trust, Defendants-Appellants,
and
Turnbull Oil, Inc.; Stephen A. Hilgers, as
Trustee of the Jack E. Hilgers Trust and as
Trustee of the Blanche A. Hilgers Trust, Defendants-Appellees.
No. 07-3233.
May 20, 2008.

5-A.23. Write the case name you would use in a full citation to the case whose Westlaw caption is shown below.

United States Court of Appeals,
Fifth Circuit.
Charles Miles, Plaintiff-Appellant,
v.
The M/V Mississippi Queen, et al., Defendants,
The Delta Queen Steamboat Company, Defendant-Appellee.
No. 83-3601.
March 1, 1985.
Rehearing Denied March 27, 1985.

5-A.24. Write the case name you would use in a full citation to the case whose Federal Reporter caption is shown at right.

In re AIR CRASH DISASTER NEAR
ROSELAWN, INDIANA ON
OCTOBER 31, 1994.

Appeal of Theresa A. SEVERIN, as Exec-
utor of the Estate of Patricia Henry,
Deceased, Roberta Spencer, Special Administrator of the Estate of Kenneth
Bartlett Spencer, Deceased, Stewart
MacKenzie, Co-Executor of the Estate
of Betty Innes Struth Tweedie, Deceased, et al.

No. 96-2130.

United States Court of Appeals,
Seventh Circuit.

Argued June 5, 1996.
Decided Sept. 19, 1996.

5-A.25. Write the case name you would use in a full citation to the case whose North Eastern Reporter caption is shown at right.

379 Ill.App.3d 795
318 Ill.Dec. 773

Albert TRTANJ and Mary Trtanj, for
the Use of State Farm Fire and Casu-
alty Company, Plaintiffs-Appellants,

v.

The CITY OF GRANITE CITY,
Defendant-Appellee.

No. 5-07-0002.

Appellate Court of Illinois,
Fifth District.

Rule 23 Order Filed Feb. 15, 2008.
Motion to Publish Granted
March 24, 2008.
March 24, 2008.

B. REPORTERS AND PAGE REFERENCES

A "reporter" is a publication containing judicial opinions from a specific court or group of courts. The second major component of a full case citation is a reference to the reporter's volume number, the abbreviated reporter name, and the initial page number on which the case begins (assuming the case is published in a print reporter, even though you may have found it online). Many cases are in fact never published in print reporters; their citations will instead provide information about the databases or Web sites in which they may be located. No matter whether a case is published in a traditional print reporter or an electronic medium, citation to particular pages within the case requires the use of pinpoint page numbers.

Volume Numbers

Volume numbers are assigned sequentially by the publisher. In print reporters, the volume number appears not only on the spine of the book, but also in the "running head" at the top of the pages of the case. When you view an electronic version of a reported case, look for the volume number set out above the case's caption. Compare the samples below, which show print and Westlaw versions of the same case published in volume 222 of the Arizona Reports and volume 213 of the Pacific Reporter, Third Series.

150 Ariz. **213 PACIFIC REPORTER, 3d SERIES** 222 Ariz. 1 **STATE of Arizona, Appellee,** v. **Julius Jarreau MOORE, Appellant.** **No. CR-07-0164-AP.** Supreme Court of Arizona, En Banc. July 24, 2009.	222 Ariz. 1, 213 P.3d 150 <u>Briefs and Other Related Documents</u> Supreme Court of Arizona, En Banc. STATE of Arizona, Appellee, v. Julius Jarreau MOORE, Appellant. No. CR-07-0164-AP. July 24, 2009.

Reporters in General

Most reporters collect only appellate opinions, but some reporters publish trial court opinions. Appendix 1, Primary Sources by Jurisdiction, lists the reporters available for each jurisdiction, in hierarchical order. Appendix 1A, West Regional Reporter Coverage, lists the states whose judicial opinions are published in each West regional reporter.

Abbreviations for reporter names are also set out in Chart 12.1, Common Reporter Abbreviations. Chart 12.1 not only provides the abbreviations for the most commonly used reporters, but it also uses a green triangle to indicate required spaces in those abbreviations.

Official and Unofficial Reporters

When you research online, you will see citations to print reporters when the case has been published. In fact, you will often see references to multiple reporters in case captions, reflecting a case's publication in both government-published (or "official") and commercially published ("unofficial") reporter sets. Note that for some states and for federal trial and intermediate appellate courts, there is no official reporter, but the cases are available in a West reporter. When you refer to cases within non-court documents such as office memos, seminar papers, or law-review articles, you will typically cite only the West reporter if the cases are available there, even though they are also published in other print and electronic sources.

If a case is available in more than one reporter and you are unsure which to cite, consult Rule 12.4(b), which provides general rules for selecting the appropriate reporter.

In contrast, when you are preparing a document to be filed with a court (e.g., a brief or a memorandum of law), you may encounter local rules that require citation to both an official reporter and one or more additional unofficial reporters in which the case is published (a practice known as "parallel citation").[1] If court rules require it, provide parallel citation.

Note that most federal and regional reporters are now in their second or third series. Be careful to correctly indicate the series, if any, with an ordinal number contraction (and see Rule 4.3, Ordinal Numbers, for guidance in their construction). If you are not careful about indicating the series, you may inadvertently send readers to the wrong text: a citation to volume 100 of the Pacific Reporter, Second Series (P.2d), will not retrieve a case that was published in volume 100 of the Pacific Reporter, Third Series (P.3d).

California and New York Reporters

Cases from California and New York present an additional consideration. California Supreme Court cases are published in two West reporters: the Pacific Reporter, which also contains cases from other states, and the California Reporter, which also contains cases from the intermediate courts of appeal in that state. Similarly, New York cases are published in two West reporters. Cases from the New York Court of Appeals appear in the North Eastern Reporter, but they and cases from intermediate appellate courts in New York also appear in West's New York Supplement. Use the regional reporter, not the state-specific reporter, if a case appears in both, unless you have been directed otherwise. Because attorneys in these two states strongly prefer citation to the California Reporter or the New York Supplement, even for non-court documents, find out which reporter you are expected to use.

---

[1] Consult Appendix 2 for jurisdiction-specific information about parallel citation requirements, and see Chapter 15, which contains exercises to help you master parallel citations when court rules require their use.

United States Supreme Court Reporters

Opinions from the United States Supreme Court present another special situation. If the case is available in the Court's official reporter, the United States Reports, cite that source. If it has not yet been published there, you may cite an unofficial publication source, following the order of preference listed in Rule 12.4(c).

In your reading, you may encounter references to named reporters for United States Supreme Court cases from the nineteenth century (e.g., Cranch, Dallas, Wheaton, and others, described more fully in Sidebar 12.4, Names and Dates of Early United States Supreme Court Reporters). Should you cite one of these older cases, omit reference to the named reporter and refer solely to the United States Reports version.

Unpublished Opinions

You will often encounter judicial opinions that are not reproduced in the standard print reporters. An "unpublished" opinion is a judicial decision that the issuing court has not designated for publication. The term "unpublished" is something of a misnomer, as many of these opinions are in fact available to the public, most often through electronic media. Some appear in a special West print reporter, the Federal Appendix, which prints unpublished opinions by many federal circuit courts of appeal. The cases may appear on judicial Web sites. Furthermore, both Westlaw and LexisNexis offer many unpublished opinions of appellate courts and some trial courts in their electronic databases.

The primary reason for not publishing certain opinions is that the courts who wrote them do not consider them to be noteworthy. Courts have claimed that these opinions neither add to our understanding of a rule's operation, nor develop new law, nor extend the application of existing law. And because such judicial opinions are deemed to have no precedential effect, many jurisdictions have limited or even prohibited their citation.

That situation is changing, however. Federal Rule of Appellate Procedure 32.1 requires the federal circuit courts of appeal to permit the citation of unpublished opinions issued on or after January 1, 2007. Older unpublished opinions may be cited *if* the circuit's local rules or internal operating procedures so allow (although they may still be considered no more than persuasive authority). Similarly, many state courts now permit the citation of unpublished opinions. If you wish to cite an unpublished opinion, check the jurisdiction's current court rules or internal operating procedures to determine whether any citation restrictions apply.

Unless a local rule specifies a particular format for citing an unpublished opinion (and many do),[2] follow Rule 12.12 (if you are citing cases available only on LexisNexis or Westlaw); Rule 12.14 (if citing cases in Federal Appendix); or Rule 12.15 (if citing cases available only on the Internet, such as a court's Web site), depending on the source in which you found the opinion.

Do not confuse unpublished cases with cases that *are* designated for publication, but which have *not yet* been assigned to a specific reporter volume and pager. A case that will eventually be published should be cited according to Rule 12.13, setting out:

- the case name;
- the docket number, if desired;
- three underlined spaces representing the unassigned volume number;

---

[2] Local rules are addressed in Chapter 15.

- the reporter abbreviation;
- three additional underlined spaces representing the unknown initial page number;
- a parallel citation to the case's Westlaw or LexisNexis identifier, if available; and
- a parenthetical containing the court's abbreviated name and the exact date (month, day, and year) of the opinion.

For guidance, see the examples in Rule 12.13.

Table Cases

A "table case" is a form of unpublished opinion stating just the disposition of the case, published in a West reporter table titled "Table of Decisions Without Reported Opinions." You will often find the court's actual opinion, however, on LexisNexis or Westlaw. For table cases cited in print reporters, append the parenthetical "(table)" to the end of the citation. If you are citing the opinion in its LexisNexis or Westlaw version, however, provide the volume, reporter, and page location of the print table, the parenthetical "(table)," a citation to the unique database identifier for the service, and a court/date parenthetical. Examples of each are shown in Rule 12.14(a).

Cases in Other Media

Electronic research methods often return information concerning a case's location not only in a print reporter, but also in one or more looseleaf services, as shown in the example from Westlaw below:

16 So.3d 922, 107 Fair Empl.Prac.Cas. (BNA) 197, 34 Fla. L. Weekly D1604

A looseleaf service collects a variety of legal materials in a specific subject area, and it is frequently updated. The name "looseleaf" derives from the easy addition or removal of individual pages from the binder format used by many such services. Do not cite cases appearing in a looseleaf service unless they are not available in standard print reporters, Westlaw, or LexisNexis. Consult Rule 28.0, Looseleaf Services and Reporters, for guidance and examples.

The citation format for looseleaf case citations is similar to the format for reporter citations, but not identical. After the case name, provide the looseleaf's volume number and its name, abbreviated in accordance with Appendix 3 (which means you should not rely on the abbreviations shown in other sources). In parentheses, provide the name of the publisher and the date of the decision. If the publisher name is not listed in Chart 28.1, use Appendix 3 to construct its abbreviation.

Page References

Case citations should provide two important page references: the initial page and a pinpoint page. The initial page tells the reader where in the reporter the case begins. When you refer to specific material *within* a case, add a pinpoint page reference to help readers quickly locate it. Make pinpoint references as precise as possible. Sidebar 5.1, Importance of Using Pinpoint References, explains the benefits—to you and your readers—of such references.

Other rules provide guidance for specific situations, such as Rule 5.3, Citing Consecutive Pages; Rule 5.4, Citing Scattered Pages; and Rule 7.0, Citing Footnotes and Endnotes.

Remember that the *Manual* lets you choose whether to represent a span of pages by retaining all digits on both sides of the span (e.g., 1287–1288) or by dropping repetitious digits but keeping the last two digits on the right side of the span (e.g., 1287–88). Sidebar 5.2 addresses the differences in using hyphens, en dashes (–), and "to" when indicating spans of pages.

Westlaw and LexisNexis databases often provide researchers with page number references to both official and unofficial reporter versions of a case, shown with one or more asterisks in the text of the electronic version. These page references, known as "star pages," indicate the pinpoint locations of cited material in the indicated reporters or databases. When you cite a case that contains star pagination for more than one reporter, be careful to match the star pages to the right reporter. Omit the asterisks from page references when you cite a *print reporter* that you found online. If you cite a case that is only available on LexisNexis or Westlaw, insert the word "at" after the database identifier. Use one asterisk before a pinpoint reference to a single page and two asterisks before a pinpoint reference to two or more pages. See Rules 5.5 and 12.12(b) and their examples.

You may sometimes wish to cite material from non-majority opinions, such as dissents or concurrences. Such citations must still provide the initial page of the opinion, and not only provide the pinpoint page reference to the material cited, but also append an explanatory parenthetical to the citation (whether it is a full citation or a short form) setting out the author's surname and title and indicating the nature of the non-majority opinion (e.g., dissenting, concurring in part). For more information, see Rule 12.11, Parenthetical Information, and Chart 12.2, Abbreviations for Titles of Judges and Other Judicial Officials.

If you are citing a case available only in a looseleaf reporter, provide pinpoint references according to the numbering system used by the looseleaf, which may be page numbers, paragraph numbers, report numbers, or other subdivisions. For more explanation and examples, see Rule 28.1(e).

EXERCISE SET 5-B

BASIC LEVEL: REPORTERS AND PAGE REFERENCES

Before beginning Exercise Set 5-B Basic Level, review the following and keep the *Manual* at hand as you work through the exercises:

- Rule 12.3, Reporter Volume
- Rule 12.4, Reporter Abbreviation

- Chart 12.1, Common Reporter Abbreviations
- Rule 12.5, Page Numbers

To complete the exercises, you may also need to refer to the following:

- Rule 2.2, Spacing for Abbreviations
- Rule 4.3, Ordinal Numbers
- Rule 5.1, Initial Pages

- Rule 5.2, Pinpoint Pages
- Rule 5.3, Citing Consecutive Pages
- Rule 5.4, Citing Scattered Pages

5-B.1. Which of the following correctly refers to a case beginning at page 867 in Volume 466 of the North Eastern Reporter, Second Series?

a. 466 N.E.2d 867
b. 466 N.E. 2d. 867
c. 466 N.E. 2nd 867
d. 466 N.E.2nd 867

5-B.2.   Which of the following correctly refers to a case beginning at page 789 in Volume 965 of the Southern Reporter, Second Series?

    a. 965 S.2d 789
    b. 965 So. 2d 789
    c. 965 So.2d 789
    d. 965 So.2d. 789

5-B.3.   Your brief cites a case published in Volume 259 of the first series of the South Western Reporter, beginning at page 369. How should you cite this reporter and initial page?

    a. 259 S. W. 369
    b. 259 Sw. 369
    c. 259 S.W. 369
    d. 259 S.W.1st 369

5-B.4.   Which of the following correctly refers to a case beginning at page 562 in Volume 176 of the Federal Rules Decisions?

    a. 176 Fed. R. Dec. 562
    b. 176 F. R. Dec. 562
    c. 176 F. R. D. 562
    d. 176 F.R.D. 562

5-B.5.   Your research on accomplice liability for crimes has led you to an older Pennsylvania case, *Commonwealth v. Strantz*. It was published in volume 195 of the Atlantic Reporter, beginning at page 75. How should you cite the reporter and initial page?

    a. 195 Atl. 75
    b. 195 A.2d 75
    c. 195 A. 75
    d. 195 A. Rep. 75

5-B.6.   Your brief to the bankruptcy court in the District of New Jersey cites a 1986 opinion by that court, *In re Mason*. The case begins at page 297 of volume 66 of the Bankruptcy Reporter. Your argument makes specific reference to material at page 301. How should your full citation to this case indicate the reporter and the initial and pinpoint page references?

    a. 66 Bankr. Rep. 297, at 301
    b. 66 Bankr. R. 297, 301
    c. 66 B.R. 297, 301
    d. 66 B.R. 297, 301

5-B.7.   The West digest entry for a case you are quoting shows the following citation format:

    Hernandez v. City Wide Insulation of Madison, Inc., 508 F.Supp.2d 682.

The quotation is from page 689. How should your full citation to this case indicate the reporter and the initial and pinpoint page references?

    a. 508 F. Supp. 2d 682, 689
    b. 508 F. Supp. 682, 689
    c. 508 F.Supp.2d 689
    d. 508 F.2d 689

5-B.8. The Ninth Circuit case of *Howard v. Cupp* begins at page 510 of volume 747 of the Federal Reporter, Second Series. You wish to quote the well-settled Ninth Circuit rule that "there is no fundamental right to a preliminary hearing." This language appears at page 510. How should your full citation to this case indicate the reporter and the initial and pinpoint page references?

    a. 747 Fed.2d 510
    b. 747 F.2d 510
    c. 747 F.2d 510, 510
    d. 747 Fed. 2d 510, at 510

5-B.9. Your office memo discusses a Sixth Circuit case published in volume 240 of West's Federal Appendix and beginning at page 70. It quotes material from page 73. How should your full citation to this case indicate the reporter and the initial and pinpoint page references?

    a. 240 F. App. 73
    b. 240 Fed. App. at 73
    c. 240 Fed. Appx. 70, 73
    d. 240 F. Appx. 70–73

5-B.10. In a brief to a federal district court, you cite the case of *Flood v. Silfies* for a definition of "local agency." The definition begins at page 1074 and continues on page 1075. The case is reported in volume 933 of the Atlantic Reporter, Second Series, beginning at page 1072. Assume that this is your brief's first citation to *Flood*. How should your full citation to this case indicate the reporter and the initial and pinpoint page references?

    a. 933 A.2d 1074–75
    b. 933 A.2d 1072, 1074 & 1075
    c. 933 A.2d 1072, 1074–1075
    d. 933 A.2d 1072, 1074–5

EXERCISE SET 5-B

INTERMEDIATE LEVEL: REPORTERS AND PAGE REFERENCES

Before beginning Exercise Set 5-B Intermediate Level, review the following and keep the *Manual* at hand as you work through the exercises:

- Rule 12.3, Reporter Volume
- Rule 12.4, Reporter Abbreviation
- Rule 12.5, Page Numbers
- Rule 12.11, Parenthetical Information
- Rule 12.12, Cases Published Only on LexisNexis or Westlaw

- Rule 12.13, Cases Not Yet Reported
- Rule 12.14(b), Cases in Federal Appendix
- Rule 28.0, Looseleaf Services and Reporters
- Chart 12.1, Common Reporter Abbreviations
- Chart 28.1, Abbreviations for Looseleaf Publishers

To complete the exercises, you may also need to refer to the following:

- Rule 2.2, Spacing for Abbreviations
- Rule 4.3, Ordinal Numbers
- Rule 5.0, Page and Location Numbers

5-B.11. You work in a New York law firm, and you are writing an office memo about defamation. You cite a case whose Westlaw caption shows the following reporters: 10 N.Y.3d 271, 885 N.E.2d 884, 856 N.Y.S.2d 31, 36 Media L. Rep. 2106, 2008 N.Y. Slip Op. 02675. Which reporter is your supervising attorney going to prefer that you use in the citation?

a. N.Y.3d
b. N.E.2d
c. N.Y.S.2d
d. Media L. Rep.

5-B.12. Your research leads you to the case decided by the United States District Court for the Western District of Missouri whose Westlaw caption is shown below. Which of the following full citations is correct to use in citing this case?

> Not Reported in F.Supp.2d, 2008 WL 795443 (W.D.Mo.)
> United States District Court, W.D. Missouri, Saint Joseph Division.
> Laura Christine RICHEY, Plaintiff,
> v.
> JIM HAWK TRUCK TRAILER, INC., Defendant.
> No. 07-6008-CV-SJ-FJG.
> March 20, 2008.

a. *Richey v. Jim Hawk Truck Trailer, Inc.*, ___ F. Supp. 2d ___ (W.D. Mo. Mar. 20, 2008).
b. *Richey v. Jim Hawk Truck Trailer, Inc.*, 2008 WL 795443 (W.D. Mo. Mar. 20, 2008).
c. *Richey v. Jim Hawk Truck Trailer, Inc.*, 2008 WL 795443, ___ F. Supp. 2d ___ (W.D. Mo. Mar. 20, 2008).
d. *Richey v. Jim Hawk Truck Trailer, Inc.*, ___ F. Supp. 2d ___, 2008 WL 795443 (W.D. Mo. Mar. 20, 2008).

5-B.13. You wish to cite the United States Supreme Court case *Craig v. Boren* in a paper for a Constitutional Law course. You find the case in West's Supreme Court Reporter, whose running head and caption are shown here. Which of the following full citations is correct to use in citing this case?

a. 97 S. Ct. 451
b. 429 U.S. 190
c. 50 L. Ed. 2d 397
d. 429 U.S. 190, 97 S. Ct. 451, 50 L. Ed. 2d 397

429 U.S. 190	CRAIG v. BOREN	451
	Cite as 97 S.Ct. 451 (1976)	

429 U.S. 190, 50 L.Ed.2d 397
Curtis CRAIG et al., Appellants,
v.
David BOREN, etc., et al.
No. 75–628.
Argued Oct. 5, 1976.
Decided Dec. 20, 1976.
Rehearing Denied Feb. 22, 1977.
See 429 U.S. 1124, 97 S.Ct. 1161.

5-B.14. You are writing a seminar paper about termination of parental rights. Researching in Westlaw, you discover a case decided by the Iowa Supreme Court that displays the following caption. Which of the following full citations is correct to use in citing page *4 of this case?

— N.W.2d ——, 2010 WL 323032 (Iowa)
Only the Westlaw citation is currently available.

NOTICE: THIS OPINION HAS NOT BEEN RELEASED FOR PUBLICATION IN THE PERMANENT LAW REPORTS. UNTIL SO RELEASED, IT IS SUBJECT TO CORRECTION, MODIFICATION OR WITHDRAWAL.
Supreme Court of Iowa.
In the Interest of P.L., Minor Child,
O.L.-V., Father, Appellant,
State of Iowa, Appellee.
No. 09-1036.
Jan. 29, 2010.

a. *In re P.L.*, ___ N.W.2d ___, 4 (Iowa Jan. 29, 2010).
b. *In re P.L.*, 2010 WL 323032 at *4 (Iowa Jan. 29, 2010).
c. *In re P.L.*, ___ N.W. 2d ___, 2010 WL 323032 at *4 (Iowa Jan. 29, 2010).
d. *In re P.L.*, ___ N.W. 2d ___, 2010 WL 323032, at *4 (Iowa Jan. 29, 2010).

5-B.15. You wish to quote and cite the language **in bold** from the dissenting opinion of Justice Maynard in the 1997 West Virginia Supreme Court case, *Baugh v. Merritt*, reported in volume 489 of the South Eastern Reporter, Second Series, beginning at page 775. Justice Maynard's dissent begins on page 780. Which of the following full citations is correct to use in citing this quotation?

My real complaint is the law which the majority cites in deciding this case. They rely heavily on *Overfield v. Collins*, 199 W.Va. 27, 483 S.E.2d 27 (1996). I was not here when *Overfield* was decided in December 1996, and accordingly, had no opportunity to dissent in that case. I certainly would have, however, and since I couldn't then, I will dissent now, in the instant case.

Some of *Overfield* is bad law. It **creates two different standards for determining custody of a child, depending on whether a **783 *401 parent who transferred custody did so on a temporary or a permanent basis.**

a. *Baugh v. Merritt*, 489 S.E.2d 775, 782–83 (W. Va. 1997) (Maynard, J., dissenting).
b. *Baugh v. Merritt*, 489 S.E.2d 775, 780 (W. Va. 1997) (Maynard, J., dissenting).
c. *Baugh v. Merritt*, 489 S.E.2d 780, 782–83 (W. Va. 1997) (Maynard, J., dissenting).
d. *Baugh v. Merritt*, 489 S.E.2d 775, 780, 782–83 (W. Va. 1997) (Maynard, J., dissenting).

5-B.16. In an office memorandum, you are quoting from page *4 of the unpublished opinion whose Westlaw caption is shown below. Which of the following full citations is correct?

120 Hawai'i 49, 200 P.3d 418 (Table), 2009 WL 190711 (Hawai'i App.)
Unpublished Disposition
Intermediate Court of Appeals of Hawai'i.
Eleonora E. KELIIPULEOLE, Plaintiff-Appellee,
v.
Shelly M. RUTT, Defendant-Appellant (Civil No. 1RC06-1-3501).
Eleonora E. Keliipuleole, Plaintiff-Appellee,
v.
Shelly M. Rutt, Defendant-Appellant (Civil No. 1RC06-1-445).
Nos. 28214, 28215.
Jan. 28, 2009.
As Amended March 3, 2009.

a. *Keliipuleole v. Rutt*, 120 Haw. 49, 200 P.3d 418 (Table), 2009 WL 190711 at *4 (Haw. App. 2009).
b. *Keliipuleole v. Rutt*, 200 P.3d 418 (table), 2009 WL 190711 at *4 (Haw. App. 2009).
c. *Keliipuleole v. Rutt*, 200 P.3d 418 (Table) (Haw. App. 2009).
d. *Keliipuleole v. Rutt*, 2009 WL 190711 at *4 (Haw. App. 2009) (table).

5-B.17. You are writing an office memorandum about employment discrimination against Hispanics, and you wish to cite the case of *Gregorio Garza, Jr. v. Laredo Independent School District*, an unpublished decision of the United States Court of Appeals for the Fifth Circuit, filed on January 30, 2009. Despite its unpublished status, you found the court's decision in Westlaw at the database identifier 2009 WL 221258. You also found it in volume 243, page 648 of the Education Law Reporter, a looseleaf published by West. It also appears in volume 309 of the Federal Appendix, beginning at page 806. Which of the following full citations will you use in the office memo?

a. *Garza v. Laredo Indep. Sch. Dist.*, 2009 WL 221258 (5th Cir. Jan. 30, 2009).

b. *Garza v. Laredo Indep. Sch. Dist.*, 309 Fed. Appx. 806 (5th Cir. 2009).

c. *Garza v. Laredo Indep. Sch. Dist.*, 243 Educ. L. Rep. (West) 648 (5th Cir. Jan. 30, 2009).

d. *Garza v. Laredo Indep. Sch. Dist.*, 309 Fed. Appx. 806, 243 Educ. L. Rep. (West) 648, 2009 WL 221258 (5th Cir. Jan. 30, 2009).

5-B.18. Using Westlaw to researching the right of publicity, you find a case with the caption shown below. You wish to cite the discussion in the passage shown in the box. What volume, reporter, and page should you use when citing the case?

— F.3d ——, 2010 WL 1039872 (C.A.9 (Cal.)), 10 Cal. Daily Op. Serv. 3565
United States Court of Appeals,
Ninth Circuit.
Paris HILTON, Plaintiff-Appellee,
v.
Hallmark CARDS, a Missouri corporation, Defendant-Appellant.
No. 08-55443.
Argued and Submitted May 6, 2009.
Filed March 23, 2010.

> The potential reach of the transformative use defense is broad. The form of the expression to which it applies "[is] not confined to parody and can take many forms," including "fictionalized portrayal . . . heavy-handed lampooning . . . [and] subtle social criticism." *Id.* at 809 (citations omitted). Nor should courts "be concerned with the quality of the artistic contribution-vulgar forms of expression fully qualify for First Amendment protection." *Id.* It is thus irrelevant whether Hallmark's card qualifies as parody [FN13] or high-brow art. Nor does it matter that Hallmark sought to profit from the card; the only question is whether the card is transformative. *Cf. Winter,* 134 Cal.Rptr.2d 634, 69 P.3d at 479 ("The question is whether the work is transformative, not how it is marketed.").
>
> *11 [27] We think it clear that Hallmark may raise the transformative use defense. The applicability of the defense, however, does not preclude Hilton from showing the "minimal merit" needed to defeat Hallmark's motion to strike.[FN14] Only if Hallmark is entitled to the defense *as a matter of law* can it prevail on its motion to strike.

a. — F.3d —, at ** 10–11

b. — F.3d —, *10–11

c. ___ F.3d ___, 2010 WL 1039872 at *10–11

d. ___ F.3d ___, 2010 WL 1039872 at **10–11

EXERCISE SET 5-B

EXPERT LEVEL: REPORTERS AND PAGE REFERENCES

Before beginning Exercise Set 5-B Expert Level, review the following and keep the *Manual* at hand as you work through the exercises:

- Rule 12.3, Reporter Volume
- Rule 12.4, Reporter Abbreviation
- Chart 12.1, Common Reporter Abbreviations
- Sidebar 12.4 (Early Supreme Court Reporters)
- Rule 12.5, Page Numbers
- Rule 28.0, Looseleaf Services and Reporters
- Chart 28.1, Abbreviations for Looseleaf Publishers

To complete the exercises, you may also need to refer to the following:

- Rule 2.2, Spacing for Abbreviations
- Rule 5.0, Page and Location Numbers

Be prepared to consult Appendix 1, Primary Sources by Jurisdiction, for some of the questions.

5-B.19. You wish to cite material at page 124 of the opinion whose caption is shown below. Write the volume, reporter, and initial and pinpoint page references from the full case citation.

---

122   275 BANKRUPTCY REPORTER

appeared. An appropriate remand order accompanies this memorandum.

In re ARDENT, INC., et al., Debtors.

No. 01-02086.

ORDER

For the reasons set forth in the accompanying memorandum, it is this 6th day of March 2002,

United States Bankruptcy Court, District of Columbia.

Nov. 16, 2001.

5-B.20. You found the following Ohio case on LexisNexis, and it's one which you believe will be persuasive authority in a brief you are writing to the Kentucky Court of Appeals. Write the volume, reporter, and initial page references that should appear in the full case citation in your brief.

47 Ohio App. 2d 103, *; 352 N.E.2d 149, **;
1975 Ohio App. LEXIS 5866, ***; 1 Ohio Op. 3d 206

ROSSMAN, APPELLANT, v. ROSSMAN, APPELLEE

No. 34267

Court of Appeals of Ohio, Eighth Appellate District, Cuyahoga County

47 Ohio App. 2d 103; 352 N.E.2d 149; 1975 Ohio App. LEXIS 5866; 1 Ohio Op. 3d 206

December 18, 1975, Decided

5-B.21. In conducting research for a paper on the Supreme Court's reliance on international law, you found a law review article with the following citation to a United States Supreme Court case:

> *The Nereide*, 13 U.S. (9 Cranch.) 388, 422-23 (1815) (stating that United States courts "are bound by the law of nations, which is part of the law of the land.").

After confirming its accuracy, you have decided to use the quotation from the case in your paper. Write the volume, reporter, and initial and pinpoint page references that should appear in your full case citation to *The Nereide.*

5-B.22. You are writing a brief in support of a motion for summary judgment to the United States District Court for the Eastern District of Michigan, and you wish to cite a case decided by that court on April 7, 2008, *Center Capital Corp. v. Marlin Air, Inc.* The case was not published in the Federal Supplement, but it is available in volume 66 of the Uniform Commercial Code Reporting Service, beginning at page 139. You wish to quote language on page 140. The publisher of this looseleaf reporter is Clark Boardman Callaghan. Write the volume, reporter, initial page, and pinpoint page number references for a full citation from the looseleaf reporter.

C. COURT NAMES AND DATES

The third component of a full case citation is a parenthetical reference to the court issuing the opinion and the year the opinion was issued.

Court Names

You will usually insert an abbreviation for the court's name in the parenthetical. Although court names display great variety, the *ALWD Citation Manual* uses consistent forms for their abbreviations. The easiest way to determine the abbreviation for a court name is to look it up in either Appendix 1, Primary Sources by Jurisdiction, which provides summary information for all primary authorities in a particular jurisdiction, including the pattern to use for subdivisions of intermediate courts, or Appendix 4, Court Abbreviations, which provides state and federal court name abbreviations. (Never use the general abbreviations in Appendix 3 to represent a court, and never rely on an abbreviation shown in another publication, which may not follow current *ALWD Citation Manual* rules.)

Two special situations make it unnecessary to insert the court name in a parenthetical reference:

- First, because opinions of the United States Supreme Court typically appear in specialized reporters (e.g., United States Reports, Supreme Court Reporter), the only time it is necessary to include the Court's abbreviation in the parenthetical is when the case appears in United States Law Week (U.S.L.W.), because it also publishes cases from other courts.
- Second, there is no need to indicate the court when the case citation uses a state-specific reporter whose name clearly signals the court who issued the opinion (e.g., Nevada Reports, West Virginia Reports). Such state-specific reporters' most common use is in parallel citations.

When you cite a West regional reporter, however, it is essential to provide the court reference, because each reporter contains the decisions of many *different states'* courts. For example, the North Eastern Reporter contains decisions from appellate courts in Illinois, Indiana, Massachusetts, New York, and Ohio. (For the states in the other regional reporters, see Appendix 1A, West Regional Reporter Coverage.) Similarly, the Federal Reporter, the Federal Supplement, the Federal Appendix, the Bankruptcy Reporter, and similar publications and looseleafs contain decisions from different federal courts, making it vital to include the court abbreviation in the parenthetical.

Many states divide their intermediate appellate courts into districts, divisions, counties, or departments. Such subdivisions feature distinguishing names or numbers (e.g., Division II; Second District; or Warren County). Even though some captions indicate smaller subdivisions, the abbreviation should refer only to the largest division of the court, as reflected in Appendix 1B, State Appellate Court Divisions. Note that although Appendix 4 sets out court abbreviations, it does not indicate the pattern to use for subdivisions, if any. Therefore, it's wise to consult Appendix 1 for the abbreviations and format used in each state. For cited divisions, follow the naming or numbering system used in that jurisdiction, but abbreviate ordinal numbers as shown in Rule 4.3. Note that occasionally a case's caption may not display a court division even though the Appendix 1 entry shows that format. When that happens, simply omit reference to the division.

Dates

Citations to cases in print reporters must indicate the year the case was decided. Although most captions show only the date of the decision, some display additional dates, such as the date the case was submitted for decision, or the date it was orally argued, or the date the court denied rehearing, to name a few (see example at right). In those instances, look for a verb that signals the date the original opinion came down, such as "decided" or "filed." Ignore other dates.

For cases that are available solely in online or looseleaf publications, always provide the exact date, using the abbreviation of the month (see Appendix 3(A), Calendar Divisions), day, and year.

> Bob E. CARPENTER, C.D. Consulting and Operating Company, and C.D. Roustabout Company and Equipment Sales, Petitioners,
>
> v.
>
> CIMARRON HYDROCARBONS CORPORATION, Respondent.
>
> No. 01-0002.
>
> Supreme Court of Texas.
>
> Argued Nov. 28, 2001.
>
> Decided Dec. 31, 2002.
>
> Opinion Concurring in Judgment and Dissenting
> Opinion Filed July 3, 2002.
>
> Rehearing Denied April 3, 2003.

EXERCISE SET 5-C

BASIC LEVEL: COURT NAMES AND DATES

Before beginning Exercise Set 5-C Basic Level, review the following and keep the *Manual* at hand as you work through the exercises:

- Rule 4.3, Ordinal Numbers
- Rule 12.6, Court Abbreviation
- Rule 12.4, Reporter Abbreviation
- Rule 12.7, Date

Be prepared to consult Appendix 1, Primary Sources by Jurisdiction, Appendix 1B, State Appellate Court Divisions, or Appendix 4, Court Abbreviations, for some of the questions.

5-C.1. Which of the following court/date parentheticals should be used in citing a case decided in 2005 by the Supreme Judicial Court of Massachusetts?

    a. (Sup. Jud. Ct. Mass. 2005)
    b. (Mass. Sup. Jud. Ct. 2005)
    c. (Mass Sup. Jud. 2005)
    d. (Mass. 2005)

5-C.2. Which of the following court/date parentheticals should be used in citing a case decided in 2004 by the United States Court of Appeals for the District of Columbia Circuit?

    a. (D.C. Cir. 2004)
    b. (D.D.C. 2004)
    c. (Dist. Columbia Cir. 2004)
    d. (U.S. Ct. App. D.C. Cir. 2004)

5-C.3. Which of the following court/date parentheticals should be used in citing the case whose caption from the North Western Reporter, Second Series, appears at right?

    a. (WI App 2008)
    b. (Wis. App. 2007)
    c. (Wis. App. 2008)
    d. (Wis. Ct. App. 2007)

2008 WI App 126

Richard G. McLELLAN, Rick Bogle, and Primate Freedom Project, Plaintiffs–Respondents–Cross–Appellants[†]

v.

Roger L. CHARLY, Defendant–Appellant–Cross–Respondent.

No. 2007AP1120.

Court of Appeals of Wisconsin.

Submitted on Briefs Dec. 7, 2007.

Opinion Filed July 17, 2008.

5-C.4. Using LexisNexis, you locate the case whose caption is shown below. You wish to cite the case in your brief to the United States District Court for the Northern District of Illinois. Which of the following court/date parentheticals should be used in its citation?

MICHEL v. LOUISIANA

NO. 32

SUPREME COURT OF THE UNITED STATES

350 U.S. 91; 76 S. Ct. 158; 100 L. Ed. 83; 1955 U.S. LEXIS 37

Argued November 8–9, 1955
December 5, 1955

a. (1955)
b. (La. 1955)
c. (U.S. 1955)
d. (U.S. (La.) 1955)

5-C.5. This case whose caption appears at right was published in the Atlantic Reporter, Second Series. Which of the following court/date parentheticals should be used in its citation?

> **ALPERT v. ALPERT.**
>
> Supreme Judicial Court of Maine.
> Nov. 26, 1946.

a. (Me. 1946)
b. (S.Ct. Me. 1946)
c. (Sup. Jud. Ct. Me. 1946)
d. (Sup. Jud. Ct. of Me. 1946)

5-C.6. Your memo cites the North Eastern Reporter, Second Series, version of the case whose caption is shown at right. Which of the following court/date parentheticals should be used in its citation?

> 336 Ill.App.3d 702
> 271 Ill.Dec. 127
>
> Claudia **MEJIA**, Independent Adm'r of the Estate of Luis G. Mejia, Deceased, Plaintiff–Appellant,
>
> v.
>
> **WHITE GMC TRUCKS, INC.**, formerly known as White Trucks of Chicago, Inc., Defendant (Volvo GM Heavy Truck Corporation, Defendant–Appellee).
>
> No. 1-00-0073.
>
> Appellate Court of Illinois, First District, Third Division.
>
> Dec. 31, 2002.

a. (1st Dist. 2002)
b. (1st Dist. 3rd Div. 2002)
c. (Ill. App. 1st Dist. 3d Div. 2002)
d. (Ill. App. 1st Dist. 2002).

5-C.7. In researching a question about appointment of counsel for criminal defendants, you located the following case on Westlaw. It is published in volume 536 of the Federal Supplement 2d, beginning at page 1070. Which of the following court/date parentheticals should be used in its citation?

United States District Court,
D. South Dakota,
Central Division.
Bryan Ward WHITEPIPE, Petitioner,
v.
Douglas WEBER, Warden, South Dakota State Penitentiary, Respondent.
No. CIV 06-3018.
Nov. 29, 2007.

a. (D.S.D. 2007)
b. (Dist. S. Dak. 2007)
c. (U.S. Dist. S. D. Nov. 29, 2007)
d. (S.D. C. Div. 2007)

5-C.8. Researching in LexisNexis, you found a reference to a case decided by the United States Supreme Court that will be very helpful to your argument. The LexisNexis reference is shown below. Which of the following court/date parentheticals should be used in its citation?

Followed by:
Argencourt v. United States, 78 F.3d 14, 1996 U.S. App. LEXIS 4619
(1st Cir. R.I. 1996)

a. (1st Cir. R.I. 1996)
b. (1st Cir. 1996)
c. (C.C.A. 1 1996)
d. (U.S. App. 1st 1996)

EXERCISE SET 5-C

INTERMEDIATE LEVEL: COURT NAMES AND DATES

Before beginning Exercise Set 5-C Intermediate Level, review the following and keep the *Manual* at hand as you work through the exercises:

- Rule 12.4, Reporter Abbreviation
- Rule 12.6, Court Abbreviation
- Rule 12.7, Date
- Rule 12.15, Cases on the Internet

- Rule 12.18, Unreported Cases
- Sidebar A4.2 (in Appendix 4), Dissecting a Federal District Court Abbreviation

Be prepared to consult Appendix 1, Primary Sources by Jurisdiction, Appendix 1B, State Appellate Court Divisions, or Appendix 4, Court Abbreviations, for some of the questions.

5-C.9. Your online research has led you to an annotation in American Law Reports ("A.L.R."). After reading the case in its cited West reporter, you decide to use it in your memo. The A.L.R. annotation appears below. Which of the following court/date parentheticals should be used in the case's citation?

> Use by the agents of a freight terminal proprietor of a lifting device known as a "hilo" having a capacity of 3,000 pounds, in order to lift the rear end of a transformer weighing in excess of 8,500 pounds, during which process it came down on the hand of a trucker on the premises to pick it up for delivery elsewhere, was held sufficient evidence of negligence to take the case to the jury and thereby to affirm a judgment for the injured trucker, in Rosillo v Erie R. Co. (1956, CA2 NY) 239 F2d 760, the court apparently applying New York law.

a. (1956, CA2 NY)
b. (C.A.2 (N.Y.) 1956)
c. (Cir. 2 1956)
d. (2d Cir. 1956)

5-C.10. You found the following entry in a West digest. After reading the case, which was decided by the New York Supreme Court, Appellate Division, Second Department, you decided to use it in a memo, citing the New York Supplement, Second Series, reporter version shown in the entry. Which of the following court/date parentheticals should be used in its citation?

> **N.Y.A.D.2 Dept. 2007.** The fact that a defect may be open and obvious does not negate a landowner's duty to maintain its premises in a reasonably safe condition, but may raise an issue of fact as to the plaintiff's comparative negligence.—Ruiz v. Hart Elm Corp., 844 N.Y.S.2d 80.

a. (A.D.2 Dept. 2007)
b. (App. Div. 2d Dept. 2007)
c. (N.Y. App. Div. 2007)
d. (N.Y. App. Div. 2d Dept. 2007)

5-C.11. A terms-and-connectors search on Westlaw yielded 120 results. After reading the sixth case in the list, you decided to use it. The Westlaw research display is shown below. Which of the following court/date parentheticals should be used in its citation?

> **ʜ 6. U.S. v. Garcia-Ortiz,**
> 528 F.3d 74, C.A.1 (Puerto Rico), June 10, 2008 (NO. 06-1923)

   a. (C.A. 1 (Puerto Rico), June 10, 2008)
   b. (C.A. 1 2008)
   c. (1st Cir. June 10, 2008)
   d. (1st Cir. 2008)

5-C.12. Your research located the slip copy of a case whose caption is shown below. Only the electronic version on Westlaw was available at the time. Which of the following court/date parentheticals should be used in its citation?

> United States District Court,
> M.D. Georgia,
> Columbus Division.
> Kenneth CLAY, Plaintiff,
> v.
> Robert WADKINS, et al., Defendants.
> No. 4:09-CV-02 (CDL).
> Feb. 5, 2009.

   a. (M.D. Ga. Feb. 5, 2009)
   b. (M.D. Ga. 2009)
   c. (M. Dist. Ga. Feb. 5, 2009)
   d. (M.D. Ga. Columbus Div. 2009)

EXERCISE SET 5-C

EXPERT LEVEL: COURT NAMES AND DATES

Before beginning Exercise Set 5-C Expert Level, review the following and keep the *Manual* at hand as you work through the exercises:

- Rule 12.6, Court Abbreviation
- Rule 12.7, Date
- Rule 12.12, Cases Published Only on LexisNexis or Westlaw

- Rule 12.13, Cases Not Yet Reported
- Rule 12.18, Unreported Cases
- Sidebar A4.2 (in Appendix 4), Dissecting a Federal District Court Abbreviation

Be prepared to consult Appendix 1, Primary Sources by Jurisdiction, Appendix 1B, State Appellate Court Divisions, or Appendix 4, Court Abbreviations, for some of the questions.

5-C.13. Write the court/date parenthetical for a full citation to the case from the Pacific Reporter, Second Series, whose caption is shown at right.

> In the Matter of the ADOPTION OF B.R.H., a minor.
>
> Chris C. WADKINS and Janice L. Wadkins, Appellees,
>
> v.
>
> Bobbie L. HOLCOM, Appellant.
>
> No. 73398.
>
> Released for Publication by Order of the Court of Appeals of Oklahoma, Division No. 2.
>
> Court of Appeals of Oklahoma, Division No. 2.
>
> Dec. 10, 1991.

5-C.14. You are writing a brief and you wish to cite a case published in volume 546 of the Federal Supplement, Second Series, which begins at page 681. Its caption on Westlaw appears below. Write the court/date parenthetical for a full citation to the case.

> United States District Court,
> W.D. Missouri,
> Central Division.
> UNITED STATES of America, Plaintiff,
> v.
> Robert Joseph SMART, Defendant.
> No. 06-4073-01-CR-C-SOW.
> March 10, 2008.

5-C.15. Write the court/date parenthetical for a full citation to the case whose caption is shown below.

— So.2d ——, 2008 WL 5195040 (Ala.Civ.App.)
Only the Westlaw citation is currently available.
NOT YET RELEASED FOR PUBLICATION.

Court of Civil Appeals of Alabama.
Alvin JOHNSON and The Johnson Realty Company, Inc.
v.
Darryl HALL, Sr., and Sondra D. Hall.
2070927.
Dec. 12, 2008.

5-C.16. Write the court/date parenthetical for a full citation to the case whose caption is shown below.

622   **50 MILITARY JUSTICE REPORTER**

UNITED STATES, Petitioner,

v.

**Master Sergeant James J. EWING,
United States Air Force,
Respondent.**

Misc. Dkt. No. 98-06.

U.S. Air Force Court of Criminal Appeals.

23 Nov. 1998.

ported by the record or clearly erroneous, and court is without authority to find facts in addition to those found by the military judge.

4. Military Justice ⬅748

Accused would be subject to conviction for making and uttering worthless checks to casinos in return for United States currency if, at the time the accused made or uttered the checks, he knew that he did not or would not have sufficient funds in his account for payment in full upon presentment, and if he made or uttered the checks with the intent to

D.   SUBSEQUENT HISTORY

Law-trained readers always want to know if the precedential value of a cited case has been affected by later decisions, whether negatively or positively. This is why you must append certain types of information indicating a case's *subsequent history*, if any exists, to its full citation. Subsequent history is never appended to a case's short-form citation. Rule 12.8(a), Actions to include, sets out examples of relevant forms of subsequent history with their abbreviations. The list is not exclusive. Any history that similarly affects a case should be appended even if the precise phrase is not listed in Rule 12.8(a).

On the other hand, some forms of procedural history should be omitted because they do not affect the precedential value of a case and are typically irrelevant to the reader's interest in the case. Such irrelevant information includes history related to remands and rehearings (whether granted or denied). See Rule 12.8(b), Actions to exclude, for a list of procedural history you can exclude. In addition, any history that *preceded* the current opinion does not affect the opinion's precedential value. It therefore is information the reader rarely needs, and its inclusion in a citation is never mandatory. For more information about prior history, see Rule 12.9.

Denial of Discretionary Review

Several subsections of Rule 12.8 direct writers to include certain history only if the cited case was decided *within the last two years. See* Rule 12.8(a)(4)–(5), (7)–(8). What is so special about the two-year period? It is special because the United States Supreme Court and many state supreme courts have discretion to accept or reject requests for appellate review of lower court decisions. Such a request (which may be called a "petition for review" or a "petition for a writ of certiorari") necessarily keeps a case alive until the higher court makes a final decision regarding its fate. The review process may take as long as two years, although most cases are resolved in less time. The denial of discretionary review is not particularly momentous in itself. It is certainly *not* the equivalent of a case being affirmed or reversed. For that reason, once the period in which a case might have been reviewed by a higher court has concluded, the denial of review is typically no longer relevant. Therefore, omit denials of discretionary review in citations to cases decided more than two years ago.

Change of Case Name

As a case moves up the procedural appellate ladder, its name rarely changes. Thus there is no need to set out the case name from the subsequent history unless the case name in the subsequent action is different from that of the cited case. Perhaps a party was substituted, or one of the litigants in a multi-party case assumed a primary position in subsequent appeals. In these instances, even though the case itself is the same, its name changes as part of its later history on appeal. When a case name changes, insert the Latin phrase *sub nom.* ("under the name of") before the new name. For example, in 1987, the Ninth Circuit decided *Jeffers v. Ricketts.* The case was appealed to the United States Supreme Court, who reversed the Ninth Circuit's decision under the name *Lewis v. Jeffers.* The citation to the Ninth Circuit case should therefore be *Jeffers v. Ricketts,* 832 F.2d 476 (9th Cir. 1987), *rev'd sub nom. Lewis v. Jeffers,* 497 U.S. 764 (1990).

Overruled cases are a different matter. The case ended; no further appeals were (or could have been) taken. But some time later, in *another case,* the same court, or a higher court of the jurisdiction, rejected the rule from the prior decision, thus **overruling** it. Because this situation always involves two different cases, you must provide the name of the later case in the subsequent history, but not with the phrase "sub nom." For example, in 2002, the United States Supreme Court overruled a 115-year-old precedent. The citation to the older case bears the name of the overruling case as a key component of its subsequent history: *Ex parte Bain,* 121 U.S. 1 (1887), *overruled, U.S. v. Cotton,* 535 U.S. 625 (2002).

Citators

To discover whether a case has subsequent history that must be appended to a citation, use a citator, either online (Westlaw KeyCite, LexisNexis Shepard's) or in print (Shepard's). As shown in some of this chapter's exercises, KeyCite marks the **cited case** with a blue arrow ➡. Beneath the cited case, KeyCite **status flags** alert the researcher to subsequent history or treatment:

- The red flag ▶ warns that the case is no longer good law for at least one of the points of law it contains. A red flag means that the citation will likely need to add subsequent history.

- The yellow flag ▷ warns that the case or administrative decision has some negative *treatment* (usually because a court disagrees with the reasoning or applicability of the case), but it has not been reversed or overruled. No subsequent history is needed for yellow-flagged cases.
- The blue "H" **H** tells researchers that the case has some *history*; this history may have preceded the cited case (prior history), or it may have developed after the cited case was decided (subsequent history). You will have to read the cases to find out what kind of history is involved (e.g., the case was later affirmed by a higher court). Relevant subsequent history should be cited.
- The green "C" **c** signals that the case has been *cited* by subsequent references, but those subsequent references do not represent direct history or negative treatment, and therefore, are not to be cited as subsequent history.

LexisNexis researchers may choose either "Shepard's for Validation (KWIC)" or "Shepard's for Research (Full)." The KWIC result will suffice for determining whether a case has subsequent history. If the researcher wants prior history or is interested in seeing all the citing references to the case, then it is better to select the "full" option.

At the top of the results page, Shepard's displays a symbol in front of the cited case:

- The red stop sign ● alerts the researcher that the cited case has negative subsequent history. The stop sign means that the citation will likely need to add subsequent history.
- The yellow triangle △ indicates possible negative *treatment*; it does not indicate negative *history*. No subsequent history is needed for negative treatment.
- The Q square **Q** indicates that the cited authority has been *questioned* in some way by later citing authorities. For example, a later case may have distinguished the cited authority, or the cited authority may have been cited in a dissenting opinion. No subsequent history reference is needed.
- The blue diamond ◆ indicates positive *treatment*; it does not indicate subsequent *history*. While this symbol tells the researcher that later authorities have looked favorably upon the cited case, such positive treatment does not affect the case's precedential weight or effect, and therefore, no subsequent history reference is needed.

Review your legal research textbook for more detailed information about using citators.

EXERCISE SET 5-D

BASIC LEVEL: SUBSEQUENT HISTORY

Before beginning Exercise Set 5-D Basic Level, review the following and keep the *Manual* at hand as you work through the exercises:

• Rule 12.8, Subsequent History
• Rule 12.9, Prior History
• Rule 12.10, Additional Rules Concerning Subsequent and Prior History
• Sidebar 12.6, Information about Denials of Certiorari

5-D.1. Your memo cites *United States v. Lopez*, 2 F.3d 1342 (5th Cir. 1993), a case to which the United States Supreme Court granted certiorari in 1994, and which it affirmed in 1995 in volume 514, United States Reports, page 549. Which of the following is the correct full citation to the Fifth Circuit case?

   a. *U.S. v. Lopez*, 2 F.3d 1342 (5th Cir. 1993).
   b. *U.S. v. Lopez*, 2 F.3d 1342 (5th Cir. 1993), 514 U.S. 549 (1995).
   c. *U.S. v. Lopez*, 2 F.3d 1342 (5th Cir. 1993), *aff'd*, 514 U.S. 549 (1995).
   d. *U.S. v. Lopez*, 2 F.3d 1342 (5th Cir. 1993), *cert. granted* (1994), *aff'd*, 514 U.S. 549 (1995).

5-D.2. The United States District Court for the District of Maryland decided *O'Connor v. United States* in 1994. One year later, the United States Court of Appeals for the Fourth Circuit affirmed that decision. The KeyCite entry is shown below. Which of the following is the correct full citation to the district court case?

   ➡ <u>1</u> KeyCited Citation:
   O'Connor v. U.S., 159 F.R.D. 22 (D.Md. Nov 29, 1994) (NO. CIV.A. PJM 94-1341)
     Affirmed by
   H <u>2</u> O'Connor v. U.S., 54 F.3d 773 (4th Cir.(Md.) May 19, 1995) (TABLE, TEXT IN WESTLAW, NO. 95-1060)

   a. *O'Connor v. U.S.*, 159 F.R.D. 22 (D. Md. 1994).
   b. *O'Connor v. U.S.*, 54 F.3d 773 (4th Cir. 1995).
   c. *O'Connor v. U.S.*, 159 F.R.D. 22, *aff'd*, *O'Connor v. U.S.*, 54 F.3d 773 (4th Cir. 1995).
   d. *O'Connor v. U.S.*, 159 F.R.D. 22 (D. Md. 1994), *aff'd*, 54 F.3d 773 (4th Cir. 1995).

5-D.3. In KeyCiting a case from the Eighth Circuit, you see the following direct history on screen. You are using the case to demonstrate how a well-settled rule has been applied to facts similar to those in your client's case. Which of the following is the correct full citation to the case?

   ➡ KeyCited Citation:
   U.S. v. Hardy, 393 F.3d 747 (8th Cir.(Iowa) Dec 28, 2004) (NO. 04-1875), rehearing and rehearing en banc denied (Dec 08, 2005)

   a. *U.S. v. Hardy*, 393 F.3d 747 (8th Cir. 2004).
   b. *U.S. v. Hardy*, 393 F.3d 747 (8th Cir. 2005).
   c. *U.S. v. Hardy*, 393 F.3d 747 (8th Cir. 2004), *reh'g denied* (2005).
   d. *U.S. v. Hardy*, 393 F.3d 747 (8th Cir. 2004), *reh'g denied and reh'g en banc denied* (8th Cir. 2005).

5-D.4. Your opponent's brief cites a 1989 Mississippi Supreme Court case captioned "Robert S. Minnick, Petitioner, versus the State of Mississippi, Respondent," published at 551 So. 2d 77. Being a smart advocate who checks citations, you discover that the case was overruled in 1991, in the Mississippi Supreme Court case of "Michael Warren Willie versus the State of Mississippi," reported at 585 So. 2d 660. When you reveal this error to the Court, how will you correctly cite the *Minnick* case?

a. *Minnick v. State*, 551 So. 2d 77 (Miss. 1989).
b. *Minnick v. State*, 551 So. 2d 77 (Miss. 1989), *rev'd*, 585 So. 2d 660 (Miss. 1991).
c. *Minnick v. State*, 551 So. 2d 77 (Miss. 1989), *rev'd sub nom. Willie v. State*, 585 So. 2d 660 (Miss. 1991).
d. *Minnick v. State*, 551 So. 2d 77 (Miss. 1989), *overruled*, *Willie v. State*, 585 So. 2d 660 (Miss. 1991).

5-D.5. You are writing a brief seeking to prevent the termination of your client's parental rights. An important case in your brief is *Jones v. Garrett*, 92 S.W.3d 835 (Tenn. 2002). When you check the case on KeyCite, you find the result set out below. Which of the following is the correct full citation to the Tennessee Supreme Court's decision in *Jones v. Garrett*?

> ▶ 1 Jones v. Garrett, 2001 WL 1398193 (Tenn.Ct.App. Nov 09, 2001) (NO. E2000-00196-COA-R3CV), appeal granted (Apr 01, 2002)
> *Judgment Reversed by*
> ➡ 2 KeyCited Citation:
> **Jones v. Garrett**, 92 S.W.3d 835 (Tenn. Dec 30, 2002) (NO. E2000-00196-SC-R11CV)

a. *Jones v. Garrett*, 92 S.W.3d 835 (Tenn. 2002).
b. *Jones v. Garrett*, 92 S.W.3d 835 (Tenn. 2002), *rev'g* 2001 WL 1398193 (Tenn. App. Nov. 9, 2001).
c. *Jones v. Garrett*, 2001 WL 1398193 (Tenn. App. Nov. 9, 2001), *rev'd*, *Jones v. Garrett*, 92 S.W.3d 835 (Tenn. 2002).
d. *Jones v. Garrett*, 2001 WL 1398193 (Tenn. App. Nov. 9, 2001), *rev'd*, 92 S.W.3d 835 (Tenn. 2002).

5-D.6. When you checked *In re Villa Marina Yacht Harbor, Inc.* for subsequent history, you found this result on KeyCite. Which of the following is the correct full citation to the First Circuit case?

> ➡ 1 KeyCited Citation:
> **In re Villa Marina Yacht Harbor, Inc.**, 984 F.2d 546 (1st Cir.(Puerto Rico) Feb 02, 1993) (NO. 92-2041, 92-2051)
> *Certiorari Denied by*
> H 2 Chase Manhattan Bank v. Villa Marina Yacht Harbor, Inc., 510 U.S. 818, 114 S.Ct. 71, 126 L.Ed.2d 40, 62 USLW 3212, 62 USLW 3244 (U.S.Puerto Rico Oct 04, 1993) (NO. 92-1883)

a. *In re Villa Marina Yacht Harbor, Inc.*, 984 F.2d 546 (1st Cir. 1993).
b. *In re Villa Marina Yacht Harbor, Inc.*, 984 F.2d 546 (1st Cir. 1993), *rev'd*, 510 U.S. 818 (1993).
c. *In re Villa Marina Yacht Harbor, Inc.*, 984 F.2d 546 (1st Cir. 1993), *cert. denied*, 510 U.S. 818 (1993).
d. *In re Villa Marina Yacht Harbor, Inc.*, 984 F.2d 546 (1st Cir. 1993), *cert. denied sub nom. Chase Manhattan Bank v. Villa Marina Yacht Harbor, Inc.*, 510 U.S. 818 (1993).

5-D.7. When you Shepardized *United States v. Horvath* for your memo, you found the following result. Which of the following is the correct full citation to *Horvath*?

> ✥ United States v. Horvath, 157 F.3d 131, 1998 U.S. App. LEXIS 24518 (2d Cir. N.Y. 1998)
> 2ND CIRCUIT—COURT OF APPEALS
> **4. Cited by:**
> Green v. United States, 260 F.3d 78, 2001 U.S. App. LEXIS 16920 (2d Cir. N.Y. 2001)
> LexisNexis Headnotes HN4

    a. *U.S. v. Horvath*, 157 F.3d 131 (2d Cir. 1998), *aff'd sub nom. Green v. U.S.*, 260 F.3d 78 (2d Cir. 2001).

    b. *U.S. v. Horvath*, 157 F.3d 131 (2d Cir. 1998), *aff'd*, 260 F.3d 78 (2d Cir. 2001).

    c. *U.S. v. Horvath*, 157 F.3d 131 (2d Cir. 1998).

    d. *U.S. v. Horvath*, 157 F.3d 131 (2d Cir. 1998), *cited by Green v. U.S.*, 260 F.3d 78 (2d Cir. 2001).

5-D.8. Your brief to the United States District Court for the District of New Jersey cites *United States v. Bethea*, 834 F. Supp. 659 (D.N.J. 1992). When you KeyCite *Bethea*, you discover the following direct history. Which of the following is the correct full citation to the District of New Jersey case?

> ➡ 1 KeyCited Citation:
> **U.S. v. Bethea**, 834 F.Supp. 659 (D.N.J. Dec 21, 1992) (NO. CR. A.90-0328-003HAA)
>   *Judgment Affirmed by*
> H 2 U.S. v. Bethea, 6 F.3d 780 (3rd Cir.(N.J.) Aug 20, 1993) (Table, NO. 93-5001)
>   *Certiorari Denied by*
> H 3 Bethea v. U.S., 510 U.S. 1061, 114 S.Ct. 732, 126 L.Ed.2d 695, 62 USLW 3453
> (U.S. Jan 10, 1994) (NO. 93-6860)

    a. *U.S. v. Bethea*, 834 F. Supp. 659 (D.N.J. 1992), *aff'd*, 6 F.3d 780 (3d Cir. 1993), *cert. denied*, 510 U.S. 1061 (1994).

    b. *U.S. v. Bethea*, 834 F. Supp. 659 (D.N.J. 1992), *aff'd*, 6 F.3d 780 (3d Cir. 1993).

    c. *U.S. v. Bethea*, 6 F.3d 780 (3d Cir. 1993), *aff'g*, 834 F. Supp. 659 (D.N.J. 1992).

    d. *U.S. v. Bethea*, 834 F. Supp. 659 (D.N.J. 1992), *aff'd sub nom. Bethea v. U.S.*, 510 U.S. 1061 (1994).

5-D.9. You are writing a seminar paper on drug warnings, so you were glad to find this law review article on the topic: Victor E. Schwartz et al., *Marketing Pharmaceutical Products in the Twenty-First Century: An Analysis of the Continued Viability of Traditional Principles of Law in the Age of Direct-to-Consumer Advertising*, 32 Harv. J.L. & Pub. Policy 333 (2009). Footnote 179 of that article provides this citation to a case you want to mention in your paper, formatted as shown here:

> Haste v. Am. Home Prods. Corp., 577 F.2d 1122, 1124 (10th Cir. 1978), *cert. denied*, 439 U.S. 955 (1978).

Which of the following is the correct full citation to *Haste*?

    a. *Haste v. Am. Home Prods. Corp.*, 577 F.2d 1122, 1124 (10th Cir. 1978), *cert. denied* 439 U.S. 955 (1978).

    b. *Haste v. Am. Home Prods. Corp.*, 577 F.2d 1122, 1124 (10th Cir.), *cert. denied*, 439 U.S. 955 (1978).

    c. *Haste v. Am. Home Prods. Corp.*, 577 F.2d 1122, 1124 (10th Cir. 1978).

    d. *Haste v. Am. Home Prods. Corp.*, 439 U.S. 955 (1978), *certifying question to* 577 F.2d 1122, 1124 (10th Cir. 1978).

5-D.10. You work for the district attorney in Bibb County, Georgia, and you are responding to a defendant's brief that argues he was denied his right to a speedy trial. Using LexisNexis, you found the case whose caption and Shepard's result (in the box) are shown below. Which of the following is the correct full citation to *Brown v. State*?

⚠ Brown v. State, 277 Ga. App. 169 (Copy w/ Cite)

277 Ga. App. 169, *; 626 S.E.2d 128, **;
2006 Ga. App. LEXIS 19, ***; 2006 Fulton County D. Rep. 210
BROWN v. THE STATE.

A05A2230.

COURT OF APPEALS OF GEORGIA

277 Ga. App. 169; 626 S.E.2d 128; 2006 Ga. App. LEXIS 19; 2006 Fulton
County D. Rep. 210

January 9, 2006, Decided

PRIOR HISTORY: [***1] Armed robbery, etc. Houston Superior Court.
Before Judge Nunn.

DISPOSITION: Judgment affirmed.

Distinguished by:
Hardeman v. State, 280 Ga. App. 168, 633 S.E.2d 595, 2006 Ga. App. LEXIS 783,
2006 Fulton County D. Rep. 2166 (2006) LexisNexis Headnotes HN4

280 Ga. App. 168 p.172
633 S.E.2d 595 p.599

---

a. *Brown v. State*, 626 S.E.2d 128 (Ga. App. 2006).
b. *Brown v. State*, 626 S.E.2d 128, *aff'd*, (Ga. App. 2006).
c. *Brown v. State*, 626 S.E.2d 128, *aff'd*, 633 S.E.2d 595 (Ga. App. 2006).
d. *Brown v. State*, 626 S.E.2d 128, *distinguished by Hardeman v. State*, 633 S.E.2d 595 (Ga. App. 2006).

EXERCISE SET 5-D

INTERMEDIATE LEVEL: SUBSEQUENT HISTORY

Before beginning Exercise Set 5-D Intermediate Level, review the following and keep the *Manual* at hand as you work through the exercises:

- Rule 12.8, Subsequent History
- Rule 12.9, Prior History
- Rule 12.10, Additional Rules Concerning Subsequent and Prior History
- Sidebar 12.6, Information about Denials of Certiorari

5-D.11. In 1961, as shown in the Southern Reporter caption below, the Florida Supreme Court denied a petition for habeas corpus. In 1963, the United States Supreme Court reversed the decision under a slightly different name, *Gideon v. Wainwright*, reported at 372 U.S. 335. Which of the following is the correct full citation to the **original** Florida case?

a. *Gideon v. Cochran*, 135 So. 2d 746 (Fla. 1961).

b. *Gideon v. Wainwright*, 372 U.S. 335 (1963), *rev'g* 135 So. 2d 746 (Fla. 1961).

c. *Gideon v. Cochran*, 135 So. 2d 746 (Fla. 1961), *rev'd sub nom.* *Gideon v. Wainwright*, 372 U.S. 335 (1963).

d. *Gideon v. Wainwright*, 135 So. 2d 746 (Fla. 1961), *rev'd*, 372 U.S. 335 (1963).

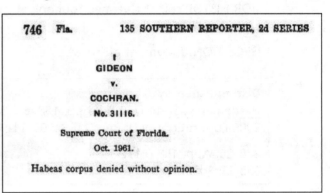

> **746 Fla.**   **135 SOUTHERN REPORTER, 2d SERIES**
>
> GIDEON
>
> v.
>
> COCHRAN.
>
> No. 31116.
>
> Supreme Court of Florida.
>
> Oct. 1961.
>
> Habeas corpus denied without opinion.

5-D.12. LexisNexis displayed the ● symbol at the top of *State v. Luurtsema*, 811 A.2d 223 (Conn. 2002). When you clicked the symbol, you saw that the Connecticut Supreme Court overruled *Luurtsema* in 2008 in the case of *State v. Salamon*, 949 A.2d 1092. Which of the following is the correct full citation to *Luurtsema*?

a. *State v. Luurtsema*, 811 A.2d 223 (Conn. 2002), *overruled*, 811 A.2d 223 (Conn. 2002).

b. *State v. Luurtsema*, 811 A.2d 223 (Conn. 2002), *overruled*, *State v. Salamon*, 949 A.2d 1092 (Conn. 2008).

c. *State v. Luurtsema*, 811 A.2d 223 (Conn. 2002), *overruled sub nom. State v. Salamon*, 949 A.2d 1092 (Conn. 2008).

d. *State v. Salamon*, 949 A.2d 1092, *reversing State v. Luurtsema*, 811 A.2d 223 (Conn. 2002).

5-D.13. The Eighth Circuit decided *Wade v. Haynes* in 1981. Two years later the case was affirmed, although under a slightly different name, as shown in its KeyCite entry. Which of the following is the correct full citation to the 1981 case?

> ➡ <u>1</u> KeyCited Citation:
> **Wade v. Haynes**, 663 F.2d 778, 9 Fed. R. Evid. Serv. 352 (8th Cir.(Mo.) Nov 09, 1981) (NO. 80-2120, 80-2131)
> > *Certiorari Granted by*
> ⊢ <u>2</u> Smith v. Wade, 456 U.S. 924, 102 S.Ct. 1968, 72 L.Ed.2d 439 (U.S.Mo. Apr 19, 1982) (NO. 81-1196)
> > *AND Judgment Affirmed by*
> ▷ <u>3</u> Smith v. Wade, 461 U.S. 30, 103 S.Ct. 1625, 75 L.Ed.2d 632 (U.S.Mo. Apr 20, 1983) (NO. 81-1196)

   a. *Wade v. Haynes*, 663 F.2d 778 (8th Cir. 1981), *cert. granted sub nom. Smith v. Wade*, 456 U.S. 924 (1982), *aff'd*, 461 U.S. 30 (1983).

   b. *Wade v. Haynes*, 663 F.2d 778 (8th Cir. 1981), *aff'd sub nom. Smith v. Wade*, 461 U.S. 30 (1983).

   c. *Wade v. Haynes*, 663 F.2d 778 (8th Cir. 1981), *cert. granted*, 456 U.S. 924 (1982), *aff'd*, 461 U.S. 30 (1983).

   d. *Smith v. Wade*, 663 F.2d 778 (8th Cir. 1981), *aff'd*, 461 U.S. 30 (1983).

5-D.14. You used KeyCite to update *Campbell v. Monaco Coal Mining Co.*, a case decided by the Ohio Court of Common Pleas. The result is shown below. Which of the following is the correct full citation to the 1948 case ?

> ➡ 1 KeyCited Citation:
> **Campbell v. Monaco Coal Min. Co.**, 85 N.E.2d 138, 53 Ohio Law Abs. 481, 39 O.O. 207 (Ohio Com.Pl. Apr 26, 1948) (NO. 11414)
> > *Appeal Dismissed by*
> ⊢ 2 Campbell v. Monaco Coal Mining Co., 151 Ohio St. 380, 85 N.E.2d 800, 39 O.O. 216 (Ohio Mar 16, 1949) (NO. 31689)

   a. *Campbell v. Monaco Coal Mining Co.*, 85 N.E.2d 138 (Ohio Com. Pleas 1948).

   b. *Campbell v. Monaco Coal Mining Co.*, 85 N.E.2d 138 (Ohio Com. Pleas 1948), *appeal dismissed*, (Ohio 1949).

   c. *Campbell v. Monaco Coal Mining Co.*, 85 N.E.2d 138 (Ohio Com. Pleas 1948), *appeal dismissed*, 85 N.E.2d 800 (Ohio 1949).

   d. *Campbell v. Monaco Coal Mining Co.*, 85 N.E.2d 800 (Ohio 1949), *dismissing appeal*, 85 N.E.2d 138 (Ohio Com. Pleas 1948).

5-D.15. Imagine that it is May 7, 2010, and you are writing a brief to a federal district court arguing an issue concerning choice-of-law rules in class-action suits. The brief will be filed by May 12, 2010. In the brief, you wish to cite the Sixth Circuit case whose KeyCite result is shown below. Which of the following is the correct full citation to the Sixth Circuit case?

H 1
Montgomery v. Wyeth, 540 F.Supp.2d 933 (E.D.Tenn. Mar 19, 2008) (NO. 1:05-CV-323)
Judgment Affirmed by
➡ 2
KeyCited Citation:
Montgomery v. Wyeth, 580 F.3d 455, Prod.Liab.Rep. (CCH) P 18,278 (6th Cir.(Tenn.) Aug 28, 2009) (NO. 08-5701), rehearing and rehearing en banc denied (Oct 23, 2009)
Certiorari Denied by
H 3
Montgomery v. Wyeth, 130 S.Ct. 1896, 176 L.Ed.2d 403, 78 USLW 3447, 78 USLW 3543, 78 USLW 3548 (U.S. Mar 22, 2010) (NO. 09-856)

a. *Montgomery v. Wyeth*, 580 F.3d 455 (6th Cir. 2009), *cert. denied*, 130 S. Ct. 1896 (2010).

b. *Montgomery v. Wyeth*, 580 F.3d 455 (6th Cir. 2009), *aff'g* 540 F.Supp.2d 933 (E.D. Tenn. 2008), *cert. denied* (U.S. Mar. 22, 2010).

c. *Montgomery v. Wyeth*, 540 F. Supp. 2d 933 (E.D. Tenn. 2008), *aff'd*, 580 F.3d 455 (6th Cir. 2009), *cert. denied*, 130 S. Ct. 1896, 176 L. Ed. 2d 403, 78 U.S.L.W. 3447, 78 U.S.L.W. 3543, 78 U.S.L.W. 3548 (Mar. 22, 2010).

d. *Montgomery v. Wyeth*, 580 F.3d 455 (6th Cir. 2009), *reh'g and reh'g en banc denied* (2009), *cert. denied*, 130 S. Ct. 1896, 176 L. Ed. 2d 403, 78 U.S.L.W. 3447, 78 U.S.L.W. 3543, 78 U.S.L.W. 3548 (2010).

EXERCISE SET 5-D

EXPERT LEVEL: SUBSEQUENT HISTORY

Before beginning Exercise Set 5-D Expert Level, review the following and keep the *Manual* at hand as you work through the exercises:

- Rule 12.8, Subsequent History
- Rule 12.9, Prior History
- Rule 12.10, Additional Rules Concerning Subsequent and Prior History
- Sidebar 12.6, Information about Denials of Certiorari

5-D.16. Write the full citation for the First Circuit case whose KeyCite result is shown below.

➡ 1 KeyCited Citation:
Foman v. Davis, 292 F.2d 85, 4 Fed.R.Serv.2d 1069 (1st Cir.(Mass.) Jun 26, 1961) (NO. 5808)
  Certiorari Granted by
H 2 Foman v. Davis, 368 U.S. 951, 82 S.Ct. 396, 7 L.Ed.2d 385 (U.S.Mass. Jan 08, 1962) (NO. 548)
  AND Judgment Reversed by
▷ 3 Foman v. Davis, 371 U.S. 178, 83 S.Ct. 227, 9 L.Ed.2d 222, 6 Fed.R.Serv.2d 1234 (U.S.Mass. Dec 03, 1962) (NO. 41)
  On Remand to
H 4 Foman v. Davis, 316 F.2d 254 (1st Cir.(Mass.) Apr 24, 1963) (NO. 5808)

5-D.17. You are responding to a brief that deals with the use of a special master's findings, but not the underlying evidence, at trial. Your opponent cited *Festo Corp. v. Shoketsu Kinzoku Kogyo Kabushiki Co.*, 72 F.3d 857 (Fed. Cir. 1995). When you updated the case, however, you found that in 1997, the United States Supreme Court vacated the case on other grounds, as set out in volume 520 of the United States Reports, beginning at page 1111. Write the full citation to *Festo Corp.*

5-D.18. *Layman v. State*, the case whose caption is shown at right, was published in Volume 658 of the South Eastern Reporter, Second Series, beginning at page 320. When you updated the case, you discovered that it had no subsequent history other than what is shown in this caption, and that the published case in fact modified the earlier attorneys' fees order. Assume that you are writing a brief to the United States Court of Appeals for the Fourth Circuit. Write the brief's full citation to *Layman*.

376 S.C. 434

Nancy S. LAYMAN, David M. Fitzgerald, Vicki K. Zelenko, Wyman M. Looney, Nancy Ahrens, James Haynes, and Janice Franklin, on behalf of themselves and all others similarly situated, Respondents/Appellants

v.

The STATE of South Carolina and The South Carolina Retirement System, Appellants/Respondents.

No. 26427.

Supreme Court of South Carolina.

Heard Sept. 19, 2007.

Decided Jan. 28, 2008.

Rehearing Denied March 10, 2008.

Opinion Modifying Attorneys' Fees March 10, 2008.

5-D.19. You are working as a research assistant for a law professor writing an article about antitrust issues. The professor cited the Pennsylvania district court version of *Hanover Show, Inc. v. United Shoe Machinery Corp.* in his manuscript, but he neglected to check the subsequent history of the case. Being an astute research assistant, you remembered to do that. The KeyCite result is shown below. Write the corrected full citation to *Hanover Shoe.*

➡ 1 KeyCited Citation:
Hanover Shoe, Inc. v. United Shoe Machinery Corp., 245 F.Supp. 258 (M.D.Pa. Apr 28, 1965) (NO. CIV. 5395)
    Judgment Vacated by
▶ 2 Hanover Shoe, Inc. v. United Shoe Machinery Corp., 377 F.2d 776 (3rd Cir.(Pa.) Apr 11, 1967) (NO. 15626, 15627)
    Certiorari Granted by
н 3 Hanover Shoe Inc. v. United Shoe Machinery Corp., 389 U.S. 818, 88 S.Ct. 86, 19 L.Ed.2d 68 (U.S.Pa. Oct 09, 1967) (NO. 335, 463)
    AND Judgment Affirmed in Part, Reversed in Part by
▷ 4 Hanover Shoe, Inc. v. United Shoe Machinery Corp., 392 U.S. 481, 88 S.Ct. 2224, 20 L.Ed.2d 1231 (U.S.Pa. Jun 17, 1968) (NO. 335, 463)

5-D.20. You are writing a paper for an upper-level seminar, Constitutional Issues in Criminal Law, dealing with the requirement that a search warrant must be issued by "detached and neutral magistrate." One of the important cases your paper discusses is *McCommon v. State.* Although the United States Supreme Court denied certiorari, as shown in the KeyCite result below, that decision was not unanimous. Justices Brennan and Marshall wrote, in dissent, that "the Court's refusal to take this case [is] particularly disturbing in light of the good faith exception to the Fourth-Amendment exclusionary rule created by *United States v. Leon . . . .*" On your answer sheet, write the full citation to the Mississippi Supreme Court's decision in *McCommon v. State.*

➡ 1 KeyCited Citation:
McCommon v. State, 467 So.2d 940 (Miss. Apr 24, 1985) (NO. 55240)
Certiorari Denied by
н 2 McCommon v. Mississippi, 474 U.S. 984, 106 S.Ct. 393, 88 L.Ed.2d 345 (U.S.Miss. Nov 12, 1985) (NO. 85-8)

E.   SHORT-FORM CITATIONS

Although they are necessary, citations interrupt the flow of the text. Legal readers are accustomed to jumping citations, slowing down to read them only when they need to glean specific information about the authority. This is one of the reasons it is preferable to place citations into their own sentences, rather than embedding them in the text.

The first time you cite a case in a legal document, give it a full citation, as required by Rule 11.1(c)(1). Once you have cited a case in full, however, you may be able to provide readers a shorter reference to the case, which not only saves paper and ink, but, even better, gives readers a shorter citation hurdle to clear. Therefore, the key to using short-form citations is gauging their helpfulness to the reader. If it is possible that a reader may be confused or inconvenienced by a short-form citation (or a particular type of short-form citation), it should not be used.

The most popular—and the shortest—of all short-form citations is *id.* The short form *id.* is an abbreviation for the Latin term "*idem*," meaning "the same" (i.e., that which is *id*entical to what has already been cited). Use *id.* when you wish to cite the same source used in the previous citation. *Id.* stands for everything in the citation that is the same. If the pinpoint page reference changes, however, insert the preposition "at" and the new page number, as shown in Rule 11.3(e).

Italicize or underline *id.* (and its period!) according to the typeface style you have chosen for case names. Capitalize *id.* only when it is the first word of a citation sentence; in other instances, such as in citation clauses, in citations following a signal, or within string citations, do not capitalize *id.* Consult Rule 11.3(c), Typeface; Rule 11.3(d), Capitalization; Rule 43.1(b), Citation clauses; Rule 43.1(c), Embedded citations; Rule 43.3(a)(1) (defining "string citation"); Rule 44.2(c) (providing short-form example); and Rule 45.3(c), Short-form citations.

When one or more citations to other authorities have intervened between your current citation to a case and its last citation, do not use *id.*, as readers cannot readily determine which of the preceding authorities you are citing again. In that instance, you must use a short form that clearly signals where to find the cited material. As Rule 11.4 explains, the term *supra* ("above") can only be used to refer to a secondary source cited in an earlier footnote or endnote. It is never correct to use *supra* to refer to a previously cited case (or other primary authority). Instead, you must construct a "longer" short form.

If you have not referred to the case's name in the textual sentence supported by the citation, your short form must include the name of one of the parties (typically the first), followed by the volume, reporter abbreviation, and pinpoint page reference, as shown in Rule 12.21(b). In contrast, if a reference to the case's name does appear in the textual sentence supported by the citation, all you need to supply is the volume, reporter abbreviation, and pinpoint page reference, as shown in Rule 12.21(c).

If the original case citation refers to its publication in an online database provider, follow the examples set out in Rule 12.21(d). If the original citation is to a slip opinion, follow the examples in Rule 12.21(e).

EXERCISE SET 5-E

BASIC LEVEL: SHORT-FORM CITATIONS

Before beginning Exercise Set 5-E Basic Level, review the following and keep the *Manual* at hand as you work through the exercises:

- Rule 11.0, Introduction to Full and Short Citation Formats
- Rule 12.20, Short Citation Format

To complete the exercises, you may also need to refer to the following:

- Rule 5.0, Page and Location Numbers

5-E.1. In discussing an issue on page 5 of your memo, you refer to *Sneed v. Stovall*, 22 S.W.3d 277, 281 (Tenn. App. 2000). In the next paragraph, you cite this case again, quoting a rule found at page 280. You have cited no other sources on page 5 of your memo. Which of the following is *the best* short-form citation to use for the second reference to *Sneed*?

   a. *Sneed v. Stovall*, 22 S.W.3d at 280.
   b. *Sneed*, 22 S.W.3d at 280.
   c. *Sneed* at 280.
   d. *Id.* at 280.

5-E.2. You are writing a memo concerning the revocation of a doctor's hospital privileges. You cite a New Jersey case, *In re License of Fanelli*, reported at 803 A.2d 1146, and then a sentence later, cite a Washington case, *Amunrud v. Board of Appeals*, which appears at 143 P.3d 571. You then cite and discuss two statutes. The next time you cite the *Fanelli* case in this section of the memo, you're referring to page 1152. You have not used the case name in the sentence supported by the citation. Which of the following is *the best* short-form citation to use for the second reference to *Fanelli*?

    a. *Fanelli*, 803 A.2d at 1152.

    b. *Fanelli, supra* at 1152.

    c. *Id.*, 803 A.2d at 1152.

    d. *Id.* at 1152.

5-E.3. An office memo analyzes claims for attorneys' fees in the litigation of a commercial lease. It cites *Exxess Electronixx v. Heger Realty Corp.*, 75 Cal. Rptr. 2d 376, 382 (App. 2d Dist. 1998). The very next textual sentence explicitly refers to *Exxess Electronixx* and quotes a sentence from the case, found at page 382. Which of the following is *the best* short-form citation to use for the second reference to *Exxess Electronixx*?

    a. *Exxess Electronixx*, 75 Cal. Rptr. 2d 376, 382.

    b. 75 Cal. Rptr. 2d at 383.

    c. *Id.* at 382.

    d. *Id.*

5-E.4. You work for a judge whose draft of an opinion has cited *Bruce's Juices, Inc. v. American Can Co.*, 330 U.S. 743 (1947). After four intervening citations to other authorities, the judge wrote the following short form reference in her draft: *Bruce's Juices, Inc., supra* at 757. She did not use the case's name in the sentence supported by that citation. Because the judge knows you are good at citations, she's given you permission to correct any errors you find in her work. Which of the following citations to *Bruce's Juices* is correct in this situation?

    a. *Id.* at 757.

    b. *Bruce's Juices* at 757.

    c. *Bruce's Juices, Inc.*, 330 U.S. at 757.

    d. *Bruce's Juices v. Am. Can Co.*, 330 U.S. at 757.

5-E.5. Your course paper addresses the "deadly weapon enhancement" courts consider in sentencing. Footnote 23 cites *State v. Schelin*, 14 P.3d 893 (Wash. App. Div. 3 2000), *aff'd*, 55 P.3d 632 (Wash. 2002). In the same section of the paper, the next reference to *Schelin* comes in footnote 27, citing page 895. Which of the following citations is *the best* to use?

    a. [27] *Schelin*, 14 P.3d at 895.

    b. [27] *Schelin, supra*, at 895.

    c. [27] *Schelin*, 14 P.3d at 895, *aff'd*, 55 P.3d 632 (Wash. 2002).

    d. [27] *State v. Schelin, supra* n. 23, at 895.

5-E.6. Your brief to a Montana trial court argues two points: (A) that the defendant breached the implied duty of good faith and fair dealing; and (B) that the notice of sale was procedurally inadequate. In part A of the brief, you discuss the Montana case whose caption is shown below, citing page 122. You then go on to discuss and cite three other mandatory authorities in part A, explaining the application of all four cases to the facts of the case before the court. After discussing and citing a statute and another case, you cite page 124 of *Knucklehead Land Co.* Which of the following is *the best* citation to use?

   a. *Knucklehead Land Co.* at 124.
   b. *Knucklehead Land Co.*, 172 P.3d at 124.
   c. *Knucklehead Land Co. v. Accutitle, Inc.*, 172 P.3d at 124.
   d. *Knucklehead Land Co. v. Accutitle, Inc.*, 172 P.3d 116, 124 (Mont. 2007).

> 2007 MT 301
> 340 Mont. 62
> **KNUCKLEHEAD LAND COMPANY, INC., a Montana corporation, Plaintiff and Appellant,**
> v.
> **ACCUTITLE, INCORPORATED, a Montana corporation, d/b/a American Title and Escrow; and Flathead County Title Company, a Montana corporation, Defendants, Third–Party Plaintiffs and Appellees,**
> v.
> **Shapiro & Meinhold, L.L.P., Third–Party Defendant.**
> No. DA 06–0561.
> Supreme Court of Montana.
> Submitted on Briefs May 23, 2007.
> Decided Nov. 20, 2007.

5-E.7. A brief cites *Jerich v. New Orleans Saints*, 776 So. 2d 1283, 1284-85 (La. App. 5th Cir. 2000), in part A. It then goes on to discuss two other Louisiana cases. Two pages later, and still in part A, the brief returns to *Jerich*, referring to it by name in the text and discussing material at page 1288. Which of the following citations is *the best* for the second citation to *Jerich*?

   a. *Jerich v. New Orleans Saints*, 776 So. 2d 1283, 1288 (La. App. 5th Cir. 2000)
   b. 776 So. 2d 1283, 1288 (La. App. 5th Cir. 2000)
   c. 776 So. 2d at 1288.
   d. *Id.* at 1288.

5-E.8. A brief to the United States Court of Appeals for the Fourth Circuit discusses the following cases, one by one, in the same section of the argument: *U.S. v. Collins*, 372 F.3d 629 (4th Cir. 2004); *U.S. v. Whittington*, 26 F.3d 456 (4th Cir. 1994); and *U.S. v. Ruhe*, 191 F.3d 376 (4th Cir. 1999). Without specifically mentioning the case by name, the text of the argument then returns to the 1994 case for an additional point, citing page 463. Which of the following citations is *the best* to use for the second reference to the 1994 case?

   a. *Whittington* at 463.
   b. *U.S.*, 26 F.3d at 463.
   c. *Whittington*, 26 F.3d at 463.
   d. *U.S. v. Whittington*, 26 F.3d 456, 463 (4th Cir. 1994).

5-E.9. You are trying to get a summary judgment order overturned on appeal. Your brief includes the passage shown below. The source of the final sentence in the passage is *Mack Trucks, Inc. v. Tamez,* as indicated by the reference "**Citation.**" Which of the following citations uses *the best* format for citing page 581 of that case?

> In reviewing a summary-judgment order, appellate courts must consider all the evidence in the light most favorable to the non-moving party, crediting evidence favorable to that party if reasonable jurors could do so, and disregarding contrary evidence unless reasonable jurors could not. *Mack Trucks, Inc. v. Tamez,* 206 S.W.3d 572, 582 (Tex. 2006). Evidence raises a genuine issue of fact if reasonable and fair-minded jurors could differ in their conclusions. *Goodyear Tire & Rubber Co. v. Mayes,* 236 S.W.3d 754, 756 (Tex. 2007). It is error for a court of appeals to consider testimony admitted only for a bill of exceptions when it reviews a trial court's decision to exclude expert testimony on causation. **Citation.**

a. *Mack Trucks, Inc. v. Tamez,* 206 S.W.3d 572, 581 (Tex. 2006).
b. *Mack Trucks, Inc.,* 206 S.W.3d at 581.
c. 206 S.W.3d at 581.
d. *Id.* at 581.

5-E.10. In a paper on the topic of leases, the citations are in footnotes. Footnote 21 contains a "string citation," as shown below. Although *Hanson v. Boeder* is not identified by name in the text, Footnote 22 cites that case, referring to page 286. Which of the following citations is *the best* to use for Footnote 22?

[21] *See generally Kanter v. Safran,* 68 So. 2d 553 (Fla. 1953); *Atkinson v. Rosenthal,* 598 N.E.2d 666 (Mass. App. 1992); *Hanson v. Boeder,* 727 N.W.2d 280 (N.D. 2007).
[22] _____

a. [22] *Id.* at 286.
b. [22] *Hanson* at 286.
c. [22] *Hanson,* 727 N.W.2d at 286.
d. [22] *Hanson v. Boeder,* 727 N.W.2d 280, 286 (N.D. 2007).

EXERCISE SET 5-E

INTERMEDIATE LEVEL: SHORT-FORM CITATIONS

Before beginning Exercise Set 5-E Intermediate Level, review the following and keep the *Manual* at hand as you work through the exercises:

- Rule 11.0, Introduction to Full and Short Citation Formats
- Rule 12.8, Subsequent History

- Rule 12.10, Additional Rules Concerning Subsequent and Prior History
- Rule 12.11, Parenthetical Information
- Rule 12.20, Short Citation Format

5-E.11. The following passage comes from an office memorandum which considers the ethical duties of lawyers and their staff to protect client confidences. It contains a full citation to *Arkansas v. Dean Foods Products Co.* The final sentence in the passage refers to material at page 385 of the *Dean Foods* case. Which of the following citations should go into the "**Citation**" reference?

> Because of this high standard of confidence and because of the nature of legal representation and advocacy, there arises an irrefutable presumption that confidences were disclosed in an attorney-client relationship. *Ark. v. Dean Foods Prods. Co.*, 605 F.2d 380, 384 (8th Cir. 1979), *overruled in part on other grounds*, *In re Multi-Piece Rim Prods. Liab. Litig.*, 612 F.2d 377 (8th Cir. 1980). A client has a right to expect that any disclosures and any other information obtained by the attorney will be held in strict confidence, and more importantly, will not be used against her. **Citation**.

a. *Dean Foods Prods.*, 605 F.2d at 385, *overruled in part on other grounds*, *In re Multi-Piece Rim Prods. Liab. Litig.*, 612 F.2d 377 (8th Cir. 1980).

b. *Id.* at 385, *overruled in part on other grounds*, *In re Multi-Piece Rim Prods. Liab. Litig.*, 612 F.2d 377 (8th Cir. 1980).

c. *Id.* at 385.

d. *Id.*

5-E.12. A brief to the Oklahoma Supreme Court cites pages 86–87 of *McCormick v. Union Pacific Railroad Co.*, the Colorado Court of Appeals case whose KeyCite entry is shown below. The very next citation in the brief is to the same case, but at pages 87–88. Which of the following citations is *best* to use for the second reference to *McCormick*?

> ⇒ <u>1</u> KeyCited Citation:
> **McCormick v. Union Pacific R. Co.**, 983 P.2d 84, 141 Oil & Gas Rep. 474, 98 CJ C.A.R. 6132 (Colo.App. Dec 10, 1998) (NO. 97CA1625), rehearing denied (Feb 25, 1999), certiorari granted (Sep 13, 1999)
> *Judgment Affirmed by*
> ⊢ <u>2</u> McCormick v. Union Pacific Resources Co., 14 P.3d 346, 146 Oil & Gas Rep. 226, 2000 CJ C.A.R. 6385 (Colo. Nov 28, 2000) (NO. 99SC243), as modified (Dec 14, 2000)

a. *McCormick v. Union P. R.R. Co.*, 983 P.2d 84, 87–88 (Colo. App. 1998), *aff'd sub nom.* *McCormick v. Union P. Resources Co.*, 14 P.3d 346 (Colo. 2000).

b. *McCormick* at 87–88, *aff'd*, 14 P.3d 346 (Colo. 2000).

c. *McCormick* at 87–88.

d. *Id.* at 87–88.

5-E.13–18. An office memo uses the following cases to illustrate certain legal principles. On your answer sheet, write the appropriate short-form citation for each reference:

Case references:

> Case A: *Hancock v. Finch*, 9 A.2d 811 (Conn. 1939).
> Case B: *Falby v. Zarembski*, 602 A.2d 1 (Conn. 1992).
> Case C: *Murphy v. Buonato*, 679 A.2d 411 (Conn. App. 1996).
> Case D: *Malone v. Steinberg*, 89 A.2d 213 (Conn. 1952).

Excerpt:

The Connecticut dog-bite statute places strict liability on any owner or keeper of any dog that does damage to another person's body or property. Conn. Gen. Stat. Ann. § 22-357 (West 2001). To be considered the keeper of the dog, one must possess or harbor the dog. Conn. Gen. Stat. § 22-237(b) (West 2001). "Possession" is defined as having nothing less than "dominion and control" of the dog. *Hancock v. Finch*, 9 A.2d 811, 812 (Conn. 1939). One who is not the owner of a dog but who affords "lodging, shelter, or refuge to it" is considered a keeper through harboring. *Falby v. Zarembski*, 602 A.2d 1, 2 (Conn. 1992). The court has defined "harboring" as lodging, sheltering or giving refuge to a dog. [**5-E.13. Case A, page 811.**] To be in a position to lodge, shelter, or provide refuge for an animal, it is necessary for one to exert some control over the area of the property in which the dog lives. [**5-E.14. Case B, page 4.**]

The amount of time the animal is sheltered is not significant. In one case, a man allowed a dog to live in his home for one week while its owner was on vacation. *Murphy v. Buonato*, 679 A.2d 411, 413 (Conn. App. 1996). The dog bit him within twenty-four hours after its arrival at his home, but because he had allowed the dog to take shelter in his home, he was, nonetheless, determined to be the harborer of the dog. [**5-E.15. Case C, page 416.**] In another Connecticut case, a couple owned a dog for three years before giving it to another family. *Malone v. Steinberg*, 89 A.2d 213, 214 (Conn. 1952). The dog found its way back to its original home from time to time. On the occasion of one such return, the dog ran at an elderly man, causing him to fall and injure his wrist. [**5-E.16. Case D, page 214.**] The original owners were found to harbor the dog because they gave shelter and refuge to the animal when it returned to their home. [**5-E.17. Case D, pages 215–216.**]

When landlords exert any type of care or control over a dog while permitting its presence on the property, they will be considered as harborers. In *Falby*, however, the court noted that the "mere acquiescence in the dog's presence within the leased premises, unaccompanied by any evidence of caretaking of the dog or actual control over its actions, could not afford a basis for their strict liability as keepers under the statute." [**5-E.18. Case B, page 4.**]

EXERCISE SET 5-E

EXPERT LEVEL: SHORT-FORM CITATIONS

> Before beginning Exercise Set 5-E Expert Level, review the following and keep the *Manual* at hand as you work through the exercises:
>
> - Rule 11.0, Introduction to Full and Short Citation Formats
> - Rule 12.11, Parenthetical Information
> - Rule 12.20, Short Citation Format

5-E.19. A bar journal article discusses the dissenting opinion of Utah Court of Appeals Judge Russell W. Bench in a case that was subsequently reversed. The dissent is cited in footnote 3 of the article, as shown below. In support of an explicit reference to *Visser* in the text of the article, the author cites the same page of Judge Bench's dissent again in footnote 5. On your answer sheet, write the citation to *Visser* in footnote 5.

[3] *State v. Visser*, 973 P.2d 998, 1003 (Utah App. 1999) (Bench, J., dissenting), *rev'd*, 22 P.3d 1242 (Utah 2000).
[4] *State v. Dean*, 57 P.3d 1106, 1109 (Utah App. 2002).
5 _____

5-E.20. A paper for a course in Criminal Procedure cites a case that is not yet published in a print reporter, although it is available online. Footnote 15 contains the paper's first citation to the case: *Ritchie v. Krasner*, ___P.3d___, 2009 WL 1065195 at **3–4 (Ariz. App. Div. 1 Apr. 21, 2009). Footnote 16 cites the fifth page of the case. Write the citation from footnote 16 on your answer sheet.

5-E.21–25. Read the following excerpt from a seminar paper, which cites authorities in footnotes. For each of the indicated footnotes below, write the appropriate short-form citation for the case reference, including its pinpoint reference, on your answer sheet:

Case references:

Case A: *Vernonia Sch. Dist. 47J v. Acton*, 515 U.S. 646 (1995).
Case B: *Chandler v. Miller*, 520 U.S. 305 (1997).
Case C: *Skinner v. Ry. Lab. Execs.' Assn.*, 489 U.S. 602 (1989).

Excerpt:

State-compelled collection and testing of student urine specimens constitutes a "search" under the Fourth Amendment,[1] and it intrudes upon expectations of privacy that society has long recognized as reasonable.[2] As these intrusions are searches under the Fourth Amendment, the ultimate measure of their constitutionality is "reasonableness."[3] Judging whether a particular search meets this reasonableness standard depends on balancing its impact on a person's Fourth Amendment right against the legitimate governmental interests promoted by the search.[4]

To be reasonable under the Fourth Amendment, a search ordinarily must be based on individualized suspicion of wrongdoing.[5] However, as the Court has recognized, "particularized exceptions to the main rule are sometimes warranted based on 'special needs, beyond the normal need for law enforcement.'"[6] Authorities do not have to demonstrate an actual drug abuse problem, although some showing of a problem supports an assertion of a special need for a suspicionless general search program.[7]

Skinner dealt with federal regulations that not only required blood and urine tests of rail employees involved in train accidents, but also authorized railroads to administer breath and urine tests to employees who violated certain safety rules.[8]

Footnotes:
[1]*Vernonia Sch. Dist. 47J v. Acton*, 515 U.S. 646, 652 (1995).
[2]*Chandler v. Miller*, 520 U.S. 305, 313 (1997).
[3][5-E.21. Case A, page 652.]
[4]*Skinner v. Ry. Lab. Execs.' Assn.*, 489 U.S. 602, 619 (1989).
[5][5-E.22. Case A, page 671.]
[6][5-E.23. Case B, page 313 (quoting Case C, page 619).]
[7][5-E.24. Case B, page 319.]
[8][5-E.25. Case C, pages 608–612.]

CHAPTER

6

CONSTITUTIONS, STATUTES,

AND ORDINANCES

Constitutions, statutes, and ordinances are intended to apply broadly to all who come within their jurisdictional scope. They also operate in an expansive temporal sense, as their application extends from the date of their adoption or enactment to the present. In fact, they are intended to apply into the future, until such time as they are amended, repealed, or superseded.

A citation to a constitution, statute, or ordinance usually refers to the law currently in force. At times, however, researchers need to cite historical sources of constitutions or statutory materials. For example, it may be necessary to discuss the version of a statute before it was amended, or it may be useful to examine a version as it was enacted by the legislative body before being codified.

Although the traditional preference in legal writing has been to cite these materials in their official print versions, many researchers—including you, perhaps—are now using electronic resources for their research. Some electronic sources are now official. The *Manual* provides guidance for citing both print and electronic versions.

This chapter provides basic-, intermediate-, and expert-level exercises for citations to current and historical constitutions, amendments, statutes, session laws, and ordinances in a variety of jurisdictions and publications.

A.   CONSTITUTIONS

As Rule 13.2 demonstrates, a full citation to a constitution begins with the abbreviated name of the jurisdiction it serves, followed by the abbreviation "Const." and a pinpoint reference, in ordinary type. Abbreviate the jurisdiction as shown in Appendix 3(B), United States and World Geography. For the pinpoint reference, indicate the article, amendment, section, paragraph, or clause you are citing, being as specific as possible and using the subdivision abbreviations in Appendix 3(C). When constitutions are referenced in textual sentences, however, they should not be abbreviated, as explained in Sidebar 13.1, Referring to Constitutions in Text.

Use Roman numerals for articles and amendments in the United States Constitution; use Arabic numbers for its smaller divisions, such as sections and clauses. For state constitutions, follow the numbering system used in an official source (which usually, but not always, will use Roman numerals and Arabic numbers in the same fashion as the United States Constitution). Now would also be a good time to refresh yourself on Rule 6.0, Citing Sections and Paragraphs. Rule 13.2(b) displays several examples of federal and state constitutional provisions as they should appear in citation sentences, including pinpoint references.

When you cite a current constitution, omit any reference to a date. Dates are omitted because a constitution operates from the time of its enactment until such time as it is amended or repealed. Rule 13.0 refers to constitutions "currently in force" because in the course of their histories, many states replaced their constitutions with entirely new documents. More often, however, constitutions are altered via the processes of amendment and repeal of specific provisions.

Citations to historical constitutions or provisions no longer part of a current constitution require parenthetical explanation, including the date on which the constitution or provision was amended, repealed, or superseded, as shown in the example for Rule 13.2(d).

EXERCISE SET 6-A

BASIC LEVEL: CONSTITUTIONS

Before beginning Exercise Set 6-A Basic Level, review the following and keep the *Manual* at hand as you work through the exercises:

- Rule 13.0, Constitutions
- Sidebar 13.1, Referring to Constitutions in Text

To complete the exercises, you may also need to refer to the following:

- Rule 1.1, Typeface Choices
- Rule 6.0, Citing Sections and Paragraphs

Throughout the exercise set, use Appendix 3, General Abbreviations, as appropriate.

6-A.1. Choose the correct abbreviation for the Oklahoma Constitution.

    a. *Oklahoma Const.*
    b. Okla. Const.
    c. OK Const.
    d. Ok. Const.

6-A.2. Choose the correct abbreviation for the Constitution of the Commonwealth of Kentucky.

    a. Commw. Ken. Const.
    b. *Ken. Const.*
    c. Const. Cmmw. Ky.
    d. Ky. Const.

6-A.3. In a brief, you write, "The Maine Constitution guarantees that park lands in the state may not be reduced or their uses substantially altered unless at least two-thirds of the legislature agrees." The current Maine Constitution was adopted in 1820. The provision concerning park lands appears in Article IX, section 23. Choose the correct citation to support this statement.

    a. Maine Const., Art. IX, Sec. 23 (1820).
    b. Me. Const. Art. IX, § XXIII.
    c. Me. Const. art. IX, § 23.
    d. Me. Const. art. IX, § XXIII.

6-A.4. You are writing a seminar paper that analyzes the Seventeenth Amendment to the United States Constitution. Although the amendment was first proposed in 1789 by James Madison, it did not become part of the Constitution until it was ratified by Michigan in 1992. Which of the following correctly cites the amendment?

    a. U.S. Const., 17th amend. (ratified 1992).
    b. U.S. Const. amend. XVII (1992).
    c. U.S.A. Const. Amend. 17.
    d. U.S. Const. amend. XVII.

6-A.5. You work as a research assistant for one of your professors. The professor is studying the Montana legislature for an article she is writing. She refers to the current Montana Constitution in the following sentence from her article. Which of the following correctly refers to the constitution in that sentence?

    According to _____, the Senate must have at least forty members, but not more than fifty, and the House requires at least eighty, but not more than one hundred members.

    a. Mont. Const. art. V, § 2
    b. article V, section 2 of the Montana Constitution
    c. Mont. Const. article V, section 2
    d. Mont. Const. Art. V, Sec. II

EXERCISE SET 6-A

INTERMEDIATE LEVEL: CONSTITUTIONS

> Before beginning Exercise Set 6-A Intermediate Level, review the following and keep the *Manual* at hand as you work through the exercises:
>
> • Rule 13.0, Constitutions
> • Sidebar 13.1, Referring to Constitutions in Text
>
> To complete the exercises, you may also need to refer to the following:
>
> • Rule 1.1, Typeface Choices
> • Rule 6.0, Citing Sections and Paragraphs
>
> Throughout the exercise set, use Appendix 3, General Abbreviations, as appropriate.

6-A.6. The preamble to the current Minnesota Constitution states, "We, the people of the state of Minnesota, grateful to God for our civil and religious liberty, and desiring to perpetuate its blessings and secure the same to ourselves and our posterity, do ordain and establish this Constitution." Which of the following correctly cites the preamble?

    a. Minn. Const. preamble.
    b. Minn. Const. art. I.
    c. Minn. Const. preamb.
    d. Minn. Const., pre.

6-A.7. Article I, Section 8, Clause 3 of the United States Constitution states that Congress has the power to regulate commerce with foreign nations, among the states, and with the Native American tribes. This clause is popularly known as the "Commerce Clause." Which of the following correctly cites the Commerce Clause?

    a. U.S. Constitution Art. I, Sec. 8, Cl. 3.
    b. U.S. Const. art. I, § 8, cl. 3.
    c. U.S. Const. art. I, § VIII, cl. III.
    d. U.S. Const. Com. Cl., Art. 1, § 8, cl. 3.

6-A.8. In researching the power of the President of the United States to declare martial law in times of emergency, you find an online source containing the citation, "U.S. Const. Art. I, § 9, Cl. 2." Although these numbers are accurate, how should you refer to this constitutional provision in a textual sentence in the body of your seminar paper?

    a. U.S. Constitution, article 1, § 9, cl. 2
    b. United States Constitution article I, section 9, clause 2
    c. U.S. Const., art. I, sec. 9, cl. 2
    d. U.S. Constitution, Article I, § 9, cl. 2

6-A.9. You are writing a paper that discusses New Hampshire's "right of revolution," set out in Part 1, article 10 of that state's current constitution, which became effective June 2, 1784, when it replaced the state's previous 1776 constitution. Which of the following correctly cites this provision?

    a. N.H. Const. pt. 1, art. 10 (1784).
    b. N.H. Const. art. I (1784).
    c. N.H. Const. Part I, art. X.
    d. N.H. Const. pt. 1, art. 10.

6-A.10. You want to cite the provision declaring "paramount allegiance" to the federal government in Article 5 of the third of Maryland's four constitutions, which was adopted in October 1864 during the Civil War, but repealed by Article II of the current constitution, adopted in September 1867. Which of the following correctly cites this provision?

    a. MD. Const. 3d art. V.
    b. Art. V, Md. Const. (1864).
    c. Md. Const. art. 5 (repealed 1867 by Md. Const. art. II).
    d. Md. Const. of 1864, art. 5, *repealed by* Md. Const. of 1867, art. II.

EXERCISE SET 6-A

EXPERT LEVEL: CONSTITUTIONS

Before beginning Exercise Set 6-A Expert Level, review the following and keep the *Manual* at hand as you work through the exercises:

• Rule 13.0, Constitutions
• Sidebar 13.1, Referring to Constitutions in Text

To complete the exercises, you may also need to refer to the following:

• Rule 1.1, Typeface Choices
• Rule 6.0, Citing Sections and Paragraphs

Throughout the exercise set, use Appendix 3, General Abbreviations, as appropriate.

6-A.11. You are writing about Nebraska's unicameral legislature. Write the citation to Article III, section 1 of the current Constitution of Nebraska. This section was adopted in 1875, and it was amended in 1912, 1934, and 2000.

6-A.12. Your research concerns the Twentieth Amendment to the United States Constitution, popularly known as the "Lame Duck Amendment." This amendment became part of the current Constitution on February 6, 1933, when it was ratified by a sufficient number of the states. Write the full citation to this amendment.

6-A.13. Your seminar paper discusses the initiative and referendum procedure in New York, and you wish to provide examples from the state's history. Write the citation to Article I, section 13 of the New York Constitution, which was repealed by vote of the people on November 6, 1962.

6-A.14. The headnote shown at right comes from *Powell v. Cusimano*, 326 F. Supp. 2d 322 (D. Conn. 2004). Write the full citation to the cited constitutional provision, making any necessary changes for the citation to comply with *ALWD Citation Manual* rules.

> **18. Prisons** ⟜4(7)
>
> Taking of prisoner's artificial hair extensions pursuant to policy classifying artificial hair extensions as contraband was not an unreasonable search and seizure in violation of Connecticut Constitution. Conn.Const. Art. 1, § 7.

6-A.15. The headnote shown at right comes from *Constructors Association of Western Pennsylvania v. Kreps*, 573 F.2d 811 (3d Cir. 1978). Write the full citation to the cited constitutional provisions, making any necessary changes for the citation to comply with *ALWD Citation Manual* rules.

> **8. Civil Rights** ⟜2.1
>
> Both Thirteenth and Fourteenth Amendments empower Congress to enact legislation to remedy racial discrimination. U.S.C.A.Const. Amends. 13, 14.

B. STATUTORY CODES

A statute is typically cited to its official codified version. A statutory "code" is a collection of statutes in a single jurisdiction, arranged by an organizational system, usually topical. Every government, both federal and state, has at least one "official code" for its statutes.

Given the variety of titles that states have assigned to their statutory codes and the existence of both official and unofficial codes published by different entities, not to mention the diversity of organizational and numbering methods employed, statutory citations can be somewhat challenging. Examine several jurisdictions' entries in Appendix 1 to get a sense of the variety. Statutory code titles may refer to terms such as Code, Century Code, Compiled Laws, Compiled Statutes, General Laws, General Statutes, Official Code, Revised Code, Revised Statutes, or even the [Subject Matter] Code.

Use ordinary typeface in statutory citations. Although citation to official codes is preferable, you are permitted to cite unofficial sources. Appendix 1 sets out abbreviations and citation templates for the official and unofficial codes in each jurisdiction. Official codes are marked with a green star.

Follow the organizational and numbering schemes employed by the code you are citing. You may first wish to outline the statute to ensure that you understand its organization. Pay close attention to the arrangement of numbers or letters in the statute. Distinctions between main sections and subordinate subsections are not always obvious. Most codes use the section symbol (§) before a set of numbers to indicate a main section. If you are citing multiple sections, use two section symbols (§§), as explained in Rule 6.6. Each citation should provide a pinpoint reference to the main section, and if applicable, the subsection(s) you are referencing; see the examples in Rule 14.2(d).

A few states put subject matter titles into their codes. Subject matter titles in Kansas, Maryland, and Texas statutes abbreviate words that appear in Appendix 3(E). For Louisiana, use the abbreviations listed in that state's entry in Appendix 1. For California and New York, use the abbreviations in those states' entries in Appendix 2.

Full citations to statutory codes conclude with a parenthetical containing the date of the code's publication, and often, a publisher. The publisher's name is required for all unofficial codes and for many official codes. The templates in Appendix 1 display publisher names where they are needed. The date in the parenthetical indicates the date of *the publication* being cited, not the date of the statute's enactment. Therefore, citations to the same statute in different sources will likely display different dates. For example, the following citations to the same Arkansas statute reflect the different publishers and the different publication dates of official and unofficial code volumes:

Ark. Code Ann. § 4-28-202 (Lexis 2001).
Ark. Code Ann. § 4-28-202 (West 2004).

Similarly, dates for federal statutes in print will likely differ depending on whether you are citing the official code (U.S.C.) or one of the unofficial codes (U.S.C.A. or U.S.C.S.). Updates for statutes' print versions typically appear in supplements, either tucked into the main volume's back pocket (the basis for the term "pocket part") or separately bound in a pamphlet. Some publishers reprint an entire statute in the supplement if any part of the statute is amended; other publishers furnish only the new language or other changes in the supplement. To refer readers to an entire statute, you may be able to cite just the supplement, or you may need to cite both the bound volume and the supplement. (For guidance in citing main volumes, supplements, or both, see Rule 8.0, Supplements.)

The legal profession has traditionally preferred citations to print sources, but increasingly researchers are using electronic sources for their research. If you cite a statute's electronic version, you must follow Rules 14.5(a) and 14.5(b) with regard to the publisher and date (using a "current through" date for the online database). Use the date information as it appears in the electronic database, but abbreviate any words appearing in Appendix 3.

Depending on the way the jurisdiction reports its statutes' currency to the electronic publisher, the "current through" date may refer to a year, a month-day-year, a specific legislative session, or even a specific public law or act within a particular legislative session. (You may see the non-ALWD abbreviations "P.L." (public law) or "P.A." (public act) in the "current through" information; replace them with "Pub. L." or "Pub. Act," respectively.) Do not assume that the "current through" date in an electronic database will be the same date appearing in the statute's print version. And do not mix elements of print and electronic sources in the same citation. The following example shows the Arkansas statute used above cited to its LEXIS publisher/date information:

Ark. Code Ann. § 4-28-202 (LEXIS current through 2009 Reg. Sess. & updates from Ark. Code Rev. Commn. through Nov. 19, 2009).

To refer to a statute in a textual sentence, follow the guidance in Sidebar 14.2, particularly concerning words to abbreviate—or not. If you use a statutory reference as the subject of a sentence, spelling out its abbreviations will help readers recognize that you are actually discussing the statute, not citing it in support of the previous sentence.

EXERCISE SET 6-B

BASIC LEVEL: STATUTORY CODES

Before beginning Exercise Set 6-B Basic Level, review the following rules and keep the *Manual* at hand as you work through the exercises:

- Rule 14.1, Which Source to Cite
- Rule 14.2, Full Citation, Print Format for Federal Statutes Currently in Force
- Rule 14.4, Full Citation, Print Format for State Statutes
- Sidebar 14.1, Date of United States Code
- Sidebar 14.2, Referring to Statutes in the Text

To complete the exercises, you may also need to refer to the following:

- Rule 1.1, Typeface Choices
- Rule 6.0, Citing Sections and Paragraphs
- Rule 8.0, Supplements

Be prepared to consult Appendix 1, Primary Sources by Jurisdiction, for many of the questions.

6-B.1. The Idaho statute of limitations for bringing suit on a written contract is five years. This provision appears in section 5-216 of the official Idaho Code Annotated. The copyright date on the volume is 2004. Choose the correct full citation to this statute.

    a. I.C. § 5-216.
    b. Id. Code Ann. § 5-216.
    c. Idaho Code § 5-216 (2004).
    d. Idaho Code Ann. § 5-216 (Lexis 2004).

6-B.2. The Rhode Island statute governing immunization of schoolchildren is published in volume 3B of the General Laws of Rhode Island, 2001 edition, and more specifically, in section 16-38-2. Choose the correct full citation to this statute.

    a. 3B Gen. L. R.I. § 16-38-2 (2001).
    b. Gen. Laws R.I. § 16-38-2 (2001).
    c. R.I. Gen. Laws § 16-38-2 (2001).
    d. R.I. Stat. § 16-38-2 (2001).

6-B.3. The State of Georgia defines the statutory tort of "newspaper libel" in section 51-5-2 of the Official Code of Georgia Annotated. The statute appears in the 2000 main volume. Choose the correct full citation to this statute.

    a. O.C.G.A. § 51-5-2 (2000).
    b. Off. Code Ga. Ann. § 51-5-2 (main vol. 2000).
    c. Ga. Code Ann. § 51-5-2 (2000).
    d. Ga. Code Ann. § 51-5-2 (West 2000).

6-B.4. Your brief cites the following subsection of a federal statute published in the 2006 bound volume of the United States Code. Choose the correct full citation to this subsection of the statute.

> 16 U.S.C. § 823b. Enforcement
> (a) Monitoring and investigation
> The Commission shall monitor and investigate compliance with each license and permit issued under this subchapter and with each exemption granted from any requirement of this subchapter. The Commission shall conduct such investigations as may be necessary and proper in accordance with this chapter. After notice and opportunity for public hearing, the Commission may issue such orders as necessary to require compliance with the terms and conditions of licenses and permits issued under this subchapter and with the terms and conditions of exemptions granted from any requirement of this subchapter.

    a. 16 U.S.C. § 823b (2006).
    b. 16 U.S.C. § 823b(a) (2006).
    c. 16 U.S.C. § 823(b)(a) (2006).
    d. 16 U.S.C. §§ 823(b), (a) (2006).

6-B.5. You represent a man who has been charged by the State of South Carolina with obtaining the certificate of title to a 1995 Kawasaki jet ski by fraud or misrepresentation, as defined by section 50-23-201 of that state's statutory compilation, the Code of Laws of South Carolina 1976 Annotated. The statute originated in Act 344 of 2008, and it is published in the 2009 cumulative supplement, a pocket part to the main volume. It does not appear in the main volume itself. Choose the correct full citation to this statute.

    a. S.C. Code Ann. § 50-23-201 (Supp. 2009).
    b. Code of Laws of S.C. § 50-23-201 (Supp. 2009).
    c. S.C. Code Laws § 50-23-201 (1976).
    d. S.C. Code § 50-23-201 (1976 & Supp. 2009).

6-B.6. You are writing an appellate brief to the Alabama Supreme Court concerning the execution of a deed. The brief cites an Alabama statute from the main volume published by the Michie Company in 1991. Choose the correct full citation to this statute.

    a. Alabama Code 35-4-20 (Michie main vol. 1991).
    b. Ala. Code § 35-4-20 (Lexis 1991).
    c. ALA. CODE § 35-4-20 (West 1991).
    d. Ala. Code Ann. § 35-4-20 (1991).

6-B.7. Your brief in support of a motion for summary judgment argues that the Colorado Governmental Immunity Act gives your client immunity from tort liability. You rely on section 24-10-106(1)(a), which waives a public entity's immunity from tort actions "for injuries resulting from . . . [t]he operation of a motor vehicle, owned or leased by such public entity, by a public employee while in the course of employment." That section of the state's official code, the Colorado Revised Statutes, appears in a bound volume published in 2009. Choose the correct full citation to this statute.

    a. Colo. Rev. Stat. § 24-10-106(1)(a) (Lexis 2009).
    b. Colo. Rev. Stat. Ann. § 24-10-106(1)(a) (West 2009).
    c. Colo. Rev. Stat. § 24-10-106(1)(a) (2009).
    d. § 24-10-106(1)(a), C.R.S. 2009.

6-B.8.   As a member of your law school's honor council, you have volunteered to write an item for the student bar association newsletter about state laws prohibiting various forms of plagiarism. You refer to a Virginia statute in the following sentence from your article. Choose the correct full citation to the statute in that sentence.

If a student in Virginia reasonably knows that another person will submit an academic paper for credit, _____ prohibits him from preparing or selling such a paper.

a. Va. Code Ann. § 18.2-505(a) (Lexis 2009)
b. Va. Code Ann. section 18.2-505(a) (2009)
c. Virginia statute § 18.2-505(a) (Lexis 2009)
d. Virginia Code Annotated section 18.2-505(a) (Lexis 2009)

6-B.9.   Your boss has asked you to research guardianship laws for several states and find their provisions for the ways a guardianship may terminate. In California, termination is governed by section 1600 of the Probate Code. The set of California statutes in your office is the unofficial version published by West. The guardianship termination provision is in volume 52A, which has no date on the spine of the volume, but which has a 2002 copyright date. Choose the correct full citation to this version of the statute.

a. 52A Cal. Code Ann. § 1600 (2002).
b. Cal. Code Ann. vol. 52A, § 1600 (Westlaw 2009).
c. Cal. Probate Code Ann. § 1600 (2002).
d. Cal. Probate Code Ann. § 1600 (West 2002).

6-B.10.   In researching the crime of embezzlement, you find a Massachusetts statute that applies to bank officers and employees. This statute appears at page 223 of main volume 44A in the multi-volume set of the Massachusetts General Laws Annotated, published by West, and is assigned to Chapter 266, section 52. No date is on the spine of the volume or the title page. The copyright date of the volume is 2008. This statute was last amended in 1934. Choose the correct full citation to this statute.

a. 44A Mass. Gen. Ls. Ann. 233 (West 2008).
b. Mass. Gen. Laws Ann. ch. 266, § 52 (West 2008).
c. Mass. Gen. Laws ch. 266, § 52 (1934).
d. M.G.L.A. 44A-266-52 (West 1934).

EXERCISE SET 6-B

INTERMEDIATE LEVEL: STATUTORY CODES

Before beginning Exercise Set 6-B Intermediate Level, review the following rules and keep the *Manual* at hand as you work through the exercises:

- Rule 14.1, Which Source to Cite
- Rule 14.2, Full Citation, Print Format for Federal Statutes Currently in Force
- Rule 14.4, Full Citation, Print Format for State Statutes
- Rule 14.5, Statutes Available on Electronic Databases
- Sidebar 14.1, Date of United States Code
- Sidebar 14.2, Referring to Statutes in the Text

To complete the exercises, you may also need to refer to the following:

- Rule 1.1, Typeface Choices
- Rule 6.0, Citing Sections and Paragraphs
- Rule 8.0, Supplements

Be prepared to consult Appendix 1, Primary Sources by Jurisdiction, for many of the questions.

6-B.11. Your research of tax laws governing non-profit corporations leads you to section 501 of the Internal Revenue Code, which appears in its entirety in the 2009 Cumulative Annual Pocket Part to the bound volumes covering sections 501 to 640 of Title 26 of the United States Code Annotated. Choose the correct full citation to subsection (c)(3) of this version of the statute.

a. 26 U.S.C.A. § 501(c)(3) (2009).
b. 26 I.R.C. § 501(c)(3) (West Supp. 2009).
c. I.R.C. § 501(c)(3) (West Supp. 2009).
d. 26 U.S.C. § 501(c)(3) (2009).

6-B.12. Your paper on sex offender registration refers to section 14071 of title 42 of the United States Code Service. Your research source was the online LEXIS database, which was current through a specific 2010 session law. Choose the correct full citation for this version of the statute.

a. Title 42 United States Code Service, sec. 14071(current through Public Law 111-145, approved Mar. 4, 2010).
b. 42 U.S. Code Serv. § 14071 (LEXIS 2010).
c. 42 U.S.C. § 14071 (current through P.L. 111-145, Mar. 4, 2010).
d. 42 U.S.C.S. § 14071 (LEXIS current through Pub. L. 111-145, approved Mar. 4, 2010).

6-B.13. The New Hampshire Whistleblowers' Protection Act shields from retaliation employees who report violations of state or federal law. This law, which was enacted in 1987, is codified in section 275-E:2. Your library does not have a copy of New Hampshire's official code, but you do find the statute in the 2008 Replacement Edition of "New Hampshire Revised Statutes Annotated," which Lexis publishes. Choose the correct full citation to the whistleblower law.

a. N.H. Rev. Stat. Ann. § 275-E:2 (Lexis 1987).
b. N.H. Rev. Stat. Ann. § 275-E:2 (Lexis 2008).
c. N.H. Rev. Stat. Ann. § 275-E:2 (Lexis 1955).
d. N.H. Rev. Stat. Ann. § 275-E:2 (Lexis Repl. 2008).

6-B.14. The national pastime is, not surprisingly, regulated by national laws. Subsection (c) of Title 15, section 26b gives major league baseball players standing to sue for antitrust violations. At the time you found this statute in the United States Code Annotated database on Westlaw, it displayed the following notation: "Current through P.L. 111-149 (excluding P.L. 111-147 and 111-148) approved 3-25-10." Choose the correct full citation to this version of the statute.

    a. 15 U.S.C. § 26(b)(c) (current through P.L. 111-149, Mar. 25, 2010).

    b. 15 U.S.C.A. § 26b, c (West, WL current through Mar. 25, 2010).

    c. U.S.C.A. Tit. 15, § 26b(c) (Mar. 25, 2010).

    d. 15 U.S.C.A. § 26b(c) (West, WL current through Pub. L. 111-21 (excluding Pub. L. 111-47 & Pub. L. 111-148) approved Mar. 25, 2010).

6-B.15. Your research on lotteries led you to a statute permitting the United States Postal Service to issue subpoenas to aid in its investigations of suspected illegal activities. You refer to a federal statute in the following sentence from your memo. Choose the correct full citation to the statute in that sentence.

> The United States Postal Service, in investigating a suspected fraudulent lottery scheme, may issue subpoenas to obtain documents. _____ permits the Postmaster General to require by subpoena the production of any records considered relevant or material to the investigation.

    a. 39 U.S.C. § 3016(a)(1)(A) (2006)

    b. Title 39 U.S.C. § 3016(a)(1)(A) (2006)

    c. Title 39, United States Code, section 3016(a)(1)(A) (2006)

    d. The Deceptive Mail Prevention and Enforcement Act, Pub. L. No. 106-168, 113 Stat. 1806 (1999), *codified at* 39 U.S.C. § 3016(a)(1)(A)

EXERCISE SET 6-B

EXPERT LEVEL: STATUTORY CODES

Before beginning Exercise Set 6-B Expert Level, review the following rules and keep the *Manual* at hand as you work through the exercises:

- Rule 14.1, Which Source to Cite
- Rule 14.2, Full Citation, Print Format for Federal Statutes Currently in Force
- Rule 14.4, Full Citation, Print Format for State Statutes
- Rule 14.5, Statutes Available on Electronic Databases
- Sidebar 14.1, Date of United States Code
- Sidebar 14.2, Referring to Statutes in the Text

To complete the exercises, you may also need to refer to the following:

- Rule 1.1, Typeface Choices
- Rule 6.0, Citing Sections and Paragraphs
- Rule 8.0, Supplement

Be prepared to consult Appendix 1, Primary Sources by Jurisdiction, for many of the questions.

6-B.16. You have used LexisNexis to retrieve a Nevada statute, a portion of which is set out below. Write the full citation for the subsection of the statute that permits a juvenile to be tried as an adult when he is charged with a "sexual assault involving the use or threatened use of force or violence against the victim."

*** THIS DOCUMENT IS CURRENT THROUGH THE 74TH (2007) SESSION AND 24TH AND 25TH SPECIAL (2008) SESSION, AND UPDATES RECEIVED FROM THE LEGISLATIVE COUNSEL BUREAU THROUGH APRIL 2009 ***

62B.390. Certification of child for criminal proceedings as adult.

1. Except as otherwise provided in subsection 2 and NRS 62B.400, upon a motion by the district attorney and after a full investigation, the juvenile court may certify a child for proper criminal proceedings as an adult to any court that would have jurisdiction to try the offense if committed by an adult, if the child:
    (a) Is charged with an offense that would have been a felony if committed by an adult; and
    (b) Was 14 years of age or older at the time the child allegedly committed the offense.
2. Except as otherwise provided in subsection 3, upon a motion by the district attorney and after a full investigation, the juvenile court shall certify a child for proper criminal proceedings as an adult to any court that would have jurisdiction to try the offense if committed by an adult, if the child:
    (a) Is charged with:
        (1) A sexual assault involving the use or threatened use of force or violence against the victim; or
        (2) An offense or attempted offense involving the use or threatened use of a firearm; and
    (b) Was 14 years of age or older at the time the child allegedly committed the offense.

6-B.17. A portion of the Westlaw version of the Illinois statute governing confidentiality of medical records is set out below. Write the full citation to this version of the statute.

---

410 ILCS 522/10-25

West's Smith-Hurd Illinois Compiled Statutes Annotated Currentness
Chapter 410. Public Health
Health Information
Act 522. Illinois Adverse Health Care Events Reporting Law of 2005
➡ 522/10-25. Confidentiality

§ 10-25. Confidentiality. Other than the annual report required under paragraph (4) of Section 10-35 of this Law, adverse health care event reports, findings of root cause analyses, and corrective action plans filed by a health care facility under this Law and records created or obtained by the Department in reviewing or investigating these reports, findings, and plans shall not be available to the public and shall not be discoverable or admissible in any civil, criminal, or administrative proceeding against a health care facility or health care professional. . . . Nothing in this Law shall preclude or alter the reporting responsibilities of hospitals or ambulatory surgical treatment centers under existing federal or State law.

CREDIT(S)
P.A. 94-242, Art. 10, § 10-25, eff. July 18, 2005.

      ·   ·   ·

Current through P.A. 96-886 of the 2010 Reg. Sess.

6-B.18. You have used the federal government's *GPO Access* Web site to retrieve a federal statute concerning a crime of embezzlement, shown at right. This online version is current through January 3, 2007. Write this version of the statute's full citation, with pinpoint reference to the subsection that defines the person to whom the statute applies.

> **TITLE 18—CRIMES AND CRIMINAL PROCEDURE**
> **PART I—CRIMES**
> **CHAPTER 9—BANKRUPTCY**
>
> Sec. 153. Embezzlement against estate
>
>   (a) Offense.—A person described in subsection (b) who knowingly and fraudulently appropriates to the person's own use, embezzles, spends, or transfers any property or secretes or destroys any document belonging to the estate of a debtor shall be fined under this title, imprisoned not more than 5 years, or both.
>
>   (b) Person to Whom Section Applies.—A person described in this subsection is one who has access to property or documents belonging to an estate by virtue of the person's participation in the administration of the estate as a trustee, custodian, marshal, attorney, or other officer of the court or as an agent, employee, or other person engaged by such an officer to perform a service with respect to the estate.

6-B.19. You have used Westlaw to retrieve a Michigan statute, a portion of which is set out below. Write the full citation for the subsection of the statute requiring an electronic prescription to include "[a]n electronic signature or other identifier that specifically identifies and authenticates the prescriber or the prescriber's authorized agent."

> Michigan Compiled Laws Annotated Currentness
> Chapter 333. Health
> Public Health Code (Refs & Annos)
> ⬛ Article 15. Occupations
> ⬛ Part 177. Pharmacy Practice and Drug Control (Refs & Annos)
> ➡ **333.17754. Electronic transmissions of prescriptions; confidentiality safeguards; original prescription**
>
> Sec. 17754. (1) Except as otherwise provided under article 7 [FN1] and the federal act, a prescription may be transmitted electronically as long as the prescription is transmitted in compliance with the health insurance portability and accountability act of 1996, Public Law 104-191, [FN2] or regulations promulgated under that act, 45 CFR parts 160 and 164, by a prescriber or the prescriber's authorized agent and the data are not altered or modified in the transmission process. The electronically transmitted prescription shall include all of the following information:
>
> (a) The name, address, and telephone number of the prescriber.
> (b) The full name of the patient for whom the prescription is issued.
> (c) An electronic signature or other identifier that specifically identifies and authenticates the prescriber or the prescriber's authorized agent.
> (d) The time and date of the transmission.
> (e) The identity of the pharmacy intended to receive the transmission.
> (f) Any other information required by the federal act or state law.
>
>   .   .   .
>
> CREDIT(S)
> P.A.1978, No. 368, § 17754, added by P.A.2006, No. 672, Imd. Eff. Jan. 10, 2007.
>
>   .   .   .
>
> The statutes are current through P.A.2010, No. 31, of the 2010 Regular Session, 95th Legislature.

6-B.20. You have used a LEXIS database to retrieve the same Michigan statute addressed in Question 6-B.19. Although the text of the statute is the same as in the Westlaw version, the following statement appears at the top of the LEXIS electronic version: "THIS DOCUMENT IS CURRENT THROUGH P.A. 23 OF THE 2010 LEGISLATIVE SESSION." On your answer sheet, write the full citation for the LEXIS version of the statute, including the pinpoint reference.

C. SESSION LAWS AND SLIP LAWS

A "session law" is an enactment of a legislative body that has been published in a collection of all the enactments of a particular legislative session. A "slip law" is an act that has not yet been placed in such a collection, often because the legislature is still assembled and has not completed its term of work. Slip laws and session laws typically represent the most recent work of the legislative body.

Session laws are designated as public laws or private laws. A public law (abbreviated "Pub. L.," or as termed by some states, "Pub. Act") is a law that applies generally to all persons. A private law (abbreviated "Priv. L.") applies only to a specific individual or group. Each act is assigned a public law or private law number, representing the order in which it was passed by the particular Congress or state legislature that enacted it. The vast majority of session laws are public laws (and only public laws are later codified).

Federal session laws are officially published in print in a collection known as Statutes at Large (abbreviated "Stat."). Prior to their official publication, they may be available through a source such as United States Code Congressional and Administrative News (abbreviated "U.S.C.C.A.N."), U.S. Law Week, or a public or commercial online database.

Rule 14.7 displays the components of a citation to a federal session law. Use ordinary type for all components. Begin with the abbreviation for public law or private law (Pub. L. or Priv. L.), followed by an Arabic number corresponding to the number of the Congress that passed the act, a hyphen, and a second Arabic number representing the chronological order in which the act was passed; see Rule 14.7(b). For example, the forty-ninth public law passed by the One Hundred Seventh Congress is rendered as Pub. L. 107-49. To the extent possible, augment the basic citation with pinpoint references to section numbers of the act itself and to page numbers in Statutes at Large; see Rule 14.7(f).

Rule 14.11 explains full citation format for a federal slip law. Begin with the public law or private law number, and add a parenthetical with the exact date of enactment. If you can, provide a parallel reference to an unofficial source in which the slip law may be found, such as U.S.C.C.A.N., U.S. Law Week, or a public or commercial online database. If you know the volume of the Statutes at Large in which the slip law will be published, add that information parenthetically, as shown in the example for Rule 14.11(b).

State session laws and slip laws are available in a variety of sources. Your law library may have the hard-bound volumes of the session laws, or you may be able to access PDFs of those volumes through a law library's HeinOnline subscription. Many states place unofficial versions of their session laws on governmental Web sites. While these versions are useful for quick research, cite an official source if possible. Consult the specific jurisdiction's entry in Appendix 1 for the abbreviations and formats to use in citing state session laws.

Because it is preferable to cite statutes to the codes to which they are assigned, as provided in Rule 14.1(a), you are likely to discuss and cite session laws in only two situations: (a) when the statute is new and not yet available in a code; or (b) even if the statute is codified, when you want to discuss it in the form in which it was originally enacted by the legislative body.

EXERCISE SET 6-C

BASIC LEVEL: SESSION LAWS AND SLIP LAWS

Before beginning Exercise Set 6-C Basic Level, review the following rules and keep the *Manual* at hand as you work through the exercises:

- Rule 14.1, Which Source to Cite
- Rule 14.7, Full Citation Format for Federal Session Laws Currently in Force
- Rule 14.9, Full Citation Format for State Session Laws

To complete the exercises, you may also need to refer to the following:

- Rule 6.0, Citing Sections and Paragraphs

Be prepared to consult Appendix 1, Primary Sources by Jurisdiction, for certain questions.

6-C.1. The One Hundred Ninth Congress enacted its twenty-first public law on July 9, 2005, to prohibit the sending of unsolicited advertisements via facsimile (junk faxes). This session law is published in volume 119 of Statutes at Large, beginning at page 359. Section 2(d) appears at page 361. Choose the correct full citation to section 2(d).

    a. P. L. 109th-21st, § 2(d), 119 STAT. 359, 361 (2005).
    b. P.L. 109-21, § 2(d), 119 Stat. 359, 361 (July 9, 2005).
    c. Pub. L. No. 109-21, § 2(d), 119 Stat. 359, 361 (2005).
    d. Pub.L. No.109-21, § 2(d), 119 Stat. 359, 361 (2005).

6-C.2. On November 13, 1998, the One Hundred Fifth Congress passed Public Law No. 105-394, also known as the "Assistive Technology Act of 1998." The act was later published in volume 112 of Statutes at Large, beginning at page 3627. The purposes of the act are set out in section 2(b), at pages 3630 to 3631. Choose the correct full citation to section 2(b).

    a. Pub. L. No. 105-394, § 2(b), 112 Stat. 3627, 3630–3631 (1998).
    b. Pub. L. 105-394, § 2(b), 112 Stat. at Large 3630–3631 (1998).
    c. P. L. No. 105-394, § 2(b), 112 Stat. 3627, 3630–31 (1998).
    d. P.L. No.105-394, 112 Stat. 3627, 3630–31, at § 2(b) (Nov. 13, 1998).

6-C.3. Your research concerns a Minnesota session law signed by that state's governor on May 9, 2006, which prohibits the disruption of a funeral, burial service, or memorial service. It begins at page 33 of the 2006 volume of Laws of Minnesota. Choose the correct full citation to this session law.

    a. Minn. L. 33 (May 9, 2006).
    b. P.L. Minn. at 33 (2006).
    c. 2006 Minn. Sess. L. Serv. ch. 33 (West).
    d. 2006 Minn. Laws 33.

6-C.4. Your research required you to find Chapter 65, Senate Bill No. 192, which is an act from pages 181–182 of the 1995 Session Laws of Kansas. The bill was enacted on March 27, 1995. Choose the correct full citation to this session law.

    a. 1995 Sess. Laws Kan. Chap. 65.
    b. 1995 Kan. Sess. Laws 181.
    c. Kan. Sess. Ls. ch. 65, at 181–182 (1995).
    d. Kan. Stat. § 65 (1995).

EXERCISE SET 6-C

INTERMEDIATE LEVEL: SESSION LAWS AND SLIP LAWS

Before beginning Exercise Set 6-C Intermediate Level, review the following rules and keep the *Manual* at hand as you work through the exercises:

- Rule 14.1, Which Source to Cite
- Rule 14.7, Full Citation Format for Federal Session Laws Currently in Force
- Rule 14.9, Full Citation Format for State Session Laws
- Rule 14.11, Full Citation Format for Federal Slip Laws

To complete the exercises, you may also need to refer to the following:

- Rule 1.1, Typeface Choices
- Rule 6.0, Citing Sections and Paragraphs

Be prepared to consult Appendix 1, Primary Sources by Jurisdiction, for certain questions.

6-C.5. You are writing a paper about the Religious Freedom Restoration Act of 1993, which was enacted by the One Hundred Third Congress in Public Law No. 103-141, published in volume 107 of Statutes at Large, beginning at page 1488. Choose the correct full citation to section 3 of that Public Law, which also appears at page 1488.

    a. Relig. Freedom Rest. Act of 1993, P.L. No. 103-141, § 3, 107 Stat. 1488, at 1488.

    b. Religious Freedom Restoration Act of 1993, Pub. L. No. 103-141, § 3, 107 Stat. 1488, 1488.

    c. Religious Freedom Restoration Act, Pub. L. No. 103-141, § 3, 107 Stat. at 1488 (1993).

    d. *Religious Freedom Restoration Act of 1993*, P. L. No. 103-141, § 3, 107 Stat. 1488, 1488.

6-C.6. On February 11, 2009, Congress passed the DTV Delay Act, postponing the changeover from analog to digital television broadcasts until June 12, 2009. The DTV Delay Act was designated as Public Law No. 111-4. You found the slip law in the April 2009 issue of U.S.C.C.A.N. It will eventually be published in volume 123 of Statutes at Large, beginning at page 112. Choose the correct full citation to this slip law in U.S.C.C.A.N.

    a. *DTV Delay Act*, Pub. L. 111-4 (Feb. 11, 2009), 2009 U.S.C.C.A.N. (123 Stat.) 112.

    b. DTV Delay Act, Pub. L. No. 111-4 (Feb. 11, 2009), 2009 U.S.C.C.A.N. (123 Stat.) 112.

    c. DTV Delay Act, Pub. L. No. 111-4 (Feb. 11, 2009), U.S.C.C.A.N. (123 Stat.) 112 (Apr. 2009).

    d. Pub. L. 111-4 (June 12, 2009), 123 Stat. 112 (2009 U.S.C.C. & A.N. Apr. 2009).

6-C.7. The One Hundred Forty-Fourth Delaware General Assembly approved House Bill 475 to amend certain portions of the Delaware Code. The governor signed the bill into law on July 9, 2008. The new law was later published in volume 76 of the Laws of Delaware (2008), as chapter 335. Choose the correct full citation to section 2 of this session law.

    a. H.B. 475, ch. 335, § 2, Del. Laws (2008).

    b. Ch. 335, § 2, 76 Del. Laws (July 9, 2008).

    c. 76 Del. Laws ch. 335, § 2 (2008).

    d. Vol. 76, Del. Laws ch. 335, § 2 (2008).

6-C.8. The One Hundred Ninth Congress passed a private law giving a life estate to a widow occupying certain property within Rocky Mountain National Park. This was the first private law of that session of Congress, and it was later published in the 2006 edition of Statutes at Large, in volume 120, beginning at page 3705. Choose the correct full citation to this private law.

   a. Priv. L. No. 109-1, 120 Stat. 3705 (2006).
   b. Pvt. L. 109-1, 120 Stat. 3705 (2006).
   c. P.L. No. 109-1, 120 Stat. 3705 (2006).
   d. Priv. Law 109-1, vol. 120, Stat. at Large 3705 (2006).

EXERCISE SET 6-C

EXPERT LEVEL: SESSION LAWS AND SLIP LAWS

Before beginning Exercise Set 6-C Expert Level, review the following rules and keep the *Manual* at hand as you work through the exercises:

• Rule 14.7, Full Citation Format for Federal Session Laws Currently in Force
• Rule 14.9, Full Citation Format for State Session Laws

Be prepared to consult Appendix 1, Primary Sources by Jurisdiction, for certain questions.

6-C.9. The Fifty-Ninth General Assembly of North Dakota amended section 62.1-02-04 of the North Dakota Century Code when it passed House Bill number 1086 to exempt private security personnel from a statute prohibiting possession of firearms in liquor establishments or gaming sites. The act was passed on March 30, 2005, and subsequently published in the 2005 edition of Laws of North Dakota, at page 2085. Write the full citation to this session law, but omit parenthetical reference to the statute that was amended.

6-C.10. No doubt due to the extreme shortage of rhinoceroses and tigers in the wilds of America, in 2002, the One Hundred Seventh Congress reauthorized the Rhinoceros and Tiger Conservation Act of 1994. The new act, titled the Rhinoceros and Tiger Conservation Reauthorization Act of 2001, was designated as Public Law No. 107-112, and it was subsequently published in the 2002 edition of Statutes at Large, beginning at page 2097 of volume 115. You wish to cite section 5 of the session law, which appears at page 2098. Write the full citation to the session law, including its title.

D. ORDINANCES

Citations to local and municipal ordinances are constructed in a similar manner to federal and state statutes; see Rule 18.1 and its examples. If the ordinance is **codified**, begin the citation with the abbreviated name of the local or municipal code, omitting prepositions such as "of" or "for." If the local or municipal government's name is not part of the code's title, add it.

Following the code abbreviation, insert a parenthetical with the abbreviation for the state in which the governmental unit is located. Follow the code's numbering system to indicate its sections, articles, chapters, etc., using abbreviations from Appendix 3(C), Subdivisions. End with a parenthetical reference to the year of the code's publication, or if the code is only available online, provide its "current through" date.

The citation format for an **uncodified** ordinance is somewhat different because it begins with the name of the political subdivision, such as a city, followed by the state abbreviation set off by commas. Next, set out the ordinance number. If the ordinance is not numbered, set out its name in italics. Do not abbreviate any words in the name of the ordinance. Conclude the citation with a date parenthetical that provides the exact date of the ordinance's enactment (month, day, year); see Rule 18.2 and its examples.

Local ordinances are increasingly being published only in electronic format. Sidebar 18.1 provides Web site addresses for many such sources. You may also find ordinances for some of the larger municipalities in Westlaw and LexisNexis databases.

The exercises in this section are for all levels.

EXERCISE SET 6-D

ALL LEVELS: ORDINANCES

Before beginning Exercise Set 6-D All Levels, review the following rules and keep the *Manual* at hand as you work through the exercises:

- Rule 18.1, Full Citation Format for Codified Ordinances
- Rule 18.2, Full Citation for Uncodified Ordinances
- Sidebar 18.1, Locating Ordinances on the Internet

To complete the exercises, you may also need to refer to the following:

- Rule 1.1, Typeface Choices
- Rule 6.0, Citing Sections and Paragraphs

6-D.1. Section 6.04.020 of the Municipal Code of Bullhead City, Arizona, governs the reporting of animal bites. The ordinance is published online, current through February 16, 2010. Select the correct full citation to the ordinance.

    a. Bullhead City, Ariz., Mun. Ordin. Code § 6.04.020 (current through Feb. 16, 2010).
    b. Bullhead City (Ariz.) Code Ordin. § 6.04.020 (2008).
    c. Bullhead City, Ariz., Mun. Code § 6.04.020 (Feb. 16, 2008).
    d. Bullhead City Mun. Code (Ariz.) § 6.04.020 (current through Dec. 16, 2008).

6-D.2. The city of Troy, Montana, publishes its uncodified, but numbered, ordinances on the Internet. Ordinance No. 582 governs construction standards for mobile homes and manufactured housing in that city. This ordinance was enacted by the city council on January 11, 2006. Select the correct full citation to the ordinance.

    a. Troy (Mont.) Ordin. 582 (2006).
    b. Troy Code (Mont.) § 582 (2006).
    c. Troy, Mont., Ordin. 582 (Jan. 11, 2006).
    d. Troy, Mont., Ordin. *Providing Construction Standards for and Location of Mobile Homes and Manufactured Housing* § 582 (Jan. 11, 2006).

6-D.3. The town of Killington, Vermont, does not codify or number its ordinances, but instead gives them titles identifying their topics. The city's "Banner Ordinance" was adopted on April 21, 2008. Select the correct full citation to section 5 of that ordinance, a provision which expressly permits the display of certain types of banners in Killington.

   a. Killington, Vt., *Banner Ordinance* § 5 (Apr. 21, 2008).
   b. Killington (Vt.) *Banner Ordin.* § 5 (2008).
   c. Killington (Vt.) "Banner Ordin." § 5 (Apr. 21, 2008).
   d. Killington, Vt., Banner Ordinance § 5 (2008).

6-D.4. Morgan City, Louisiana, publishes its ordinances online. The Web site is current through August 26, 2008. Section 122-2 of the Code of Ordinances declares abandoned or sunken vessels to be a nuisance. Select the correct full citation to the ordinance.

   a. Morgan City, La. Code § 122-2 (Aug. 26, 2008).
   b. Morgan City Code Ordin. (La.) § 122-2 (current through Aug. 26, 2008).
   c. Code Ordin. Morgan City (La.) § 122-2 (2008).
   d. Morgan City Ordin. § 122-2 (current through Ordin. No. 08-7, enacted Aug. 26, 2008).

6-D.5. The city of Waterford, Connecticut, has an ordinance prohibiting vehicles from parking on the town's streets during snowstorms. Codified as section 10.08.020, the ordinance is available online, on a Web site current through December 1, 2008. Write the full citation to the ordinance.

6-D.6. The town of Culver, Indiana, requires "wrecked, junked or abandoned automobile[s]" to be kept out of public view. The town's ordinance, titled "Unlawful to Display in Public View," is set out in the town's Code of Ordinances, at section 91.02. It was enacted on September 25, 2007. You found the ordinance online, on a Web site current through October 13, 2009. Write the full citation to the ordinance.

E.   SHORT-FORM CITATIONS

The first time you cite a constitution, statute, ordinance, session law, or slip law, provide a full citation, as required by Rule 11.1(c)(1). Thereafter, just as with citations to other forms of legal authority, you may use a short form.

Id.

The short form *id.* is the easiest to use, but it can only be used in appropriate circumstances, i.e., when you want to cite the same source you just cited in the preceding citation. Therefore, if the preceding citation was a string citation (one that joined citations to two or more sources), you cannot use *id.* because it is unclear which of the previous sources the short-form citation indicates.

Other Short-Form Citations

When *id.* is not appropriate, short-form citations for constitutions, statutes, session laws, slip laws, and ordinances are treated differently. Table 6.1 displays the applicable rules and formats to use in short-form citations to these sources.

TABLE 6.1

SHORT-FORM CITATIONS

Type of Source	*Id.*	Other Short-Form Citations
Constitutions **Rule 13.4**	To cite another subdivision of the same constitution, use "*Id.* at [subdivision]."	None. Repeat full citation.
Statutes **Rule 14.6**	To cite another subdivision of the same statute, use "*Id.* at [subdivision]."	*For documents without footnotes:* Option 1: Repeat all components of the full citation except the publisher/date parenthetical. Option 2: Keep name of statute (if any), drop code name abbreviation, and keep the section symbol and all digits/letters following it. Option 3: Drop name of statute (if any) and code name abbreviation, but keep the section symbol and all digits/letters following it. *For document with footnotes:* Repeat all components of the full citation except the publisher/date parenthetical.
Session Laws **Rule 14.10**	To cite another subdivision of the same session law, use "*Id.* at [subdivision]."	Drop name of act, if any. Repeat volume number, abbreviation for the session law source, and insert pinpoint reference after the preposition "at."
Slip Laws **Rule 14.3**	To cite another subdivision of the same slip law, use "*Id.* at [subdivision]."	Repeat all components of the full citation except the publisher/date parenthetical.
Ordinances **Rule 18.3**	To cite another subdivision of the same ordinance, use "*Id.* at [subdivision]."	*For codified ordinance:* Drop state abbreviation and date parenthetical. *For uncodified ordinance:* Repeat all components of the full citation except the date parenthetical.

EXERCISE SET 6-E

BASIC LEVEL: SHORT-FORM CITATIONS

Before beginning Exercise Set 6-E Basic Level, review the following and keep the *Manual* at hand as you work through the exercises:

- Rule 13.4, Short Citation Format [Constitutions]
- Rule 14.6, Short Citation, Print Format for Federal and State Statutes

To complete the exercises, you may also need to refer to the following:

- Rule 6.0, Citing Sections and Paragraphs

Be prepared to consult Appendix 1, Primary Sources by Jurisdiction, for some of the questions.

6-E.1.   Your brief argues that your client is immune from tort liability because the federal Volunteer Protection Act preempts state law. In support of your argument, you cite title 42 of the United States Code, section 14503(a)(1) (2006). Next, explaining why your client is not subject to the statute's exception for gross negligence, you cite the same section, but at subsection (a)(3), using a short form. Choose the correct short-form citation for the gross negligence exception.

    a. *Id.*
    b. *Id.* at (a)(3).
    c. *Id.* at § 14503(a)(3).
    d. 42 U.S.C. at § 14503(a)(3).

6-E.2.   You have used the 2000 bound volume of Vernon's Annotated Missouri Statutes to research landlord-tenant law. Describing the liability of tenants who hold over after their lease term expires, you have cited section 441.080. Your next citation is to a Missouri case, *Schnucks Carrollton Corp. v. Bridgeton Health & Fitness Inc.*, 884 S.W.2d 733 (Mo. App. E. Dist. 1984). The third citation returns to the statute. Choose the correct short form for the third citation.

    a. *Id.* at § 441.080.
    b. Mo. Rev. Stat. § 441.080.
    c. Mo. Rev. Stat. Ann. § 441.080.
    d. Mo. Rev. Stat. Ann. at § 441.080.

6-E.3.   Your criminal law paper discusses the trial-by-jury provision of the United States Constitution, set out in article III, section 2, clause 3, reproduced below. Immediately after quoting and citing the provision in full, your paper addresses the phrase, "except in Cases of Impeachment." You have not cited any other authorities in this section of the paper. Choose the correct short form for a citation to the source of the phrase.

> The Trial of all Crimes, except in Cases of Impeachment, shall be by Jury; and such Trial shall be held in the State where the said Crimes shall have been committed; but when not committed within any State, the Trial shall be at such Place or Places as the Congress may by Law have directed.

    a. U.S. Const. at art. III, § 2, cl. 3.
    b. Art. III, § 2, cl. 3.
    c. § 2, cl. 3.
    d. *Id.*

6-E.4. Article 3, section 17 of the current Constitution of the State of Mississippi declares that private property owners must be compensated when government takes their property for public use. In your memo discussing this "takings" clause, the first reference to this provision cites the constitution in full. The memo's second and third citations are to *Fratesi v. City of Indianola*, 972 So. 2d 38 (Miss. App. 2008). The fourth citation refers again to the "takings" clause. Choose the correct short form for the fourth citation.

    a. Miss. Const. art. 3, § 17.
    b. Miss. Const. at art. 3, § 17.
    c. *Id.* at art. 3, § 17.
    d. Art. 3, § 17.

6-E.5. Your brief to a Wyoming trial court discusses that state's version of the Uniform Commercial Code governing installment contracts. The brief's first citation is to the definition of "installment contract," found in section 34.1-2-612(a). The brief's second citation discusses subsection (b) of the same statute. Choose the correct short form for the citation to subsection (b).

    a. Wyo. Stat. Ann. at § 34.1-2-612(b).
    b. § 34.1-2-612(b).
    c. *Id.* at (b).
    d. Id. at (b).

EXERCISE SET 6-E

INTERMEDIATE LEVEL: SHORT-FORM CITATIONS

Before beginning Exercise Set 6-E Intermediate Level, review the following and keep the *Manual* at hand as you work through the exercises:

- Rule 13.4, Short Citation Format [Constitutions]
- Rule 14.6, Short Citation, Print Format for Federal and State Statutes
- Rule 14.10, Short Citation Format for Federal and State Session Laws
- Rule 18.3, Short Citation Format for Codified and Uncodified Ordinances

To complete the exercises, you may also need to refer to the following:

- Rule 6.0, Citing Sections and Paragraphs
- Rule 8.0, Supplements

Be prepared to consult Appendix 1, Primary Sources by Jurisdiction, for some of the questions.

6-E.6. Your memo about child support orders in the State of Washington cites section 74.20A.320 of the Revised Code of Washington Annotated, which appears in the 2009 pocket part. One paragraph later, it cites section 74.20A.330, a provision from the 2001 main volume. The memo's next citation is to section 74.20A.320 again. Choose the correct short form for the second citation to section 74.20A.320.

    a. Wash. Rev. Code Ann. § 74.20A.320 (West Supp. 2009).
    b. *Id.* at § 74.20A.320.
    c. *Id.* at § 74.20A.320 (West Supp. 2009).
    d. § 74.20A.320.

6-E.7. In Tennessee, persons who administer lie detector tests are subject to the Polygraph Examiners Act, which appears in Title 62, Chapter 27, sections 101 through 129 of the official Tennessee Code Annotated. Some sections of the act are in the 1997 bound volume, and others are in the 2008 pocket part. You are writing a law review comment about section 107, which appears in its entirety in the pocket part. Choose the correct short form for the citation to section 107.

    a. Tenn. Code Ann. § 62-27-107.
    b. Tenn. Code § 62-27-107 (1997 & Supp. 2008).
    c. Tenn. Code § 62-27-107 (Supp. 2008).
    d. § 107.

6-E.8. You have cited 18 U.S.C. § 1955 (2006) as authority for whether a local charity's "Casino Night" violates federal law regulating illegal gambling. The first citation to the statute makes a pinpoint reference to subsection (b)(2), which defines "gambling." You then cite a case. After the case citation, the next citation is to subsection (d) of the statute, which explains the forfeiture of property seized in a raid upon an illegal gambling business. Choose the correct short form for the citation to subsection (d).

    a. 18 U.S.C. § 1955(d) (2006).
    b. 18 U.S.C. § 1955(d).
    c. § (d).
    d. 1955(d).

6-E.9. Loma Linda, California, authorizes certain exceptions to its underground utilities ordinance in section 12.16.110 of the city's municipal code. One exception applies to overhead electric wires carrying more than 34,500 volts, as set out in section 12.16.110.D. Your research source for this ordinance is the LexisNexis Municipal Code Web site, current through Ordinance 682, passed January 13, 2009. Choose the correct short form for the citation to section 12.16.110.D.

    a. Loma Linda Mun. Code (Cal.) § 12.16.110.D (LEXIS current through Ordin. 682, passed Jan. 13, 2009).
    b. Loma Linda Mun. Code § 12.16.110.D.
    c. § 12.16.110.D.
    d. § D.

6-E.10. The One Hundred Eighth Congress passed the "Clean Diamond Trade Act" on April 25, 2003. Assigned as Public Law number 108-19, the act is found at pages 631 to 637 of Statutes at Large volume 117. In a short memo about the act, you first cite page 633. Your memo's second citation is to pages 634–635. The third citation refers to an international treaty. The fourth and final citation is to pages 633–634. Choose the correct short form for the fourth citation.

    a. 117 Stat. at 633–634.
    b. Pub. L. No. 108-19 at 633–634.
    c. Pub. L. No. 108-19, 117 Stat. at 633–634.
    d. *Id.* at 633–634.

EXERCISE SET 6-E

EXPERT LEVEL: SHORT-FORM CITATIONS

Before beginning Exercise Set 6-E Expert Level, review the following and keep the *Manual* at hand as you work through the exercises:

- Rule 13.4, Short Citation Format [Constitutions]
- Rule 14.6, Short Citation, Print Format for Federal and State Statutes
- Rule 14.10, Short Citation Format for Federal and State Session Laws
- Rule 18.3, Short Citation Format for Codified and Uncodified Ordinances

To complete the exercises, you may also need to refer to the following:

- Rule 6.0, Citing Sections and Paragraphs

Be prepared to consult Appendix 1, Primary Sources by Jurisdiction, for some of the questions.

6-E.11. The Texas Penal Code provides for the entrapment defense in section 8.06(a). You have cited that section in your brief, followed by a citation to *Norman v. State*, 588 S.W.2d 340 (Tex. Crim. App. 1979). The next citation in the brief refers to § 8.06(b). Using the **official code** for Texas, write the short-form citation for that subsection. Do not use *id.*

6-E.12. The Code of Ordinances for the City of Crestview Hills, Kentucky, contains the provision shown below. Write the short-form citation for the section of the ordinance that prohibits vehicles from passing over a fire hose. Do not use *id.*

---

§ 71.26 FOLLOWING EMERGENCY VEHICLES; DRIVING OVER FIRE HOSE.

(A) It shall be unlawful for the operator of any vehicle not on official duty to follow an authorized emergency vehicle, traveling in response to a fire alarm or other emergency, closer than 200 feet, or to park any vehicle within a block in any direction of the location where these vehicles are responding to a fire alarm.

(B) It shall be unlawful for the operator of any vehicle coach to drive over unprotected hose of the Fire Department when laid down on any street or private driveway, to be used at any fire, or alarm of fire, or for any other purpose, without the consent of the Fire Department official in command or on duty at such point.

6-E.13. Public Law number 104-65, the "Lobbying Disclosure Act of 1995," was enacted by the One Hundred Fourth Congress on December 19, 1995, and published at 109 Stat. 691. Your first citation is to the definition of "agency" in section 3(1), and you cite the session law in full. The second citation is to the definition of "client" in section 3(2). Determine whether the second citation should be a full citation or a short citation, and on your answer sheet, write the second citation.

6-E.14–20. On your answer sheet, write the citations—full or short, as appropriate—for the federal statutes cited at the points indicated in this excerpt from a judicial opinion. Assume that no statute has previously been cited in the opinion.

- **Citation A:** Title 42, section 12112(a) of the United States Code (2006).
- **Citation B:** Title 21, sections 801 *et seq.* of the United States Code (2006).
- **Citation C:** Title 42, section 12111(6)(A) of the United States Code (2006).
- **Citation D:** Title 42, section 12102(2)(A) of the United States Code (2006).
- **Citation E:** Title 42, section 12210(a) of the United States Code (2006).

Danville claims that his termination violated the provisions of the Americans with Disabilities Act ("ADA"), [**6-E.14, Citation A**]. The ADA prohibits discrimination by an employer "against a qualified individual with a disability because of the disability of such individual." [**6-E.15, Citation A.**] Drug addiction that substantially limits one or more major life activities is a recognized disability under the ADA. *Thompson v. Davis*, 295 F.3d 890, 896 (9th Cir. 2002). However, the ADA protects only individuals who are no longer using illegal drugs. *Campbell v. Minneapolis Pub. Hous. Auth.*, 168 F.3d 1069, 1072 n. 1 (8th Cir. 1999). The term "illegal use of drugs" means the use of drugs, the possession or distribution of which is unlawful under the Controlled Substances Act, [**6-E.16, Citation B**], but it does not include the use of a drug taken under supervision by a licensed health care professional, [**6-E.17, Citation C**].

Danville's prima facie case of employment discrimination required that he prove (1) he has a disability within the meaning of the ADA; (2) he is qualified to perform the essential functions of his job, with or without reasonable accommodation; and (3) he suffered an adverse employment action because of his disability. *Burchett v. Target Corp.*, 340 F.3d 510, 517 (8th Cir. 2003) (citations and quotation omitted). Moreover, he bears the burden to prove he is disabled. *Id.*

Danville has not met his burden on the first step of the prima facie case. More specifically, he has not shown he has a disability within the meaning of the ADA. To show that he qualifies as disabled under federal law, Danville must show that he (1) has a physical, sensory, or mental impairment which materially limits one or more major life activities; (2) has a record of such an impairment; or (3) is regarded as having such an impairment. [**6-E.18, Citation D.**] Major life activities include caring for one's self, performing manual tasks, walking, seeing, hearing, breathing, learning, and working. *Fjellestad v. Pizza Hut of Am., Inc.*, 188 F.3d 944, 948 (8th Cir. 1999). Danville's case is unique because his claimed disability has a peculiar feature. Certain behavior, while consistent with his claimed disability, also happens to be illegal. Such conduct is not protected by the ADA. Under the ADA "the term 'individual with a disability' does not include an individual who is currently engaging in the illegal use of drugs, when the covered entity acts on the basis of such use." [**6-E.19, Citation E.**]

Danville argues that he is disabled because although he is currently sober, if he were to relapse, he would then be disabled. By way of analogy, he points out that employees disabled by alcoholism are protected by the ADA, citing *Schmidt v. Safeway, Inc.*, 864 F. Supp. 991, 996 (D. Or. 1994). As the district court noted, this argument is unpersuasive and contrary to the ADA. Under the ADA, Danville is not protected from the consequences of illicit conduct explainable by his chemical dependence, such as diverting his employer's pharmaceutical supplies to his own personal use. Danville admitted to his drug counselor that he took Vicodin for his own use from the pharmacy where he worked. The ADA provides no protection from the consequences of that conduct. *See* [**6-E.20, Citation E.**]

CHAPTER

LEGISLATIVE MATERIALS

Many lawyers monitor the status of pending legislation, whether in Congress or in their own state legislatures. In addition, research needs will often call for investigation into the historical development of statutory law, the reasons prompting legislative solutions, or the processes followed. Thus, you should develop some familiarity with the sources of historical, pending, and unenacted legislation.

According to the Library of Congress, a two-year session of Congress presently sees the introduction of approximately ten thousand bills and resolutions, only 10 percent of which survive House or Senate Committee scrutiny for further consideration by the full legislative body.[1] These statistics illustrate that at any given moment, not only is there a significant amount of pending legislation, but also much legislation that will languish in committee until the legislative term concludes, never to be enacted into law.

Things are not much different in the fifty state legislatures, although in many states, the legislative bodies convene less often or for shorter periods than Congress does, thereby diminishing in some respect the sheer volume of proposed laws. For example, during the Florida Legislature's sixty-day regular session in 2009, a total of 2,369 bills and resolutions were filed, only 271 of which passed both chambers.[2]

This chapter is designed to guide your construction of citations to a variety of federal and state legislative sources. Section A provides exercises for citing bills and resolutions that are presently pending in Congress as well as bills and resolutions that were entertained by previous Congresses. Section B addresses the many types of documents that relate to the history of a bill or resolution, including such things as committee reports and prints, and transcripts of hearings or debates. State legislation and state legislative history are covered in section C. You will work with short forms for all these sources in section D.

---

[1] Lib. of Congress, *THOMAS*, http://thomas.loc.gov/ (accessed Apr. 3, 2010).
[2] *Florida Legislature—Regular Session—2009 Information Statistics Report* 1 (July 17, 2009) (available at http://199.44.254.194/data/session/2009/citator/daily/stats.pdf).

A.   FEDERAL LEGISLATION

As Sidebar 15.1 explains, new federal laws are proposed in one of four formats: the bill, the joint resolution, the concurrent resolution, and the simple resolution. The bill is the format most commonly used. A federal bill may be introduced in either the House of Representatives or the Senate. Bills are numbered in the order in which they are introduced during a legislative session. After introduction, bills are typically referred to congressional committees for further study.

Like bills, resolutions from each house are assigned a number in the order in which they are introduced during a session of Congress. A joint resolution may be introduced in either legislative chamber, but it must be approved by both houses and signed by the President in order to have the force of law. Concurrent resolutions require the agreement of both houses, but are not signed by the President; they typically concern rules applicable to both houses. A simple resolution does not require the agreement of the other house and is not signed by the President. Simple resolutions usually deal with a house's own rules.

Unless you elect to begin the citation with the title of the bill or resolution (in ordinary type, as shown in Rule 15.1(g)), a citation to federal legislation starts with an abbreviation for the type of bill or resolution (e.g., Senate Bill ("Sen."), House Concurrent Resolution ("H.R. Con. Res.")), followed by the bill or resolution number. Use the abbreviations shown in Rule 15.1(a), which may differ slightly from abbreviations you see on the documents themselves. Insert a comma, and then provide the number of Congress, using an ordinal contraction (e.g., 96th, 101st, 103d) and the abbreviation "Cong." Each Congress meets in two regular sessions, each lasting a year. Do not designate the session of Congress unless you are citing a House bill or resolution introduced before 1881 or a Senate bill or resolution introduced before 1847, as explained in Rule 15.1(d). Give a pinpoint reference, if appropriate, to the cited section(s) of the bill or resolution, and end the citation with a parenthetical setting out the exact date of the document being cited. For example, the House Joint Resolution shown here should be cited H.R. Jt. Res. 16, 111th Cong. (Jan. 8, 2009).

```
111TH CONGRESS      H. J. RES. 16
  1ST SESSION

Proposing an amendment to the Constitution of the United States to repeal
                the sixteenth article of amendment.


IN THE HOUSE OF REPRESENTATIVES
                JANUARY 8, 2009
Mr. KING of Iowa introduced the following joint resolution; which was referred
            to the Committee on the Judiciary


JOINT RESOLUTION
Proposing an amendment to the Constitution of the United
   States to repeal the sixteenth article of amendment.

1      Resolved by the Senate and House of Representatives
2  of the United States of America in Congress assembled
```

You will typically use the date of the bill's or resolution's introduction, but if the text of the bill or resolution has changed from what was originally introduced, use the date of the newer version (e.g., a version as reported by a congressional committee, a version as passed). In such instances, you may also wish to indicate parenthetically the newer status of the bill or resolution, as shown in the examples for Rule 15.1(f).

The citation form for an *enacted* simple or concurrent resolution uses the appropriate abbreviation from Rule 15.1(a), the resolution number, the ordinal number of the Congress, a date parenthetical indicating the year of its enactment, followed by an additional parenthetical containing the word "enacted." As shown in Rule 15.4 and its examples, you have the option, as a service to your readers, to add a third parenthetical citing the resolution's reprint in the Congressional Record or Statutes at Large. The Congressional Record is a daily publication of the Government Printing Office that contains the official record of congressional proceedings such as the remarks, debates, and votes of representatives and senators. At the end of a congressional session, the daily editions are compiled into a permanent bound edition. Along the same lines, the National Archives and Records Administration compiles all the session laws and prints them in Statutes at Large, which is the official permanent publication for all enacted laws and resolutions of Congress.

Once a bill or a joint resolution has been enacted by both houses of Congress and signed into law by the President, Rule 15.3 requires that it be cited as a **statute**, using Rule 14 (citing its publication in a code, or if it is not yet codified, citing it as a session law or slip law). The only exception to this requirement applies when you are documenting the legislative history of the bill or resolution. In that situation, cite the enacted bill or resolution following the examples shown in Rule 15.1.

EXERCISE SET 7-A

BASIC LEVEL: FEDERAL LEGISLATION

Before beginning Exercise Set 7-A Basic Level, review the following and keep the *Manual* at hand as you work through the exercises:

- Rule 15.1, Full Citation Format for Federal Unenacted Bills, Unenacted Simple Resolutions, and Unenacted Concurrent Resolutions
- Sidebar 15.1, Types of Proposed Laws

To complete the exercises, you may also need to refer to the following:

- Rule 4.3, Ordinal Numbers

7-A.1. On January 9, 2003, Senator Lindsey Graham of South Carolina introduced Senate Bill 110 to the One Hundred Eighth Congress. The bill, whose primary purpose was increasing the amount of student loan forgiveness and loan cancellation available to qualified teachers, was read twice and referred to the Committee on Health, Education, Labor, and Pensions. Choose the correct full citation to Senate Bill 110.

a. S.B. 108–110 (Jan. 9, 2003).
b. S. 110, 108th Cong. (2003).
c. Sen. 110, 108th Cong. (Jan. 9, 2003).
d. Sen. B. 110 (108th Cong. Jan. 9, 2003).

7-A.2. On February 6, 1991, Indiana Representative Andrew Jacobs, Jr., introduced legislation to the One Hundred Second Congress to change the national anthem from "The Star-Spangled Banner" to "America the Beautiful." House Bill 883 was immediately referred to the House Committee on Post Office and Civil Service, and on February 13, 1991, was further referred to the House Subcommittee on Census and Population, where it remained, no additional action on the bill ever taking place. Choose the correct full citation to House Bill 883.

a. H.B. 883, 102d Cong. (1991).
b. H.R. 883, 102d Cong. (Feb. 6, 1991).
c. H. 883, 102th Cong. (Feb. 13, 1991).
d. HB 883, 102th Cong. (1991).

7-A.3. The Ninety-Third Congress met from 1973 to 1975, and during its first session, Representative Olin Teague of Texas introduced House Resolution 11035, encouraging the nation's voluntary adoption of the metric system and establishing a national metric conversion board to coordinate the switch. Representative Teague introduced the resolution on October 18, 1973, but he was unsuccessful in persuading his colleagues in the House to approve the measure. Choose the correct full citation to House Resolution 11035.

a. H.R. Res. 11035, 93d Cong. (Oct. 18, 1973).
b. H. Res. 93–11035 (1973).
c. HRES 93–11035 (Oct. 18, 1973).
d. H.R. Con. Res. 11035, 93th Cong. 1st Sess. (Oct. 18, 1973).

7-A.4. On January 6, 2009, New York Representative José Serrano introduced House Concurrent Resolution 3 in the One Hundred Eleventh Congress during its first session. Expressing goals for United States residents to become proficient in English and other languages, the resolution not only promoted multilingualism and the preservation of Native American languages, it also opposed "English-only measures." Choose the correct full citation to this resolution.

a. H.R. Con. Res. 3, 111th Cong. (Jan. 6, 2009).
b. H. Res. 3, 111th Cong. (2009).
c. H. Con. Res. 3, 111st Cong. 1st Sess. (Jan. 6, 2009).
d. H.R. Con. Res. 3, 111st Cong. (2009).

7-A.5. In the second session of the One Hundred Fifth Congress, Senators Dianne Feinstein (California) and Edward Kennedy (Massachusetts) introduced Senate Bill 1611, which would have amended the Public Health Service Act to prohibit attempts at human cloning and the use of federal research funds for such attempts. The bill was introduced on February 5, 1998. Choose the correct full citation to this bill.

a. S. 1611, 105th Cong. 2d Sess. (Feb. 5, 1998).
b. SB 105–1611 (1998).
c. Sen. B. 1611, 105th Cong. (1998).
d. Sen. 1611, 105th Cong. (Feb. 5, 1998).

EXERCISE SET 7-A

INTERMEDIATE LEVEL: FEDERAL LEGISLATION

Before beginning Exercise Set 7-A Intermediate Level, review the following and keep the *Manual* at hand as you work through the exercises:

• Rule 15.1, Full Citation Format for Federal Unenacted Bills, Unenacted Simple Resolutions, and Unenacted Concurrent Resolutions
• Sidebar 15.1, Types of Proposed Laws
• Rule 15.3, Enacted Bills and Joint Resolutions
• Rule 15.4, Full Citation Format for Enacted Simple and Enacted Concurrent Resolutions

To complete the exercises, you may also need to refer to the following:

• Rule 4.3, Ordinal Numbers

7-A.6. On July 28, 1993, Ohio Representative David Mann introduced House Bill 2787 in the House of Representatives of the One Hundred Third Congress, titled the "Employment Discrimination Evidentiary Amendment of 1993." It was referred to the Committee on Education and Labor, where it remained. Choose the correct full citation to section 2 of this bill.

   a. *Employment Discrimination Evidentiary Amendment of 1993*, 103th Congress (1993–1994).
   b. Employment Discrimination Evidentiary Amendment of 1993, H.R. 2787, 103d Cong. § 2 (July 28, 1993).
   c. *Employment Discrimination Evidentiary Amendment of 1993 § 2*, H.B. 103–2787 (1993).
   d. Employment Discrimination Evidentiary Amendment of 1993, § 2, H. 2787, 103d Cong. (July 28, 1993).

7-A.7. To ensure that all members of Congress have pocket copies of the Constitution, the United States Senate agreed to the resolution shown at right. Choose the correct full citation to this resolution.

   a. 111th Congress, 1st Sess., S. Con. Res. 35 (July 24, 2009).
   b. Authorizing Printing of the Pocket Version of the United States Constitution, Sen. Con. Res. 35 (July 24, 2009).
   c. S. Con. Res. 35, 111st Cong. (July 24, 2009).
   d. Sen. Con. Res. 35, 111th Cong. (July 24, 2009).

111TH CONGRESS
1ST SESSION
S. CON. RES. 35

Authorizing printing of the pocket version of the United States Constitution.

IN THE SENATE OF THE UNITED STATES

JULY 24, 2009

Mr. SCHUMER submitted the following concurrent resolution; which was considered and agreed to

CONCURRENT RESOLUTION

Authorizing printing of the pocket version of the United States Constitution.

1   *Resolved by the Senate (the House of Representatives*
2 *concurring),*
3 SECTION 1. POCKET VERSION OF THE UNITED STATES
4   CONSTITUTION.

7-A.8. On September 25, 2003, the House and the Senate of the One Hundred Eighth Congress passed House Bill 3161, ratifying the authority of the Federal Trade Commission to establish a do-not-call registry. The President signed the act into law on September 29, 2003, creating Public Law No. 108-82, published in volume 117 of Statutes at Large, at page 1006. The act is now codified as 15 U.S.C. § 6151 (2006). Choose the correct full citation to this enactment.

a. H.R. 3161, 108th Cong. (Sept. 25, 2003).
b. Pub. L. No. 108-82, 117 Stat. 1006 (2003).
c. 15 U.S.C. § 6151 (2006).
d. H.R. 3161, 108th Cong. (2003) (enacted) (reprinted in 117 Stat. 1006).

EXERCISE SET 7-A

EXPERT LEVEL: FEDERAL LEGISLATION

Before beginning Exercise Set 7-A Intermediate Level, review the following and keep the *Manual* at hand as you work through the exercises:

- Rule 15.1, Full Citation Format for Federal Unenacted Bills, Unenacted Simple Resolutions, and Unenacted Concurrent Resolutions
- Sidebar 15.1, Types of Proposed Laws
- Rule 15.3, Enacted Bills and Joint Resolutions
- Rule 15.4, Full Citation Format for Enacted Simple and Enacted Concurrent Resolutions
- Rule 15.6, Proposed House and Senate Amendments

To complete the exercises, you may also need to refer to the following:

- Rule 4.3, Ordinal Numbers

7-A.9. You wish to cite the federal bill shown at right. Introduced by New York Representative John Hall on February 3, 2009, it requires that advertisements for cars include information about their fuel consumption and fuel costs. Write the full citation to this bill.

111TH CONGRESS
1ST SESSION

H. R. 818

To require advertising for any automobile model to display information regarding the fuel consumption and fuel cost for that model, and for other purposes.

IN THE HOUSE OF REPRESENTATIVES

FEBRUARY 3, 2009

Mr. HALL of New York introduced the following bill; which was referred to the Committee on Energy and Commerce

A BILL

To require advertising for any automobile model to display information regarding the fuel consumption and fuel cost for that model, and for other purposes.

7-A.10. You wish to cite an enacted resolution in which the House and Senate agreed to authorize "soap box derby" races on the grounds of the United States Capitol. The resolution and its reprint in Statutes at Large appear below. Write the full citation to this resolution, including a parenthetical reference to Statutes at Large.

House Calendar No. 169

108TH CONGRESS
2D SESSION

H. CON. RES. 376

[Report No. 108–469]

Authorizing the use of the Capitol Grounds for the Greater Washington Soap Box Derby.

IN THE HOUSE OF REPRESENTATIVES

MARCH 2, 2004

Mr. HOYER (for himself, Mr. WOLF, Ms. NORTON, Mr. WYNN, Mr. MORAN of Virginia, and Mr. VAN HOLLEN) submitted the following concurrent resolution; which was referred to the Committee on Transportation and Infrastructure

APRIL 22, 2004

Referred to the House Calendar and ordered to be printed

CONCURRENT RESOLUTION

Authorizing the use of the Capitol Grounds for the Greater Washington Soap Box Derby.

the Senate

118 STAT. 4046   CONCURRENT RESOLUTIONS—APR. 29, 2004

(2) urges the President to issue a proclamation calling on the people of the United States, all Federal departments and agencies, States, localities, organizations and media to annually observe a National Military Appreciation Month with appropriate ceremonies and activities; and

(3) urges the White House Commission on Remembrance, established by Congress to honor those who died in service to the United States and those who continue to serve the Nation, to work to support the goals and objectives of a National Military Appreciation Month.

Agreed to April 26, 2004.

Apr. 29, 2004
[H. Con. Res. 376]

SOAP BOX DERBY RACES—CAPITOL GROUNDS AUTHORIZATION

Resolved by the House of Representatives (the Senate concurring),

SECTION 1. AUTHORIZATION OF SOAP BOX DERBY RACES ON CAPITOL GROUNDS.

The Greater Washington Soap Box Derby Association (in this resolution referred to as the "Association") shall be permitted to sponsor a public event, soap box derby races, on the Capitol Grounds on June 19, 2004, or on such other date as the Speaker of the

B.   FEDERAL LEGISLATIVE HISTORY

Many documents are relevant to the legislative history of an enactment, including the following: the original bills or joint resolutions and their amendments, if any; House and Senate committee reports analyzing the proposed legislation and indicating the committee's recommendation whether to pass a bill; conference reports, indicating the negotiated agreement of the House and Senate on proposed legislation; transcripts of committee hearings, including witness testimony, written statements, and exhibits; transcripts of debates by members of the House or Senate; and committee prints, containing detailed studies on specific topics of interest to a committee.

When you research a statute in an annotated code, you will see references to its legislative history in the credits, annotations, statutory notes, or historical notes following the statutory text. For example, the notations under title 18, section 1962 of the United States Code Service reveal information about its enactment in 1970 and its amendment in 1988, as shown below.

---

18 U.S.C.S. § 1962

History:

(Added Oct. 15, 1970, P.L. 91-452, Title IX, § 901(a), 84 Stat. 942; Nov. 18, 1988, P.L. 100-690, Title VII, Subtitle B, § 7033, 102 Stat. 4398.)

History; Ancillary Laws and Directives:

Amendments

1988. Act Nov. 18, 1988, in subsec. (d), substituted "subsection" for "subsections"

Depending on the type of the legislative history source you are citing, you will need to consult many sections of Rule 15, as explained below:

- Cite **amendments** similarly to bills and resolutions, but note parenthetically the legislation they are intended to amend. Refer to the examples in Rule 15.6.
- Cite **congressional hearings** according to Rule 15.7 and its examples. As explained in Rule 15.1(d), a session number is required only for hearings on bills introduced before 1881 in the House or 1847 in the Senate.
- Cite **numbered congressional reports, documents, or prints** following the examples set out in Rule 15.9. Use the abbreviations listed in Rule 15.9(a) to designate the type of report, document, or print being referenced, followed by the number of the Congress, a hyphen (-) or en dash (–), and the specific number assigned to the report, document, or print. For example, the thirty-third report for the 111th Congress should be designated as 111-33. Provide the most exact date that can be discerned from the report, document, or print itself. If it has also been published in the Congressional Record or United States Code Congressional and Administrative News, you may furnish this reprint information in a parenthetical. For additional guidance on source locations in general, see Rule 15.9(g); for specific guidance on United States Code Congressional and Administrative News, see Rule 15.17.

- Cite **unnumbered reports, documents, or prints** following the examples in Rule 15.11, treating them as if they are reports written by an institutional author.
- Cite **congressional debates** to the daily or the permanent edition of the Congressional Record. Citations to the permanent edition are preferred, but it is not published until the congressional session has ended. Therefore, when it is not available, cite the daily edition. Rule 15.12 displays templates and examples for citing both the daily and the permanent editions. Citations to the daily edition must parenthetically indicate the edition and the exact date of publication. Pages in the daily edition are grouped in one of four sections, displaying a "folio prefix" abbreviation for the section (shown in parentheses after each): House (H); Senate (S); Extensions of Remarks (E); and Daily Digest (D). In contrast, citations to the permanent edition need only the year of the volume in parentheses. Also note that pages in the permanent edition do not use the prefixes.
- To cite **historical debates** occurring between 1789 and 1873, consult Rule 15.14 and the table shown there. Depending on its date, a debate may be published in the Annals of Congress, the Register of Debates, or the Congressional Globe.

    The exercises in this set are presented for all levels.

EXERCISE SET 7-B

ALL LEVELS: FEDERAL LEGISLATIVE HISTORY

> Before beginning Exercise Set 7-B All Levels, review the following and keep the *Manual* at hand as you work through the exercises:
>
> - Rule 15.1, Full Citation Format for Federal Unenacted Bills, Unenacted Simple Resolutions, and Unenacted Concurrent Resolutions
> - Rule 15.7, Full Citation Format for Congressional Hearings
> - Rule 15.9, Full Citation Format for Numbered Congressional Reports, Documents, and Prints
> - Rule 15.12, Full Citation Format for Congressional Debates Occurring after 1873
> - Rule 15.17, United States Code Congressional and Administrative News

7-B.1. During the One Hundred Fourth Congress, Utah Senator Orrin Hatch introduced Senate Bill 627 on March 27, 1995. The bill's stated purpose was "to require the general application of the antitrust laws to major league baseball." The bill was referred to the Senate Judiciary Committee, which issued a favorable report and recommended that it pass without amendment. The report, which was given the number 104–231, was ordered to be printed on February 6, 1996. No further action was ever taken. The role of the baseball commissioner is discussed in detail at page 14 of the report. Choose the correct full citation to this page of the report.

    a. S. Rpt. 104–231 1, 14 (Mar. 27, 1995).
    b. S. Rep. 104–231, at 14 (Feb. 6, 1996).
    c. Sen. Rpt. 104–231 at 14 (Feb. 6, 1996).
    d. Sen. Rept. No. 104–231 (Mar. 27, 1995).

7-B.2. On September 27, 2000, United States senators debated a proposed amendment to a bill titled the "American Competitiveness in the Twenty-First Century Act of 2000" before ultimately approving it. A portion of their debate was published in 2000, at pages 19589 through 19628 of the permanent edition of the Congressional Record, volume 146. Choose the correct full citation to these pages of the debate.

a. 146 Cong. Rec. S19589–S19628 (daily ed. Sept. 27, 2000).
b. 146 Cong. Rec. 19589–19628 (2000).
c. Cong. Rec., vol. 146, at 19589–19628 (perm. ed. 2000).
d. Cong. Rec. 146, at S19589–S19628 (Sept. 27, 2000).

7-B.3. During the summer of 2009, congressional debate on "pay-as-you-go" legislative proposals was published in the daily edition of the Congressional Record. On July 21, 2009, the Congressional Record published the remarks of North Carolina Representative Virginia Foxx in volume 155, pages H8412 to H8413. Choose the correct full citation to these remarks in the daily edition.

a. 155 Cong. Rec. H8412–H8413 (daily ed. July 21, 2009) (statement of Rep. Virginia Foxx).
b. 155 Cong. Rec. H8412–H8413 (2009) (statement of Rep. Virginia Foxx).
c. 155 Cong. Rec. at H8412–H8413 (statement of Rep. Virginia Foxx).
d. Cong. Rec., vol. 155, at H8412–H8413 (daily ed. 2009) (statement of Rep. Virginia Foxx).

7-B.4. Senate Committee Print number 61, titled *Technology Assessment in the War on Terrorism and Homeland Security: The Role of OTA*, was published in April 2002 for the Committee on Commerce, Science, and Transportation of the One Hundred Seventh Congress. At pages 34–35, the print recommends that Congress reactivate and fund the Office of Technology Assessment. Choose the correct full citation to these pages of the print.

a. S. Comm. Prt. 107–61, at 34–35 (Apr. 2002).
b. Sen. Comm. Print 107–61 at 34–35 (Apr. 2002).
c. *Technology Assessment in the War on Terrorism and Homeland Security: The Role of OTA*, 107th Cong. Sen. Prt. 61 (2002).
d. Technology Assessment in the War on Terrorism and Homeland Security: The Role of OTA, S. Print 61, 107th Cong. 34–35 (2002).

7-B.5. Shown at right is the title page of a published congressional hearing transcript. Choose the correct full citation to pages 16–17 of this document.

a. H. Hrg. 107–24, H. Comm. on Energy & Com., 107th Cong. 1st Sess. (Apr. 12, 2001).
b. H.R. Energy & Com. Comm., *H.R. 1542, The Internet Freedom and Broadband Deployment Act of 2001*, 107th Cong. 16–17 (Apr. 12, 2001).
c. H.R. 1542 Hrg. before H. Comm. Energy & Com., 107th Cong. 1st Sess., Serial No. 107-24, at 16–17 (Apr. 12, 2001).
d. *The Internet Freedom and Broadband Deployment Act of 2001*, H.R. 1542, 107th Cong. 16–17 (Apr. 12, 2001).

> **THE INTERNET FREEDOM AND BROADBAND DEPLOYMENT ACT OF 2001**
>
> **HEARING**
> BEFORE THE
> **COMMITTEE ON ENERGY AND COMMERCE**
> **HOUSE OF REPRESENTATIVES**
> ONE HUNDRED SEVENTH CONGRESS
> FIRST SESSION
> ON
> **H.R. 1542**
> APRIL 12, 2001
>
> **Serial No. 107–24**
>
> Printed for the use of the Committee on Energy and Commerce

7-B.6. On February 12, 2009, the Commercial and Administrative Law subcommittee of the House of Representative's Judiciary Committee in the One Hundred Eleventh Congress conducted an extensive hearing on House Bill 1304, the Free Speech Protection Act of 2009. Addressing the phenomenon of foreign courts trying U.S. citizens for allegedly defamatory speech, the hearing was published under the title *Libel Tourism*. The oral testimony of one witness, attorney Bruce D. Brown, appears at pages 15–16 of the published transcript. Choose the correct full citation to Mr. Brown's testimony before the subcommittee.

    a. *H.R. 1304, Libel Tourism*, H.R. Jud. Comm., Com. & Admin. L. Subcomm., 111th Cong. at 15–16 (Feb. 12, 2009).

    b. Testimony of Bruce D. Brown on H.R. 1304, *Libel Tourism*, H. Jud. Comm. & Com. & Admin. L. Subcomm. of 111st Cong., at 15–16 (Feb. 12, 2009).

    c. Subcomm. on Com. & Admin. L. of H. Comm. of Jud., *Libel Tourism*, 111st Cong. 15–16 (Feb. 12, 2009).

    d. H.R. Subcomm. on Com. & Admin. L. of Jud. Comm., *H.R. 1304, Libel Tourism*, 111th Cong. 15–16 (Feb. 12, 2009).

7-B.7. When the Senate disagreed with a proposed House amendment to a Senate bill, a group of "managers" (selected senators and representatives) were sent to a "committee of conference" to discuss and work out their differences. The managers came to an agreement and made their recommendations to the Senate and House in the document whose opening is shown at right. Choose the correct full citation to pages 35–39 of this document.

    a. Conf. Comm., *S. 454, Weapon Systems Acquisition Reform Act of 2009*, H. Rpt. 111–124 at 35–39 (2009).

    b. S. 454, *Weapon Systems Acquisition Reform Act of 2009*, 111th Cong., Rpt. 111–124, at 35–39 (2009).

    c. H.R. Conf. Rpt. 111–124 at 35–39 (May 20, 2009).

    d. H.R. Conf. Comm. Rpt. 111–124 at 35–39 (May 20, 2009).

> | 111TH CONGRESS
1st Session | HOUSE OF REPRESENTATIVES | REPORT
111–124 |
>
> **WEAPON SYSTEMS ACQUISTION REFORM ACT OF 2009**
>
> MAY 20, 2009.—Ordered to be printed
>
> Mr. SKELTON, from the committee on conference, submitted the following
>
> **CONFERENCE REPORT**
>
> [To accompany S. 454]
>
> The committee of conference on the disagreeing votes of the two Houses on the amendment of the House to the bill (S. 454), to improve the organization and procedures of the Department of Defense for the acquisition of major weapon systems, and for other purposes, having met, after full and free conference, have agreed to recommend and do recommend to their respective Houses as follows:
>
> That the Senate recede from its disagreement to the amendment of the House and agree to the same with an amendment as follows:
>
> In lieu of the matter proposed to be inserted by the House amendment, insert the following:

7-B.8. Part of the legislative history of 38 U.S.C. §§ 4096, 4097 (2006), federal statutes addressing retirement benefits for judges of the Court of Veterans Appeals, is House Report 101-189, dated July 27, 1989, and prepared by the House Committee on Veterans' Affairs. You found a copy of this report reprinted in the 1989 volume of U.S.C.C.A.N., beginning at page 560. Choose the correct full citation to pages 8–9 of the report, which correspond to pages 565–566 of the reprint.

    a. H.R. Rpt. 101–189 at 8–9 (July 27, 1989) (reprinted in 1989 U.S.C.C.A.N. 560, 565–566).

    b. H.R. Comm. Print 101–189 at 8–9 (July 27, 1989) (available in 1989 U.S.C.C.A.N. 560, 565–566).

    c. H. Rpt. 101–189 at 8–9 (reprinted in 1989 U.S.C.C.A.N. 560, 565–566 (July 27, 1989)).

    d. H.R. Comm. on Vets.' Affairs, Rpt. 101-189 at 8–9 (July 27, 1989) (reprinted in 1989 U.S.C.C.A.N. 560, 565–566).

7-B.9. In the Senate Document whose title page is shown at right, the United States Senate Historical Office published President George Washington's remarks to the American people explaining why he would not seek a third term. Write the document's full citation, including the title.

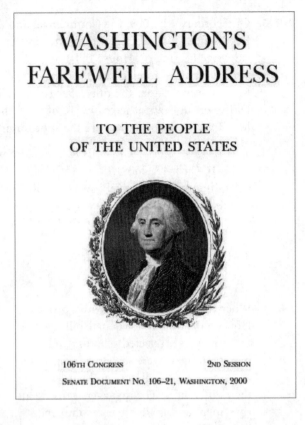

WASHINGTON'S
FAREWELL ADDRESS

TO THE PEOPLE
OF THE UNITED STATES

106TH CONGRESS   2ND SESSION
SENATE DOCUMENT NO. 106–21, WASHINGTON, 2000

7-B.10. A hearing transcript, dated September 12–15, 2005, and titled *Confirmation Hearing on the Nomination of John G. Roberts, Jr. to Be Chief Justice of the United States*, contains at pages 55–56 the nominee's statement to the Senate Judiciary Committee of the One Hundred Ninth Congress. Write its full citation, including the title.

C.   STATE LEGISLATION AND LEGISLATIVE HISTORY

The composition and operation of state legislative bodies vary greatly from one part of the country to another. Although most states have a bicameral legislative body (with an upper-chamber Senate and a lower chamber with names like the Assembly, the General Assembly, the House of Representatives, or the House of Delegates), one state—Nebraska—is unicameral (i.e., it has a single chamber). Some state legislatures meet on an annual basis; some convene biennially. The state's constitution may give the governor the power to call the legislature to convene in a special (or extraordinary) session.

For legal writers, this variety means that a single citation format for state legislation is impossible. Therefore, in order to cite an unenacted or pending bill, file, or resolution of a state legislature, you should study the examples in Rule 16.1. While you may be able to analogize the legislation you are citing to the main example shown in the rule, it is also possible that legislation you wish to cite does not possess all of the possible components shown there. In that case, cite as many of the components as are available.

Unless you elect to begin the citation with the title of the bill, file, or resolution (in ordinary typeface), a citation to state legislation starts with the Appendix 3(B) abbreviation for the state's name. Consult the list and examples in Rule 16.1(b) to find the abbreviations you will need for the type of document you are citing. Insert the number assigned to the document, followed by an abbreviation for the designation used by the legislature (e.g., Legis., Gen. Assembly). Most states use ordinal numbers to identify a specific legislature or assembly.

Like their federal counterparts, annotated state codes display historical notes or annotations indicating a state statute's legislative history. Remember that an enacted bill or resolution should not be cited in its legislative form. Instead, it should ordinarily be cited as a slip law, a session law, or a statute, depending on how far along it is in the codification process. Refer to Rule 16.3.

The exercises in this section are presented for all levels.

EXERCISE SET 7-C

ALL LEVELS: STATE LEGISLATION AND LEGISLATIVE HISTORY

Before beginning Exercise Set 7-C All Levels, review the following and keep the *Manual* at hand as you work through the exercises:

• Rule 16.1, Full Citation Format for State Unenacted Bills, Unenacted Files, and Unenacted Resolutions
• Rule 16.8, Full Citation Format for State Legislative Debates

To complete the exercises, you may also need to refer to Appendix 2, Local Court Citation Rules, and Appendix 3, General Abbreviations.

7-C.1. A piece of legislation being considered by the 128th Ohio General Assembly in its 2009–2010 regular session was House Bill 45, which would have required that drivers activate their cars' headlights when windshield wipers are operating. The bill was introduced on February 24, 2009. Choose the correct full citation to this bill.

a. Oh. H.R. 45, 128th Gen. Assembly (2009–2010).
b. Ohio H. Bill 45, 2009–2010 Reg. Sess. (Feb. 24, 2009).
c. Ohio H. 45, 128th Gen. Assembly, 2009–2010 Reg. Sess. (Feb. 24, 2009).
d. Ohio Gen. Assembly 45, 128th Sess. (Feb. 24, 2009).

7-C.2. On February 2, 2007, during the 2007 Regular Session of the Maryland General Assembly, two state senators introduced a joint resolution protesting the federal REAL ID Act of 2005 on grounds it would mandate an unfunded national driver's license and invite both identity theft and invasion of privacy. Senate Joint Resolution 5 received a hearing in a senate committee, but the Maryland House of Representatives took no action on it before the legislative session ended. Choose the correct full citation to this joint resolution.

a. Md. Jt. Res. 5, Reg. Sess. (2007).
b. Md. S. Jt. Res. 2007–5 (Feb 2, 2007).
c. Md. Sen., Reg. Sess. Jr. Res. 5 (2007).
d. Md. Sen. Jt. Res. 5, 2007 Reg. Sess. (Feb. 2, 2007).

7-C.3. On April 27, 2009, during the 2009 Regular Session of the Legislature of Louisiana, House Concurrent Resolution number 9 was introduced in the Louisiana House of Representatives, expressing the state's desire to accept funding allocated in the unemployment compensation modernization provision of the American Recovery and Reinvestment Act of 2009. The resolution was referred to the House's Committee on Labor and Industrial Relations. Choose the correct full citation to this concurrent resolution.

a. La. H. Con. Res. 9, 2009 Reg. Sess. (Apr. 27, 2009).
b. La. H.R. Con. Res. 9, H. Comm. Labor & Industrial Rel., 2009 Reg. Sess. (Apr. 27, 2009).
c. La. H. Rep. Con. Res. No. 9 (Apr. 27, 2009).
d. HLS 09RS-700, *Unemployment Comp.*, 2009 Reg. Sess. (Apr. 27, 2009).

7-C.4. In the 2007 Regular Session of the Sixtieth Legislature of the State of Washington, lawmakers considered Senate Bill 5484, introduced by Senators Jacobsen, Kline, Murray, and Poulsen on January 22, 2007. The bill would have allowed "well-behaved leashed dogs" to come into bars and other licensed establishments serving alcohol if they were accompanied by their owners. Choose the correct full citation to this bill.

a. Sen. 5484, Wash. 60th Legislature 2007 Regular Sess. (2007).
b. Wash. S–0902.1, 60th Leg. (Jan. 22, 2007).
c. Wash. Sen. 5484, 60th Legis., 2007 Reg. Sess. (Jan. 22, 2007).
d. S. 5484, 60th Legis., 2007 Reg. Sess. (Wash. Jan. 22, 2007).

7-C.5. During the 2009–2010 session of the Wisconsin Legislature, two members of the Wisconsin State Assembly, the state's equivalent of a House of Representatives, introduced "2009 Assembly Joint Resolution 6," proposing a constitutional amendment affecting the size of the legislature and gubernatorial appointment of supreme court justices. The resolution was introduced by Representatives Keller and Williams on February 5, 2009. Choose the correct full citation to this joint resolution.

a. Wis. H. Jt. Res. 6, 2009–2010 Legis. (Feb. 5, 2009).
b. Wis. St. Assembly Jt. Res. 6, 2009–2010 Legis. (Feb. 5, 2009).
c. Wis. 2009 Assembly Jt. Res. 6 (Feb. 5, 2009).
d. Wis. H.R. Jt. Res. 6, 2009–2010 Legis. (Feb. 5, 2009).

7-C.6. Before taking a vote during the Regular Session of Ninety-Second General Assembly, the Illinois Senate debated Senate Bill 1663. A transcript of the April 4, 2004, debate is available on the Illinois General Assembly's Web site, at http://www.ilga.gov/senate/transcripts/strans92/ST040402.pdf. Write the full citation to pages 30–34 of the transcript.

7-C.7. On May 20, 2008, during the 2007–2008 Session of the General Assembly of North Carolina, House Bill 2252, titled "Smoke-Free Motor Fleet," was introduced. The bill would have amended existing law that prohibits smoking in state government buildings to apply also to state-owned vehicles. Write the full citation to section 3 of this bill.

7-C.8. During the 5th Extraordinary Session of the 2005 Mississippi State Legislature, Senator Ross introduced Senate Bill 2020. This bill, introduced on September 27, 2005, would have created a one-month extension of statutes of limitation for actions filed in a specific district in that state. It died in committee. Write the full citation to section 1 of this bill.

D. SHORT-FORM CITATIONS

No matter what kind of legislative material is involved, *id.* may be used as the short-form citation in appropriate circumstances. When *id.* cannot be used, whether because the preceding citation cites two or more sources or because the preceding citation refers to another source, carefully browse Rules 15 and 16 to locate the specific short-form rule applicable to the type of document you are citing. Table 7.1 collects and summarizes the short-form rules for legislative materials that are scattered throughout Rules 15 and 16. Unless otherwise noted in the table, the short-form citation for a particular source is the same whether it appears in a document with or without footnotes.

The exercises in this section are for all levels.

TABLE 7.1

SHORT-FORM CITATIONS TO LEGISLATIVE MATERIALS

Type of Source	*Id.*	Other Short-Form Citations
Unenacted congressional bills and resolutions **Rule 15.2**	To cite another sub-division of the same bill or resolution, use "*Id.* at [subdivision]."	Repeat all components of the full citation except the date parenthetical, and insert pinpoint reference after the preposition "at."
Unenacted state bills, files, and resolutions **Rule 16.2**	To cite another sub-division of the same bill, file, or resolution, use "*Id.* at [subdivision]."	Repeat all components of the full citation except the date parenthetical, and insert pinpoint reference after the preposition "at."
Enacted congressional simple and concurrent resolutions **Rule 15.5**	To cite another sub-division of the same enacted resolution, use "*Id.* at [subdivision]."	Repeat all components of the full citation except the date parenthetical, and references, if any, to Congressional Record or Statutes at Large. Insert pinpoint reference after the preposition "at."

TABLE 7.1

(Continued)

Type of Source	*Id.*	Other Short-Form Citations
Congressional hearings **Rule 15.8**	To cite another sub-division of the same hearing, use "*Id.* at [subdivision]."	*Documents without footnotes:* Repeat all components of the full citation except the hearing title and the date parenthetical. Insert pinpoint reference after the preposition "at." *Documents with footnotes:* Following abbreviation for committee name, insert "*supra* n." followed by number of footnote containing full citation, and pinpoint reference after the preposition "at."
State legislative hearings **Rule 16.5**	To cite another sub-division of the same hearing, use "*Id.* at [subdivision]."	*Documents without footnotes:* Repeat all components of the full citation except legislature designation and the date parenthetical. Insert pinpoint reference after the preposition "at." *Documents with footnotes:* Following abbreviation for committee name, insert "*supra* n." followed by number of footnote containing full citation, and pinpoint reference after the preposition "at."
Numbered congressional reports, documents, and prints **Rule 15.10**	To cite another sub-division of the same report, document, or print, use "*Id.* at [subdivision]."	Repeat all components of the full citation except the date parenthetical, and insert pinpoint reference after the preposition "at."
State legislative reports, documents, and prints **Rule 16.7**	To cite another sub-division of the same report, document, or print, use "*Id.* at [subdivision]."	Repeat all components of the full citation except legislature designation, session designation, and the date parenthetical. Insert pinpoint reference after the preposition "at."

TABLE 7.1

(Continued)

Type of Source	*Id.*	Other Short-Form Citations
Congressional debates **Rule 15.13** **Rule 15.15**	To cite another subdivision of the same debate, use "*Id.* at [subdivision]."	Repeat all components of the full citation except the date parenthetical, and insert pinpoint reference after the preposition "at."
State legislative debates **Rule 16.9**	To cite another subdivision of the same debate, use "*Id.* at [subdivision]."	Repeat all components of the full citation except the legislature designation, session designation, location parenthetical, and date parenthetical. Insert pinpoint reference after the preposition "at."
Congressional journals **Rule 15.16**	To cite another subdivision of the same journal, use "*Id.* at [subdivision]."	Repeat all components of the full citation except the date parenthetical, and insert pinpoint reference after the preposition "at."
State legislative journals **Rule 16.10**	To cite another subdivision of the same journal, use "*Id.* at [subdivision]."	Repeat all components of the full citation except the date parenthetical, and insert pinpoint reference after the preposition "at."

EXERCISE SET 7-D

ALL LEVELS: SHORT-FORM CITATIONS

Before beginning Exercise Set 7-D All Levels, review the following and keep the *Manual* at hand as you work through the exercises:

- Rule 11.0, Introduction to Full and Short Citation Formats
- Rule 15.2, Short Citation Format for Unenacted [Congressional] Bills and Resolutions
- Rule 15.8, Short Citation Format for Congressional Hearings
- Rule 15.10, Short Citation Format for Numbered Congressional Reports, Documents, and Prints
- Rule 15.13, Short Citation Format for Congressional Debates Occurring after 1873
- Rule 16.2, Short Citation Format for State Unenacted Bills, Unenacted Files, and Unenacted Resolutions

7-D.1. In a paper you are writing that argues for greater police presence in the public schools, footnote 10 refers to the "Safe Schools Act of 1998," introduced as House Bill 4224 in the One Hundred Fifth Congress on July 15, 1998. Footnotes 11 and 12 cite Peter Price, Student Author, *When Is a Police Officer an Officer of the Law?: The Status of Police Officers in Schools*, 99 J. Crim. L. & Criminology 541 (2009). Footnote 13 cites section 2 of House Bill 4224. Which of the following is *the best* short-form citation to use in footnote 13?

    a. [13] *Id.* at § 2.
    b. [13] *Id.*, H.R. 4224 § 2, 105th Cong.
    c. [13] H.R. 4224, 105th Cong. at § 2.
    d. [13] H.R. 4224, *supra* n. 10, at § 2.

7-D.2. A brief to a federal circuit court of appeals argues that federal antitrust law was improperly invoked to deter television broadcasts of sporting events. The brief first cites Stephen F. Ross, *An Antitrust Analysis of Sports League Contracts with Cable Networks*, 39 Emory L.J. 463 (1990). The brief's second citation is to a bill introduced in the One Hundred First Congress in 1989, House of Representatives Bill 2593, the "Baseball Viewers Protection Act of 1989." The third citation in the brief again cites the bill. Which of the following citations is *the best* to use for the third citation?

    a. *Id.*
    b. *Id.*, H.R. 2593.
    c. 101st Cong. at H.R. 2593 (1989).
    d. H.R. 2593, *supra.*

7-D.3. Your seminar paper concerns federal elections, and specifically, new ideas for voting by mail (or email). Your research leads you to a bill filed in the United States House of Representatives, House Bill 281, the Universal Right to Vote by Mail Act of 2008. Although this bill's goal was to allow eligible voters to mail in their votes for federal elections, some opponents of the bill argued that it would preempt absentee-voting laws in the District of Columbia and at least twenty-two states.

On April 14, 2008, the House Committee on House Administration filed a report on this bill. The first page of the report is shown in the box. After citing the report in full in footnote 20, your paper cites a law-review article on absentee voting in footnote 21. Footnote 22 cites page 11 of the report. Which of the following citations is *the best* for citing page 12 of the report in footnote 23?

a. [23] H.R. Rpt. 110–581 at 12.

b. [23] *H.R. 281, Universal Right to Vote by Mail Act of 2008*, H. Comm. on H. Admin., H. Rpt. 110–581 at 12.

c. [23] H. Rep. 110–581, 110th Cong. 2d Sess., *supra* n. 20, at 12.

d. [23] *Id.* at 12.

110TH CONGRESS 2d Session	HOUSE OF REPRESENTATIVES	REPORT 110–581

UNIVERSAL RIGHT TO VOTE BY MAIL ACT OF 2008

APRIL 14, 2008.—Committed to the Committee of the Whole House on the State of the Union and ordered to be printed

Mr. BRADY of Pennsylvania, from the Committee on House Administration, submitted the following

R E P O R T

together with

MINORITY VIEWS

[To accompany H.R. 281]

[Including cost estimate of the Congressional Budget Office]

The Committee on House Administration, to whom was referred the bill (H.R. 281) to amend the Help America Vote Act of 2002 to allow all eligible voters to vote by mail in Federal elections, having considered the same, report favorably thereon with an amendment and recommend that the bill as amended do pass.

The amendment is as follows:

Strike all after the enacting clause and insert the following:

SECTION 1. SHORT TITLE.

This Act may be cited as the "Universal Right to Vote by Mail Act of 2008".

7-D.4. On January 21, 2009, the United States Senate Committee on Commerce, Science, and Transportation of the One Hundred Eleventh Congress conducted a hearing to consider the nomination of Ray LaHood to be Secretary of the Department of Transportation. The transcript of the hearing contains Mr. LaHood's statement to the Committee at pages 29–30. You are writing an article about members of the Obama Cabinet. You cite this hearing in full in footnote 76. The next time you cite the hearing is in footnote 81, referring to page 30. Which of the following citations is *the best* to use in footnote 81?

a. [81] *Id.* at 30.

b. [81] Sen. Comm. on Com., Sci. & Transp., 111th Cong. at 30.

c. [81] Sen. Comm. on Com., Sci. & Transp., *supra* n. 76, at 30.

d. [81] Sen. Comm. on Com., Sci. & Transp., *supra* n. 81, at 30.

7-D.5. A concurrent resolution introduced during the One Hundred Fourth Congress called for the convening of a "National Silver Haired Congress" with senior-citizen representation from every state. Senate Concurrent Resolution 52 was introduced by Senator Barbara Mikulski on April 17, 1996, and referred to the Committee on Labor and Human Resources. That committee issued a brief report, the opening of which is shown in the box. You are writing a paper discussing this legislation. Footnote 7 cites the resolution in full and the report in full in a single citation sentence. Footnote 8 cites page 2 of the report alone. Which of the following short-form citations is *the best* to use in footnote 8?

a. [8] *Id.* at 2.
b. [8] Sen. Rpt. 104–345 at 2.
c. [8] Sen. Comm. Print 104–345 at 2.
d. [8] Sen. Rpt. 104–345, at 2 (July 31, 1996).

104TH CONGRESS 2d Session	SENATE	Calendar No. 554 REPORT 104–345

RECOGNIZING AND ENCOURAGING THE CONVENING OF A NATIONAL SILVER HAIRED CONGRESS

JULY 31, 1996.—Ordered to be printed

Mrs. KASSEBAUM, from the Committee on Labor and Human Resources, submitted the following

REPORT

[To accompany S. Con. Res. 52]

The Committee on Labor and Human Resources, to which was referred the concurrent resolution (S. Con. Res. 52) to recognize and encourage the convening of a National Silver Haired Congress, having considered the same, reports favorably thereon without amendment and recommends that the concurrent resolution do pass.

7-D.6. Write a short-form citation to page S7463 in the daily edition of the Congressional Record volume shown below. Do not use *id.*

Congressional Record

United States of America

PROCEEDINGS AND DEBATES OF THE *109th* CONGRESS, SECOND SESSION

Vol. 152	WASHINGTON, THURSDAY, JULY 13, 2006	No. 91

Senate

7-D.7–12. Write the full citations—or if appropriate, short-form citations—for the state legislative materials cited in the footnotes from this article excerpt.

- **Citation A:** Nevada Assembly Bill 150, 75th Regular Session, introduced February 10, 2009
- **Citation B:** Nevada Assembly Bill 391, 75th Regular Session, introduced March 16, 2009

Although tanning-bed legislation has recently passed in other states,[1] not even blistering debate convinced lawmakers in Nevada to screen teens from their own poor judgment. Two burning pieces of legislation were introduced in that state in 2009, but neither passed before the legislature adjourned. Assembly Bill 150 would have set specific age and training guidelines for operators of "tanning equipment."[2] Assembly Bill 391, in contrast, set out minimum ages for operators and users of such equipment.[3] Despite this difference, the two bills defined "tanning equipment" in the same way, as "any device that emits ultraviolet radiation to tan human skin, including, without limitation, sunlamps, tanning booths and tanning beds."[4] In addition to its regulatory aspect, Assembly Bill 150 would have required parental consent for anyone under the age of 18 to visit a tanning establishment.[5] Assembly Bill 391, however, was even more age-restrictive, requiring parental consent for those under the age of 16,[6] and restricting those under age 14 from using such equipment unless they obtained written authorization from a physician.[7]

---

[1] *See e.g.* 2009 Ark. Acts 707.

[2] [7-D.7. **Citation A, section 14.**]

[3] [7-D.8. **Citation B.**]

[4] [7-D.9. **Citation A, section 5; Citation B, section 4.**]

[5] [7-D.10. **Citation A, section 10.**]

[6] [7-D.11. **Citation B, section 8.**]

[7] [7-D.12. **Citation B, section 9.**]

CHAPTER

ADMINISTRATIVE AND EXECUTIVE

MATERIALS

When it comes to dealing with the executive branch of government and its administrative agencies, you may need to negotiate with (or fight against) these agencies on a client's behalf, or you may work for an agency. The sources of law issued by the executive branch are not often the focus of attention in the first year of law school, yet these sources reveal the operation of government, primarily through the regulatory and adjudicative functions of the executive branch's administrative agencies, whether state or federal, and also through the opinions, orders, and proclamations of executive officials.

This chapter addresses full and short citations to sources published in the Code of Federal Regulations and the Federal Register, including current and proposed regulations, rules, and notices, and it provides exercises for both federal and state administrative codes, rules, and registers. The chapter also addresses other administrative and executive materials, such as federal and state agencies' written decisions and opinion letters; advisory opinions issued by members of the executive branch, such as attorneys general; and of course, orders, proclamations, and other documents issued by the chief executive officer, the President of the United States, or the governor of a state.

A. FEDERAL REGULATIONS

When Congress enacts legislation (whether singly or as part of a more comprehensive scheme of related acts), it often delegates the details for carrying out the legislation's goals to federal administrative agencies. For example, when the Family Smoking Prevention and Tobacco

Control Act was signed into law in June 2009, provisions of the Act not only gave the Food and Drug Administration the authority to regulate the levels of nicotine in tobacco products, but they also authorized the agency to develop rules for labeling those products, including the placement of warning labels. Each step of the rule-making process—from initial notice of proposed rules for regulating tobacco, invitations for comments, final rules, and the ultimate codification of those rules—is being published and made available for researchers' study.

Regulations promulgated by federal agencies are organized by subject in the fifty titles of the Code of Federal Regulations (abbreviated as "C.F.R."). Those titles roughly correspond (but do not exactly match) the fifty titles of the United States Code. The C.F.R. is published annually in paperbound volumes, as well as in an official online version through the Government Printing Office's *GPO Access* Web site, at http://www.gpoaccess.gov/CFR/.

Full citations for print and official electronic versions are similar. If the rule or regulation in the C.F.R. has been given a descriptive title, you may use it in the citation. If you elect to do so, put that title at the beginning of the citation in ordinary typeface. See the example in Rule 19.1(e). Otherwise, begin the full citation with the title number, followed by the abbreviation for C.F.R., a pinpoint reference, and a date parenthetical, also rendered in ordinary typeface. Note that the word "title" is used both to refer to the name given to a particular regulation and to the organizational grouping of regulations in a subject area (e.g., Title 7, Agriculture).

Indicate a pinpoint reference to the smallest applicable subdivision of the C.F.R. that you are citing (e.g., a chapter, a part, one or more sections, an appendix). As the Government Printing Office explains,

> Each title is divided into chapters, which usually bear the name of the issuing agency. Each chapter is further subdivided into parts that cover specific regulatory areas. Large parts may be subdivided into subparts. All parts are organized in sections, and most citations in the CFR are provided at the section level.[1]

Use the numbering as shown in the C.F.R. material you are citing (e.g., Roman numerals for chapters, Arabic numbers for parts and sections), as shown in Rule 19.1(c) and its examples. Consult Rules 5.0, 6.0, and 9.0, and Appendix 3(C), Subdivisions, for additional help with pinpoint references to certain types of subdivisions.

End the citation with a parenthetical reference to the year of the edition in which the regulation appears. Ordinarily, you should cite the year of the current edition. Check dates carefully. One-fourth of the titles in the C.F.R. are revised and reprinted each quarter. By the end of the calendar year, the entire C.F.R. will have been updated (e.g., titles 1–16 revised as of January 1 each year; titles 17–27 revised as of April 1; and so forth). Do not assume, for example, that just because title 7 uses the current year's date, title 42 has also been updated from the previous year's edition. If you need to cite a historic version of a rule or regulation, use the date of the edition in which that version appears.

In the official electronic version of the C.F.R., look for the title number and year in the upper corner of even-numbered pages, as shown here. If your source is an unofficial electronic database, modify the date parenthetical by adding an abbreviation for the database provider (LEXIS, WL, or GPO e-CFR), and provide the exact date through which the database is current, as shown in the examples under Rule 19.1(d).

12 CFR Ch. IX (1–1–09 Edition)

---

[1] GPO Access, *Code of Federal Regulations: About*, http://www.gpoaccess.gov/cfr/about.html (last updated Jan. 5, 2010).

EXERCISE SET 8-A

BASIC LEVEL: FEDERAL REGULATIONS

Before beginning Exercise Set 8-A Basic Level, review the following and keep the *Manual* at hand as you work through the exercises:

- Rule 19.1, Full Citation Format for Code of Federal Regulations
- Sidebar 19.1, Determining the Date of Current C.F.R. Volumes

To complete the exercises, you may also need to refer to the following:

- Rule 6.0, Citing Sections and Paragraphs
- Rule 9.3, Citing Other Subdivisions
- Appendix 3(C), Subdivisions

8-A.1. In conducting research for a paper on federal assistance to victims of natural disasters, you find a case discussing a relevant federal regulation: "FEMA is explicitly authorized to 'provide . . . direct assistance . . . to respond to the disaster-related housing needs . . . .' 44 CFR § 206.117(a)." At the time of your research, the current version of this regulation was in the October 1, 2009, print edition of the Code of Federal Regulations. Choose the correct full citation to this regulation.

    a. 44 CFR § 206.117(a).
    b. C.F.R. tit. 44, § 206.117(a) (2009).
    c. 44 C. F. R. § 206.117(a) (Oct. 1, 2009).
    d. 44 C.F.R. § 206.117(a) (2009).

8-A.2. The Federal Election Commission defines relevant terms relating to the Presidential Election Campaign Fund in part 9002 of title 11 of the Code of Federal Regulations. Choose the correct full citation to this part in the January 1, 2010, official electronic edition.

    a. C.F.R. tit. 11, § 9002 (2010).
    b. 11 C.F.R. Part 9002 (Jan. 1, 2010).
    c. 11 CFR 9002 (2010).
    d. 11 C.F.R. pt. 9002 (2010).

8-A.3. You are using Westlaw to research regulations concerning the jewelry industry. The Federal Trade Commission distinguishes between a "pearl," a "cultured pearl," and an "imitation pearl." The definition of "cultured pearl" is set out in title 16 of the Code of Federal Regulations, in section 23.18, subsection (b). Westlaw displayed the information shown below at the time of your research. Choose the correct full citation to the Westlaw version of the regulation.

> 16 C. F. R. § 23.18, 16 CFR § 23.18
> Current through March 25, 2010; 75 FR 14360

    a. 16 C.F.R. 23.18(b) (WL 2010).
    b. 16 CFR § 23.18(b) (current through Mar. 25, 2010; 75 FR 14360).
    c. 16 C. F. R. § 23.28(b) (Mar. 25, 2010).
    d. 16 C.F.R. § 23.28(b) (WL current through Mar. 25, 2010).

EXERCISE SET 8-A

INTERMEDIATE LEVEL: FEDERAL REGULATIONS

Before beginning Exercise Set 8-A Intermediate Level, review the following and keep the *Manual* at hand as you work through the exercises:

• Rule 19.1, Full Citation Format for Code of Federal Regulations
• Sidebar 19.1, Determining the Date of Current C.F.R. Volumes

To complete the exercises, you may also need to refer to the following:

• Rule 6.0, Citing Sections and Paragraphs   • Appendix 3(C), Subdivisions
• Rule 9.3, Citing Other Subdivisions

8-A.4. Title 23 of the Code of Federal Regulations governs highways, and within part 1235 of that title, regulates a uniform system for parking for persons with disabilities. In a report, you are citing the full text of three regulations that deal with displays on automobiles: section 1235.3, special license plates; section 1235.4, removable windshield placards; and section 1235.5, temporary removable windshield placards. These regulations appear on pages 514–515 of the 2009 print edition. Choose the correct full citation to this edition.

  a. 23 C.F.R. §§ 1235.3–1235.5 (2009).
  b. 23 CFR § 1235.3, § 1235.4, § 1235.5 (2009).
  c. 23 CFR §§ 1235.3–1235.5, at 514–515 (2009).
  d. 23 C.F.R. pt. 1235, §§ 1235.3–35.5 (2009).

8-A.5. Prescription drug advertisements are regulated by the Food and Drug Administration in the section of the Code of Federal Regulations whose header from the official electronic edition is shown below. Choose the correct full citation to this section and edition.

> **§ 202.1**   **21 CFR Ch. I (4–1–09 Edition)**

  a. 21 CFR Ch. I § 202.1 (4-1-09 ed.)
  b. 21 C.F.R. ch. I, § 202.1 (Apr. 1, 2009).
  c. 21 C.F.R. § 202.1 (2009).
  d. 21 CFR § 202.1 (2009).

8-A.6. Federal regulations relating to the National Aeronautics and Space Administration appear in title 14, chapter V of the Code of Federal Regulations. You are writing about development of the space shuttle program, and for historical support, you wish to cite the January 1, 1999, official print version of section 1214.702, which addresses the space shuttle commander's authority and responsibilities. Choose the correct full citation to this section and edition.

  a. 14 C. F. R. ch. V, § 1214.702 (1999).
  b. 14 C.F.R. § 1214.702 (1999).
  c. 14 C.F.R. ch. 5, § 1214.702 (Jan. 1, 1999).
  d. 14 CFR § 1214.702 (1999).

EXERCISE SET 8-A

EXPERT LEVEL: FEDERAL REGULATIONS

Before beginning Exercise Set 8-A Expert Level, review the following and keep the *Manual* at hand as you work through the exercises:

* Rule 19.1, Full Citation Format for Code of Federal Regulations
* Sidebar 19.1, Determining the Date of Current C.F.R. Volumes

To complete the exercises, you may also need to refer to the following:

* Rule 6.0, Citing Sections and Paragraphs
* Appendix 3(C), Subdivisions

8-A.7. Write the full citation for the official electronic version of the federal regulation governing "stolen or lost firearms" shown at right.

| §479.141 | 27 CFR Ch. II (4-1-09 Edition) |

Subpart J—Stolen or Lost Firearms or Documents

§ 479.141 Stolen or lost firearms.

Whenever any registered firearm is stolen or lost, the person losing possession thereof will, immediately upon discovery of such theft or loss, make a report to the Director showing the following:

(a) Name and address of the person in whose name the firearm is registered, (b) kind of firearm, (c) serial number, (d) model, (e) caliber, (f) manufacturer of the firearm, (g) date and place of theft or loss, and (h) complete statement of facts and circumstances surrounding such theft or loss.

8-A.8. You used the e-CFR on *GPO Access* to research the authority of the Secretary of Homeland Security, which is addressed in title 8, chapter 1, subchapter A, part 2, section 2.1. At the time of your research, the e-CFR home page stated that "e-CFR Data is current as of April 6, 2010." Write the full citation for this regulation.

B. PROPOSED FEDERAL REGULATIONS, RULES, AND NOTICES

As your legal research textbook no doubt explains in greater detail, you should be careful to update your research in the C.F.R. by checking for new or amended rules in the Federal Register. The Federal Register, an official news publication published on weekdays by the National Archives and Records Administration, advises researchers on a wide range of administrative documents, including notices of public meetings, proposed rulemaking, and final rules. Cite the Federal Register for final regulations that have not yet been published in the C.F.R. and also for proposed rules and administrative notices.[2]

You can find the print version of the Federal Register in law libraries, but you can also access an official online version at http://www.gpoaccess.gov/fr/. The online version contains both the current Federal Register and older volumes dating back to 1994. Unofficial online versions are available on Westlaw, LexisNexis, and HeinOnline.

Rule 19.3 displays the five components of a full citation to the Federal Register. Cite the print version and official online version in the same manner. The title of the rule or regulation is optional, but if you include it, place it first in ordinary typeface as explained in Rule 19.3(f). Next, provide the volume number, which is displayed on the cover of the print version, and at the top of each page, as shown below.

3706   Federal Register / Vol. 72, No. 17 / Friday, January 26, 2007 / Rules and Regulations

---

Ignore the issue number. Abbreviate Federal Register as "Fed. Reg.," and insert the initial page for the material cited. If possible, add a pinpoint page reference. Because the Federal Register is a daily publication, use the exact date in the date parenthetical, e.g., 72 Fed. Reg. 3706 (Jan. 26, 2007).

Pay attention to the way the administrative material is labeled in its Federal Register synopsis. The example at right shows a *final rule*. When you cite a proposed rule, however, note that Rule 19.3(d) requires the word "proposed" to be inserted in the date parenthetical.

Finally, if a proposed rule or regulation indicates that it will appear in the C.F.R., Rule 19.3(e) requires that you add a second parenthetical to the citation, containing a "to be codified" reference to the C.F.R., indicating the C.F.R. chapter, part, or section affected.

DEPARTMENT OF THE INTERIOR

Fish and Wildlife Service

50 CFR Part 14

[FWS–R9–LE–2008–0024; 99011–1224–0000–9B]

RIN 1018–AV31

Importation, Exportation, and Transportation of Wildlife; Inspection Fees, Import/Export Licenses, and Import/Export License Exemptions

AGENCY: Fish and Wildlife Service, Interior.

ACTION: Final rule

---

[2] Executive Orders, treated later in this chapter in section E, are also published in the Federal Register.

EXERCISE SET 8-B

BASIC LEVEL: PROPOSED FEDERAL REGULATIONS, RULES, AND NOTICES

Before beginning Exercise Set 8-B Basic Level, review the following and keep the *Manual* at hand as you work through the exercises:

• Rule 19.3, Full Citation Format for Federal Register

To complete the exercises, you may also need to refer to the following:

• Rule 5.0, Page and Location Numbers   • Appendix 3(C), Subdivisions

8-B.1. On July 24, 2009, the Federal Motor Carrier Safety Administration of the United States Department of Transportation published a notice that certain Japanese citizens holding commercial driver's licenses would be permitted to drive Isuzu test vehicles in the United States without obtaining an equivalent United States license. The notice was published in its entirety in volume 74 of the Federal Register on page 36809. Choose the correct full citation to this notice.

    a. 74 F. Reg. 36809 (2009).

    b. 74 Fed. Reg. 36809, 36809 (July 24, 2009).

    c. 74 FR 36809, 36809 (2009).

    d. Fed. Reg. vol. 74, at 36809 (July 24, 2009).

8-B.2. The United States Fish and Wildlife Service recently proposed a rule designating "critical habitat" for the Oregon Chub, a fish that has been on the endangered species list since 1993. Choose the correct full citation with pinpoint reference to page 10430 from the issue of the Federal Register shown below.

10412	Federal Register / Vol. 74, No. 45 / Tuesday, March 10, 2009 / Proposed Rules

DEPARTMENT OF THE INTERIOR

Fish and Wildlife Service

50 CFR Part 17

[FWS–R1–ES–2009–0010; 92210–1117–000–B4]

RIN 1018–AV87

Endangered and Threatened Wildlife and Plants; Designation of Critical Habitat for the Oregon Chub (Oregonichthys crameri)

AGENCY: Fish and Wildlife Service, Interior.

ACTION: Proposed rule.

Public Comments

We intend that any final action resulting from this proposal will be as accurate and as effective as possible. Therefore, we request comments or suggestions on this proposed rule. We particularly seek comments concerning:

1. The reasons why we should or should not designate habitat as "critical habitat" under section 4 of the Act (16 U.S.C. 1531 *et seq.*), including whether there are threats to the species from human activity, the degree of which can be expected to increase due to the designation, and whether the benefit of designation would outweigh threats to the species caused by the designation, such that the designation of critical habitat is prudent.

comment—including any personal identifying information—will be posted on the Web site. If you submit a hardcopy comment that includes personal identifying information, you may request at the top of your document that we withhold this information from public review. However, we cannot guarantee that we will be able to do so. We will post all hardcopy comments on *http://www.regulations.gov.*

Comments and materials we receive, as well as supporting documentation we used in preparing this proposed rule, will be available for public inspection at *http://www.regulations.gov*, or by appointment, during normal business hours, at the U.S. Fish and Wildlife Service, Oregon Fish and Wildlife Office

    a. Fed. Reg. vol. 74, No. 45, at 10430 (March 10, 2009) (to be codified at 50 C.F.R. pt. 17).

    b. 74 FR 10412, 10430 (proposed Mar. 10, 2009) (to be codified at 50 C.F.R. pt. 17).

    c. 74 Fed. Reg. 10412, 10430 (proposed Mar. 10, 2009) (to be codified at 50 C.F.R. pt. 17).

    d. Endangered and Threatened Wildlife and Plants; Designation of Critical Habitat for the Oregon Chub (Oregonichthys crameri), 74 Fed. Reg. 10412, 10430 (March 10, 2009) (to be codified at 50 C.F.R. pt. 17).

EXERCISE SET 8-B

INTERMEDIATE LEVEL: PROPOSED FEDERAL REGULATIONS, RULES, AND NOTICES

Before beginning Exercise Set 8-B Intermediate Level, review the following and keep the *Manual* at hand as you work through the exercises:

• Rule 19.3, Full Citation Format for Federal Register

To complete the exercises, you may also need to refer to the following:

• Rule 5.0, Page and Location Numbers
• Sidebar 5.2, Using Hyphens, En Dashes, and "to" for Spans
• Appendix 3(C), Subdivisions

8-B.3. On September 15, 2008, the Department of Agriculture's Food and Nutrition Service published a notice in the Federal Register inviting comments on the School Breakfast Program. The notice appeared in Volume 73, beginning and ending on page 53188. Choose the correct full citation.

   a. 73 Fed. Reg. 53188 (2008).
   b. Notice, 73 Fed. Reg. 53188, 53188 (Sept. 15, 2008).
   c. 73 FR 53188, 53188 (September 15, 2008).
   d. Notice, Fed. Reg. vol. 73, at 53188 (Sept. 15, 2008).

8-B.4. When the Coast Guard amended a rule governing crewmember identification on certain vessels, it published the final rule (affecting 33 C.F.R. part 160) on April 29, 2009, in volume 74 of the Federal Register, beginning on page 19135. Choose the correct full citation to pages 19140–19141 of the rule.

   a. Crewmember Identification Documents, 74 Fed. Reg. 19135, 19140–19141 (Apr. 29, 2009) (to be codified at 33 C.F.R. pt. 160).
   b. *Crewmember Identification Documents*, 74 Fed. Reg. 19135, 19140–19141 (2009) (to be codified at 33 C.F.R. pt. 160).
   c. *Crewmember Identification Documents*, 74 FR 19140–19141 (April 29, 2009) (amending 33 C.F.R. pt. 160).
   d. Crewmember Identification Documents, 74 Fed. Reg. at 19140–19141 (2009) (amending 33 C.F.R. pt. 160).

8-B.5. The Alcohol and Tobacco Tax and Trade Bureau, a branch of the Department of the Treasury, proposed a regulation governing allergen labeling for certain alcoholic beverages. It published notice, as shown at right, in the July 26, 2006, issue of the Federal Register, volume 71, on pages 42329 through 42344. Choose the correct full citation.

   a. 71 Fed. Reg. 42329, 42329–44 (July 26, 2006).
   b. Fed. Reg., Vol. 71, No. 143 (July 26, 2006), at 42329.
   c. Major Food Allergen Labeling for Wines, Distilled Spirits and Malt Beverages, 71 FR 42329, 42329–42344 (proposed July 26, 2006).
   d. Major Food Allergen Labeling for Wines, Distilled Spirits and Malt Beverages, 71 F.R. 42329, 42329–42344 (July 26, 2006) (to be codified at 27 C.F.R. Parts 4, 5 & 7).

> **DEPARTMENT OF THE TREASURY**
>
> **Alcohol and Tobacco Tax and Trade Bureau**
>
> **27 CFR Parts 4, 5, and 7**
>
> **[Notice No. 62]**
>
> **RIN 1513–AB08**
>
> **Major Food Allergen Labeling for Wines, Distilled Spirits and Malt Beverages**
>
> **AGENCY:** Alcohol and Tobacco Tax and Trade Bureau, Treasury.
>
> **ACTION:** Notice of proposed rulemaking; solicitation of comments.

EXERCISE SET 8-B

EXPERT LEVEL: PROPOSED FEDERAL REGULATIONS, RULES, AND NOTICES

Before beginning Exercise Set 8-B Expert Level, review the following and keep the *Manual* at hand as you work through the exercises:

• Rule 19.3, Full Citation Format for Federal Register

To complete the exercises, you may also need to refer to the following:

• Rule 5.0, Page and Location Numbers
• Sidebar 5.2, Using Hyphens, En Dashes, and "to" for Spans
• Appendix 3(C), Subdivisions

8-B.6. On March 9, 2009, the Financial Crimes Enforcement Network of the U.S. Department of the Treasury issued proposed rules regarding the confidentiality of a report of suspicious activity. The proposed rules are published in volume 74 of the Federal Register, beginning at page 10148. These rules, if adopted, will be codified in Title 31, Part 103, of the Code of Federal Regulations. Write the correct full citation to the proposed rules.

8-B.7. The Food and Drug Administration notice shown below comes from the official online edition of the Federal Register. Write the full citation to the notice, but omit the title.

31038   Federal Register / Vol. 74, No. 123 / Monday, June 29, 2009 / Notices

---

Dated: June 18, 2009.
Maryam I. Daneshvar,
Acting Reports Clearance Officer, Centers for Disease Control and Prevention.
[FR Doc. E9–15254 Filed 6–26–09; 8:45 am]
BILLING CODE P

DEPARTMENT OF HEALTH AND HUMAN SERVICES

Food and Drug Administration

[Docket No. FDA–2009–D–0271]

Draft Guidance for Industry on Measures to Address the Risk for Contamination by Salmonella Species in Food Containing a Pistachio-Derived Product as an Ingredient; Availability

AGENCY: Food and Drug Administration, HHS.
ACTION: Notice.

SUMMARY: The Food and Drug Administration (FDA) is announcing the availability of a draft guidance for industry entitled "Guidance for

FOR FURTHER INFORMATION CONTACT: Michael E. Kashtock, Center for Food Safety and Applied Nutrition (HFS–317), Food and Drug Administration, 5100 Paint Branch Pkwy., College Park, MD 20740, 301–436–2022.
SUPPLEMENTARY INFORMATION:

I. Background

FDA is announcing the availability of a draft guidance for industry entitled "Guidance for Industry: Measures to Address the Risk for Contamination by *Salmonella* Species in Food Containing a Pistachio-Derived Product as an Ingredient." This draft guidance is intended to clarify for manufacturers who produce foods containing a pistachio-derived product as an ingredient that there is a risk that *Salmonella* species (spp.) may be present in the incoming pistachio-derived product, and to recommend measures to address that risk. Pistachio-derived products include roasted in-shell pistachios and shelled pistachios (also called kernels) that are roasted or

of Dockets Management
and 4 p.m., Monday thr

III. Electronic Access

Persons with access t
may obtain the docume
www.regulations.gov or
www.fda.gov/FoodGuid

IV. Reference

The following referen
placed on display in th
Dockets Management (F
and Drug Administratio
Lane, rm. 1061, Rockvil
and may be seen by inte
between 9 a.m. and 4 p.
through Friday.
1. FDA, 2009, Pistachio
Salmonella, updated April

Dated: June 18, 2009.
Jeffrey Shuren,
Associate Commissioner fo Planning.
[FR Doc. E9–15202 Filed 6
BILLING CODE 4160–01–S

8-B.8. Write the correct full citation to the federal agency's notice shown below with the running head from the page on which it was published.

13436   Federal Register/Vol. 75, No. 54/Monday, March 22, 2010/Rules and Regulations

ENVIRONMENTAL PROTECTION AGENCY

40 CFR Parts 52 and 81

[EPA–R10–OAR–2008–0690; FRL–9091–5]

Approval and Promulgation of State Implementation Plans: Alaska

AGENCY: Environmental Protection Agency (EPA).

ACTION: Final rule.

C. STATE ADMINISTRATIVE CODES, RULES, AND REGISTERS

State governments have administrative agencies similar to those of the United States government, regulating a wide range of programs affecting public works and the public interest, such as administering health and human services programs, operating prisons, regulating the sales of alcoholic beverages, operating state lotteries, constructing and maintaining state highways, and collecting taxes.

Although state agencies promulgate rules or regulations much as federal agencies do, not all states codify their regulations, nor do they all publish these materials in a multi-volume compilation analogous to the Code of Federal Regulations. Many states publish their administrative materials online, although presently only a few states' online versions are deemed official.

Because the names and citation formats of state administrative codes vary widely, Rule 20 provides only general guidance to full citations of these materials. To locate the name of (and abbreviation for) a state's administrative compilation, look for the state's entry in Appendix 1. Just as it does for state statutes, Appendix 1 provides a template for citing a state's administrative rules or regulations. In addition, you may refer to Rule 19.1 as guidance for citing state materials.

Many states publish administrative registers similar in function to the Federal Register, although such registers typically are published on a more infrequent basis. Each state's administrative register, if it has one, is shown in the jurisdiction's entry in Appendix 1. Follow the format shown there for citing the state register, or if needed, analogize to Rule 19.3.

The exercises in this section are for all levels.

EXERCISE SET 8-C

ALL LEVELS: STATE ADMINISTRATIVE CODES, RULES, AND REGISTERS

Before beginning Exercise Set 8-C All Levels, review the following and keep the *Manual* at hand as you work through the exercises:

• Rule 20.1, Full Citation [Format] for State Administrative Codes
• Rule 20.3, Full Citation Format for State Administrative Registers
• Rule 38.1, Source Available in Print and Electronic Formats

Be prepared to consult Appendix 1, Primary Sources by Jurisdiction, for templates for state administrative materials.

8-C.1. When Betsy L. Child, Commissioner of the Tennessee Department of Environment and Conservation, issued emergency rules governing "clandestine drug manufacturing sites," she also issued a "Statement of Necessity" justifying their promulgation. The statement was published in Volume 30, Number 9 of the Tennessee Administrative Register on September 15, 2004, pages 19–20. Choose the correct full citation to the statement.

    a. 30 TAR 19–20 (Sept. 15, 2004).
    b. Tenn. Admin. Reg. vol. 30, at 19–20 (2004).
    c. 30 Tenn. Admin. Register 19–20 (Sept. 2004).
    d. 30 Tenn. Admin. Reg. 19–20 (Sept. 15, 2004).

8-C.2. The Utah Board of Pardons imposes certain requirements on news media attending its meetings, including the method of selection of those in attendance and the photographic, recording, or transmitting equipment they may use. These requirements are set out in Rules 671-302.1 through 671-302.9 of the Utah Administrative Code. These rules, which were adopted on November 21, 2002, are published in an official online version dated April 1, 2009. Choose the correct full citation to these rules.

    a. Utah Bd. Pardons §§ 671-302.1–671-302.9 (Nov. 21, 2002).
    b. Utah Admin. Code §§ 671-302.1 to 671-302.9 (Apr. 1, 2009).
    c. Utah Admin. Code r. 671-302.1 to 671-302.9 (Apr. 1, 2009).
    d. Utah Admin. Code R. 671-302.1 to 671-302.9 (2009).

8-C.3. At the time of your research, the Indiana Administrative Code was available in a 2009 edition. Within provisions for the "State Ethics Commission" in title 40, article 2, "State Officers and Employees," the definition of "conflict of interest" appears in section 4, subsection (g). Write the full citation for this definition.

8-C.4. You used LexisNexis to locate a California regulation setting out the procedure to follow when a state agency requests an administrative hearing. The regulation appears in title 1, section 1018 of Barclays Official California Code of Regulation. The LEXIS database indicated it was current through "Register 2010, No. 12, March 19, 2010." Write the full citation for the regulation.

D.   AGENCY DECISIONS

Many federal and state administrative agencies are charged with quasi-judicial responsibilities to resolve disputes over matters regulated by the agency. The decisions made by an agency's administrative law judge, or by an administrative board or commission, may be written up in opinion form much as cases in the judicial system are resolved and explained in written opinions.

Agency decisions appear in a variety of sources. The United States Government Printing Office publishes the official decisions of many federal agencies in hefty bound volumes such as the Reports of the Interstate Commerce Commission and the Decisions and Reports of the Securities and Exchange Commission, but there is no standardized series similar to the collection of decisions in the judicial case reporters you know so well. Many such decisions may also be accessed in unofficial versions through specialized looseleaf services and reporters,[3] or through electronic media publishers such as HeinOnline (e.g., United States Federal Agency Documents, Decisions, and Appeals collection, in PDF format), or in subject-matter databases in LexisNexis and Westlaw. In recent years, many federal and state agencies have also begun to make their decisions freely available on the Internet.

Rule 19.5 displays the components of a full citation to a federal agency decision, and Rule 20.5 does the same for state agency decisions, analogizing to the federal rule but adding the state abbreviation to the agency's name. Because an administrative adjudication is similar to a case decided in the courts, follow the guidance of Rule 12.2 for case names and Rule 12.7 for dates.

Appendix 8 lists major official federal administration publications and the abbreviations you should use in citing them. Although you should use Appendix 3 for abbreviating words in case names and abbreviating the name of the agency rendering the decision, do not use it for abbreviating the name of an administrative publication unless the publication is *not listed* in Appendix 8.

If you are citing an electronic source for the decision, analogize the citation to Rule 12.12, Cases Published Only on LexisNexis or Westlaw; Rule 12.15, Cases on the Internet; or Rule 40, World Wide Web Sites, according to the source being used.

The exercises in this section are for all levels.

---

[3] For additional information on citing administrative decisions published in looseleaf services, see Rule 28.

EXERCISE SET 8-D

ALL LEVELS: AGENCY DECISIONS

Before beginning Exercise Set 8-D Intermediate Level, review the following and keep the *Manual* at hand as you work through the exercises:

- Rule 19.5, Full Citation Format for Federal Agency Decisions
- Rule 20.5, Full Citation Format for State Agency Decisions
- Rule 38.1, Source Available in Print and Electronic Formats

To complete the exercises, you may also need to refer to the following:

- Rule 5.0, Page and Location Numbers
- Rule 6.0, Citing Sections and Paragraphs
- Rule 9.0, Graphical Material, Appendices, and Other Subdivisions
- Rule 12.2, Case Name
- Rule 12.7, Date
- Sidebar 12.3, Explanation of Commonly Used Procedural Phrases

Be prepared to consult Appendix 3, General Abbreviations, and Appendix 8, Selected Official Federal Administrative Publications, for certain questions.

8-D.1. The Securities and Exchange Commission issued an opinion permanently barring the subject shown in the caption at right from any association with the securities industry. The opinion was published in volume 54 of the United States Securities and Exchange Commission Decisions and Reports, beginning at page 25. Choose the correct full citation to this agency decision.

> IN THE MATTER OF
>
> **TED HAROLD WESTERFIELD**
>
> *File No. 3-9355. Promulgated March 1, 1999*
>
> Securities Exchange Act of 1934
>
> **OPINION OF THE COMMISSION**

    a. *In re Westerfield*, 54 SEC 25 (Sec. & Exch. Commn. 1999).

    b. *In the Matter of Westerfield*, 54 S.E.C. 25 (1999).

    c. *SEC v. Westerfield*, 54 U.S. Secs. & Exch. Commn. Decs. & Rpts. 25 (S.E.C. 1999).

    d. *Sec. & Exch. Commn. v. Westerfield*, United States Securities and Exchange Commission Decisions and Reports, vol. 54, at 25 (Sec. & Exch. Commn. Mar. 1, 1999).

8-D.2. You represent a client in deportation proceedings before the federal Board of Immigration Appeals, where you seek to overturn the immigration judge's decision to deport her to her home country. In your brief to the Board, you wish to cite one of its decisions, captioned as "*Matter of Sosa-Hernandez*," which contains useful precedent for your argument. The decision was handed down on November 12, 1993. It was published in volume 20 of Administrative Decisions under Immigration and Nationality Laws, beginning at page 758. Your brief refers to specific material on page 763. Choose the correct full citation to this agency decision.

    a. *Matter of Sosa-Hernandez*, 20 I & N Dec. 758, 763 (BIA 1993).

    b. *Matter of Sosa-Hernandez*, 20 I&N Decs. 758, 763 (BIA Nov. 12, 1993).

    c. *In re Sosa-Hernandez*, 20 I. & N. Dec. 758, 763 (Bd. Immig. Apps. 1993).

    d. *In re Sosa-Hernandez*, 20 Admin. Decs. Immig. & Nationality Ls. 758, 763 (Bd. Immig. Apps. 1993).

8-D.3. You are writing an article for a specialty journal concerning recent environmental agency decisions from around the country. You found one such decision on Westlaw, displaying the caption shown below. Choose the correct full citation to the agency decision.

2009 WL 1684914 (Tex. Com. Env. Qual.)
Texas Commission on Environmental Quality
State of Texas
*1 IN THE MATTER OF AN ENFORCEMENT ACTION CONCERNING
WEST HOUSTON AIRPORT CORPORATION
Docket No. 2007-1726-MWD-E
RN102096633
June 12, 2009
AGREED ORDER

a. *In the Matter of Enforcement Action re West Houston Airport Corp.*, No. 2007-1726-MWD-E (Tex. Com. June 12, 2009).

b. *In the Matter of Enforcement Action concerning W. Houston Airport Corp.*, 2009 WL 1684914 (Tex. Com. Env. Qual. June 12, 2009).

c. *In re Enforcement Action concerning W. Houston Airport Corp.*, 2009 WL 1684914 (Tex. Commn. Envtl. Quality June 12, 2009).

d. *In re Enforcement Action concerning West Houston Airport Corp.*, 2009 WL 1684914 (Tex. Comm. Envtl. Qual. 2009).

8-D.4. You used the Minnesota Workers' Compensation Administrative Decisions database on Westlaw (MNWC-ADMIN) to locate a decision issued on May 4, 1992, by the Minnesota Workers' Compensation Court of Appeals involving the claim of Robert T. Przybylski against the Minnesota Department of Transportation. The Westlaw caption is shown below. Write the full citation to the decision.

1992 WL 114987 (Minn.Work.Comp.Ct.App.)
Workers' Compensation Court of Appeals
State of Minnesota
*1 ROBERT T. PRZYBYLSKI, RESPONDENT
v.
MINN. DEPT. OF TRANSPORTATION, SELF–INSURED, APPELLANT
AND
WESTERN LIFE INSURANCE COMPANY,
AND
MEDCENTERS HEALTH PLAN, INTERVENORS
May 4, 1992

8-D.5. Volume 341 of Decisions and Orders of the National Labor Relations Board contains the decision whose caption is shown at right, beginning at page 492. Write the full citation to this decision, with pinpoint reference to pages 497–498.

492   DECISION OF THE NATIONAL

Hewlett Packard Company[1] *and* **United Steel Workers of America, AFL–CIO, CLC.** Case 25–CA–28591

March 29, 2004

DECISION AND ORDER

BY CHAIRMAN BATTISTA AND MEMBERS LIEBMAN AND MEISBURG

E. ADVISORY OPINIONS, EXECUTIVE ORDERS, AND OTHER EXECUTIVE DOCUMENTS

Advisory Opinions

One of the important responsibilities of attorneys general and agency counsel is to render legal opinions on questions of law requested by certain governmental officials. In the federal government, the President and certain officials in the executive branch may request such opinions. The Attorney General is not, however, authorized to deliver opinions to Congress, the Judiciary, foreign governments, or private persons. In state governments, in contrast, officials such as members of the legislature or local government leaders may be authorized to seek such opinions. These advisory opinions are not binding authority, although they may carry considerable persuasive weight; see Sidebar 19.2, Purpose of Attorney General Opinions.

The United States Attorney General also delegates authority to draft these legal opinions to the Office of Legal Counsel, a branch of the Department of Justice. Since 1977, the Government Printing Office has published annual print volumes containing selected Opinions of the Attorney General and Opinions of the Office of Legal Counsel. Opinions dating back to 1992 are also available online, through the *GPO Access* Web site, at http://www.usdoj.gov/olc/opinions.htm, although these are not official versions. The full citation format for the print version of opinions from the United States Attorney General or Office of Legal Counsel is shown in Rule 19.7.

Published opinions of state attorneys general may be found in a variety of sources, including commercial databases such as LexisNexis or Westlaw, state government Web sites, or print publications. For example, opinions of the Arkansas Attorney General are published in their official version in the Arkansas Register, and they are also available in an unofficial online version at http://www.ag.arkansas.gov/opinions/, and in unofficial commercial databases such as LexisNexis and Westlaw. Rule 20.7 supplies the format to use in citing state attorney general opinions. If your source is an online version on the Internet, refer to Rule 40.1, adding a parenthetical showing the Web site address. If the opinion is also published in a state administrative code or register, you may provide a parallel citation to that source.

Executive Documents

Whether the chief executive is the President of the United States or a state governor, he or she is responsible for implementing and enforcing the laws enacted by Congress or the state's legislature. The chief executive appoints the heads of the various departments (e.g., the Departments of Commerce, Defense, or Education, which are further composed of agencies, boards, bureaus, and commissions), and delegates to them the day-to-day operation of government. Even so, the President or a governor may issue specific executive orders or other documents that direct governmental activities or recognize notable events.

In the federal government, the President's executive orders are consecutively numbered, and they are published in two official sources, the Federal Register and the Code of Federal Regulations. The Federal Register is the official daily publication for executive orders, proclamations, and other presidential documents, such as determinations, memoranda, and reorganization plans. Title 3 of the Code of Federal Regulations annually compiles the signed Presidential documents from the Federal Register. Remember that the Federal Register is available in an official online version through *GPO Access*, http://www.gpoaccess.gov/fr/index.html. Presidential documents are also published in unofficial sources such as the United States Code Congressional and Administrative News ("U.S.C.C.A.N.") and commercial electronic databases.

To cite a presidential document, you may elect to begin the citation with the document's title in ordinary typeface. If you elect not to use the title (or following the title), write "Exec." followed by an abbreviation from Rule 19.9(a)(2) for the type of document, followed by the number assigned to the document, if any. If the document has been published in the C.F.R., cite that version. If it has not yet appeared in the C.F.R., cite the version in the Federal Register.

Add the initial page, followed by a pinpoint reference, if appropriate. Pinpoint pages are most common, but some documents may be divided into sections. See the examples shown in Rule 19.9, Full Citation Format for Executive Orders, Proclamations, Determinations, Memoranda, Notices, and Reorganization Plans.

Whether you are citing federal or state executive documents, pay close attention to the date. The citation's date depends on the source being cited. If you cite a freestanding document that is dated (e.g., a governor's executive order published on a state Web site), use the date of the order or document. If the order or document is included within a larger publication (e.g., the C.F.R. or a state administrative register), use the date of the publication. Depending on the nature of the publication, the date may be the year it was published or an exact date. If the document has been reprinted in another source, such as U.S.C.C.A.N., you may provide a separate "reprinted in" parenthetical with a citation to the reprint source.

The same sorts of documents are issued by governors. Rule 20.9 directs users citing such materials to analogize to Rules 19.9 and 19.12. If the document is available on the Internet, you may include a parenthetical reference that cites its electronic location; see Rule 38.1 and its examples.

The exercises in this section are for all levels.

EXERCISE SET 8-E

ALL LEVELS: ADVISORY OPINIONS, EXECUTIVE ORDERS, AND OTHER EXECUTIVE DOCUMENTS

Before beginning Exercise Set 8-E Intermediate Level, review the following and keep the *Manual* at hand as you work through the exercises:

- Rule 19.7, Full Citation Format for Attorney General Opinions and Justice Department Office of Legal Counsel Opinions
- Sidebar 19.2, Purpose of Attorney General Opinions
- Rule 19.9, Full Citation Format for Executive Orders, Proclamations, Determinations, Memoranda, Notices, and Reorganization Plans
- Rule 20.7, Full Citation Format for State Attorney General Opinions
- Rule 20.9, State Executive Materials

To complete the exercises, you may also need to refer to the following:

- Rule 5.0, Page and Location Numbers
- Rule 38.1, Source Available in Print and Electronic Formats

8-E.1. On May 23, 1996, the United States Attorney General delivered an opinion to President Clinton titled "Assertion of Executive Privilege Regarding White House Counsel's Office Documents." The opinion was published in volume 20 (1996) of the Opinions of the Attorney General, beginning at page 2. Choose the correct full citation to page 4 of that opinion.

    a. 20 Op. Off. Leg. Counsel 2, 4 (1996).

    b. 20 Op. Atty. Gen. 2, 4 (1996).

    c. Atty. Gen. Op. 20-2, at 4 (May 23, 1996).

    d. Assertion of Executive Privilege Regarding White House Counsel's Office Documents, 20 U.S. Atty. Gen. Op. 2, 4 (1996).

8-E.2. The Office of Legal Counsel was asked to determine whether it would be legal for Congress to establish a national lottery, and in an opinion written by Charles J. Cooper and dated April 4, 1986, its answer was "no." The eight-page opinion, bearing the title "Congressional Authority to Adopt Legislation Establishing a National Lottery," appears in Opinions of the Office of Legal Counsel, volume 10 (1986), beginning at page 40. Choose the correct full citation to page 46 of that opinion.

    a. Charles J. Cooper, 10 Op. Off. Leg. Counsel 46 (1986).

    b. 10 Op. Off. Leg. Couns. 40, 46 (Apr. 4, 1986).

    c. Charles J. Cooper, *Congressional Authority to Adopt Legislation Establishing a National Lottery*, 10 Off. Leg. Counsel 40-46 (Apr. 4, 1986).

    d. Congressional Authority to Adopt Legislation Establishing a National Lottery, 10 Op. Off. Leg. Counsel 40, 46 (1986).

8-E.3.   In a legal opinion, the California Attorney General concluded that "[a] person appointed as an unpaid, volunteer investigator by a district attorney may qualify as a 'peace officer' provided that he or she is assigned to perform investigative duties and otherwise meets all standards imposed by law." The opinion appears in LexisNexis with the caption shown below. Choose the correct full citation to the opinion.

2007 Cal. AG LEXIS 19, *; 90 Ops. Cal. Atty. Gen. 7
OFFICE OF THE ATTORNEY GENERAL OF THE STATE OF CALIFORNIA
No. 06-204
2007 Cal. AG LEXIS 19; 90 Ops. Cal. Atty. Gen. 7
January 5, 2007

a. Off. Atty. Gen. of St. of Cal., No. 06-204, 2007 Cal. AG LEXIS 1 (Jan. 5, 2007).
b. Cal. Atty. Gen. Op. No. 06-204, 2007 Cal. AG LEXIS 1; 90 Ops. Cal. Atty. Gen. 7 (Jan. 5, 2007).
c. Cal. Atty. Gen. Op. No. 06-204, 2007 Cal. AG LEXIS 1 (Jan. 5, 2007).
d. Atty. Gen. Op. 06-204, 90 Ops. Cal. Atty. Gen. 7 (Jan. 5, 2007) (available at 2007 Cal. AG LEXIS 1).

8-E.4.   On July 26, 2000, President George W. Bush signed an executive order with the title "Increasing the Opportunity for Individuals with Disabilities to Be Employed in the Federal Government." This order bears the number 13163. It is published in title 3 of the Code of Federal Regulations, 2001 edition, beginning at page 285. Choose the correct full citation to this executive order.

a. EO 13163, 3 CFR 285 (July 26, 2000).
b. Increasing the Opportunity for Individuals with Disabilities to Be Employed in the Federal Government, Exec. Or. 13163, 3 C.F.R. 285 (2001).
c. Exec. Or. No. 13163, 3 CFR 285 (2001).
d. George W. Bush, Increasing the Opportunity for Individuals with Disabilities to Be Employed in the Federal Government, 3 Code Fed. Reg. No. 13163 (July 26, 2000).

8-E.5.   On February 6, 2009, President Barack Obama signed an executive order addressing the government's use of "project labor agreements" in large-scale construction projects. This executive order was assigned the number 13502. It was published in the February 11, 2009, issue of the Federal Register, in volume 74, beginning on page 6985. Choose the correct full citation to this executive order.

a. Barack Obama, Executive Order No. 13502, Fed. Reg. vol. 74, at 6985 (Feb. 6, 2009).
b. Exec. Or. 13502, 74 Fed. Reg. 6985 (Feb. 11, 2009).
c. Exec. Or. 13502, 3 C.F.R. 6985 (Feb. 6, 2009).
d. EO 13502, 74 FR 6985 (Feb. 11, 2009).

8-E.6.   Volume 39 of the Pennsylvania Bulletin, published January 24, 2009, contains Executive Order No. 2008-09. The executive order appears in its entirety on page 406. Establishing the Governor's Food Safety Council, the order was signed by Edward G. Rendell, Governor of the Commonwealth of Pennsylvania, on December 17, 2008. Choose the correct full citation to the executive order.

a. Penn. Exec. Or. 2008-09 (Dec. 17, 2008).
b. Edward G. Rendell, Penn. Exec. Ordin. 2008-09, 39 Penn. Bull. 406 (Jan. 24, 2009).
c. Pa. Exec. Or. No. 2008-09, 39 Pa. Bull. 406, 406 (Jan. 24, 2009).
d. Pa. Exec. Or. No. 2008-09, 39 Pa. Bull. at 406 (Dec. 17, 2008).

8-E.7. In an advisory opinion numbered 99-00122 and dated February 25, 1999, Bill Pryor, the Alabama Attorney General, advised a prison official in that state that the governor had the power to commute a death sentence to the lesser sentences of life or life without parole. This opinion is published on a governmental Web site in Alabama, at http://www.ago.alabama.gov/pdfopinions/99-00122.pdf. Write the full citation for the opinion and provide its online location in a parenthetical.

8-E.8. Write the full citation to the source of the presidential document shown below.

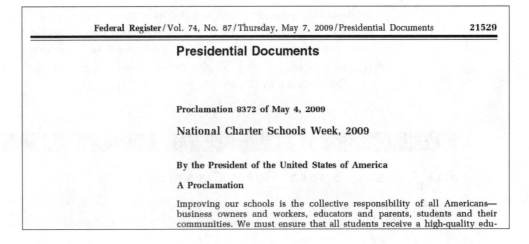

Federal Register / Vol. 74, No. 87 / Thursday, May 7, 2009 / Presidential Documents   21529

Presidential Documents

Proclamation 8372 of May 4, 2009

National Charter Schools Week, 2009

By the President of the United States of America

A Proclamation

Improving our schools is the collective responsibility of all Americans— business owners and workers, educators and parents, students and their communities. We must ensure that all students receive a high-quality edu-

F. SHORT-FORM CITATIONS

The hardest thing about constructing short-form citations to federal and state administrative and executive materials is locating the applicable rules. Because Rules 19 and 20 address so many kinds of authorities, there is no single short-form rule that applies across the board. Instead, you will find the rule you need immediately after the details for creating a full citation for a specific source.

For most federal administrative and executive materials, if *id.* is not an appropriate short-form citation, you must use a longer alternative that includes all of the full-citation elements except the date parenthetical. The preposition "at" is inserted before the pinpoint reference.

These "long" short forms are necessary for citations to the following:

- the Code of Federal Regulations (Rule 19.2);
- the Federal Register (Rule 19.3);
- Attorney General and Office of Legal Counsel opinions (Rule 19.8); and
- Executive Orders and other executive documents (Rule 19.10).

Similarly, state administrative and executive materials use this longer format when *id.* is inappropriate. Analogize to the federal rules; drop the date parenthetical from the full citation and add "at" before the pinpoint reference. Applicable rules and their federal analogs include the following:

- state administrative codes (Rule 20.2; analogize to Rule 19.2);
- state administrative registers (Rule 20.4; analogize to Rule 19.4);

- state attorney general opinions (Rule 20.8; analogize to Rule 19.8); and
- state executive materials (Rule 20.9; analogize to Rule 19.10).

The short-form citations for reported decisions by federal and state administrative agencies, however, are treated analogously to short-form citations for cases. In fact, Rules 19.6 and 20.6 simply advise users constructing short-form citations to federal or state agency decisions to "[f]ollow Rule 12.20."

No matter what the source, however, remember the short form *id.* and use it if appropriate. If *id.* is not appropriate, use the longer short form indicated by the applicable rule. *Supra* is never an appropriate short form to use with primary authorities from one of the branches of government. Even if you are writing a document with footnotes, do not use *supra* to send readers back to an earlier full citation of the source, as explained in Rule 11.4(b).

The exercises in this section are for all levels.

EXERCISE SET 8-F

ALL LEVELS: SHORT-FORM CITATIONS

Before beginning Exercise Set 8-F All Levels, review the following and keep the *Manual* at hand as you work through the exercises:

- Rule 11.3, *Id.* as a Short Citation
- Rule 11.4, *Supra* as a Short Citation
- Rule 19.2, Short Citation Format for Code of Federal Regulations
- Rule 19.4, Short Citation Format for Federal Register
- Rule 19.10, Short Citation Format for Executive Orders, Proclamations, Determinations, Memoranda, Notices, and Reorganization Plans

8-F.1. On July 28, 2009, the National Highway Traffic Safety Administration published a correction to a final rule in volume 74 of the Federal Register, set out in its entirety on page 37176. The synopsis of the final rule appears at right. In a memorandum describing recent administrative rule changes, you cite the corrected rule. Two citations later, after discussing a federal statute and a different regulation, you cite this rule a second time. Choose *the best* short-form citation to the rule.

> **DEPARTMENT OF TRANSPORTATION**
>
> **National Highway Traffic Safety Administration**
>
> **49 CFR Part 571**
>
> **[Docket No. NHTSA–2009–0116]**
>
> **RIN 2127–AK35**
>
> **Federal Motor Vehicle Safety Standards; Door Locks and Door Retention Components, Correction**
>
> **AGENCY:** National Highway Traffic Safety Administration (NHTSA), Department of Transportation (DOT).
> **ACTION:** Final rule; correction.

  a. *Id.* at 37176.
  b. 74 Fed. Reg. at 37176 (to be codified at 49 CFR Part 571).
  c. 74 Fed. Reg. at 37176 (July 28, 2009).
  d. 74 Fed. Reg. at 37176.

8-F.2. You are writing a memorandum concerning federal tax laws as they affect married couples. Your memo cites the provision of the Code of Federal Regulations that deals with spouses filing separate returns, shown below. Your memo's first citation is to subsection (a) of the regulation. The memo's second citation is also to subsection (a). Choose *the best* short-form citation to the regulation.

---

§ 1.4–3   **26 CFR Ch. I (4–1–09 Edition)**

of adjusted gross income and he elects to take the standard deduction, he will be deemed to have elected to pay the tax under section 3 if it is subsequently determined that his correct adjusted gross income is less than $5,000.

(c) [Reserved]

(d) *Change of election.* For rules relating to a change of election to pay, or not to pay, the optional tax imposed under section 3, see section 144 (b) and the regulations thereunder.

[T.D. 6500, 25 FR 11402, Nov. 26, 1960, as amended by T.D. 6581, 26 FR 11677, Dec. 6, 1961; T.D. 7269, 38 FR 9295, April 13, 1973]

§ 1.4–3 Husband and wife filing separate returns.

(a) *In general.* If the separate adjusted gross income of a husband is less than $5,000 and the separate adjusted gross income of his wife is less than $5,000, and if each is required to file a return, the husband and the wife must each elect to pay the optional tax imposed under section 3 or neither may so elect. If the separate adjusted gross income of each spouse is $5,000 or more, then

ard deduction by husband and wife, see part IV (section 141 and following), subchapter B, chapter 1 of the Code, and the regulations thereunder.

(b) *Taxable years beginning after December 31, 1963, and before January 1, 1970.* (1) In the case of a husband and wife filing a separate return for a taxable year beginning after December 31, 1963, and before January 1, 1970, the optional tax imposed by section 3 shall be—

(i) For taxable years beginning in 1964, the lesser of the tax shown in Table IV (relating to the 10-percent standard deduction for married persons filing separate returns) or Table V (relating to the minimum standard deduction for married persons filing separate returns) of section 3(a), and

(ii) For a taxable year beginning after December 31, 1964, and before January 1, 1970, the lesser of the tax shown in Table IV (relating to the 10-percent standard deduction for married persons filing separate returns) or Table V (relating to minimum standard deduction

---

    a. 26 C.F.R. Ch. 1, § 1.4-3(a) (Apr. 1, 2009).

    b. 26 CFR Ch. 1, at § 1.4-3(a).

    c. *Id.* at 26 C.F.R. § 1.4-3(a).

    d. *Id.*

8-F.3. A federal statute, 23 U.S.C. § 158, establishes the "National Minimum Drinking Age." Congress gave the National Highway Traffic Safety Administration the authority to implement this statute. Its regulations appear in volume 23 of the Code of Federal Regulations. You are citing the regulation's definition of "public possession," set out in section 1208.3. Your brief cites the Westlaw version of the regulation, current through April 2, 2010, and then cites an article by Mary Pat Treuthart, *Lowering the Bar: Rethinking Underage Drinking,* 9 N.Y.U. J. Legis. & Pub. Policy 303 (2006). The brief's next citation again refers to section 1208.3. Choose *the best* citation for the brief's **second** reference to section 1208.3.

    a. 23 C.F.R. at § 1208.3.

    b. *Id.* at § 1208.3 (Westlaw current through Apr. 2, 2010).

    c. *See supra* at § 1208.3.

    d. *Id.* (Westlaw current through Apr. 2, 2010).

8-F.4. Another section of your brief about the National Minimum Drinking Age discusses the history of the act, quoting the following sentence from the proposed rule, which appeared in volume 50 of the September 27, 1985, Federal Register, on page 39140: "In addition to the increase in drinking age, Congress and the President expressed overwhelming concern for the continuing 'blood border' problem that exists when young people can drive from one State to another and purchase alcoholic beverages which are otherwise prohibited to them." Without citing any intervening authorities, the brief then quotes a second sentence from the same page of the Federal Register: "A uniform national drinking age will solve the problem that now occurs when teenagers in one State with a drinking age of 21 easily drive into another State with a lower age limit, consume alcohol, and drive home." Choose *the best* citation for the **second** quotation.

a. 50 Fed. Reg. at 39140 (Sept. 27, 1985).

b. 50 Fed. Reg., *supra*, at 39140.

c. *Id.*

d. *Id.* at 39140.

8-F.5-10. Read the following excerpt from a seminar paper that uses footnotes. On your answer sheet, write the appropriate full or short-form citations for the authorities and their pinpoint references listed below.

> **Citation A:** Executive Order 13292, published on March 25, 2003, in volume 68 of the Federal Register beginning at page 15315.
> **Citation B:** Executive Order 12958, published on April 17, 1995, in volume 60 of the Federal Register beginning at page 19825.

Although governmental documents are ordinarily available to the public via the Freedom of Information Act, each federal agency bears the burden of justifying its decision to withhold records or portions of records.[1] Accordingly, agencies will argue that they are entitled to shield records from disclosure that must, "under criteria established by an Executive order[,] . . . be kept secret in the interest of national defense or foreign policy."[2]

In his first term, President George W. Bush issued Executive Order 13292, classifying information as "top secret," "secret," and "confidential" in the interests of national security.[3] While the purpose of the executive order was to amend existing procedures[4] and to prescribe "a uniform system for classifying, safeguarding, and declassifying national security information, including information relating to defense against transnational terrorism,"[5] it did not permit classification to conceal violations of law, to save persons from embarrassment, or to shield information that does not implicate national security interests.[6]

The executive order allows classification only if four conditions are met, including "damage to the national security."[7] The phrase "damage to the national security" means "harm to the national defense or foreign relations of the United States from the unauthorized disclosure of information, taking into consideration such aspects of the information as the sensitivity, value, utility, and provenance of that information."[8]

---

[1] 5 U.S.C. § 552 (2006).

[2] *Id.* at § 552(b)(1).

[3] [**8-F.5. Citation A, full citation, section § 1.2(a).**]

[4] [**8-F.6. Citation B, full citation.**]

[5] [**8-F.7. Citation A, at page 15315.**]

[6] [**8-F.8. Citation A, at section 1.7.**]

[7] [**8-F.9. Citation A, at section 1.1(a)(4).**]

[8] [**8-F.10. Citation A, at section 6.1(j).**]

CITING SECONDARY SOURCES AND

PRACTICE MATERIALS

Part 3 provides exercises covering secondary sources—those that explain, interpret, locate, and comment on the law. There are three reasons why the secondary sources are grouped in this part of the *Companion*: these sources are often cited in briefs, memoranda, and other forms of legal writing, including scholarly legal writing, to help explain the law; are primarily used by researchers to educate themselves about the law on a given topic; and operate as tools of research by helping locate the applicable law.

The first chapter in Part 3 begins with the secondary sources most familiar to law students: books and treatises. Some looseleafs are also covered in this chapter because they resemble books and treatises. The next chapter covers legal periodicals. And the remaining chapters in Part 3 cover other secondary sources such as the American Law Reports, legal dictionaries, and encyclopedias.

CHAPTER

BOOKS, TREATISES,

AND LOOSELEAFS

In this chapter, you will practice working with each of the major components of citations for books, treatises, and looseleafs, but first, you will need a little more general information about these sources. For example, what is the difference between a book and a treatise? Basically, treatises—and looseleafs, for that matter—are *types* of books. Legal books "range from multi-volume specialized treatises and detailed surveys to short monographs on specific issues or limited aspects of practice in particular jurisdictions."[1] A treatise is traditionally a multi-volume set, which provides an "exhaustive coverage of particular fields of law."[2]

Looseleafs "provide a treatise-type function, explaining the basic doctrines of a subject area."[3] They typically contain multiple types of sources—primary and secondary—from multiple jurisdictions. At one time, the difference between treatises and looseleafs was that treatises were bound volumes and looseleafs were binders, but as more and more books, treatises, and looseleafs find their way online, this distinction no longer remains true. Looseleafs contain a wealth of information. When you cite a looseleaf, look at the *nature* of the material contained within the looseleaf. If the looseleaf contains cases or administrative decisions, use Rule 28 to cite the material. If the nature of the material resembles books or treatises, use Rule 22 to cite the material, which is the focus of this chapter.

---

[1] Kent C. Olson, *Principles of Legal Research (Successor to* How to Find the Law, *9th Edition)* § 10.4, 344 (West 2009).

[2] *Id.* at 344–345.

[3] *Id.* at 345.

A. AUTHORS AND TITLES

The first component in a book, treatise, or looseleaf citation is the author's name. The author could be a single author, multiple authors, or an organization; in some cases, the author may be unknown or not listed. Rule 22.1(a) provides guidance on presenting the author's name. Present the name as it appears on the document, using designations such as "Sr." or "III," but omitting titles of respect, such as "Hon." If the author's name is not listed or is unknown, start the full citation with the title.

The second component of a book, treatise, or looseleaf citation is the title. Keep four general concepts in mind when formatting titles:

- Capitalize words in the title according to Rules 3.1 and 3.4.
- If the title is followed by a subtitle, you may choose to include the subtitle in the citation. Insert a colon and one space between the title and subtitle. If the title ends with a question mark or exclamation point, however, do not insert the colon. According to Rule 3.1(b)(3), capitalize the first word of the subtitle, no matter what it is, because it is the first word after a colon.
- Italicize words in the title, with two exceptions:
  - When a title includes an italicized case name or publication name, Rule 1.6 applies. Put the case or publication name in ordinary typeface, as shown in the examples for Rule 1.6.
  - When a title includes an italicized foreign word that is not incorporated into normal English (as explained in Rule 1.8), put the foreign word in ordinary typeface.
- And finally, use Rule 3.1(c) for the proper capitalization of hyphenated words. Always capitalize the first word. The word that follows a hyphen is also capitalized unless it is an article, preposition, or conjunction.

The exercises below help you identify and construct the author and title components in full citations to books, treatises, and looseleafs.

EXERCISE SET 9-A

BASIC LEVEL: AUTHORS AND TITLES

Before beginning Exercise Set 9-A Basic Level, review the following and keep the *Manual* at hand as you work through the exercises:

- Rule 22.1(a), Author's name
- Rule 22.1(b), Title

To complete the exercises, you may also need to refer to the following:

- Rule 1.6, Italicized Material within Italicized Material
- Rule 3.1, Words in Titles
- Rule 3.4, Capitalization in Selected Non-English Languages
- Appendix 3, General Abbreviations
- Appendix 5, Abbreviations for Legal Periodicals

9-A.1. In 1914, Justice Louis Dembitz Brandeis wrote a book titled *Other People's Money and How the Bankers Use It*. Justice Brandeis's name appears on the title page as Louis D. Brandeis. How should his name appear in a full citation to the book?

    a. Justice Louis Dembitz Brandeis
    b. Justice Louis D. Brandeis
    c. Louis D. Brandeis
    d. Louis Dembitz Brandeis

9-A.2. Gregory Tillet, Ph.D., and Brendan French wrote a book titled *Resolving Conflict: A Practical Approach*. The authors' names appear on the title page as Gregory Tillet, Ph.D., and Brendan French. How should their names appear in a full citation to the book?

    a. Gregory Tillet, Ph.D., & Brendan French
    b. Gregory Tillet & Brendan French
    c. Brendan French & Gregory Tillet
    d. Gregory Tillet and Brendan French

9-A.3. The following information is from the cover of a book. Use the information to answer the next two questions.

> A PRACTICAL GUIDE TO
> # APPELLATE
> # ADVOCACY
>
> Second Edition
>
> Mary Beth Beazley

9-A.3.a. How should the author's name appear in the full citation?

    a. Mary Beth Beazley
    b. Beazley, Mary Beth
    c. Mary Beazley
    d. Beazley, Mary

9-A.3.b. How should the title appear in the full citation?

    a. A PRACTICAL GUIDE TO APPELLATE ADVOCACY
    b. A Practical Guide to Appellate Advocacy
    c. *A Practical Guide To Appellate Advocacy*
    d. *A Practical Guide to Appellate Advocacy*

9-A.4.   The following information is from the cover of a book. Use the information to answer the next three questions.

FOURTH EDITION

Clear

and Effective

Legal

Writing

Veda R. Charrow
Myra K. Erhardt
Robert P. Charrow

9-A.4.a.   Which of the following is a correct presentation of the authors' names?

a. Veda R. Charrow, Myra K. Erhardt, and Robert P. Charrow
b. Veda R. Charrow, Myra K. Erhardt, & Robert P. Charrow
c. Veda R. Charrow, Myra K. Erhardt & Robert P. Charrow
d. Robert P. Charrow, Veda R. Charrow & Myra K. Erhardt

9-A.4.b.   **True or False:** In a full citation to the book pictured before question 9-A.4, the authors' names could also be presented as: Veda R. Charrow et al.,

a. True
b. False

9-A.4.c.   Which is the correct presentation of the title?

a. *Clear And Effective Legal Writing*
b. *Clear and Effective Legal Writing*

9-A.5.   A book was co-authored by Rebecca C. Morgan and the National Academy of Elder Law Attorneys, Inc. Which of the following is the correct presentation of the authors' names?

a. Rebecca C. Morgan and National Academy of Elder Law Attorneys, Inc.
b. Rebecca C. Morgan & Natl. Acad. Elder L. Atty., Inc.
c. Rebecca C. Morgan & Natl. Acad. Eld. L. Attys., Inc.
d. Rebecca C. Morgan & Natl. Acad. Elder L. Attys., Inc.

9-A.6. A popular legal writing text, *A Practical Guide to Legal Writing & Legal Method*, has five authors. The authors are listed on the title page as shown below. Which of the following is a correct presentation of the authors' names?

John C. Dernbach
Widener University School of Law

Richard V. Singleton II
Blank Rome LLP

Cathleen S. Wharton
University of Georgia School of Law

Joan M. Ruhtenberg
Indiana University School of Law at Indianapolis

Catherine J. Wasson
Widener University School of Law

    a. John C. Dernbach, Widener University School of Law, et al.,
    b. John C. Dernbach, Joan M. Ruhtenberg, Richard V. Singleton, Catherine J. Wasson & Cathleen S. Wharton,
    c. John C. Dernbach, Richard V. Singleton II, Cathleen S. Wharton, Joan M. Ruhtenberg & Catherine J. Wasson,
    d. John C. Dernbach, Widener University School of Law, Richard V. Singleton II, Blank Rome LLP, Cathleen S. Wharton, University of Georgia School of Law, Joan M. Ruhtenberg, Indiana University School of Law at Indianapolis & Catherine J. Wasson, Widener University School of Law,

9-A.7. There is an additional way to present three or more authors' names. Using the names of the authors for the textbook discussed in the previous question, provide the alternative way to present the authors' names on your answer sheet.

9-A.8. The following information is from the title page of a book. How should the author's name be presented in a full citation?

    a. The University of Chicago Press
    b. The U. of Chi. Press
    c. U. Chi. Press
    d. The citation should not contain an author name.

The Chicago Manual of Style
15th edition
The University of Chicago Press Chicago and London

EXERCISE SET 9-A

INTERMEDIATE LEVEL: AUTHORS AND TITLES

Before beginning Exercise Set 9-A Intermediate level, review the following and keep the *Manual* at hand as you work through the exercises:

- Rule 22.1(a), Author's name
- Rule 22.1(b), Title

To complete the exercises, you may also need to refer to the following:

- Rule 1.6, Italicized Material within Italicized Material
- Rule 3.1, Words in Titles
- Rule 3.4, Capitalization in Selected Non-English Languages
- Appendix 3, General Abbreviations
- Appendix 5, Abbreviations for Legal Periodicals

9-A.9. The following information is from the cover of a book. How should the title appear in a full citation?

a. *Deconstructing Legal Analysis*
b. *Deconstructing Legal Analysis: a 1L primer*
c. *Deconstructing Legal Analysis A 1L Primer*
d. *Deconstructing Legal Analysis: A 1L Primer*

> Aspen Publishers
>
> DECONSTRUCTING
> ## Legal Analysis
>
> A 1L PRIMER

9-A.10. The following information is from the cover of a looseleaf. How should the title appear in the full citation?

a. *HIPAA—A Guide To Health Care Privacy and Security Law*
b. *HIPAA: A Guide to Health Care Privacy and Security Law*
c. HIPAA: A Guide to Health Care Privacy and Security Law
d. HIPAA—A GUIDE TO HEALTH CARE PRIVACY AND SECURITY LAW

> # HIPAA
>
> A GUIDE TO
> HEALTH CARE PRIVACY
> AND SECURITY LAW

9-A.11. Rewrite the following title, using the correct typeface (use underlining for italics) and capitalization:

> clean air act: step-by-step compliance

9-A.12. Rewrite the following title, using the correct typeface (use underlining for italics) and capitalization:

> de facto segregation and civil rights: struggle for legal and social equality

9-A.13. Rewrite the following title, using the correct typeface (use underlining for italics) and capitalization:

AFTER *BROWN*

THE RISE AND RETREAT OF

SCHOOL DESEGREGATION

EXERCISE SET 9-A

EXPERT LEVEL: AUTHORS AND TITLES

Before beginning Exercise Set 9-A Expert Level, review the following and keep the *Manual* at hand as you work through the exercises:

- Rule 22.1(a), Author's name
- Rule 22.1(b), Title

To complete the exercises, you may also need to refer to the following:

- Rule 1.6, Italicized Material within Italicized Material
- Rule 3.1, Words in Titles
- Rule 3.4, Capitalization in Selected Non-English Languages
- Appendix 3, General Abbreviations
- Appendix 5, Abbreviations for Legal Periodicals

9-A.14. The following information is from the cover of a book. Use the information to answer the next two questions.

MEDICAL RECORDS AND THE LAW

THIRD EDITION

William H. Roach, Jr.
and
The Aspen Health Law and
Compliance Center

9-A.14.a. Write the authors' names as they should appear in a full citation.

9-A.14.b. Write the title as it should appear in a full citation. (Use underlining to show italics.)

9-A.15. The following information comes from an electronic looseleaf on Westlaw. Write the authors' names as they should appear in a full citation.

Modern Tort Law: Liability and Litigation
Database Updated June 2009

J.D. Lee, Barry Lindahl

Chapter 14. Jurisdictional Considerations in Modern Tort Law

§ 14:11. Jurisdiction over the person; constitutional requirements

Under the United States Constitution, a state can exercise jurisdiction over an individual only if there are sufficient minimum contacts between the state and the individual so that it is reasonable for the state to exercise jurisdiction.

.   .   .

9-A.16. The following information comes from an online treatise on LexisNexis. Write the title as it should appear in the full citation. (Use underlining to show italics.)

Copyright 2007 John Wiley & Sons, Inc.
All Rights Reserved

Bankruptcy & Insolvency Taxation

Third Edition

SECTION: CHAPTER TEN

LENGTH: 34010 words

HEADLINE: Tax Procedures and Litigation

BYLINE:
GRANT W. NEWTON
ROBERT LIQUERMAN

B. VOLUMES AND PINPOINT REFERENCES

Make the pinpoint reference as specific as possible. When you work with books, treatises, and looseleafs, the pinpoint reference can be much more than just a page or span of pages. For example, the pinpoint reference could be a footnote, an appendix, a table, or other graphical material, as explained in Rules 7.0 and 9.0. Note these additional tips about pinpoint references:

- If there is a section number and a page number, the section number should precede the page number, as shown in Rule 6.1(b).
- If the title ends in a numeral and the pinpoint reference is a page number, insert a comma after the title and the word "at" before the page number. Doing so lets the reader distinguish between the end of the title and the pinpoint page, as explained in Rule 5.2(b)(3).

For additional examples of the types of pinpoint references in books, treatises, and looseleafs, see the examples in Rule 22.1(c).

When books, treatises, and looseleafs are published in multi-volume sets, the citation must include a reference to the volume number. Immediately after the title, insert the abbreviation "vol." and the volume number.

Books and treatises are updated by pocket parts (updates inserted in the back of the volume) or separate supplements. If you are citing the supplement instead of the main volume, use the abbreviation "Supp." before the publication date in the parenthetical, as shown in Rule 8.0.

The exercises below help you identify pinpoint reference information in citations and construct some of the more common pinpoint references.

EXERCISE SET 9-B

BASIC LEVEL: VOLUMES AND PINPOINT REFERENCES

Before beginning Exercise Set 9-B Basic Level, review the following and keep the *Manual* at hand as you work through the exercises:

• Rule 22.1(c), Pinpoint reference

To complete the exercises, you may also need to refer to the following:

• Rule 5.0, Page and Location Numbers
• Rule 6.0, Citing Sections and Paragraphs
• Rule 7.0, Citing Footnotes and Endnotes
• Rule 8.0, Supplements
• Rule 9.0, Graphical Material, Appendices, and Other Subdivisions

9-B.1.   Use the information in the following full citation to answer the three questions below.

> Daniel J. Solove, *The Digital Person: Technology and Privacy in the Information Age* 59–61 (N.Y.U. Press 2004).

9-B.1.a.   Identify the pinpoint reference in the citation above, and explain what the pinpoint reference refers to (chapter, section, page(s), etc.).

9-B.1.b.   Is the citation referring to the main volume or a supplement?
     a. Main volume
     b. Supplement
     c. Both

9-B.1.c.   Suppose you want to cite page 75. Write only the pinpoint reference that would appear in the full citation.

9-B.2.   Use the information in the following full citation to answer the four questions below.

> William A. Kaplin & Barbara A. Lee, *The Law of Higher Education* vol. 2, ch. 9 (4th ed., John Wiley & Sons, Inc. 2006).

9-B.2.a.   Identify the pinpoint reference in the citation above, and explain what the pinpoint reference refers to (chapter, section, page(s), etc.).

9-B.2.b.   Is the citation referring to the main volume or a supplement?
     a. Main volume
     b. Supplement
     c. Both

9-B.2.c.   **True or False:** This book has at least two volumes.

     a. True
     b. False

9-B.2.d.   Suppose instead you want to refer to section 9.4.2 of volume 2. Write the full pinpoint reference.

9-B.3.   Suppose you wanted to refer to section 14:11 of an online treatise. Write the full pinpoint reference.

EXERCISE SET 9-B

INTERMEDIATE LEVEL: VOLUMES AND PINPOINT REFERENCES

Before beginning Exercise Set 9-B Intermediate Level, review the following and keep the *Manual* at hand as you work through the exercises:

• Rule 22.1(c), Pinpoint reference

To complete the exercises, you may also need to refer to the following:

• Rule 5.0, Page and Location Numbers
• Rule 6.0, Citing Sections and Paragraphs
• Rule 7.0, Citing Footnotes and Endnotes
• Rule 8.0, Supplements
• Rule 9.0 Graphical Material, Appendices, and Other Subdivisions

9-B.4.   Use the information in the following full citation to answer the two questions below.

> Robert A. Feldman & Raymond T. Nimmer, *Drafting Effective Contracts: A Practitioner's Guide* § 2.02[E], 2-26 to 2-30 (2d ed., Aspen Publishers Supp. 2009).

9-B.4.a.   Identify the pinpoint reference in the citation above, and explain what the pinpoint reference refers to (chapter, section, page(s), etc.).

9-B.4.b.   Is the citation referring to the main volume or a supplement?
     a. Main volume
     b. Supplement

9-B.5.   Use the information in the following full citation to answer the two questions below.

> Kelly Lynn Anders, *The Organized Lawyer* 104 n. 1 (Carolina Academic Press 2009).

9-B.5.a.   Identify the pinpoint reference in the citation above, and explain what the pinpoint reference refers to (chapter, section, page(s), etc.).

9-B.5.b.   You want to refer to footnotes 1 through 10, which appear on pages 104 to 105 in the pinpoint reference. Using this information, write only the pinpoint reference component of a full citation.

9-B.6. Identify the pinpoint reference in the citation below, and explain what the reference refers to (chapter, section, page(s), etc.).

> John T. Boese, *Civil False Claims and Qui Tam Actions* vol. 2, app. F, F-1 to F-5 (3d ed., Aspen Publishers 2010).

9-B.7. Identify the pinpoint reference in the citation below, and explain what the reference refers to (chapter, section, page(s), etc.).

> William A.V. Clark, *Immigrants and the American Dream: Remaking the Middle Class* 9, fig. 1.2 (Guilford Press 2003) (summarizing "[t]he characteristics of new single-family homes").

EXERCISE SET 9-B

EXPERT LEVEL: VOLUMES AND PINPOINT REFERENCES

Before beginning Exercise Set 9-B Expert Level, review the following and keep the *Manual* at hand as you work through the exercises:

• Rule 22.1(c), Pinpoint reference

To complete the exercises, you may also need to refer to the following:

• Rule 5.0, Page and Location Numbers
• Rule 6.0, Citing Sections and Paragraphs
• Rule 7.0, Citing Footnotes and Endnotes
• Rule 8.0, Supplements
• Rule 9.0, Graphical Material, Appendices, and Other Subdivisions

9-B.8. You want to refer to a table that appears on page 48, in Chapter 2 of a particular source. The table is number 2.3 and is titled "Educational attainment by immigration status." Write only the pinpoint reference component of a full citation.

9-B.9. You want to refer to an illustration that appears on page 96 of a particular source. The illustration is number 6. Write only the pinpoint reference component of a full citation.

9-B.10. You want to refer to a graph that appears on page 375 as a part of Appendix C of a particular source. The graph is number A-7. Write only the pinpoint reference component for a full citation.

C. PUBLICATION INFORMATION

The parenthetical at the end of a full citation for a book, treatise, or looseleaf contains the publication information, and depending upon the source, the parenthetical could contain some or all of the following information:

• editor or editions;
• translator or translators;

- edition;
- printings;
- publisher;
- supplement; and
- date.

The parenthetical of a full citation to a book, treatise, or looseleaf contains, at minimum, a publisher and a date; however, if a source contains all the different types of publication information presented above, the information should be presented in the order listed. This chapter focuses on the four most common types of publication information: editor(s), edition, publisher, and date, as summarized in Table 9.1 below.

The basic-level exercises help you identify the different types of "publication information" that appears in the parenthetical. In the intermediate- and expert-level exercises, you will construct the parentheticals that appear in a full citation.

TABLE 9.1	
PUBLICATION INFORMATION FOR PARENTHETICALS	
Editor or editors **Rule 22.1(d)**	Even if the source has an author, include any editor(s) listed on the front cover or the title page. Present the editor's full name, followed by the abbreviation "ed." and a comma. For more than one editor, use the abbreviation "eds."
Edition **Rule 22.1(f)**	Indicate editions other than the original or first. Use an ordinal number or other appropriate abbreviation (e.g., "rev." for revised) before the abbreviation "ed."
Publisher **Rule 22.1(i)**	Provide the name of the publisher. The name may be abbreviated, using Appendix 3. Omit information, if any, about an office or division of the publisher. There is no comma between the publisher and the supplement or date information.
Supplement **Rule 8**	If you are citing a supplement, insert the abbreviation "Supp." between the publisher information and the publication date.
Date **Rule 22.1(j)**	Provide the date of publication on the title page or the copyright page. Typically, only the year is needed.

EXERCISE SET 9-C

BASIC LEVEL: PUBLICATION INFORMATION

Before beginning Exercise Set 9-C Basic Level, review the following and keep the *Manual* at hand as you work through the exercises:

- Rule 22.1(d), Editor
- Rule 22.1(f), Edition
- Rule 22.1(i), Publisher
- Rule 22.1(j), Date

To complete the exercises, you may also need to refer to the following:

- Rule 4.3, Ordinal Numbers
- Rule 8.0, Supplements
- Appendix 3, General Abbreviations

9-C.1. Use the information in the following full citation to answer the three questions below.

Derek Bruff, *Teaching with Classroom Response Systems: Creating Active Learning Environments* 205–207 (Jossey-Bass 2009).

9-C.1.a. Identify the publisher of the book.

9-C.1.b. Identify the date that the book was published.

9-C.1.c. **True or False:** The book has an editor.

a. True
b. False

9-C.2. Use the information in the following full citation to answer the four questions below.

Teaching the Law School Curriculum ch. 11 (Steven Friedland & Gerald F. Hess eds., Carolina Academic Press 2004).

9-C.2.a. Identify the editor or editors of the book.

9-C.2.b. Identify the publisher of the book.

9-C.2.c. Identify the date the book was published.

9-C.2.d. **True or False:** The book citation does not contain an author name.

a. True
b. False

9-C.3. Use the information in the following full citation to answer the three questions below.

>Mary Miles Prince, *Bieber's Dictionary of Legal Abbreviations* 23 (5th ed., William S. Hein & Co. 2001).

9-C.3.a. Identify the edition of the book.

9-C.3.b. Identify the book's publisher.

9-C.3.c. Identify the date the book was published.

9-C.4. Use the information in the following full citation to answer the four questions below.

>Leslie W. Abramson & James J. Alfini, *Judicial Conduct and Ethics* § 3.12, 17 (3d ed., Lexis Cum. Supp. 2001).

9-C.4.a. Identify the edition of the book.

9-C.4.b. Identify the book's publisher.

9-C.4.c. Identify the date the book was published.

9-C.4.d. **True or False:** The writer is citing the supplement.

>a. True
>b. False

EXERCISE SET 9-C

INTERMEDIATE LEVEL: PUBLICATION INFORMATION

Before beginning Exercise Set 9-C Intermediate Level, review the following and keep the *Manual* at hand as you work through the exercises:

- Rule 22.1(d), Editor
- Rule 22.1(f), Edition
- Rule 22.1(i), Publisher
- Rule 22.1(j), Date

To complete the exercises, you may also need to refer to the following:

- Rule 4.3, Ordinal Numbers
- Rule 8.0, Supplements
- Appendix 3, General Abbreviations

9-C.5. Using the publisher information provided below, write the publisher's name for the parenthetical.

>Aspen Law & Business
>A Division of Aspen
>Publishers, Inc.

9-C.6.   Using the publisher information provided below, write the publisher's name for the parenthetical.

OXFORD
UNIVERSITY PRESS

9-C.7.   The publisher for the book *Best Practices for Legal Education: A Vision and a Road Map* is Clinical Legal Education Association. Write the publisher's name for the parenthetical.

9-C.8.   The publisher for the book *The Lawyer's Quick Guide to E-Mail* is provided below. Write the publisher's name for the parenthetical.

> Law Practice Management Section
> American Bar Association

9-C.9.   Using the title page presented below, write the complete publication parenthetical for this book.

APPELLATE
ADVOCACY
IN A NUTSHELL

Second Edition

By
Alan D. Hornstein
Professor of Law
University of Maryland
School of Law

West
Group

St. Paul, Minn.
1998

9-C.10. Using the title page presented below (and a publication date of 2007), write the complete publication parenthetical for this book.

> # BOILERPLATE
> ### The Foundation of Market Contracts
>
> Edited by
> ### OMRI BEN-SHAHAR
> Kirkland and Ellis Professor of Law and Economics
> University of Michigan Law School
>
> Cambridge
> University Press

EXERCISE SET 9-C

EXPERT LEVEL: PUBLICATION INFORMATION

Before beginning Exercise Set 9-C Expert Level, review the following and keep the *Manual* at hand as you work through the exercises:

- Rule 22.1(d), Editor
- Rule 22.1(f), Edition

- Rule 22.1(i), Publisher
- Rule 22.1(j), Date

To complete the exercises, you may also need to refer to the following:

- Rule 4.3, Ordinal Numbers
- Rule 8.0, Supplements
- Appendix 3, General Abbreviations

9-C.11. Construct the parenthetical that should appear at the end of a full citation. (The publication date is 2004.)

> # CONTROLLING IMMIGRATION
>
> ## A Global Perspective
>
> ### Second Edition
>
> Edited by
> Wayne A. Cornelius, Takeyuki Tsuda,
> Philip L. Martin, and James F. Hollifield
>
> STANFORD UNIVERSITY PRESS, STANFORD, CALIFORNIA

9-C.12. Construct the parenthetical that should appear at the end of a full citation. (The publication date is 2009.)

LEGALLY SPEAKING

REVISED AND UPDATED EDITION

40 Powerful
Presentation
Principles
Lawyers
Need to Know

DAVID J. DEMPSEY, JD

KAPLAN PUBLISHING
New York

9-C.13. While researching in an online library catalog, you find a book titled *Children and the Law: Rights & Obligations* by Thomas A. Jacobs. The book was published by Thomson/West in 2008. On the cover and title page of the book, you find a lot of additional information, including the following:

- 2008 Cumulative Supplement, issued in May 2008
- Volume 2
- By Thomas A. Jacobs, Commissioner/Judge Pro-Tem, Maricopa County Superior Court
- © Thomas Reuters/West, 2008

Using this information, construct the parenthetical that should appear at the end of the full citation.

9-C.14. While researching in an online law library catalog, you find a novel titled *A Mad Desire to Dance*. The novel was published by Alfred A. Knopf in 2009. The novel is the first American edition and was translated from French by Catherine Temerson. Construct the parenthetical that should appear at the end of a full citation.

D. | WORKS IN A COLLECTION

Sometimes a book contains a collection of shorter works by one or more authors. The full citation to a shorter work within a collection is similar to the full citation to a book, with two differences:

- The author and title of the shorter work precede the citation information for the larger work. (Typically, the citation for the larger work starts with the author's name; however, if the larger work does not have an author, the author and title of the shorter work comes before the title of the larger work.)

- The pinpoint reference in the full citation needs more information. The pinpoint reference will contain the initial page of the shorter work (so that the reader can find where the shorter work starts) and the pinpoint reference for the cited information.

Citing a work in a collection can be challenging for even the most expert legal writer. A tip to assist the novice legal author: keep Rule 22.1(m) in front of you as you are determining which information needs to be in the citation. Work your way through the list of components in the sample in Rule 22.1(m) from the beginning to the end. Omit any components in Rule 22.1(m) that are not relevant to the source you are citing—either in the shorter work or in the larger work, as Rules 22.1(l) and 22.1(m) explain.

To construct the full citation to a collected work, you will need to use all the tools that you have learned thus far in this chapter. The exercises in this section help you identify the components of the full citation and construct full citations to collected works. The exercises in this set are for all levels.

EXERCISE SET 9-D

ALL LEVELS: WORKS IN A COLLECTION

> Before beginning Exercise Set 9-D All Levels, review the following and keep the *Manual* at hand as you work through the exercises:
>
> • Rule 22.1(m), Collected Works of Several Authors
>
> To complete the exercises, you may also need to refer to the following:
>
> • Other rules cross-referenced in Rule 22.0

9-D.1. Use the information in the following full citation to answer the five questions below.

> Harvey Jassem, *The Turning Tide: Electronic Media Regulatory Principles Then and Now*, in Susan J. Drucker & Gary Gumpert, *RealLaw@Virtual Space: Communication Regulation in Cyberspace* 23, 25–27 (2d ed., Hampton Press, Inc. 2005).

9-D.1.a. Who is the author of the shorter work?
a. Harvey Jassem
b. Susan J. Drucker
c. Gary Gumpert
d. Susan J. Drucker & Gary Gumpert

9-D.1.b. Who is the author of the larger work?

    a. Harvey Jassem
    b. Susan J. Drucker
    c. Gary Gumpert
    d. Susan J. Drucker & Gary Gumpert

9-D.1.c. What is the title of the shorter work?

    a. *The Turning Tide: Electronic Media Regulatory Principles Then and Now*
    b. *RealLaw@Virtual Space: Communication Regulation in Cyberspace*

9-D.1.d. What is the title of the larger work?

    a. *The Turning Tide: Electronic Media Regulatory Principles Then and Now*
    b. *RealLaw@Virtual Space: Communication Regulation in Cyberspace*

9-D.1.e. Identify which page the shorter work starts on and the pinpoint reference.

9-D.2. Use the information in the following full citation to answer the five questions below.

Carrie Menkel-Meadow, *Is There an Honest Lawyer in the Box? Legal Ethics on TV*, in *Lawyers in Your Living Room! Law on Television* 37, 44 (Michael Asimow ed., ABA 2009).

9-D.2.a. Who is the author of the shorter work?
    a. The citation to the shorter work does not contain an author name.
    b. Carrie Menkel-Meadow
    c. Michael Asimow

9-D.2.b. Who is the author of the larger work?

    a. The citation to the larger work does not contain an author name.
    b. Carrie Menkel-Meadow
    c. Michael Asimow

9-D.2.c. What is the title of the shorter work?

    a. *Lawyers in Your Living Room!*
    b. *Lawyers in Your Living Room! Law on Television*
    c. *Is There an Honest Lawyer in the Box?*
    d. *Is There an Honest Lawyer in the Box? Legal Ethics on TV*

9-D.2.d. What is the title of the larger work?

    a. *Lawyers in Your Living Room!*
    b. *Lawyers in Your Living Room! Law on Television*
    c. *Is There an Honest Lawyer in the Box?*
    d. *Is There an Honest Lawyer in the Box? Legal Ethics on TV*

9-D.2.e. Identify which page the shorter work starts on and the pinpoint reference.

9-D.3. Using the information provided below, construct the full citation to the work within a collection, referring to page 215.

Information about the collection
(published in 2002):

> # Environmental Dispute Resolution
>
> An Anthology of
> Practical Solutions
>
> Editors
> Ann L. MacNaughton
> Jay G. Martin
>
> Section of Environment, Energy, and Resources
> American Bar Association

Information about the smaller work:

> **Chapter 10**
> **Is Mediation a Better Alternative for**
> **the Resolution of International**
> **Environmental Disputes?** 207
>
> Nancy A. Oretskin and Ann L. MacNaughton

9-D.4. Using the information provided below, construct the full citation to the work within a collection, referring to pages 131 through 132.

Information about the collection
(published in 2009):

> # Homeland Security
>
> LEGAL AND POLICY ISSUES
>
> Joe D. Whitley and Lynne K. Zusman, Editors
>
> Section of Administrative Law and Regulatory Practice
> American Bar Association

Information about the smaller work:

> Chapter 7
> 2008: The Year of Increased Worksite Enforcement 123
> *Dawn M. Lurie, Mahsa Aliaskari, and Joe Whitley*

9-D.5. Using the information provided below, construct the full citation to the work within a collection, referring to section 13.2, pages 337 through 340.

Information about the collection
(published in 2002):

Information about the smaller work:

Taking Sides on Taking Issues

Public and Private Perspectives

Thomas E. Roberts
Editor

Section of State and Local Government Law
American Bar Association

Chapter 13

Applying *Nollan/Dolan* to Impact Fees: A Case for the *Ehrlich* Approach   333

Daniel J. Curtin, Jr. and Cecily T. Talbert

9-D.6. Using the information provided below, construct the full citation to the work within a collection, referring to figure 2 on page 273.

Information about the collection:

Information about the smaller work:

Native American Law and Colonialism, Before 1776 to 1903

Edited with introductions by
John R. Wunder
University of Nebraska-Lincoln

GARLAND PUBLISHING, INC.
New York & London
1996

263   The White Man's Justice: Native Americans and the Judicial System of San Diego County, 1870-1890

Richard W. Crawford

E. SHORT-FORM CITATIONS

Once you provide a full citation to a book, treatise, or looseleaf, you can thereafter use a short-form citation—either *id.*, a short citation, or *supra*. Short-form citations save space, but the form must still contain enough information for the reader to find the source and the information within the source.

Whenever appropriate, use *id.*, which means "the same." In documents *without* footnotes, it is appropriate to use *id.* to refer to the same single source that was last cited (the "immediately preceding authority," described in Rule 11.3(b)(4)(a)). In documents *with* footnotes, it is appropriate to use *id.* to refer to the same single source that was last cited in the same footnote or the single source cited in the preceding footnote, as shown in Rule 11.3(b)(4)(b). If the preceding citation or footnote cites more than one source, or if you have cited intervening sources, *id.* is not appropriate. When *id.* is not appropriate, the correct short-form citation depends on whether your document has footnotes.

Short-Form Citations in Documents *without* Footnotes

Short-form citations for books, treatises, or looseleafs have three components:

* the last name(s) of the author(s) (or just the first author's last name and the phrase "et al.";
  see the examples in Rule 22.2(c));
* the title of the book, treatise, or looseleaf; and
* the pinpoint reference, after the word "at."

If the title is long, you may provide a "hereinafter" format in square brackets after the *full citation* to tell the reader what the "shortened" title will be in the short-form citations, as shown in Rule 11.4(d)(1)(a).

To cite a work in a collection, use the same three components listed above; however, the author's name and title will refer to the author and title of the shorter work.

Short-Form Citations in Documents *with* Footnotes

Short-form citations for books, treatises, or looseleafs in documents with footnotes have the same three components listed above; however, use *supra* and the footnote number in place of the title. For example, if you provide the full citation to a book in footnote 17 of a document and then cite the same book in footnote 104, the second component of the short-form citation will be "*supra* n. 17."

When you are writing documents that have footnotes, the "hereinafter" notation serves a second purpose. If a footnote contains citations to two sources by the same author—two books, for example—"hereinafter" can be used to distinguish the two sources. For more information and examples of "hereinafter," see Rule 11.4(d).

To cite a work in a collection in documents with footnotes, use *supra* with the shorter work as well as the larger work. The short-form citation contains the same three components listed above; however, the author's last name and title could refer to either the shorter work or the larger work, depending upon the situation. See the example in Rule 22.3(b).

The exercises below help you construct the short-form citations for sources that appear in both documents with footnotes and without footnotes.

EXERCISE SET 9-E

BASIC LEVEL: SHORT-FORM CITATIONS

Before beginning Exercise Set 9-E Basic Level, review the following and keep the *Manual* at hand as you work through the exercises:

• Rule 22.2, Short Citation Format for Works Other Than Those in a Collection
• Rule 22.3, Short Citation Format for Works in a Collection

To complete the exercises, you may also need to refer to the following:

• Rule 11.1, Full Citation Format
• Rule 11.2, Short Citation Format
• Rule 11.3, *Id.* as a Short Citation, specifically subsections (a)–(e), and (g)
• Rule 11.4, *Supra* as a Short Citation

9-E.1. Use the information in the following full citation to answer the two questions below.

Ian Gallacher, *A Form and Style Manual for Lawyers* 83 (Carolina Academic Press 2005).

9-E.1.a. The full citation appears in a document *without* footnotes. Later in the document, after referring to other sources, you want to refer to this book again, specifically page 106. Which of the following short-form citations is correct?
a. Ian Gallacher, *A Form and Style Manual for Lawyers* at 106.
b. Gallacher, *supra* at 106.
c. Ian Gallacher, *A Form and Style Manual for Lawyers* 106 (Carolina Academic Press 2005).
d. Gallacher, *A Form and Style Manual for Lawyers* at 106.

9-E.1.b. The same source appears in a document *with* footnotes, and the full citation appears in footnote 42. Later in the document, you want to refer to this book again in footnote 73, at page 106. Which of the following short-form citations is correct?
a. Gallacher, *A Form and Style Manual for Lawyers* at 106.
b. Gallacher, *supra* n. 42, at 106.
c. Gallacher, *supra* n. 73, at 106.
d. Gallacher, *supra* at 106.

9-E.2. Use the information in the following full citation to answer the two questions below.

Charles R. Calleros, *Legal Method and Writing* 282 (5th ed., Aspen Publishers 2006).

9-E.2.a.   The full citation appears in a document *without* footnotes. Later in the document, after referring to other sources, you want to refer to this book again, specifically pages 301 to 304. Which of the following short-form citations is correct?

a. Calleros, *Legal Method and Writing* at 301–304.
b. Calleros, *Legal Method and Writing*, at 301, 302, 303, and 304.
c. Calleros, *supra* at 301–304.
d. Charles R. Calleros, *Legal Method and Writing*, at 301–304.

9-E.2.b.   The same source appears in a document *with* footnotes, and the full citation appears in footnote 8. Later in the document, you want to refer to this book again in footnote 22, at pages 301 to 304. Which of the following short-form citations is correct?

a. Calleros, *Legal Method and Writing* at 301–304.
b. Calleros, *supra* at 301–304.
c. Calleros, *supra* n. 22, at 301–304.
d. Calleros, *supra* n. 8, at 301–304.

9-E.3.   Use the information in the following full citation to answer the two questions below.

Clint Bolick, *Sunshine Replaces the Cloud*, in *The Future of School Choice* 55, 62 (Paul E. Peterson ed., Hoover Inst. Press 2003).

9-E.3.a.   The full citation appears in a document *without* footnotes. Later in the document, after referring to other sources, you want to refer to the shorter work again, specifically page 70. Which of the following short-form citations is correct?

a. Bolick, *Sunshine Replaces the Cloud*, in *The Future of School Choice*, at 70.
b. Bolick, *Sunshine Replaces the Cloud* at 70.
c. Bolick, *supra*, at 70.
d. Bolick, *supra*, in *The Future of School Choice*, at 70.

9-E.3.b.   The full citation appears in a document *with* footnotes, in footnote 45. You would like to refer to the shorter work again in footnote 103, at page 70. Which of the following short-form citations is correct?

a. Bolick, *Sunshine Replaces the Cloud* at 70.
b. Bolick, *Sunshine Replaces the Cloud*, *supra* n. 45, at 70.
c. Bolick, *supra* n. 45, at 70.
d. Bolick, *supra* n. 103, at 70.

EXERCISE SET 9-E

INTERMEDIATE LEVEL: SHORT-FORM CITATIONS

Before beginning Exercise Set 9-E Intermediate Level, review the following and keep the *Manual* at hand as you work through the exercises:

- Rule 22.2, Short Citation Format for Works Other Than Those in a Collection
- Rule 22.3, Short Citation Format for Works in a Collection

To complete the exercises, you may also need to refer to the following:

- Rule 11.1, Full Citation Format
- Rule 11.2, Short Citation Format
- Rule 11.3, *Id.* as a Short Citation, specifically subsections (a)–(e), and (g)
- Rule 11.4, *Supra* as a Short Citation

9-E.4. Use the information in the following full citation to answer the two questions below.

> Elizabeth Fajans & Mary R. Falk, *Scholarly Writing for Law Students: Seminar Papers, Law Review Notes and Law Review Competition Papers* 7 (3d ed., Thomson/West 2000) [hereinafter *Scholarly Writing*].

9-E.4.a. The full citation appears in a document *without* footnotes. Later in the document, after referring to other sources, you want to refer to this book again, specifically pages 99 to 100. Which of the following short-form citations is correct?

- a. Elizabeth Fajans & Mary R. Falk, *Scholarly Writing for Law Students: Seminar Papers, Law Review Notes and Law Review Competition Papers* at 99–100.
- b. Fajans & Falk, *Scholarly Writing for Law Students: Seminar Papers, Law Review Notes and Law Review Competition Papers* at 99–100.
- c. Fajans & Falk, *Scholarly Writing* at 99–100.
- d. Fajans & Falk, *supra* at 99–100.

9-E.4.b. The same source appears in a document *with* footnotes, specifically footnote 113. Later in the document, you want to refer to this book again in footnote 136, specifically pages 99 to 100. Which of the following short-form citations is correct?

- a. Elizabeth Fajans & Mary R. Falk, *supra* n. 113, at 99–100.
- b. Fajans & Falk, *supra* n. 136, at 99–100.
- c. Fajans & Falk, *supra*, at 99–100.
- d. Fajans & Falk, *supra* n. 113, at 99–100.

9-E.5. Use the information in the following full citation to answer the two questions below.

David Delaney, *Race, Place, and the Law 1836–1948*, at 50 (U. Tex. Press 1998).

9-E.5.a. The full citation appears in a document *without* footnotes. Later in the document, after citing other sources, you want to cite this book again, referring to page 50. Which of the following short-form citations is correct?

    a. Delaney, *Race, Place, and the Law 1836–1948*, at 50.
    b. Delaney, *Race, Place, and the Law 1836–1948*.
    c. David Delaney, *supra*.
    d. Delaney, *supra* at 50.

9-E.5.b. The full citation appears in a document *with* footnotes, specifically footnote 67. You want to refer to this book again in footnote 70, at page 50. Which of the following short-form citations is correct?

    a. Delaney, *Race, Place, and the Law 1836*–1948 at 50.
    b. Delaney, *supra* at 50.
    c. Delaney, *supra* n. 67.
    d. Delaney, *supra* n. 67, at 50.

9-E.6. Use the information in the following full citation to answer the two questions below.

    Thomas A. Cotton, *Nuclear Waste Story: Setting the Stage*, in *Uncertainty Underground: Yucca Mountain and the Nation's High-Level Nuclear Waste* 29, 36 (Allison M. Macfarlane & Rodney C. Ewing eds., MIT Press 2006) [hereinafter *Uncertainty Underground*].

9-E.6.a. The full citation appears in a document *without* footnotes. Later in the document, after referring to other sources, you want to refer to this book again, but to a different shorter work—William M. Murphy's *Regulating the Geologic Disposal of High-Level Nuclear Waste at Yucca Mountain*. The shorter work begins at page 45, and you want to refer to page 48. Which of the following short-form citations is the correct citation for the Murphy work?

    a. William M. Murphy, *Regulating the Geologic Disposal of High-Level Nuclear Waste at Yucca Mountain*, in *Uncertainty Underground*, at 48.
    b. William M. Murphy, *Regulating the Geologic Disposal of High-Level Nuclear Waste at Yucca Mountain*, in *Uncertainty Underground*, *supra*, at 48.
    c. William M. Murphy, *Regulating the Geologic Disposal of High-Level Nuclear Waste at Yucca Mountain*, in *supra*, at 48.
    d. William M. Murphy, *Regulating the Geologic Disposal of High-Level Nuclear Waste at Yucca Mountain*, in *id.* at 48.

9-E.6.b. The same source appears in a document *with* footnotes, specifically footnote 3. Later in the document (and *id.* is not appropriate), you want to refer to this book again, but to the shorter work by William M. Murphy, *Regulating the Geologic Disposal of High-Level Nuclear Waste at Yucca Mountain*. You want to refer to this work in footnote 50. The shorter work starts on page 45, and you want to refer to page 48. Which of the following short-form citations is correct?

    a. William M. Murphy, *Regulating the Geologic Disposal of High-Level Nuclear Waste at Yucca Mountain*, in *Uncertainty Underground*, *supra*, at 48.
    b. William M. Murphy, *Regulating the Geologic Disposal of High-Level Nuclear Waste at Yucca Mountain*, in *Uncertainty Underground*, at 48.
    c. William M. Murphy, *Regulating the Geologic Disposal of High-Level Nuclear Waste at Yucca Mountain*, in *Uncertainty Underground*, *supra* n. 3, at 48.
    d. William M. Murphy, *Regulating the Geologic Disposal of High-Level Nuclear Waste at Yucca Mountain*, in *Uncertainty Underground*, *supra* n. 50, at 48.

EXERCISE SET 9-E

EXPERT LEVEL: SHORT-FORM CITATIONS

Before beginning Exercise Set 9-E Expert Level, review the following and keep the *Manual* at hand as you work through the exercises:

• Rule 22.2, Short Citation Format for Works Other Than Those in a Collection
• Rule 22.3, Short Citation Format for Works in a Collection

To complete the exercises, you may also need to refer to the following:

• Rule 11.1, Full Citation Format
• Rule 11.2, Short Citation Format
• Rule 11.3, *Id.* as a Short Citation, specifically subsections (a)–(e), and (g).
  Rule 11.4, *Supra* as a Short Citation

9-E.7.   This question has three parts. Use the information provided below to answer the questions.

THE PRACTICE
OF LAW SCHOOL:

Getting in and Making the Most
of Your Legal Education

Christen Civiletto Carey, Esq.
and
Professor Kristen David Adams

2003

ALM Publishing

9-E.7.a.   Write the full citation for the book pictured above. Assume the pinpoint reference is page 15.

9-E.7.b.   You want to cite the same book again in a document *without* footnotes. Assuming that *id.* is not appropriate, provide the short-form citation with a pinpoint reference to pages 439 to 441.

9-E.7.c.   You want to cite the same book again in a document *with* footnotes. The full citation was provided in footnote 28, and the short-form citation will appear in footnote 51. Assuming that *id.* is not appropriate, provide the short-form citation with a pinpoint reference to pages 439 to 441.

9-E.8. The information provided below comes from HeinOnline. Use it to answer the three questions.

The title page for the collection:

> CELEBRATION LEGAL ESSAYS
> *By Various Authors*
>
> To Mark the Twenty-fifth Year
> of Service of
>
> John H. Wigmore
>
> As Professor of Law in
> Northwestern University
>
> Chicago
> Northwestern University Press
> 1919

The titles for the shorter works:
This essay starts on page 113.

> PART IV
> LEGAL EDUCATION
> _____
> SOME ESSENTIALS OF A
> MODERN LEGAL EDUCATION
> By John Bradley Winslow

This essay starts on page 435.

> PART X
> PRIVATE LAW
> _____
> CONSIDERATION IN EQUITY
> By Roscoe Pound

9-E.8.a. You are interested in referring to the Winslow essay in this collection titled "Some Essentials of a Modern Legal Education," specifically information found on page 114. Provide the full citation to the Winslow essay.

9-E.8.b. In a document *without* footnotes, you would like refer to the Winslow essay again later in the document (using *id.* is not appropriate). Provide the short-form citation to the essay, referring to pages 117 to 118.

9-E.8.c. In a document *with* footnotes, you would like to refer to another essay within this source, specifically the Pound essay titled "Consideration in Equity." The information is in the source's footnote 17, on page 440. Your document's full citation to the source is in footnote 246, and you would like to refer to the essay a second time in footnote 253. Provide the short-form citation to the Pound essay.

LEGAL PERIODICALS

This chapter provides practice with each of the major components of legal periodical citations. There are many types of legal periodicals, such as law reviews and law journals, bar association journals, magazines, bulletins, and newsletters. Rule 23, which covers legal periodicals, is also used to cite non-legal periodicals.

The components of legal periodical citations are almost identical to the components of book, treatise, and looseleaf citations. This chapter revisits and re-emphasizes components that were introduced in Chapter 9 such as author and title, pinpoint reference, and date. This chapter also introduces a new component—periodical abbreviations. You will also learn how to cite legal periodicals that are "working papers" or published on the Social Sciences Research Network ("SSRN").

A. AUTHORS AND TITLES

The first component in a legal periodical citation is the author's name. As discussed in Chapter 9, the author could be a single author or multiple authors, or in some cases, the author may be unknown or not listed. Present the author's full name including designations such as "Jr." or "II," but do not include titles of respect or an author's degree information.

There is one difference from the author name discussed in Chapter 9; sometimes, the author of a law review or journal article is a student. If that is the case, the phrase "Student Author" is placed after a comma that follows the author name. Determining whether the author is a student can sometimes be challenging. Sidebar 23.1 discusses several guidelines to help you identify student-written articles. In addition to noticing where the articles are published (e.g., at the end of the law review or journal issue), and the designation of the article (e.g., casenote, note, comment, or recent development), you may find other clues to determine whether the article was written by a student:

- The author's name may not appear until the end of the article.
- The first footnote of the article (sometimes referred to as the "bio footnote") may describe the author's background. Look for a description such as "J.D. expected," which indicates that the student had not graduated from law school at the time the article was published.
- If the article provides an abstract after the title, review the abstract for key phrases such as a description of the author's background or the article's designation.

The second component of a legal periodical citation is the title. Although titles were covered in Chapters 3 and 9, this section of Chapter 10 revisits the common rules. Here are some guidelines to help you format the titles of legal periodicals:

- As mentioned in Rule 23.1(b)(1), present the title as it appears in the article, except for the capitalization, which you may need to correct. Do not abbreviate or omit words from the title.
- If the article does not have a title, use the designation provided by the periodical—"Book Review," "Essay," "Commentary," for example—as seen in Rule 23.1(b)(2).
- Italicize the title, but not a case or publication name within the title or foreign words not incorporated into normal English. These words should be presented in ordinary typeface. See Rules 1.6 and 1.8 for additional guidance.
- If the article title includes a subtitle, place a colon and one space between the title and the subtitle. Newspaper articles often use a semi-colon to separate the title and subtitle. If that is the case, retain the original punctuation. If the title concludes with end punctuation such as a question mark or exclamation point, omit the colon between the title and the subtitle.
- According to Rule 23.1(b)(4), a comma in ordinary typeface follows the title of the article. However, if the title concludes with end punctuation such as an exclamation point or question mark, omit the comma after the title.
- If the title ends with a quotation mark, the only punctuation that goes inside the quotation mark is that punctuation that is part of the title. The comma that indicates the end of the title should be placed outside the quotation mark, unless the title ends with an exclamation point or a question mark. In that case, there should be no comma after the title.

The exercises below help you identify and construct the author and title components in citations to periodicals.

EXERCISE SET 10-A

BASIC LEVEL: AUTHORS AND TITLES

Before beginning Exercise Set 10-A Basic Level, review the following and keep the *Manual* at hand as you work through the exercises:

- Rule 23.1(a), Author's name
- Rule 23.1(b), Title

To complete the exercises, you may also need to refer to the following:

- Rule 1.6, Italicizing Material within Italicized Material
- Rule 1.8, Italicizing Foreign Words

If a question involves capitalizing words in a title, double underline the first letter of each word that should be capitalized. Use proofreader's marks. For example: shifting paradigms of lawyer honesty

10-A.1. Double-underline the first letter of each word that should be capitalized in the following title:

a legal duty to disclose individual research findings to research subjects?

10-A.2. Double-underline the first letter of each word that should be capitalized in the following title:

let's talk: critical aspects of the anti-contact rule for lawyers

10-A.3. The Honorable Richard A. Posner, United States Court of Appeals for the Seventh Circuit judge, wrote an essay that was published in the *Duke Law Journal*. How should Judge Posner's name appear in the full citation?

a. Honorable Richard A. Posner
b. Judge Richard A. Posner
c. Richard A. Posner, Judge
d. Richard A. Posner

10-A.4. Use the information provided below to answer the following three questions.

> CASENOTES
> *SHER V. LAFAYETTE INSURANCE CO.:* **A TOTAL VICTORY FOR INSURANCE COMPANIES?**

10-A.4.a. Is the author a student?

a. Yes
b. No

10-A.4.b. Explain how you arrived at your answer to Question 10-A.4.a. above.

10-A.4.c. Write the title of the article, double-underlining the first letter of each word that should be capitalized.

10-A.5. Robert G. Morvillo, Barry A. Bohrer, and Barbara L. Balter wrote an essay published in the *American Criminal Law Review*. How should their names appear in the full citation?

    a. Robert G. Morvillo et al.,
    b. Morvillo, Robert G., Bohrer, Barry A., and Balter, Barbara L.,
    c. Robert G. Morvillo, Barry A. Bohrer, and Barbara L. Balter
    d. Morvillo et al.,

10-A.6. Using the information in the text box below, write the author and title for the full citation to this article. Double-underline the first letter of each word that should be capitalized.

NOW PERFORMING IN A COURTROOM NEAR YOU: THE ELDERLY EYEWITNESS! TO BELIEVE OR NOT TO BELIEVE THAT IS THE QUESTION
John W. Clark III, Ph.D. and Roger Enriquez

EXERCISE SET 10-A

INTERMEDIATE LEVEL: AUTHORS AND TITLES

Before beginning Exercise Set 10-A Intermediate level, review the following and keep the *Manual* at hand as you work through the exercises:

• Rule 23.1(a), Author's name
• Rule 23.1(b), Title

To complete the exercises, you may also need to refer to the following:

• Rule 1.6, Italicizing Material within Italicized Material
• Rule 1.8, Italicizing Foreign Words

If a question involves capitalizing words in a title, double underline the first letter of each word that should be capitalized. Use proofreader's marks. For example: shifting paradigms of lawyer honesty

10-A.7. Use the information provided below to answer the following two questions.

THE INTERNATIONAL CONVENTION FOR THE SUPPRESSION OF ACTS OF NUCLEAR TERRORISM: WHO RATIFIES AND WHY?

Derrick L. Clarke

Abstract

Are there common characteristics of the United Nations member states' behavior when deciding to ratify the International Convention for the Suppression of Acts of Nuclear Terrorism? International treaty theories have suggested several explanations of state behavior when deciding to ratify this convention. To test this hypothesis, this Comment's statistical analyses builds upon an earlier study performed by Kendall W. Stiles and Adam Thayne, *Compliance with International Law: International Law on Terrorism at the United Nations*, 41 Cooperation & Conflict 153 (2006), by focusing strictly on the impact of United States bilateral trade relations while examining other governance and economic capacity indicators. Ultimately, the results of this study reveal that strong bilateral trade relations of the United Nations member states with the United States exhibit the strongest characteristic of ratifying countries.

10-A.7.a. Is the author a student?

  a. Yes
  b. No

10-A.7.b. Briefly explain your answer to Question 10-A.7.a. above.

10-A.8. Using the information in the text box below, write the author and title of the article. (The author is not a student.)

> **Book Review**
>
> Leona D. Jochnowitz

10-A.9. Write the following title, double-underlining the first letter of each word that should be capitalized.

  out of sight, but not out of mind: how executive order 13,233 expands executive privilege while simultaneously preventing access to presidential records

10-A.10. Write the title for the article shown below. Double-underline the first letter of each word that should be capitalized.

> **CASEBOOK REVIEW**
>
> The Wide World of Torts: Reviewing Franklin & Rabin's *Tort Law and Alternatives*
>
> *Bernard W. Bell*

10-A.11. Write the names of the authors from the article shown below as they should appear in a full citation. (Robert M. Wilsey and Hillary A. Taylor are students.)

> Articles
>
> SEEKING BEST PRACTICES AMONG INTERMEDIATE COURTS OF APPEAL: A NASCENT JOURNEY
>
> W. Warren H. Binford, Preston C. Greene, Maria C. Schmidlkofer, Robert M. Wilsey, Hillary A. Taylor

EXERCISE SET 10-A

EXPERT LEVEL: AUTHORS AND TITLES

Before beginning Exercise Set 10-A Expert Level, review the following and keep the *Manual* at hand as you work through the exercises:

- Rule 23.1(a), Author's name
- Rule 23.1(b), Title

To complete the exercises, you may also need to refer to the following:

- Rule 1.6, Italicizing Material within Italicized Material
- Rule 1.8, Italicizing Foreign Words

If a question involves capitalizing words in a title, double underline the first letter of each word that should be capitalized. Use proofreader's marks. For example: shifting paradigms of lawyer honesty

10-A.12. Use the information in the text box below, and write the author and title as they should appear in a full citation. Double-underline the first letter of each word that should be capitalized.

STUDENT NOTE AND COMMENT: EX-POST-BOOKER: RETROACTIVE APPLICATION OF FEDERAL SENTENCING GUIDELINES

NAME: Christine M. Zeivel*

10-A.13. Use the information in the text box below, and write the author and title as they should appear in a full citation. Double-underline the first letter of each word that should be capitalized.

Comment: Southwestern Bell Telephone, L.P. v. City of Houston: Has The Fifth Circuit Barred the Use of a § 1983 Claim to Enforce Section 253 of the Telecommunications Act of 1996?

NAME: Christopher J. Costello

10-A.14. Use the information provided below, and write the author and title as they should appear in a full citation. Double-underline the first letter of each word in the title that should be capitalized.

Top of the first page of the article

First footnote on the first page of the article

NOTES

RATIONALIZING HARD LOOK REVIEW
AFTER THE FACT

INTRODUCTION

A fundamental illogic of administrative law is that courts strictly review agencies' determinations of fact and policy but defer to their interpretations of law.[1] Presumably, the opposite should be the case: judges should pay closer attention to their specialty — the law — and less to areas in which they have no particular expertise, such as those with scientific and technical aspects. This is not, however, how judicial review
to agencie
determina
been frequ
ating dela

[1] *See* Stephen Breyer, *Judicial Review of Questions of Law and Policy*, 38 ADMIN. L. REV. 363 (1986); Thomas J. Miles & Cass R. Sunstein, *The Real World of Arbitrariness Review*, 75 U. CHI. L. REV. 761, 772 (2008) ("If we attend to the distinctive competence of agencies and courts, the opposite conclusion might seem hard to resist: questions of law are for judicial resolution, whereas questions of policy and fact should be resolved by agencies."). *Compare* Chevron U.S.A. Inc. v. Natural Res. Def. Council, Inc., 467 U.S. 837, 843-44 (1984), *with* Motor Vehicle Mfrs. Ass'n v. State Farm Mut. Auto. Ins. Co., 463 U.S. 29, 43 (1983).

The only information provided on the last page of the article

1930   *HARVARD LAW REVIEW*   [Vol. 122:1909

sion of missing rationales for administrative policy ex post. Though only a modest step, this proposal would effectively soften aspects of the hard look doctrine while leaving the bulk of the doctrine in place.

10-A.15. The text box below shows the beginning of a recent development article published in volume 38 of the *Stetson Law Review*, starting on page 753. "Land Use Planning & Zoning: Takings" is the subheading in the section. Below the subheading is the citation to the case being discussed in the recent development. Write the author and title of this recent development.

Land Use Planning & Zoning: Takings

Drake v. Walton County,
2009 WL 981218 (Fla. 1st Dist. App. Apr. 14, 2009)

This is the author information from the last page of the recent development, page 738

Matthew E. Kahn

B. PERIODICAL ABBREVIATIONS

After the author and title, the next component is information about the periodical in which the article can be found. The reader needs three pieces of information—the volume number, the periodical abbreviation, and the initial page.

Volume number: After the title of the article, include the volume number of the periodical if one is available. Use Arabic numbers, even if the periodical uses Roman numerals. If the volume number for a law review is not available, use the publication year in place of the volume number. (If the year is used as the volume number, do not repeat the year at the end of the full citation in the date parenthetical.) Some legal periodicals, like newspapers, do not have volume numbers, or the volume number is not readily available. If that is the case, provide the periodical abbreviation immediately following the title.

Periodical abbreviation: After the volume number (or title, if a volume number is not available), include the abbreviation for the periodical. There are two ways to determine the periodical abbreviation:

- Look for the name of the periodical in Appendix 5.
- If the periodical is not listed in Appendix 5, use the spacing conventions explained in Rule 2.2 and the abbreviations in Appendix 3 to create the periodical abbreviation.

In the fourth edition of the *Manual*, you will find some alternative abbreviations in Appendices 3(E) and 5. These abbreviations, or more accurately, "contractions," contain apostrophes. For example, the word "international" can be abbreviated as "int'l" or "intl." You may use either the abbreviations or the contractions for words in a periodical title, but you must be consistent in the form that you use. The *Companion* uses the abbreviations.

When you construct citations to newspapers and newsletters, include information about the newspaper's place of publication if the place is not evident from the periodical title or the place is not well known. Similarly, include information about the issuing organization that publishes a newsletter. Both types of information—the place of publication of a newspaper and the issuing organization of a newsletter—should be placed in a parenthetical that follows the periodical abbreviation.

A note on periodical names that have titles and subtitles: Because Rule 23.1(d) directs you to "omit colons, and everything following them, that may appear within the title [of the periodical]," do not include subtitles in the periodical abbreviation. For example, Appendix 5 shows the periodical abbreviation for the journal, *Asian Pacific American Law Journal: UCLA School of Law*, as "Asian P. Am. L.J." The subtitle "UCLA School of Law" is not part of the abbreviation.

Initial page: After the periodical abbreviation, provide the initial page of the article.

The exercises below help you identify and construct the periodical abbreviation component—volume number, periodical abbreviation, and initial page—of citations to periodicals.

EXERCISE SET 10-B

BASIC LEVEL: PERIODICAL ABBREVIATIONS

Before beginning Exercise Set 10-B Basic Level, review the following and keep the *Manual* at hand as you work through the exercises:

- Rule 23.1(d), Periodical abbreviation

To complete the exercises, you may also need to refer to the following:

- Rule 2.0, Abbreviations
- Appendix 3, General Abbreviations
- Appendix 5, Abbreviations for Legal Periodicals

10-B.1. A print copy of a 2008 issue of *The John Marshall Journal of Computer and Information Law* displays the volume number XXVI on the cover. How should you present the volume number in the full citation?

a. XXVI
b. 26
c. Use the date of the issue instead of the volume number, 2008.
d. No volume number should be included in the full citation.

10-B.2. Which of the following is the correct abbreviation for the *Fordham Intellectual Property, Media & Entertainment Law Journal*?

a. Fordham Intellectual Property, Media & Entertainment Law Journal
b. Fordham Intell. Prop., Media & Ent. L. J.
c. Fordham Intell. Prop. Media & Ent. L.J.
d. Fordham Intell. Prop., Media & Ent. L.J.

10-B.3. Which of the following is the correct abbreviation for the *Boston College Law Review*?

a. Boston College Law Review
b. B.C.L.Rev.
c. B.C.L. Rev.
d. B.C. L. Rev.

10-B.4. Explain the spacing (or lack thereof) between the abbreviations of the words in the answer you chose to Question 10-B.3. above, and provide the applicable rule number(s).

10-B.5. **True or False:** The abbreviation for the *Chicago Sun Times* needs a parenthetical after it to identify the place of publication.

a. True
b. False

10-B.6. **True or False:** The abbreviation for *The Second Draft*, a publication of the Legal Writing Institute, needs a parenthetical after it to identify the issuing organization.

a. True
b. False

EXERCISE SET 10-B

INTERMEDIATE LEVEL: PERIODICAL ABBREVIATIONS

Before beginning Exercise Set 10-B Intermediate Level, review the following and keep the *Manual* at hand as you work through the exercises:

• Rule 23.1(d), Periodical abbreviation

To complete the exercises, you may also need to refer to the following:

• Rule 2.0, Abbreviations
• Appendix 3, General Abbreviations
• Appendix 5, Abbreviations for Legal Periodicals

10-B.7. Write the abbreviation for *Berkley Business Law Journal.*

10-B.8. Write the abbreviation for *Southern Methodist University Law Journal.*

10-B.9. Write the abbreviation for *Journal of Law, Information and Science.*

10-B.10. Write the abbreviation for *Advocates' Quarterly.*

EXERCISE SET 10-B

EXPERT LEVEL: PERIODICAL ABBREVIATIONS

Before beginning Exercise Set 10-B Expert Level, review the following and keep the *Manual* at hand as you work through the exercises:

• Rule 23.1(d), Periodical abbreviation

To complete the exercises, you may also need to refer to the following:

• Rule 2.0, Abbreviations
• Appendix 3, General Abbreviations
• Appendix 5, Abbreviations for Legal Periodicals

10-B.11. Write the abbreviation for *Berkeley Journal of Gender, Law & Justice.*

10-B.12. Write the abbreviation for *Roman Legal Tradition.*

10-B.13. Write the abbreviation for *Administrative & Regulatory Law News.*

10-B.14. Write the abbreviation for *Law & Justice: The Christian Law Review.*

C. PINPOINT REFERENCES

After the initial page of the article, place a comma and a space and provide a pinpoint reference for the information you are citing. As discussed in Chapter 3 and reiterated throughout other chapters, the pinpoint reference is *very* important. The pinpoint reference could be a single page or multiple scattered pages, a footnote or multiple footnotes, or graphical material such as a table, figure, chart, or appendix. Use Rules 5.0, 6.0, 7.0, and 9.0 as needed when providing pinpoint references.

On some occasions, you may not want to cite a single article within an issue; instead, you may want to cite an entire issue because the issue contains "an entire symposium, colloquium, survey, or special issue," as discussed in Rule 23.1(g). In this instance, the initial page is the first page of the symposium and you do not need a pinpoint reference.

The exercises below help you identify and construct pinpoint references for citations to periodicals.

EXERCISE SET 10-C

BASIC LEVEL: PINPOINT REFERENCES

Before beginning Exercise Set 10-C Basic Level, review the following and keep the *Manual* at hand as you work through the exercises:

- Rule 23.1(e), Page numbers
- Rule 23.1(g), Symposia, colloquia, survey issues, and special issues

To complete the exercises, you may also need to refer to the following:

- Rule 5.0, Page and Location Numbers
- Rule 7.0, Citing Footnotes and Endnotes
- Rule 9.0, Graphical Material, Appendices, and Other Subdivisions

10-C.1. Identify the pinpoint reference in the following short-form citation.

> Gallacher, *supra* n. 153, at 16, 17.

10-C.2. Explain the difference between the pinpoint reference in the citation in Question 10-C.1 above and the following pinpoint reference: 16–17. Provide the applicable rule number(s).

10-C.3. Identify the pinpoint reference in the following citation.

> Joanne Dugan, *Choosing the Right Tool for Internet Searching: Search Engines vs. Directories*, 14 Persp. 111, 111 n. 1 (2006).

10-C.4. Identify the pinpoint reference in the following citation.

> Vanessa Baird & Tonja Jacob, *How the Dissent Becomes the Majority: Using Federalism to Transform Coalitions in the U.S. Supreme Court*, 59 Duke L.J. 183, 205 tbl. 1 (2009).

10-C.5. Identify the pinpoint reference in the following citation.

> Theodore Eisenberg & Geoffrey P. Miller, *Reversal, Dissent, and Variability in State Supreme Courts: The Centrality of Jurisdictional Source,* 89 B.U. L. Rev. 1451, 1474–1475 fig. 1 (2009).

10-C.6. Identify the pinpoint reference in the following citation.

> Raymond Shih Ray Ku et al., *Does Copyright Law Promote Creativity? An Empirical Analysis of Copyright's Bounty,* 62 Vand. L. Rev. 1669, app. 3 (2009).

10-C.7. **True or False:** The pinpoint page you want to refer to is the same page as the initial page of the article. In that case, you still need to repeat the pinpoint page in the full citation.

> a. True
> b. False

EXERCISE SET 10-C

INTERMEDIATE LEVEL: PINPOINT REFERENCES

> Before beginning Exercise Set 10-C Intermediate Level, review the following and keep the *Manual* at hand as you work through the exercises:
>
> • Rule 23.1(e), Page numbers
> • Rule 23.1(g), Symposia, colloquia, survey issues, and special issues
>
> To complete the exercises, you may also need to refer to the following:
>
> • Rule 5.0, Page and Location Numbers
> • Rule 7.0, Citing Footnotes and Endnotes
> • Rule 9.0, Graphical Material, Appendices, and Other Subdivisions

10-C.8. Professor Marilyn R. Walter's article, in volume 43 of the *Journal of Legal Education,* starting on page 569, is titled "Retaking Control over Teaching Research." You refer to footnote 1 of the article, which is also on page 569. Fill in the blanks in the full citation.

> Marilyn R. Walter, *Retaking Control over Teaching Research,* 43 J. Leg. Educ. _____, _____ (1993).

10-C.9. Still using the article from the question above, you now refer to footnotes 40 to 47, which appear on pages 575 and 576. Fill in the blanks in the full citation.

> Marilyn R. Walter, *Retaking Control over Teaching Research,* 43 J. Leg. Educ. _____, _____ (1993).

10-C.10. An article by Susan Franck is published in volume 86 of the *North Carolina Law Review*, starting at page 1. You refer to table 3, on page 40. Fill in the blanks in the full citation.

> Susan D. Franck, *Empirically Evaluating Claims about Investment Treaty Arbitration*, 86 N.C. L. Rev. _____, _____ (2007).

EXERCISE SET 10-C

EXPERT LEVEL: PINPOINT REFERENCES

Before beginning Exercise Set 10-C Expert Level, review the following and keep the *Manual* at hand as you work through the exercises:

- Rule 23.1(e), Page numbers
- Rule 23.1(g), Symposia, colloquia, survey issues, and special issues

To complete the exercises, you may also need to refer to the following:

- Rule 5.0, Page and Location Numbers
- Rule 7.0, Citing Footnotes and Endnotes
- Rule 9.0, Graphical Material, Appendices, and Other Subdivisions

10-C.11. You are citing an article that starts at page 408 of the *Maine Law Review*, volume 59. Specifically, you refer to pages 408, 411, and 426 to 429 in the full citation. Write the initial page and pinpoint reference components of a full citation to the article.

10-C.12. You are referring to three footnotes from an article that starts at page 589 of the *Washington University Law Quarterly*, volume 80. You cite footnotes 1 and 2, which appear on page 589, and footnote 18, on page 593. Write the initial page and pinpoint reference components of a full citation to the article.

10-C.13. You are referring to table A, at page 660, and the appendix, at pages 677 and 678, of an article published in volume 16 of the *Columbia Journal of Gender and Law*. The article starts at page 643. Write the initial page and pinpoint reference components of the full citation.

10-C.14. Write the initial page of the Symposium shown below, as needed in a full citation to the entire symposium.

Legal Writing
The Journal of the
Legal Writing Institute

D.   DATE

The date of the article is presented at the end of the full citation, in parentheses. Whether the year that the article was published is sufficient or whether something more is needed depends upon whether the article is published in a consecutively paginated or a non-consecutively paginated journal. Typically, legal periodicals are published in issues, and a certain number of issues make up a volume (usually corresponding to a calendar or academic year). For example, the *Student Lawyer*, a publication of the American Bar Association, is published once a month for nine months. And nine issues comprise a volume. A new volume starts in September of each year. Another example is the *Stetson Law Review*, in which a volume contains three issues that are published during an academic year.

The difference between a consecutively paginated and a non-consecutively paginated journal is whether each issue starts on page 1. If each issue begins on page 1, the journal is non-consecutively paginated. If pages in the second issue in a volume begin where the first issue left off, the journal is consecutively paginated.

Because issues of non-consecutively paginated journals start over at page 1, the reader needs more information in the date parenthetical to find the article. Use the exact date as provided on the cover or first page of the issue. How do you determine whether the journal you are citing is non-consecutively paginated? Look for a green star next to the journal's title in Appendix 5. If the journal is not listed in Appendix 5, look at the pagination of the previous issue of the journal and compare it to the issue you are citing. Most newspapers, newsletters, and bar association journals are non-consecutively paginated journals, whereas most law reviews or journals are consecutively paginated.

The exercises below help you identify and construct the date component of citations to periodicals. This set of exercises is for all levels.

EXERCISE SET 10-D

ALL LEVELS: DATE

Before beginning Exercise Set 10-D All Levels, review the following and keep the *Manual* at hand as you work through the exercises:

• Rule 23.1(f), Date

To complete the exercises, you may also need to refer to the following:

• Appendix 5, Abbreviations for Legal Periodicals

10-D.1. Is the *ABA Journal* a consecutively or non-consecutively paginated periodical?

a. consecutively paginated
b. non-consecutively paginated

10-D.2. Is the *Brigham Young University Law Review* a consecutively or non-consecutively paginated periodical?

a. consecutively paginated
b. non-consecutively paginated

10-D.3. Is the *Family Advocate* a consecutively or non-consecutively paginated periodical?

a. consecutively paginated
b. non-consecutively paginated

10-D.4. Is the *Indianapolis Star* a consecutively or non-consecutively paginated periodical?

a. consecutively paginated
b. non-consecutively paginated

10-D.5. Is the journal in the following citation consecutively or non-consecutively paginated?

Mark Curriden & Patrick Higginbotham, *Judges and Journalists: Defusing Tensions and Building Relationships*, 46 Judges' J. 10, 13 (Spring 2007).

a. consecutively paginated
b. non-consecutively paginated

10-D.6. Is *The Journal of Law, Medicine & Ethics* a consecutively or non-consecutively paginated periodical?

   a. consecutively paginated
   b. non-consecutively paginated

10-D.7. Write the date parenthetical for a full citation to an article published in the periodical issue shown below.

> # For The Defense
> ---
> Vol. 51, No. 5   May 2009

10-D.8. Write the date parenthetical for a full citation to an article published in the periodical issue shown below.

> **School Law Bulletin**
> Winter 2008 · Volume 39, No. 1

10-D.9. Write the date parenthetical for a full citation to an article published in the periodical issue shown below.

> THE CHRONICLE OF HIGHER EDUCATION • DECEMBER 11, 2009

10-D.10. Write the date parenthetical for a full citation to an article published in the periodical issue shown below.

> # Law/Technology
> **1st Quarter 2009**
> **Volume 42 / Number 1**

E. FORTHCOMING WORKS, WORKING PAPERS, AND SSRN

Given the time needed to publish print periodicals, you may need to cite an article that is "forthcoming" or working papers or articles posted on Internet databases such as SSRN (the Social Science Research Network). Keeping in mind the primary goal of citations—that the reader be able to find the source and the information provided within the source—you must give the reader more information to find these types of articles. Table 10.1 summarizes the additional information needed.

The exercises below help you construct the citations to forthcoming works and working papers, which may appear on SSRN. The exercises in this set are for all levels.

TABLE 10.1

FORTHCOMING WORKS, WORKING PAPERS, AND SSRN

Forthcoming Works Rule 36.0	A work is "forthcoming" when it is scheduled for publication, but the issue has not yet appeared in print. • Use the same citation format as will be used when the article is published, but if the volume number or initial page is not available, insert three underlined spaces in the place where the volume number or initial page should appear. • Include the word "forthcoming" at the beginning of the date parenthetical. • Providing a pinpoint reference is a little more difficult with forthcoming works. If the unpublished manuscript is available, add a parenthetical at the end of the full citation. In the parenthetical, provide the pinpoint reference in the unpublished manuscript, and include any other information that will help the reader find the manuscript, such as "on file with the Author" or "on file with Law Review."
Unpublished Works and Working Papers Rule 37.0	Citations to working papers, typically found on SSRN, are similar to a book citation. • Provide the author's name, the title of the paper, and the pinpoint reference, and then in a parenthetical, include the following information: the sponsoring organization, the phrase "Working Paper," and if available, the paper number—all before the date. • Add another parenthetical after the date parenthetical that provides the reader with more information about where the paper can be found on the Internet (URL) or on SSRN.

EXERCISE SET 10-E

ALL LEVELS: FORTHCOMING WORKS, WORKING PAPERS, AND SSRN

Before beginning Exercise Set 10-E All Levels, review the following and keep the *Manual* at hand as you work through the exercises:

• Rule 36.0, Forthcoming Works
• Rule 37.0, Unpublished Works and Working Papers

To complete the exercises, you may also need to refer to the following:

• Appendix 3, General Abbreviations
• Appendix 5, Abbreviations for Legal Periodicals

10-E.1. What information is missing from the following full citation?

> Michael J. Higdon, *Something Judicious This Way Comes . . . The Use of Foreshadowing as a Persuasive Device in Judicial Narrative* 4–5 (2009) (available at http://ssrn.com/abstract=1454887).

a. The name of the sponsoring organization
b. The phrase "Working Paper"
c. The working paper number, if available
d. All of the above

10-E.2. The following information is available about an article that you would like to cite:

Author:	Ellen S. Podgor, Professor of Law, Stetson University College of Law
Article title:	White Collar Innocence: Irrelevant in the High Stakes Risk Game
Article's status:	Forthcoming in the Chicago-Kent Law Review in 2010

Write the full citation to the article, citing pages 2 through 8 of the manuscript, which is available on SSRN.

10-E.3. Write the full citation to the working paper shown below.

**How the Separation of Powers Doctrine
Shaped the Executive**

by

Louis J. Sirico, Jr.

**Villanova University School of Law
Public Law and Legal Theory
Working Paper No. 2008-24**

May 2008

This article is a working paper.

This paper can be downloaded without charge from
the Social Science Research Network Electronic
Paper Collection at
http://ssrn.com/abstract=1139122

10-E.4. Write the full citation to the forthcoming article shown below.

Drexel University Earle Mack School of Law
Legal Studies Research Paper Series
2009-A-23

"Muddy Waters:
The Supreme Court and the Clear Statement Rule for
Spending Clause Legislation"

Terry Jean Seligmann

This article will be published at:
Tulane Law Review, (May 2010)

This article can be downloaded without cost from
the Drexel University Earl Mack School of Law Legal
Studies Research Paper Series
at http://www.ssrn.com/link/Drexel-U-LEG.html

F.   SHORT-FORM CITATIONS

After the full citation to a legal periodical article, you can use a short-form citation—either *id.*, a "short citation," or *supra.* Use *id.* when appropriate; otherwise, whether you should use a "short citation" or *supra* depends upon whether the document has footnotes. If the document does not have footnotes, the short citation has four components:

- Author's last name (or authors' last names, or first author's last name and the phrase "et al.," if the phrase was used in the full citation);
- Volume number;
- Periodical abbreviation; and
- The word "at" and the pinpoint reference.

If the document has footnotes, the same types of information go into the short-form citation; however, the volume number and periodical abbreviation components are replaced with "*supra* n. *X*," where *X* is the footnote number in which the full citation to the article originally appeared.

The exercises below help you identify and construct short-form citations to periodicals.

EXERCISE SET 10-F

BASIC LEVEL: SHORT-FORM CITATIONS

Before beginning Exercise Set 10-F Basic Level, review the following and keep the *Manual* at hand as you work through the exercises:

- Rule 23.2, Short Citation Format [Legal and Other Periodicals]
- Rule 36.2, Short Citation Format [Forthcoming Works]
- Rule 37.2, Short Citation Format for Unpublished Works

To complete the exercises, you may also need to refer to the following:

- Rule 11.2, Short Citation Format
- Rule 11.3, *Id.* as a Short Citation, specifically subsections (a)–(e), and (g)
- Rule 11.4, *Supra* as a Short Citation, specifically subsections (a)–(c)

10-F.1.   Use the following full citation to answer the two questions below.

> Cass R. Sunstein et al., *Ideological Voting on Federal Courts of Appeals: A Preliminary Investigation*, 90 Va. L. Rev. 301, 337–343 (2004).

10-F.1.a.   Assume that the citation appears in a document without footnotes and you would like to cite the article again, but referring to pages 340 to 343. Which of the following is the correct short-form citation?

a. Cass R. Sunstein, David Schkade & Lisa Michelle Ellman, 90 Va. L. Rev. at 340–343.
b. Sunstein, Schkade & Ellman, 90 Va. L. Rev. at 340–343.
c. Cass R. Sunstein et al., 90 Va. L. Rev. at 340–343.
d. Sunstein et al., 90 Va. L. Rev. at 340–343.

10-F.1.b. Assume that the citation appears in a document with footnotes, specifically footnote 33. You would like to refer to the article again in footnote 102, specifically pages 340 to 343. Which of the following is the correct short-form citation?

    a. Sunstein et al., 90 Va. L. Rev. at 340–343.

    b. Sunstein et al., *supra* at 340–343.

    c. Sunstein et al., *supra* n. 33, at 340–343.

    d. Cass R. Sunstein, David Schkade & Lisa Michelle Ellman, *supra* n. 33, at 340–343.

10-F.2. Use the following full citation to answer the two questions below.

> M. Tae Phillips, Student Author, *Un-Equal Protection: Preferential Admissions, Treatment for Athletes,* 60 Ala. L. Rev. 751, 760 (2009).

10-F.2.a. You are writing a document with no footnotes, and after citing the article in full, you would like to refer to it, after citing other sources, at page 751. Which of the following short-form citations is correct?

    a. Phillips, 60 Ala. L. Rev. at 751.

    b. Phillips, Student Author, 60 Ala. L. Rev. at 751.

    c. Phillips, 60 Ala. L. Rev. 751.

    d. Philips, Student Author, 60 Ala. L. Rev. 751.

10-F.2.b. You are writing a document with footnotes, and your full citation to the article appeared in footnote 60. You would like to refer to the article again, after citing other sources, at page 751. Which of the following short-form citations is correct?

    a. Phillips, *supra* at 751.

    b. Phillips, *supra* n. 60, at 751.

    c. Phillips, Student Author, *supra* at 751.

    d. Philips, Student Author, *supra* n. 60, at 751.

EXERCISE SET 10-F

INTERMEDIATE LEVEL: SHORT-FORM CITATIONS

Before beginning Exercise Set 10-F Intermediate Level, review the following and keep the *Manual* at hand as you work through the exercises:

- Rule 23.2, Short Citation Format [Legal and Other Periodicals]
- Rule 36.2, Short Citation Format [Forthcoming Works]
- Rule 37.2, Short Citation Format for Unpublished Works

To complete the exercises, you may also need to refer to the following:

- Rule 11.2, Short Citation Format
- Rule 11.3, *Id.* as a Short Citation, specifically subsections (a)–(e), and (g)
- Rule 11.4, *Supra* as a Short Citation, specifically subsections (a)–(c)

10-F.3.   Use the information provided below from Westlaw to answer the following three questions. (Note: the author is *not* a student.)

---

10 Fordham J. Corp. & Fin. L. 407

Fordham Journal of Corporate and Financial Law
2005

Essay

407 ANTI-DUMPING CIRCUMVENTION IN THE EU AND THE US: IS THERE A FUTURE FOR MULTILATERAL PROVISIONS UNDER THE WTO?

Lucia Ostoni

10-F.3.a.   Provide the full citation to the article, assuming that you would like to refer to footnote 29, at page 412.

10-F.3.b.   Assume that the document that you are writing has no footnotes and you have provided the full citation to the article. You would like to refer to the article again later in the document after providing citations to other sources. Specifically, you would like to refer to footnote 93 at page 425 and footnote 110 at page 427. Provide the short-form citation to the article.

10-F.3.c.   The document you are writing has footnotes, and you have provided the full citation in footnote 107. You would like to refer to the article again in your document's footnote 125, specifically footnote 93 at page 425 and footnote 110 at page 427. *Id.* is not appropriate. Provide the short-form citation to the article.

10-F.4. The box below displays information from an article published in *The Federal Lawyer*, volume 55, starting at page 51. Use it to answer the following three questions:

Practical Lessons from a "Made for TV" Patent Litigation: The Trial of *Yeda Research and Development Co. Ltd v. ImClone Systems Inc. and Aventis Pharmaceuticals Inc.*

By Nicholas Groombridge and Brian Paul Gearing

This is the information from the bottom corner of the page.

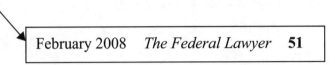

February 2008   *The Federal Lawyer*   **51**

10-F.4.a. Provide the full citation to the article, specifically referring to pages 53 to 55.

10-F.4.b. The document you are writing has no footnotes, and you have provided the full citation to the article. You would like to refer to the article again later in the document, and *id.* is not appropriate. You would like to refer to page 51. Write the short-form citation to the article.

10-F.4.c. Assume that the document that you are writing has footnotes and you have provided the full citation to the article in footnote 57. You would like to refer to the article again in footnote 63, specifically page 51. *Id.* is not appropriate. Provide the short-form citation to the article.

EXERCISE SET 10-F

EXPERT LEVEL: SHORT-FORM CITATIONS

Before beginning Exercise Set 10-F Expert Level, review the following and keep the *Manual* at hand as you work through the exercises:

- Rule 23.2, Short Citation Format [Legal and Other Periodicals]
- Rule 36.2, Short Citation Format [Forthcoming Works]
- Rule 37.2, Short Citation Format for Unpublished Works

To complete the exercises, you may also need to refer to the following:

- Rule 11.2, Short Citation Format
- Rule 11.3, *Id.* as a Short Citation, specifically subsections (a)–(e), and (g)
- Rule 11.4, *Supra* as a Short Citation, specifically subsections (a)–(c)

10-F.5. Use the information provided below to answer the following three questions.

St. John's University School of Law
LEGAL STUDIES RESEARCH PAPER NO. 08-0129

Nova Southeastern University
SHEPARD BROAD LAW CENTER RESEARCH
PAPER NO. 08-010

**The Blind Leading the Blind: What If
They're Not All Visual or Tactile Learners?**

Robin Boyle
St. John's University School of Law

James B. Levy
*Nova Southeastern University—Shepard Broad Law
Center*

This paper can be downloaded free of charge from the
Social Science Research Network at:
http://ssrn.com/abstract=1121352

10-F.5.a. Write the full citation to the paper, specifically referring to page 1.

10-F.5.b. You are writing a paper that does not have footnotes, and you have already provided the full citation to this paper. Later in the document, after citing other sources, you want to refer to this paper again, specifically page 2. Write the short-form citation.

10-F.5.c. You are writing a document that has footnotes, and the full citation to this paper appears in footnote 65. You want to refer to this paper a second time in footnote 71, at page 2. Write the short-form citation.

10-F.6. Use the information provided below from Westlaw to answer the following three questions. (The author is *not* a student.)

---

17 Int'l J. Refugee L. 833

International Journal of Refugee Law
December, 2005

Book Review

***833** MARGARET PHELAN AND JAMES GILLESPIE, IMMIGRATION LAW HANDBOOK, OXFORD: OXFORD UNIVERSITY PRESS, 4TH EDITION 2005, XVII + 1170PP. ISBN 0-19-928473 3

Robin M. White
University of Dundee

10-F.6.a. Write the full citation to the article, specifically referring to page 833.

10-F.6.b. You are writing a document that does not have footnotes, and you provided the full citation to the article. Later in the document, after citing other sources, you refer to the article a second time, but to pages 833 and 835. Provide the short-form citation to the article.

10-F.6.c. You are writing a document that has footnotes, and you provided the full citation to the article in footnote 146. You refer to the article a second time in footnote 152, specifically page 834. Write the short-form citation to the article.

10-F.7. Use the information provided below from LexisNexis to answer the following three questions.

For Judges on Facebook, Friendship Has Limits The New York Times
December 11, 2009 Friday

Copyright 2009 The New York Times Company
The New York Times

December 11, 2009 Friday
Late Edition—Final

SECTION: Section A; Column 0; National Desk; Pg. 25

BYLINE: By **JOHN SCHWARTZ**

10-F.7.a. Write the full citation to the article.

10-F.7.b. You are writing a document that does not have footnotes, and you have already provided the full citation to the article. Later in the document, after citing other sources, you want to refer to the article again. Write the short-form citation to the article.

10-F.7.c. The document you are writing has footnotes, and the full citation to the article appears in footnote 138. Later in the document, you refer to the article a second time in footnote 142. Write the short-form citation to the article.

10-F.8. The information provided below is from the Columbia Journal of Gender and Law. Use it to answer the following three questions about the article by Pat K. Chew and Lauren K. Kelley-Chew (who is a student).

Table of Contents

Volume 16	2007	Number 3

The Subtle Side of Sexism
Deborah L. Rhode 613

Subtly Sexist Language
Pat K. Chew & Lauren K. Kelley-Chew 643

10-F.8.a. Write the full citation to the article, with pinpoint reference to graphs 1 and 2, found at pages 664 and 666, respectively.

10-F.8.b. The document you are writing does not have footnotes, and you have already provided the full citation to the article. Later in the document, after citing other sources, you refer to the article a second time, specifically to graph 1, at page 664, and the entire appendix. Write the short-form citation to the article.

10-F.8.c. The document you are writing has footnotes, and the full citation to the article appears in footnote 232. You refer to the article a second time in footnote 248, referring to graph 2, at page 666, and the entire appendix. Write the short-form citation to the article.

CHAPTER

11

GENERAL WORKS

Chapter 11 addresses works that you will frequently consult as you begin a new project. Many are intended to provide a sweeping overview of the law; others collect the law of several jurisdictions into a single source; and still others prescribe ideal or standardized versions of laws on specific topics, in hopes that they will be adopted across jurisdictions. And many function as excellent research tools, assisting you in finding relevant mandatory or persuasive authority.

These general works—including Restatements, model laws, encyclopedias, and annotations, among others—exhibit some qualities similar to statutory codes, some qualities similar to books and treatises, and some qualities similar to periodicals. Many feature unique characteristics of their own as well. Therefore, although these works are addressed in specific *ALWD Citation Manual* rules, you will also find cross-references to rules in the *Manual* on analogous works.

The chapter begins by examining the citation features of Restatements, uniform laws, and model laws, all covered in Rule 27.0. You will then work with citations to general reference works such as dictionaries (Rule 25.0), encyclopedias (Rule 26.0), and annotations (Rule 24.0). The last section of the chapter focuses on short-form citations for all these works.

RESTATEMENTS, UNIFORM LAWS, AND MODEL LAWS

Restatements

Restatements are compendia of the law on particular subjects, drafted by members of the American Law Institute ("ALI").[1] Their goal is to represent the most generally accepted view of American common law on those subjects. A Restatement is not primary authority because it is not a source of law published by a governmental branch, but it is highly persuasive. Many state courts have "adopted" a particular Restatement section when they are faced with a common-law issue that a Restatement addresses.

The full citation format for a Restatement is shown in Rule 27.1. Because all Restatements are authored by ALI members on its behalf, the citation omits an author name, even if one is shown. Begin with the specific Restatement's full title in italics, including its subtitle, if any. If you cite a Restatement series other than the first, insert the spelled-out ordinal number of the series in parentheses after the word Restatement, as shown in the examples in Rule 27.1(a).

Even though some Restatements are published in multiple volumes, the section numbering within a Restatement is continuous. Therefore, omit reference to the volume number in the pinpoint reference, and simply cite in ordinary typeface the section number(s) you are referencing. If you cite a subdivision within a section, such as a comment or an illustration, include its pinpoint reference in the citation. See the examples in Rule 27.1(b). And if you need assistance with the pinpoint references, go to Rule 6.0, Citing Sections and Paragraphs, or Rule 9.0, Graphical Material, Appendices, and Other Subdivisions.

End the citation by adding a parenthetical with the date of the specific volume's publication, not the date of the entire Restatement's adoption or promulgation, which may be different. If you cite a particular *draft* of a Restatement, indicate that draft in the date parenthetical. For examples and guidance, refer to Rule 27.1(c).

Uniform Laws

Uniform laws are products of the National Conference of Commissioners on Uniform State Laws ("NCCUSL"). The NCCUSL's goal for a uniform law is to see it enacted by a majority of state legislatures, thereby achieving a significant measure of uniformity across the United States on the law's subject matter. The best-known set of uniform laws is the Uniform Commercial Code, but more than one hundred other uniform laws have been enacted in one or more states. Uniform laws that have been adopted by at least one state are included in the multi-volume Uniform Laws Annotated ("U.L.A."). Volumes are updated by pocket parts and annual supplements.

---

[1] For a list of covered subjects, see Sidebar 27.1, Subject Matters of Restatements.

Cite a uniform law according to Rule 27.4. Set out its title in ordinary typeface, abbreviating any words that appear in Appendix 3 and omitting any articles or prepositions not needed for clarity. For example, the Uniform Management of Public Employee Retirement Systems Act should be rendered as "Unif. Mgt. Pub. Employee Ret. Sys. Act." Provide a pinpoint reference to the section(s) being cited, followed by a comma, and if it is possible, a reference to the volume and page(s) of U.L.A. containing the cited material. See the examples in Rule 27.4(c). End with a date parenthetical referring to the copyright date of the U.L.A. volume or supplement being cited; if you cannot provide the U.L.A. date, however, use the date of the uniform act's adoption or most recent amendment. See the examples in Rule 27.4(c), (d).

When you refer to a particular state's enactment of a uniform law, simply cite it in the same manner you would cite any other statute from that state. Refer to Rules 14.4 and 14.6, and follow the template shown in Appendix 1 for that state's statutes. See the examples in Rule 27.4(f).

Model Laws

Organizations such as the American Bar Association, the American Law Institute, and the American Academy of Matrimonial Lawyers, to name just a few, have drafted model codes, acts, and rules for states' adoption. Model laws are cited similarly to federal statutes.

Use Appendix 3 to find applicable abbreviations for words in the title of the model law, and set out the abbreviated name of the model law in ordinary typeface. Model acts and codes are typically divided by sections; model rules may use different subdivisions. Consult Rules 5.0, 6.0, or 9.0 for guidance on pinpoint references, depending on the form of subdivisions used in the source. End the citation with a parenthetical indicating the abbreviated name of the organization that promulgated the model law or rule, followed by the year shown in the publication being cited. If you cite a tentative or proposed draft, indicate that status as well in the date parenthetical. See the examples in Rule 27.3(c), (d). The exercises in this set are for all levels.

EXERCISE SET 11-A

ALL LEVELS: RESTATEMENTS, UNIFORM LAWS, AND MODEL LAWS

> Before beginning Exercise Set 11-A All Levels, review the following and keep the *Manual* at hand as you work through the exercises:
>
> • Rule 27.1, Full Citation Format for Restatements
> • Rule 27.3, Model Codes and Acts
> • Rule 27.4, Uniform Laws
>
> To complete the exercises, you may also need to refer to the following:
>
> • Rule 5.0, Page and Location Numbers
> • Rule 6.0, Citing Sections and Paragraphs
> • Rule 9.3, Citing Other Subdivisions
> • Rule 14.2, Full Citation, Print Format for Federal Statutes Currently in Force
> • Appendix 3, General Abbreviations

11-A.1. The Supreme Court of Tennessee adopted section 90 of the original Restatement of Contracts in *Alden v. Presley*, 637 S.W.2d 862, 864 (Tenn. 1982). This Restatement was published in 1932. Choose the correct full citation to this Restatement section.

   a. Restatement (First) of Contracts § 90 (1932).
   b. *Restatement of Contracts* § 90 (1932).
   c. Restatement (1st) of Contracts, § 90 (1932).
   d. *Restatement of Contracts* § 90 (1st ed. 1932).

11-A.2. In the American Bar Association's 2009 edition of the Model Rules of Professional Conduct, Rule 3.7 sets out the general prohibition against lawyers serving as witnesses, unless certain exceptions apply. Subsection (a)(2) excepts "testimony relat[ing] to the nature and value of legal services rendered in the case." Choose the correct full citation to this model rule and subsection.

   a. Model R. Prof. Conduct 3.7(a)(2) (ABA 2009).
   b. Am. Bar Assn., Model Rules Prof. Conduct 3.7(a)(2) (2009).
   c. *Model R. Prof. Conduct* § 3.7(a)(2) (Am. Bar Assn. 2009 ed.).
   d. Rule 3.7(a)(2), ABA Model R. Prof. Conduct (2009).

11-A.3. Section 4(b) of the Uniform Marital Property Act states the presumption that all property owned by spouses is marital property. This uniform act is published in volume 9A of the Uniform Laws Annotated, at page 116. The volume indicates that it was copyrighted in 1998 by West Group. Choose the correct full citation to this section of the uniform act.

   a. Unif. Mar. Prop. Act § 4(b) (West Group 1998).
   b. *Uniform Marital Property Act*, 9A U.L.A. § 4(b) (1998).
   c. Unif. Marital Prop. Act § 4(b), 9A U.L.A. 116 (1998).
   d. 9A Unif. Laws Ann. § 4(b), at 116 (West 1998).

11-A.4. The topic of duress as a defense is covered by the section of the Model Penal Code shown below. The American Law Institute approved this language on May 24, 1962. The section is published at page 37 of the Model Penal Code's 1985 main volume. Choose the correct full citation to the subsection concerning recklessness.

Section 2.09. Duress.

   (1) It is an affirmative defense that the actor engaged in the conduct charged to constitute an offense because he was coerced to do so by the use of, or a threat to use, unlawful force against his person or the person of another, that a person of reasonable firmness in his situation would have been unable to resist.

   (2) The defense provided by this Section is unavailable if the actor recklessly placed himself in a situation in which it was probable that he would be subjected to duress. The defense is also unavailable if he was negligent in placing himself in such a situation, whenever negligence suffices to establish culpability for the offense charged.

---

     a. MPC § 2.09, *Duress*, at (2) (Am. L. Inst. 1985).
     b. Am. L. Inst., Model Penal Code § 2.09.2, at 37 (1962).
     c. *Model Penal Code* § 2.09(2), at 37 (ALI 1962).
     d. Model Penal Code § 2.09(2) (ALI 1985).

11-A.5. You are writing a case note for the law review. The note's background section discusses the approach taken by the third Restatement of Unfair Competition toward deceptive marketing, specifically citing section 2. The American Law Institute issued this Restatement on May 11, 1993; it published the volume containing section 2 in 1995. Choose the correct full citation to this section of the Restatement.

     a. Restatement of Unfair Competition, § 2 (3d ed., Am. Law Inst. 1993).
     b. Restatement (3d) of Unfair Competition § 2 (1995).
     c. *Restatement of the Law of Unfair Competition 3d*, at § 2 (ALI 1993).
     d. *Restatement (Third) of Unfair Competition* § 2 (1995).

11-A.6. Section 9-4-1 of the Official Code of Georgia Annotated (2007 edition) is based on section 12 of the Uniform Declaratory Judgments Act, which is published in volume 12A of the Uniform Laws Annotated (2008), beginning at page 752. Choose the correct full citation to the Georgia statute.

     a. Unif. Decl. Judms. Act, 12A U.L.A. § 12 (2008).
     b. Ga. Code Ann. § 9-4-1 (2007).
     c. O.C.G.A. § 9-4-1 (2007), 12A U.L.A. § 12 (2008).
     d. Uniform Declaratory Judgments Act § 12, 12A U.L.A. 752 (2008).

11-A.7. You are writing an essay comparing the original and amended versions of section 2-204 of the Uniform Commercial Code, which addresses the formation of a contract for the sale of goods. Section 2-204 was amended in 2003. You do not have access to the Uniform Laws Annotated. Write the full citation to the amended version of the section.

11-A.8. In *Generaux v. Dobyns*, 134 P.3d 983, 988 (Or. App. 2006), the Oregon Court of Appeals quoted a Restatement, as shown below.

> *See Restatement (Third) of Trusts* § 12 comment c (2003) ("Where no consideration is paid for the creation of the trust, it is sufficient to show that the settlor was induced by mistake to create the trust, although neither the trustee nor the beneficiary shared in the mistake or had reason to know of it.")

Write the full citation to section 12 of the cited Restatement, comment c, replacing the court's citation with correct *ALWD Citation Manual* format. You may rely on the date of the Restatement shown in the court's quotation.

B. DICTIONARIES, ENCYCLOPEDIAS, AND A.L.R. ANNOTATIONS

Law dictionaries, legal encyclopedias, and American Law Reports annotations are secondary reference works that are popular with legal researchers. Not only do they explain terms and concepts, but they also often contain citations to key sources that can help researchers locate applicable primary authorities.

Dictionaries

You are probably familiar with *Black's Law Dictionary*, but you may not realize that it has some competition. Your law library probably contains several different dictionaries—some general in scope, others targeted to specialized topics. Rule 25.0 addresses not only these legal dictionaries, but also nonlegal dictionaries.

Cite dictionaries analogously to books. Set out the author name (if any is displayed) in ordinary typeface, followed by the dictionary's title, in italics. Provide a pinpoint reference to the page(s) on which the cited material appears. Add a parenthetical that sets out the dictionary's named editor (if any), its edition (if later than the first), the abbreviated name of the publisher (using Appendix 3 for abbreviations), and the year of publication. See Rule 25.1 for examples of dictionary citations, and study Rule 22.0 for analogous examples of citations to books. Depending on the way the work is subdivided and the specific type of material you are citing, you may also need to consult Rules 5.0, 6.0, or 9.0 for pinpoint references.

Legal Encyclopedias

Rule 26.0 governs citations to legal encyclopedias that do not have a named author. The best-known general encyclopedias of law are American Jurisprudence, Second Edition (abbreviated as "Am. Jur. 2d"), and Corpus Juris Secundum (abbreviated as "C.J.S."), and each is composed of multiple volumes. Alternatively, you may find yourself working with a legal encyclopedia for the laws of a particular state (e.g., Encyclopedia of Mississippi Law, South Carolina Jurisprudence).

Despite the fact that a particular encyclopedia entry may display the name of its author (e.g., Alan J. Jacobs, who wrote *Newspapers, Periodicals, and Press Associations* for Am. Jur. 2d or Jack K. Levin, who wrote *Certiorari* for C.J.S.), the full citation to the entry omits the author's name and instead begins with the number of the encyclopedia volume in which the material appears. Some volume numbers are accompanied by a letter (e.g., 11A, 14B). Include the letter if it is present.

Following the volume number, set out the abbreviated name of the encyclopedia in ordinary typeface, and, if you are citing the second or later series of the encyclopedia, the ordinal contraction for that series (e.g., "Cal. Jur. 3d").[2] Refer to Chart 26.1, Selected Encyclopedia Abbreviations, for examples.

Next in the citation is the complete name of the title or main topic, as shown on the initial page of the entry, written in italics. Do not abbreviate any words in the title or topic name. Even though an encyclopedia's main topics are often subdivided into smaller sub-topics, omit reference to the name of a subtopic. Instead, simply insert a section symbol for the pinpoint reference, followed by the section number, as shown in Rule 26.1(c)(2), (e)(3). If the encyclopedia is not divided into sections, cite the relevant page numbers, as you do with a book or treatise.

The final element of the citation is the date parenthetical. Use the year of the specific volume's publication, not the copyright date of the full set, which may be different. If the cited material came from a pocket part or supplement, provide the date of the supplement. Refer to Rule 8.0, Supplements, for guidance.

Finally, note that to cite a single-volume or multi-volume work that is wholly attributed to the same author(s), you should follow Rule 22.0, Books, Treatises, and Other Nonperiodic Materials.

A.L.R. Annotations

A favorite tool of legal researchers is the American Law Reports series on legal topics, popularly known as "A.L.R." Now in its sixth series for state law and its second series for federal law, A.L.R. publishes analyses of specific legal topics. The analyses are referred to as "annotations" because they are accompanied by commentaries, citations to authorities, and case synopses. Although annotations are most useful when you are seeking an overview of a topic or citations to primary authorities on an issue, you may cite the annotations themselves as secondary authority, particularly when you wish to direct readers to a single source identifying all known cases on an issue as of the annotation's date of publication.

In citations to annotations, treat author names in the same manner as authors of books, following Rule 22.1(a). Although an annotation typically displays the author's J.D. degree appended to his or her name on the annotation's title page, omit reference to the degree. An older annotation may not identify its author. In such instances, omit reference to an author, and begin the citation with the title, as shown in Rule 22.1(a)(3)(c).

Do not omit or abbreviate any words in the title of an annotation. Despite the way the title may be rendered in the annotation itself, capitalize words according to the guidelines set out in Rule 3.1, and put the title in italics.

Because annotations are published in a series, provide both the number of the bound volume and the appropriate abbreviation and ordinal contraction for the particular series the volume belongs to, as shown in Chart 24.1, Abbreviations for A.L.R. Series. Because each bound volume contains a number of individual annotations, a full citation provides the cited annotation's initial page number, followed by pinpoint references to specific pages within the annotation, if any. Although the *Manual* cross-references Rule 23.1(e) from periodicals

---

[2] Ordinal contractions are explained in Rule 4.3.

for page numbering, you should also consult Rules 5.2, 5.3, and 5.4 for guidance on pinpoint references to specific pages, consecutive pages, and scattered pages.

Annotations in bound volumes are typically updated with pocket parts, or if the pocket part is too large to insert in the volume's back pocket, with a separate paperbound supplement. Although you will see both month and year on the title pages for these supplements, the citation refers just to the year. For additional information about citing supplements, see Rule 8.0.

The A.L.R. annotations that are available in bound volumes are also available online in Westlaw and LexisNexis databases. Although they are cited in almost the same manner, citations to the electronic versions should append a parenthetical indicating the name of the database, as shown in the examples for Rule 24.1(f).

A form of online-only annotations is available solely on Westlaw. Known as "e-annotations," these works highlight current hot topics. Because they do not exist in print, they cannot be cited in the same manner as A.L.R. annotations in bound volumes. Follow the instructions in Rule 24.3. Begin with the author name, if it is shown. In place of a volume number, use the year, followed by the series indicator. Pinpoint references will refer to one or more specific sections, as e-annotations are not paginated. The following example demonstrates a full citation to an e-annotation:

Jay M. Zitter, *Liability for Injury on, or in Connection with, Escalator*, 2002 A.L.R.5th 24, § 15.

The exercises in this set are for all levels.

EXERCISE SET 11-B

ALL LEVELS: DICTIONARIES, ENCYCLOPEDIAS, AND A.L.R. ANNOTATIONS

Before beginning Exercise Set 11-B All Levels, review the following and keep the *Manual* at hand as you work through the exercises:

- Rule 22.1(a), Author's name
- Rule 23.1(b), Title
- Rule 23.1(e), Page numbers
- Rule 24.0, A.L.R. Annotations

- Rule 25.0, Legal Dictionaries
- Rule 26.0, Legal Encyclopedias
- Chart 24.1, Abbreviations for A.L.R. Series
- Chart 26.1, Selected Encyclopedia Abbreviations

To complete the exercises, you may also need to refer to the following:

- Rule 3.1, Words in Titles
- Rule 4.3, Ordinal Numbers
- Rule 5.0, Page and Location Numbers

- Rule 6.0, Citing Sections and Paragraphs
- Rule 8.0, Supplements

11-B.1. You are writing a paper for Professor Potter's course in English Legal History. You found a definition for the phrase "cognitionibus mittendis" at page 295 of the ninth edition of *Black's Law Dictionary*. This dictionary was edited by Bryan A. Garner and published in 2009 by Thomson Reuters. Choose the correct full citation to this entry.

a. BLACK'S LAW DICTIONARY, *Cognitionibus Mittendis*, at 295 (9th ed. 2009).
b. BLACK'S LAW DICTIONARY 295 (9th ed. 2009).
c. Bryan A. Garner, *Black's Law Dictionary* 295 (9th ed., Thomson Reuters 2009).
d. *Black's Law Dictionary* 295 (Bryan A. Garner ed., 9th ed., Thomson Reuters 2009).

11-B.2.   You are editing a law review article whose author cited the third edition of *Ballentine's Law Dictionary* for its definition of the term "dunnage." You found this entry at page 382. This dictionary was edited by William S. Anderson and published by Lawyers Cooperative Publishing Company in 1969. Choose the correct full citation to this entry.

   a. William S. Anderson, BALLENTINE'S LAW DICTIONARY at 382 (1969).
   b. Anderson, William S., *Ballentine's Law Dictionary 3d*, at 382 (Lawyers Cooperative Publishing Co. 1969).
   c. BALLENTINE'S LAW DICTIONARY 382 (3d ed. 1969).
   d. *Ballentine's Law Dictionary* 382 (William S. Anderson ed., 3d ed., Laws. Coop. Publg. Co. 1969).

11-B.3.   Researching the effect of a municipality's decision to lease slips at a public dock to charter fishing boats, you find a helpful entry in volume 58, American Jurisprudence, Second Edition, in the topic *Nuisances*, written by Anne E. Melley. In particular, section 34, "Definitions," at pages 594–595 of the main volume (published in 2002), helps your understanding of what constitutes a public nuisance. Choose the correct full citation to this entry and section.

   a. *Nuisances* § 34, Am. Jur. 2d vol. 58 (2002).
   b. 58 Am. Jur. 2d *Nuisances* § 34 (2002).
   c. Anne E. Melley, 58 Am. Jur. § 34, *Nuisances:* "Definitions," (2d ed. 2002).
   d. Anne E. Melley, *Nuisances*, vol. 58, § 34, "Definitions," at 594–595 (2d ed., 2002).

11-B.4.   For a course in professional responsibility, you've been assigned to write a paper on your state's treatment of barratry. The case law is old and confusing. You turn to a legal encyclopedia for help in understanding it, finding volume 14 of Corpus Juris Secundum and its topic *Champerty and Maintenance; Barratry and Related Matters*, section 4, "Offenses compared and distinguished," written by John A. Glenn. There is no date on the spine of the volume or the title page. The copyright page shows that Thomson/West holds a copyright dated 2006. Choose the correct full citation to this section.

   a. 14 C.J.S. *Champerty and Maintenance; Barratry and Related Matters* § 4 (2006).
   b. "Offenses Compared and Distinguished," *Champerty and Maintenance; Barratry and Related Matters* vol. 14, § 4 (Thomson/West 2006).
   c. *Champerty and Maintenance*, 14 C.J.S. § 4 (2006).
   d. John A. Glenn, *Champerty and Maintenance* § 4, "Offenses compared and distinguished," C.J.S. vol. 14 (Thomson/West 2006).

11-B.5.   An annotation about the reporter's privilege, written by Jennifer J. Ho, was published in 2006 in volume 13 of American Law Reports' sixth series, beginning on page 111. The full title is displayed as LIBEL AND SLANDER: CONSTRUCTION AND APPLICATION OF THE NEUTRAL REPORTAGE PRIVILEGE. You wish to cite page 121, discussing courts who view the privilege as "superfluous, since the press is already adequately protected by the 'actual malice' standard." Choose the correct full citation to this quotation.

   a. Ho, Jennifer J. *Libel and Slander*, 13 A.L.R. 6th 111, 121 (2006).
   b. Jennifer J. Ho, *Libel and Slander: Construction and Application of the Neutral Reportage Privilege*, 13 A.L.R.6th 111, 121 (2006).
   c. Ho, Jennifer J., Libel & Slander: Constr. & Application of Neutral Reportage Privilege, 13 A.L.R. 6th 111, 121 (2006).
   d. JENNIFER J. HO, LIBEL AND SLANDER: CONSTRUCTION AND APPLICATION OF THE NEUTRAL REPORTAGE PRIVILEGE, 13 A.L.R.6th 111, 121 (2006).

11-B.6.   Your office memo cites the definition of "friable" in volume VI of *The Oxford English Dictionary*, second edition, at page 188. This dictionary was published by Clarendon Press in 1989. Its editors are J.A. Simpson and E.S.C. Weiner. Choose the correct full citation to this definition.

    a. J.A. Simpson & E.S.C. Weiner eds., *The Oxford English Dictionary*, vol. VI, at 188 (2d ed., Clarendon Press 1989).

    b. *The Oxford English Dictionary* vol. VI, 188 (J.A. Simpson & E.S.C. Weiner eds., 2d ed., Clarendon Press 1989).

    c. VI *Oxford Eng. Dict.* 188 (J.A. Simpson & E.S.C. Weiner eds., 2nd ed. 1989).

    d. Vol. VI, *OED* 188 (J.A. Simpson & E.S.C. Weiner eds., 2d ed. 1989).

11-B.7.   Conducting research for an appellate brief, you find reference to an annotation in *State v. Johnson*, 198 P.3d 769, 780 (Kan. App. 2008), as shown at right. When you obtain the print volume of the annotation, you discover that it was written by C.R. McCorkle and published in 1956. In the print volume, the full title is shown as ACCUSED'S RIGHT TO POLL OF JURY. Choose the correct full citation to this annotation.

> "[I]t is generally held that the failure to make a timely demand or request for a poll, where a reasonable opportunity to do so has been afforded, operates as a waiver of the right. Conversely, a waiver will not be implied from a failure to demand or request a poll where the defendant has not had a reasonable opportunity to make such demand or request." Annot., 49 A.L.R.2d 619, § 8 (Waiver or Loss of Right).

    a. Annot. 49 A.L.R.2d 619 (1956).

    b. C.R. McCorkle, *Waiver or Loss of Right*, 49 A.L.R.2d 619 (1956).

    c. C.R. McCorkle, *Accused's Right to Poll of Jury*, 49 A.L.R.2d 619 (1956).

    d. C.R. McCorkle, Annotation, *Accused's Right to Poll of Jury: Waiver or Loss of Right*, 49 A.L.R.2d 619 (1956).

11-B.8.   You work for a law office that occasionally does immigration work. Your supervising attorney asked you to find recent sources discussing title 8, section 1447 of the United States Code. In Westlaw, you found the e-annotation whose identifying information is shown below. Choose the correct full citation to section 5(b) of this work.

> **2006 A.L.R. Fed. 2d 11 (Originally published in 2006)**
>
> **American Law Reports**
> **ALR Federal 2d**
> The ALR databases are made current by the weekly addition of relevant new cases.
>
> (This annotation has not been released for publication in ALR and is subject to revision or withdrawal).
>
> **Construction and Application of 8 U.S.C.A. § 1447 Governing Hearings on Denials of Applications for Naturalization**

    a. *Construction and Application of 8 U.S.C.A. § 1447 Governing Hearings on Denials of Applications for Naturalization*, 2006 A.L.R. Fed. 11, § 5(b) (2006).

    b. Kurtis A. Kemper, *Construction and Application of 8 U.S.C.A. § 1447 Governing Hearings on Denials of Applications for Naturalization*, 2006 A.L.R. Fed. 2d 11, § 5(b).

    c. Kurtis A. Kemper, *Construction and Application of 8 U.S.C.A. § 1447 Governing Hearings on Denials of Applications for Naturalization*, 2006 A.L.R. Fed. 2d 11, at 5(b) (Westlaw 2006).

    d. Kurtis A. Kemper, J.D., Annotation, *Construction and Application of 8 U.S.C.A. § 1447 Governing Hearings on Denials of Applications for Naturalization*, 2006 A.L.R. Federal 2d 11 (accessed on WL).

11-B.9.   In *Commonwealth v. Dykens*, 784 N.E.2d 1107, 1113 (Mass. 2003), the Supreme Judicial Court of Massachusetts approvingly cited an annotation written by Sonja Larsen when it confirmed the permissibility of jurors taking notes during trials. The court's citation is shown at right. Using the date supplied by the court, write the full citation to the print version of this annotation, with pinpoint reference to page 260 of the main volume.

> Juror notetaking has long been approved in this Commonwealth, see H.B. Zobel, The Boston Massacre 271 (1970); L.K. Wroth & H.B. Zobel, eds., 3 Legal Papers of John Adams 25 n.89 (1965); *Commonwealth v. Wilborne*, 382 Mass. 241,253, 415 N.E.2d 192 (1981); *Commonwealth v. Tucker*, 189 Mass. 457, 497, 76 N.E. 127 (1905), and in other jurisdictions, see *Commonwealth v. St. Germain*, 381 Mass. 256, 267–268, 408 N.E.2d 1358 (1980); Annot., *Taking and Use of Trial Notes By Jury*, 36 A.L.R. 5th 255–376 (1996 & Supp.2002).

11-B.10.   Volume 27 of Florida Jurisprudence 2d, a state encyclopedia published by Thomson/West, displays on its cover and spine the words "Florida Jur 2d" in gold type, but no date. The book's copyright date is 2007, and its current pocket part is dated February 2010. You wish to cite section 22, "Artificial fishing reefs," within the topic *Fish and Game*, which is treated in both the main volume and the pocket part. Write the full citation to the material in section 22.

C.   SHORT-FORM CITATIONS

This chapter has treated a variety of sources, some of which are analogous to statutes, some to books, and others to periodical articles. Not surprisingly, their short-form citations are similar to the short forms for these analogous works. Short-form rules for general works typically cross-reference analogous rules for short forms in other works, as shown in Table 11.1 below.

TABLE 11.1

SHORT-FORM CITATION RULES AND CROSS-REFERENCES

Type of Source	Rule(s) to Consult for Short Forms
Restatements	27.2 (rule and examples)
Model and Uniform Laws	14.6 (federal statutes); 27.3(c) (examples); 27.4(c) (examples)
Dictionaries	22.2 (books); 25.2 (examples)
Encyclopedias	26.2 (rule and examples)
A.L.R. annotation	23.2 (periodicals); 24.2 (examples)

Id. is always an acceptable short-form citation in the right circumstances (and if you are not quite sure what those circumstances are, review Rule 11.3). Citations in footnotes to sources cited by author name, such as dictionaries and A.L.R. annotations, may use *supra* to refer to an earlier footnote containing the full citation. Review Rule 11.4, *Supra* as a Short Citation. Footnote citations to other sources addressed in this chapter should not use *supra*.

The exercises in this set are for all levels.

EXERCISE SET 11-C

ALL LEVELS: SHORT-FORM CITATIONS

Before beginning Exercise Set 11-C All Levels, review the following and keep the *Manual* at hand as you work through the exercises:

- Rule 11.3, *Id.* as a Short Citation
- Rule 11.4, *Supra* as a Short Citation
- Rule 23.2, Short Citation Format [Legal and Other Periodicals]
- Rule 24.2, Short Citation Format [A.L.R. Annotations]
- Rule 25.2, Short Citation Format [Legal Dictionaries]
- Rule 26.2, Short Citation Format for Multivolume Encyclopedias without Authors or Editors
- Rule 27.2, Short Citation Format for Restatements
- Rule 27.3(c), [Model codes and acts, short citation options]
- Rule 27.4(c), [Uniform laws, short citation options]

To complete the exercises, you may also need to refer to the following:

- Rule 5.0, Page and Location Numbers
- Rule 9.3, Citing Other Subdivisions
- Rule 14.6, Short Citation, Print Format for Federal and State Statutes

11-C.1. You are writing a paper for a course in future interests. Footnote 6 of your paper cites the ninth edition of *Black's Law Dictionary* for the definition of "feme sole," found at page 695. Bryan A. Garner edited this dictionary, which was published by Thomson West in 2009. Footnote 7 of your paper cites page 259 of the same edition of *Black's Law Dictionary* for the definition of "cestui que trust." Choose the correct short-form citation for footnote 7.

   a. Garner, *Black's Law Dictionary* at 259.
   b. *Black's Law Dictionary* at 259.
   c. *Black's* at 259.
   d. *Id.* at 259.

11-C.2. As a teaching assistant, you are helping a legal writing professor develop an appellate problem concerning drugs found when an off-duty police officer walked his dog past a person wearing a backpack. You are drafting a memo outlining the current state of the law, with citations to authorities the legal writing students are likely to read, including legal encyclopedias. One source is volume 79 of Corpus Juris Secundum, which contains the topic "Searches," and more specifically, section 94, which talks about "dog sniff." You cite this section more than once in the text of the memo, although not consecutively. Choose the correct short-form citation for your second reference to section 94.

    a. 79 C.J.S. § 94.
    b. 79 C.J.S. at § 94.
    c. 79 C.J.S. *Searches* § 94.
    d. 79 C.J.S. at § 94, *Dog Sniff.*

11-C.3. Another source cited in the dog-sniff research memo is an annotation from volume 150 of the A.L.R.'s first federal series, written by Brian L. Porto, and titled *Use of Trained Dog to Detect Narcotics or Drugs As Unreasonable Search in Violation of Fourth Amendment.* The annotation begins at page 399. After citing the annotation in full, the memo cites a case, followed by a citation to page 407 of the annotation. Choose the correct short-form citation for page 407.

    a. *Id.* at 407.
    b. 150 A.L.R. Fed. 407.
    c. Porto, 150 A.L.R. Fed. at 407.
    d. Porto, *Use of Trained Dog to Detect Narcotics or Drugs*, 150 A.L.R. Fed. at 407.

11-C.4. A lawyer's ability to testify in a contested matter is addressed in the *Restatement (Third) of the Law Governing Lawyers* § 108 (2000). You are writing a brief seeking disqualification of counsel for proffering such testimony. After the brief cites subsection 108(a), which contains the prohibitions against the practice, it goes on to discuss a relevant case in which a lawyer was disqualified from further representing his client. The brief then cites subsection 108(b), which contains the limited exceptions that permit a lawyer to testify. Choose the correct short-form citation for subsection 108(b).

    a. § 108(b).
    b. *Restatement (Third) of the Law Governing Lawyers* § 108(b).
    c. *Id.* at § 108(b).
    d. *Restatement (3d) of L. Governing Laws.* § 108(b).

11-C.5. Arguing a strict liability issue, Part II of a brief cites the following comment from section 520 of the second Restatement of Torts. In the same section of the brief, the next citation is to a New York case. Immediately following the case citation, the brief cites the comment a second time. Choose the correct short-form citation for the second citation to the comment.

> *e. Not limited to the defendant's land.* In most of the cases to which the rule of strict liability is applicable the abnormally dangerous activity is conducted on land in the possession of the defendant. This, again, is not necessary to the existence of such an activity. It may be carried on in a public highway or other public place or upon the land of another.

a. *Restatement (Second) of Torts* § 520 cmt. e.

b. Restatement (2d) of Torts, *supra*, § 520, comment e.

c. *Id.* at comment e.

d. *Rest. (2d) Torts*, vol. 3, § 520, cmt. e.

11-C.6–14. Read the following excerpt from a paper that cites its authorities in footnotes. Assume that in earlier footnotes, the paper has **already cited in full** the four authorities listed below. In this exercise, you will write the text of several later footnotes for the paper. For the indicated footnotes, write the appropriate short-form citation for the previously cited authority and its pinpoint reference.

Previously cited authorities:

- **Citation A:** William H. Danne, Jr., *Legal Status of Posthumously Conceived Child of Decedent*, American Law Reports, Sixth Series, volume 17, initial page 593 (2006); first cited in footnote 11
- **Citation B:** Uniform Status of Children of Assisted Conception Act, Uniform Laws Annotated, volume 9C (2001); first cited in footnote 7
- **Citation C:** Uniform Parentage Act, Uniform Laws Annotated, volume 9B (Supp. 2009); first cited in footnote 5
- **Citation D:** Uniform Probate Code, Uniform Laws Annotated, volume 8 (Supp. 2009); first cited in footnote 6

The excerpt:

With today's advances in science and medicine, persons who might otherwise be unable to procreate are able to have children, whether by surrogacy arrangements or by fertilization and implant procedures. Although assisted reproduction technologies perform miracles for would-be parents, they also pose challenges for existing intestacy and social-assistance laws, which were drafted long before legislatures contemplated the effects of alternative means of conception and gestation. Courts are consequently struggling to determine whether children conceived and born as a result of those technologies have the same entitlements and rights of inheritance as children conceived and born the old-fashioned way.[15]

For example, an Arkansas statute permitting intestate succession of a child "conceived" before death of the father but born after father's death was held not to apply to a child who was conceived via *in vitro* fertilization but not implanted in the mother's uterus until after the father's death.[16] Similarly, a federal court was faced with the question whether children conceived after their father's death through *in vitro* fertilization met the definition of "natural child" under the Social Security Act.[17]

Perhaps a new and truly uniform definition of "child" is in order. The existing uniform acts are harmonious in some respects, but conflicting in others. Although it was certainly current and cutting-edge when promulgated in 1988, the Uniform Status of Children of Assisted Conception Act does not define "child," but rather, defines "assisted conception," the method used to produce the child.[18] The definition includes artificial insemination and embryo implant, but it excludes *in vitro* fertilization, even when a woman's own husband provides the sperm.[19]

The Uniform Parentage Act defines "assisted reproduction" as any method of causing pregnancy other than sexual intercourse.[20] It then goes on to define "child" as "an individual of any age whose parentage may be determined" under the Uniform Parentage Act's provisions.[21]

The Uniform Probate Code has recently added a section specifically defining the relevant terms. In a section titled, "Child Conceived by Assisted Reproduction Other Than Child Born to Gestational Carrier," the Uniform Probate Code creates a new kind of child, a "child of assisted reproduction," i.e., one "conceived by means of assisted reproduction."[22] The definition explicitly excludes, however, a child conceived by a "gestational carrier."[23] "Assisted reproduction," under the Uniform Probate Code, is broadly defined: "a method of causing pregnancy other than sexual intercourse."[24] The Uniform Probate Code acknowledges that it copied its definition of "assisted reproduction" from the Uniform Parentage Act.[25]

---

[15][**11-C.6. Citation A, pages 600–601.**]

[16]*Finley v. Astrue*, 270 S.W.3d 849, 855 (Ark. 2008).

[17]*Gillett-Netting v. Barnhart*, 371 F.3d 593, 597 (9th Cir. 2004).

[18][**11-C.7. Citation B, section 1(1), at page 368.**]

[19][**11-C.8. Citation B, section 1(1), at page 368.**]

[20][**11-C.9. Citation C, section 102(4), at page 303.**]

[21][**11-C.10. Citation C, section 102(5), at page 303.**]

[22][**11-C.11. Citation D, section 2-120(a)(2), at page 57.**]

[23][**11-C.12. Citation D, section 2-120(a)(2), at page 57.**]

[24][**11-C.13. Citation D, section 2-115(2), at page 51.**]

[25][**11-C.14. Citation D, section 2-115(2), comment, at page 51.**]

CHAPTER

12

NON-PRINT MEDIA

The landscape of legal research is undergoing change. Old boundaries are falling. New resources are beckoning. Things that used to be difficult (or expensive) to access are now easily retrieved through electronic means, and sometimes, are available at no cost. And yet, old traditions persist, particularly when it comes to citation. Print sources are familiar, reliable, and stable, and at present, the legal community's widespread preference is to cite print sources if they are available—to you *and* to your readers. Despite this traditional preference, electronic materials are gaining in popularity, scope, and availability. One reason is that the costs of acquiring, maintaining, updating, and even housing print sources have grown, and many law libraries are consequently discontinuing subscriptions to print resources. But there are other reasons. Publishers are converting former print-only publications to electronic media, and increasingly you will be using materials that do not have print counterparts.

At the same time, you will find yourself using a broader array of source materials than ever before, relying not just on traditional printed primary authorities, but also on a growing variety of secondary sources, including many non-legal materials, as well as audio and video resources that have not been—or cannot be—duplicated in words on a paper or digital page.

This chapter provides guidance for determining which available sources to cite. It provides practice not only in citing materials published in electronic sources such as Web sites and CD-ROMs, but also in citing new forms of electronic media such as electronic messaging and e-readers and in citing sources that traditionally are not publicly available in print such as speeches and recordings.

A.   ELECTRONIC MEDIA IN GENERAL

In today's research environment, many sources formerly available only in print are now available online. While an online source may be convenient for you to access, it may not be equally accessible to your readers. Thus the strong preference remains for citing print sources, particularly if you are citing a source of primary law that is readily available in print. In similar fashion, many familiar secondary materials are available online, but the accepted citation formats for most secondary works are designed to retrieve their print versions.

A significant difficulty arises if you research online and then craft a citation that *appears* to cite the print source, even though the online medium fails to provide you with accurate information for all of the components of the print-source citation. For example, a print-source citation to a codified federal statute refers to the date of publication of the volume in which the statute appears. But its online version will refer to a different date, the date through which the electronic database is current.

The preference for citing print versions does not mean that you cannot provide readers with a citation to a convenient electronic version of the source, but it does indicate that citations to electronic versions should supplement, not replace, citations to print versions. Therefore, place citations to electronic versions in an "available at [or in] . . ." parenthetical appended to the print-source citation, as shown in the examples for Rule 38.1(a), (b).

A recurring challenge is deciding which of several available electronic versions of a source is best to cite. For example, you may find that some sources are reproduced in a variety of electronic media, such as CD-ROMs, commercial databases (such as LexisNexis, Westlaw, or Loislaw), or Web sites. It is acceptable to cite only one of these media; therefore, choose to cite the medium that will be accessible to the greater number of readers. Accessibility is not the only consideration, however. You should also consider the reliability and trustworthiness of the source's author and its electronic publisher. If you have an option to do so, cite an official source.

Increasingly, official sources of primary law are appearing online. Official sources are ordinarily those published by a governmental entity. Official electronic versions of primary federal law are beginning to appear in authenticated versions on government-sponsored Web sites such as the Government Printing Office's Federal Digital System (FDsys) (http://www.gpo.gov/fdsys/search/home.action). Primary sources of state law—particularly administrative codes and regulations—are also beginning to be published in official online sources. While not all primary materials published on governmental Web sites are official versions, where they are, you should select such governmental sites (e.g., .gov or .state) sites as your preferred electronic source over commercial (.com) sites. Use Appendix 1 to determine whether an electronic source of primary law in a particular jurisdiction is official, but also be prepared to check a government's official Web site for updated information. Appendix 1 designates official codes, whether print or online, with a green star.

When choosing among different electronic sources, you must also consider the similarity of the electronic source to the original. For example, many sources are available in online versions via hypertext markup language (HTML, a form of text file). HTML-formatted sources typically do not display the original pinpoint references, particularly page numbers, as these documents are designed for reading by scrolling down the screen, rather than turning pages. You can often, however, find exact electronic reproductions of print sources, rendered in Portable Document Format (PDF). Because PDFs are digital *copies* of print sources, their contents are identical to the originals, and they display the original page numbers. Thus, if you have a choice between a PDF and an HTML online version, cite the PDF.

The ready availability of a source in print or electronic format is also a significant factor to consider. It is increasingly acceptable to use electronic media to cite uncommon or hard-to-locate sources such as wire service reports, state administrative materials, out-of-state newspapers, and foreign sources. The best-known and most widely used electronic media are LexisNexis and Westlaw. However, other Web-based research services also offer search engines and online libraries for federal and state primary materials. Among these other services are Casemaker, Fastcase, Loislaw, and VersusLaw. Many state bar associations furnish these research services to subscribers as a benefit of membership.

The *ALWD Citation Manual* provides citation formats for cases published only on LexisNexis or Westlaw (Rule 12.12) and cases available only on the Internet (Rule 12.15). Online statutory citations are treated in Rule 14.5. Rule 39.0 governs citation of secondary sources that are published on Westlaw or LexisNexis. Many such sources are assigned unique identifiers by those electronic publishers. Rule 23.1 provides guidance for citing electronic journals. For other sources that are only available in an electronic format, consult Rules 39.0, 40.0, 41.0, and 42.0, depending on the nature of the source.

EXERCISE SET 12-A

BASIC LEVEL: ELECTRONIC MEDIA IN GENERAL

Before beginning Exercise Set 12-A Basic Level, review the following and keep the *Manual* at hand as you work through the exercises:

- Rule 12.12, Cases Published Only on LexisNexis or Westlaw
- Rule 12.15, Cases on the Internet
- Rule 14.5, Statutes Available on Electronic Databases
- Rule 38.0, General Information about Online and Electronic Citation Formats
- Sidebar 38.1, Accessing and Preserving Electronic Sources
- Rule 39.0, Westlaw and LexisNexis [non-case materials]

12-A.1. Assuming it is available in all of the following sources, which is the *best source* for citing a law review article?

    a. a bound copy from the law review in which it was published

    b. a download from Westlaw's JLR database

    c. a printout of the author's manuscript posted on the Social Sciences Research Network (SSRN)

    d. a PDF from HeinOnline

12-A.2. Assuming it is available in all of the following sources, which is the *best source* for citing a case decided by the Illinois Supreme Court in a brief to the Wisconsin Supreme Court?

    a. a print copy of West's Illinois Decisions

    b. a download from LexisNexis

    c. a print copy from the North Eastern Reporter

    d. a download from Fastcase

12-A.3. Assuming it is available in all of the following sources, which is the *best source* for citing a case decided by the United States Court of Appeals for the First Circuit?

     a. a reprint in American Law Reports
     b. the First Circuit's Web site
     c. the Government Printing Office's *GPO Access* Web site
     d. the Federal Reporter

12-A.4. Assuming it is available in all of the following sources, which is the *best source* for citing an unpublished case decided by the United States Court of Appeals for the Seventh Circuit?

     a. the Westlaw version from the CTA-7 database
     b. the Federal Appendix
     c. the Seventh Circuit's Web site
     d. a looseleaf reporter

12-A.5. Assuming it is available in all of the following sources, which of the following Web sites is the *best source* for citing the Kentucky statute of limitations for personal injury actions?

     a. http://www.lrc.ky.gov/statrev/frontpg.htm
     b. http://www.statutes-of-limitations.com/state/kentucky
     c. http://www.expertlaw.com/library/limitations_by_state/Kentucky.html
     d. http://law.findlaw.com/state-laws/civil-statute-of-limitations/kentucky/

12-A.6. Assuming it is available in all of the following sources, which of the following is the *best source* for citing a Nevada statute?

     a. West's Nevada Revised Statutes Annotated
     b. Nevada Revised Statutes Annotated (LexisNexis)
     c. Nevada Revised Statutes
     d. the Nevada legislature's Web site, http://search.leg.state.nv.us/nrs/SearchNRS.html

12-A.7. Assuming it is available in all of the following sources, which of the following is the *best source* for citing a New Jersey statute?

     a. *New Jersey Law Network*, http://www.njlawnet.com/njstatutes.html
     b. New Jersey Statutes Annotated (West)
     c. FindLaw, *New Jersey Laws*, http://law.findlaw.com/state-laws/new-jersey/
     d. New Jersey Legislature Web site, http://www.njleg.state.nj.us/Default.asp, *select* Statutes

12-A.8. Assuming it is available in all of the following sources, which of the following is the *best source* for citing an opinion by the United States Supreme Court?

     a. United States Supreme Court Web site, *Opinions*, http://www.supremecourt.gov/opinions/opinions.aspx
     b. Cornell University Law School, Legal Information Institute, *Supreme Court*, http://www.law.cornell.edu/supct/
     c. FindLaw, *US Supreme Court Opinions*, http://www.findlaw.com/casecode/supreme.html
     d. United States Law Week

12-A.9. Assuming it is available in all of the following sources, which is the *best source* for citing a federal session law?

    a. United States Law Week

    b. United States Code Congressional and Administrative News

    c. the United States Code Service; Code, Const, Rules, Conventions & Public Laws library on LexisNexis

    d. Statutes at Large

12-A.10. Assuming it is available in all of the following sources, which is the *best source* for citing a story in a specific issue of the Concord Monitor, a New Hampshire newspaper?

    a. Web site of the Concord Monitor, http://www.concordmonitor.com/

    b. the Westlaw database for the Concord Monitor, CONCORDMONT

    c. the LexisNexis library, New Hampshire News Publications, file NHNEWS

    d. the Twitter feed for the Concord Monitor, http://twitter.com/conmonitornews

EXERCISE SET 12-A

INTERMEDIATE LEVEL: ELECTRONIC MEDIA IN GENERAL

Before beginning Exercise Set 12-A Intermediate Level, review the following and keep the *Manual* at hand as you work through the exercises:

- Rule 12.12, Cases Published Only on LexisNexis or Westlaw
- Rule 12.15, Cases on the Internet
- Rule 14.5, Statutes Available on Electronic Databases
- Rule 23.1(i), Electronic journals
- Rule 38.0, General Information about Online and Electronic Citation Formats
- Sidebar 38.1, Accessing and Preserving Electronic Sources
- Rule 39.0, Westlaw and LexisNexis [non-case materials]

Be prepared to consult Appendix 1, Primary Sources by Jurisdiction, for many of the questions.

12-A.11. Which of the following states has an official online statutory compilation?

    a. Alabama

    b. Georgia

    c. Kansas

    d. Utah

12-A.12. Which of the following states has an official online statutory compilation?

    a. Delaware

    b. Louisiana

    c. Maine

    d. New Hampshire

12-A.13. Which of the following states has official online case reports?

    a. Arkansas
    b. Illinois
    c. Louisiana
    d. Virginia

12-A.14. You wish to cite *Taking the "Long View" on the Fourth Amendment: Stored Records and the Sanctity of the Home*, an article by Jack I. Lerner and Deirdre K. Mulligan. It was published on February 2, 2008, as the third article in the 2008 volume of the Stanford Technology Law Review, an electronic journal. The article is located at http://stlr.stanford.edu/pdf/lerner-mulligan-long-view.pdf. Choose the correct full citation to this electronic article.

    a. Jack I. Lerner & Deirdre K. Mulligan, *Taking the "Long View" on the Fourth Amendment: Stored Records and the Sanctity of the Home*, Stanford Tech. L. Rev., Feb. 2, 2008, available at http://stlr.stanford.edu/pdf/lerner-mulligan-long-view.pdf.
    b. Jack I. Lerner & Deirdre K. Mulligan, *Taking the "Long View" on the Fourth Amendment: Stored Records and the Sanctity of the Home*, http://stlr.stanford.edu/pdf/lerner-mulligan-long-view.pdf.
    c. Jack I. Lerner & Deirdre K. Mulligan, *Taking the "Long View" on the Fourth Amendment: Stored Records and the Sanctity of the Home*, 2008 Stan. Tech. L. Rev. 3 (Feb. 2, 2008), http://stlr.stanford.edu/pdf/lerner-mulligan-long-view.pdf.
    d. Jack I. Lerner & Deirdre K. Mulligan, *Taking the "Long View" on the Fourth Amendment: Stored Records and the Sanctity of the Home*, 2008 Stan. Tech. L. Rev. 3 (2008) (available at http://stlr.stanford.edu/pdf/lerner-mulligan-long-view.pdf).

12-A.15. You wish to cite a trial-court opinion that is only available electronically. Its LexisNexis caption is shown below. Choose the correct full citation to this opinion.

> *2009 U.S. Dist. LEXIS 115029,* *
>
> AZALEA SOLO, on behalf of herself and all others similarly situated in California, and MEGHAN EVELAND, on behalf of herself and all others similarly situated in Pennsylvania, Plaintiffs, v. BAUSCH & LOMB INC., Defendant.
>
> MDL No. 1785, C/A No. 2: 06-MN-77777-DCN, C/A No. 2:06-CV-02716-DCN
>
> UNITED STATES DISTRICT COURT FOR THE DISTRICT OF SOUTH CAROLINA, CHARLESTON DIVISION
>
> 2009 U.S. Dist. LEXIS 115029
>
> September 25, 2009, Decided
> September 25, 2009, Filed

    a. *Solo v. Bausch & Lomb Inc.*, MDL No. 1785, C/A No. 2:06-MN-77777-DCN, C/A No. 2: 06-CV-02716-DCN (D.S.C. Sept. 25, 2009).
    b. *Solo v. Bausch & Lomb Inc.* (D.S.C. Sept. 25, 2009), available at 2009 U.S. Dist. LEXIS 115029.
    c. *Solo v. Bausch & Lomb Inc.*, 2009 U.S. Dist. LEXIS 115029 (D.S.C. Sept. 25, 2009).
    d. *Solo v. Bausch & Lomb Inc.*, U.S. Dist. LEXIS at 115029 (D.S.C. 2009).

EXERCISE SET 12-A

EXPERT LEVEL: ELECTRONIC MEDIA IN GENERAL

Before beginning Exercise Set 12-A Expert Level, review the following and keep the *Manual* at hand as you work through the exercises:

- Rule 12.12, Cases Published Only on LexisNexis or Westlaw
- Rule 12.15, Cases on the Internet
- Rule 14.5, Statutes Available on Electronic Databases
- Rule 23.1(i), Electronic journals
- Rule 38.0, General Information about Online and Electronic Citation Formats
- Rule 39.0, Westlaw and LexisNexis [non-case materials]

Be prepared to consult Appendix 1, Primary Sources by Jurisdiction, for many of the questions.

12-A.16. In 1989, William C. Thompson and Simon Ford wrote an article about DNA and genetic testing for the Virginia Law Review, which published the article in 1989, in volume 75, beginning at page 45. Westlaw gives it the unique identifier 75 VALR 45 and the title, DNA TYPING: ACCEPTANCE AND WEIGHT OF THE NEW GENETIC IDENTIFICATION TESTS. Write the preferred full citation to this article.

12-A.17. Write the preferred full citation to the opinion whose LexisNexis caption is shown below.

---

62 F.R.D. 581, *; 1973 U.S. Dist. LEXIS 11251, **;
19 Fed. R. Serv. 2d (Callaghan) 666; 88 L.R.R.M. 2756

Charles N. BUCHHOLTZ et al., Plaintiffs v. SWIFT AND COMPANY et al., Defendants

No. 4-71-Civ. 602

UNITED STATES DISTRICT COURT FOR THE DISTRICT OF MINNESOTA, FOURTH DIVISION

62 F.R.D. 581; 1973 U.S. Dist. LEXIS 11251; 19 Fed. R. Serv. 2d (Callaghan) 666; 88 L.R.R.M. 2756;
75 Lab. Cas. (CCH) P10,479

November 2, 1973

12-A.18. Write the preferred full citation to the Utah statute providing citizens with the right to injure or kill a dog that is attacking certain domesticated or protected wild animals. The statute's number is 18-1-3. It is available on the Web site of the Utah Legislature, http://le.utah.gov/~code/TITLE18/htm/18_01_000300.htm, a site that was last updated on December 31, 2009.

B.   NON-PRINT SOURCES

Web Sites and Blogs

Given the amazing variety of materials available on the Internet, you might think that their citations would be complicated to construct or to decode. Fortunately, that is not the case. A full citation to a Web site has five components:

- author (or if unavailable, the site's owner);
- name of site (main title or top-level heading);
- a pinpoint reference (if available);
- URL (the Uniform Resource Locator, or the exact address on the Web); and
- exact date.

Cite blogs in the same way, but in addition to the blog's name, provide the title of the specific blog entry being cited. See Rule 40.3 and its examples.

Author names for Web sites and blogs are not always prominently displayed, so follow the *Manual*'s advice to explore the site before deciding that no author name is available. If there is in fact no individual author name available, indicate the site's owner, which may be an individual or an organization. You may abbreviate any words in an organization's name that appear in Appendix 3. Refer to Rule 40.1 for many examples of Web site citations.

Be careful in presenting a Web site's Uniform Resource Locator (URL). If the URL is not accurately set out, the reader may not be able to locate the source. Many URLs are longer than a single line of text. If you must break the URL, try to do so *after* a slash or *before* a period. Do not hyphenate the break. In some cases, you may need to provide readers with keystroke identifiers and, possibly, search terms to access the materials online, because you cannot furnish a direct URL or because the URL is extremely long. Rule 40.1(d)(3) describes methods for citing Web materials using keystroke identifiers.

In presenting the date, refer to the date of the Web source itself, but if that is not available, use the date the Web site was last modified or updated, or the date on which the researcher accessed the material. For blog postings, wikis, and similar sources, also provide the exact time of the posting or the last modification to the entry, using the 24-hour clock (e.g., 08:30, which represents 8:30 a.m., or 14:00, which represents 2:00 p.m.). Additional examples are provided in Rules 40.3(a) and 40.5.

CD-ROMs and E-Readers

Before citing material on a CD-ROM or e-reader, see whether it is also available in a print format. Because such materials are not generally accessible to the public, cite the electronic medium only where no print format exists for such material. When citations to these electronic media are called for, follow the examples and cross-references in Rule 42.0.

Electronic Mail and Messages

Email and electronic messages are increasingly popular forms of correspondence. Rule 41.0 provides detailed guidance for citing such electronic letters, analogizing them to unpublished letters and memoranda, which are treated in Rule 32.0. You will likely need to refer to both rules to construct a full citation to such a source.

Microformed Materials

A "microform" is an image of text or graphics that has been photographically reduced in size for storage. Storage media for microforms include cards ("microfiche") or reels of film ("microfilm"), commonly requiring special readers and printers to view and copy the materials. If the source is available in regular print format, do not cite a microform, although you may provide such a citation as a parenthetical supplement to a regular print citation. If the source is only available in microform, however, consult Rule 35.0 for general guidance, and follow analogous rules for the source in print (e.g., Rule 22.0 for books; Rule 32.0 for letters).

Speeches, Interviews, Recordings, and Presentations

To cite an audio, video, or other source that has not been transcribed in words and published, use the following rules: Rule 30.0, Speeches, Addresses, Oral Presentations, and Live Performances; Rule 31.0, Interviews; Rule 33.0, Video and Visual Sources; and Rule 34.0, Audio Sources. "New media" sources such as YouTube videos, podcasts, PowerPoint slideshows, video blog posts, and vodcasts are covered in Rule 33.3.

EXERCISE SET 12-B

BASIC LEVEL: NON-PRINT SOURCES

> Before beginning Exercise Set 12-B Basic Level, review the following and keep the *Manual* at hand as you work through the exercises:
>
> - Rule 30.0, Speeches, Addresses, Oral Presentations, and Live Performances
> - Rule 31.0, Interviews
> - Rule 33.0, Video and Visual Sources
> - Rule 34.0, Audio Sources
>
> - Rule 35.0, Microformed Materials
> - Rule 40.0, World Wide Web Sites
> - Rule 41.0, Electronic Mail and Messages
> - Rule 42.0, CD-ROMs and E-Readers

12-B.1. On its Web site, the Supreme Court of the United States posts links to official transcripts of the oral arguments it hears. This Web page, titled *Arguments Transcripts*, is found at the URL http://www.supremecourt.gov/oral_arguments/argument_transcripts.aspx. Although the site contains transcripts going back to the October Term of 2000, at the time of your access, the page containing the links bore the date April 7, 2010. Which of the following full citations to that page is correct?

    a. *Arguments Transcripts*, www.supremecourt.gov/oral_arguments/argument_transcripts.aspx (Apr. 7, 2010).

    b. S. Ct., *Arguments Transcripts*, http://www.supremecourt.gov/oral_arguments/argument_transcripts.aspx (Apr. 7, 2010).

    c. U.S. Sup. Ct., *Arguments Transcripts*, <www.supremecourt.gov/oral_arguments/argument_transcripts.aspx> (Apr. 7, 2010).

    d. Sup. Ct. of U.S., Arguments Transcripts (Apr. 7, 2010), available at http://www.supremecourt.gov/oral_arguments/argument_transcripts.aspx.

12-B.2. You consulted Wikipedia for an entry concerning a fictional animal that was the subject of an elaborate hoax, the "Hotheaded Naked Ice Borer." The Wikipedia entry is available at the following URL: http://en.wikipedia.org/wiki/Hotheaded_Naked_Ice_Borer. A notation at the bottom of the Web page states, "This page was last modified on 27 February 2010 at 21:01." Choose the correct full citation.

    a. Wikipedia, http://en.wikipedia.org/wiki/Hotheaded_Naked_Ice_Borer (last edited Feb. 27, 2010).

    b. *Hotheaded Naked Ice Borer*, Wikipedia, http://en.wikipedia.org/wiki/ Hotheaded_Naked_Ice_Borer (accessed Feb. 27, 2010).

    c. Wikipedia, *Hotheaded Naked Ice Borer*, http://en.wikipedia.org/wiki/ Hotheaded_Naked_Ice_Borer (last modified Feb. 27, 2010, 21:01).

    d. Wikipedia, *Hotheaded Naked Ice Borer*, www.en.wikipedia.org/wiki/ Hotheaded_Naked_Ice_Borer (last modified Feb. 27, 2010, 9:01 p.m.).

12-B.3. Legal-writing specialist Benjamin Opipari blogs about writing and running in his blog, Literary Legs. At 7:29 a.m. on January 25, 2010, Mr. Opipari posted an entry titled *This Is Clearly Overuse*. The URL for the entry is http://www.benopipari.com/literary_legs/2010/01/clearly.html. Choose the correct full citation.

    a. "This Is Clearly Overuse," Literary Legs, http://www.benopipari.com/literary_legs/2010/01/ clearly.html (accessed Jan. 25, 2010).

    b. Benjamin Opipari, Literary Legs, *This Is Clearly Overuse*, http://www.benopipari.com/ literary_legs/2010/01/clearly.html (Jan. 25, 2010, 07:29).

    c. Opipari, Benjamin. *This Is Clearly Overuse*, in *Literary Legs*, <http://www.benopipari.com/ literary_legs/2010/01/clearly.html> (posted 7:29 a.m., Jan. 25, 2010).

    d. Benjamin Opipari, *Literary Legs, This Is Clearly Overuse*, http://www.benopipari.com/ literary_legs/2010/01/clearly.html (Jan. 25, 2010) (7:29 a.m.).

12-B.4. In 1993, the British rock singer Sting recorded an album titled *Ten Summoner's Tales* for A & M Records, Inc. Which of the following citations correctly refers to a compact disc version of the album?

    a. A & M Records, Inc., Sting, *Ten Summoner's Tales* (CD, 1993).

    b. Sting & A & M Records, Inc., *Ten Summoner's Tales* (1993).

    c. Sting, *Ten Summoner's Tales* (A & M Records, Inc. 1993) (CD).

    d. Sting, CD, *Ten Summoner's Tales* (A & M Records, Inc. 1993).

12-B.5. High on many people's favorite lawyer-movie lists is *My Cousin Vinny*, a film starring Joe Pesci and Marisa Tomei (who won a best-supporting actress Oscar for her work), produced by Palo Vista Productions and released in 1992. Choose the correct full citation to this film.

    a. *My Cousin Vinny*, Motion Picture (Palo Vista Prods. 1992).

    b. Palo Vista Productions, *My Cousin Vinny* (1992).

    c. Palo Vista Prods., *My Cousin Vinny*, Motion Picture (1992).

    d. *My Cousin Vinny* (Palo Vista, 1992).

EXERCISE SET 12-B

INTERMEDIATE LEVEL: NON-PRINT SOURCES

Before beginning Exercise Set 12-B Intermediate Level, review the following and keep the *Manual* at hand as you work through the exercises:

- Rule 30.0, Speeches, Addresses, Oral Presentations, and Live Performances
- Rule 31.0, Interviews
- Rule 33.0, Video and Visual Sources
- Rule 34.0, Audio Sources

- Rule 35.0, Microformed Materials
- Rule 40.0, World Wide Web Sites
- Rule 41.0, Electronic Mail and Messages
- Rule 42.0, CD-ROMs and E-Readers

12-B.6. *The AILA Immigration Practice Toolbox* is a commercially published CD-ROM. Edited by Davis C. Bae, it was published in November 2009 by the American Immigration Lawyers Association (AILA). Choose the correct full citation to this source.

a. AILA & Davis C. Bae, ed., *The AILA Immigration Practice Toolbox* (3d ed. 2009).

b. *The AILA Immigration Practice Toolbox* (Davis C. Bae ed., 3d ed., Am. Immig. Laws. Assn. 2009) (CD-ROM).

c. Davis C. Bae ed., CD-ROM, *The AILA Immigration Practice Toolbox* (3d ed., Am. Immig. Laws. Assn. 2009).

d. Davis C. Bae & Am. Immig. Laws. Assn. (AILA), *The AILA Immigration Practice Toolbox* (3d ed. 2009) (CD-ROM).

12-B.7. A request for $85.4 million to develop the Gamma-ray Large Area Space Telescope appears in the *2007 Budget Request of the National Aeronautics and Space Administration.* The budget request document is available on NASA's Web site, at the following URL: http://www.nasa.gov/pdf/ 142458main_FY07_budget_full.pdf. You accessed the Web site on March 9, 2010. Choose the correct full citation to the budget request document.

a. *2007 Budget Request Natl. Aeronautics & Space Admin.*, <http://www.nasa.gov/pdf/ 142458main_FY07_budget_full.pdf> (Mar. 10, 2010).

b. Nat. Aeronautics & Space Admin., *2007 Budget Request of the National Aeronautics and Space Administration*, <http://www.nasa.gov>, Mar. 10, 2010.

c. Natl. Aeronautics & Space Admin., *2007 Budget Request of the National Aeronautics and Space Administration*, http://www.nasa.gov/pdf/142458main_FY07_budget_full.pdf (accessed Mar. 10, 2010).

d. National Aeronautics and Space Administration, *2007 Budget Request* (available at http:// www.nasa.gov/pdf/142458main_FY07_budget_full.pdf).

12-B.8. A classmate tells you about a video by poet Taylor Mali on the use (or misuse) of a word processing program's spell-check feature, *The The Impotence of Proofreading*. Mali posted the video on his YouTube channel, Taylor Mali, on August 14, 2008; you watched it on April 30, 2010. The URL is http://www.youtube.com/watch?v=OonDPGwAyfQ. You know your legal writing professor is going to love it, and you want to cite it correctly when you send her the link. Chews (er, choose) the correct full citation to the video.

a. Taylor Mali, YouTube, *The The Impotence of Proofreading* (Taylor Mali posted Aug. 14, 2008) (available at http://www.youtube.com/watch?v=OonDPGwAyfQ).

b. YouTube, *The The Impotence of Proofreading*, by Taylor Mali, available at http://www.youtube.com/watch?v=OonDPGwAyfQ (Apr. 30, 2010).

c. Taylor Mali, *The The Impotence of Proofreading*, YouTube, Taylor Mali channel <www.youtube.com/watch?v=OonDPGwAyfQ> (accessed Apr. 30, 2010).

d. Mali, Taylor, *The The Impotence of Proofreading*, <http://www.youtube.com/watch?v=OonDPGwAyfQ> (Taylor Mali, accessed Apr. 30, 2010).

12-B.9. Which of the following citations correctly indicates an email message sent at 10:15 a.m. Central Daylight Time, July 16, 2010, from Alphonse Hughes, Director of the Bureau of Independent Research Associates, to Penelope Brother, on the topic *2013 Buenos Aires Conference*, a copy of which is on file with Ms. Brother?

a. Alphonse Hughes, Dir. Bureau of Indep. Research Assocs., *Email to Penelope Brother*, re: *2013 Buenos Aires Conference* (July 16, 2010) (copy on file with Ms. Brother).

b. Email from Alphonse Hughes, Dir. Bureau of Indep. Research Assocs., *2013 Buenos Aires Conference* (July 16, 2010, 10:15 a.m. CDT) (on file with Penelope Brother).

c. Alphonse Hughes, Dir. Bureau of Indep. Research Assocs., *email re 2013 Buenos Aires Conference*, to Penelope Brother (July 16, 2010, 10:15 a.m. CDT).

d. Email from Alphonse Hughes, Dir. Bureau of Indep. Research Assocs., to Penelope Brother, *2013 Buenos Aires Conference* (July 16, 2010, 10:15 a.m. CDT) (copy on file with Penelope Brother).

12-B.10. You wish to cite pages 40–41 of an LL.M. thesis that is unpublished, but available on microform. The author is Mario L. Barnes, who was a student at the University of Wisconsin–Madison in 2004 when he wrote *The Stories We Did Not Tell: Identity, Family Silence and the Legal Re-Creation of Inequality*. The microform was issued by William S. Hein & Co. as part of *Hein's Legal Theses and Dissertations* and given the unique identifier 017-00338. Choose the correct full citation to the microform.

a. Mario L. Barnes, *The Stories We Did Not Tell: Identity, Family Silence and the Legal Re-Creation of Inequality* 40–41 (unpublished LL.M. thesis, U. Wis.–Madison 2004) (microformed on William S. Hein & Co., Hein's Legal Theses and Dissertations 017-00338).

b. Barnes, Mario L. *The Stories We Did Not Tell: Identity, Family Silence and the Legal Re-Creation of Inequality*, at 40–41 (William S. Hein & Co. 2004) (microform).

c. Mario L. Barnes, Microform, *The Stories We Did Not Tell: Identity, Family Silence and the Legal Re-Creation of Inequality* 40–41 (microformed on William S. Hein & Co., Hein's Legal Theses and Dissertations 017-00338).

d. Mario L. Barnes, *The Stories We Did Not Tell: Identity, Family Silence and the Legal Re-Creation of Inequality* 40–41 (unpublished LL.M. thesis, U. Wis.–Madison 2004).

EXERCISE SET 12-B

EXPERT LEVEL: NON-PRINT SOURCES

Before beginning Exercise Set 12-B Expert Level, review the following and keep the *Manual* at hand as you work through the exercises:

- Rule 30.0, Speeches, Addresses, Oral Presentations, and Live Performances
- Rule 31.0, Interviews
- Rule 33.0, Video and Visual Sources
- Rule 34.0, Audio Sources

- Rule 35.0, Microformed Materials
- Rule 40.0, World Wide Web Sites
- Rule 41.0, Electronic Mail and Messages
- Rule 42.0, CD-ROMs and E-Readers

12-B.11. Write the full citation to the Wikipedia entry, "Earthquake," available at http://en.wikipedia.org/wiki/Earthquake. At the time you accessed it, a notation at the bottom of the Web page stated, "This page was last modified on 21 April 2010 at 15:20."

12-B.12. Write the full citation to a telephone interview with United States Supreme Court Associate Justice Sonia Sotomayor, conducted on January 22, 2011.

12-B.13. On March 14, 2010, Roger B. McNeale gave a speech in Kansas City, Missouri. The title of the speech was "No Time for Delay: Health Care Costs Are Climbing." The speech was not recorded. Write the full citation to the speech.

12-B.14. Write the full citation to the Beatles' album *Rubber Soul*, released in 1965 by Capitol Records in a 33 rpm L.P. format.

CHAPTER 13

COURT RULES, ETHICS OPINIONS,

AND JURY INSTRUCTIONS

This chapter focuses on the three sources covered in Rule 17.0: Court Rules, Ethics Rules and Opinions, and Jury Instructions. As you work through the different components of the citations in this chapter, you should begin to notice some similarities to citations discussed earlier in the *Companion* such as pinpoint references and abbreviations in the names of sources. These exercises continue to reinforce skills that you have learned throughout this *Companion*.

A. COURT RULES

For court rules—those currently in force and those no longer in force—the full citation has at least two components:

- Code abbreviation
- Rule number

And for court rules no longer in force, an additional component is a parenthetical that contains the reason why the rule is no longer in force and the year in which the rule lost effect.

Create the code abbreviation by using abbreviations in Appendix 3 and following the spacing guidelines discussed in Rule 2.2. When creating the abbreviation, omit prepositions and articles not needed for clarity. Because the rule number is the pinpoint reference, it is necessary to be as specific as possible and to include the section or subsection of the rule to which you are referring. If you refer to the notes, comments, history, internal operating procedures, or similar information, provide that pinpoint reference after the rule number as well. The exercises below help you construct the full citations for court rules.

EXERCISE SET 13-A

BASIC LEVEL: COURT RULES

Before beginning Exercise Set 13-A Basic Level, review the following and keep the *Manual* at hand as you work through the exercises:

• Rule 17.1, Full Citation Format for Rules Currently in Force

To complete the exercises, you may also need to refer to the following:

• Rule 2.2, Spacing for Abbreviations
• Rule 6.4, Subsections and Subparagraphs

• Rule 6.8, Citing Consecutive Subdivisions within a Single Section or Paragraph
• Appendix 3, General Abbreviations

13-A.1. **True or False:** A full citation to a rule currently in force, like Rule 104 of the Federal Rules of Evidence, must have a date parenthetical that includes the current year.

    a. True
    b. False

13-A.2. In title III of the Federal Rules of Criminal Procedure, you will find Rule 6, which discusses grand juries. Which of the following is the correct full citation to that rule?

    a. Fed. R. Crim. P. tit. III, R. 6.
    b. Fed. R. Crim. P. III(6).
    c. Fed. R. Crim. P. 6.
    d. F.R. Crim. P. 6.

13-A.3. Which of the following is the correct full citation to the rule regarding withdrawing library books, Rule 262 of the Colorado Court Rules?

    a. Colorado Court Rules 262.
    b. Colo. Ct. Rs. 262.
    c. 262 Colo. Ct. R.
    d. Colo. Ct. R. 262.

13-A.4. Which of the following is the correct full citation to Delaware Family Court Civil Procedure Rule 7, subsection (a)?

    a. Del. Fam. Ct. Civ. P. R. 7(a).
    b. Del. Fam. Ct. Civ. P. R. 7 (a).
    c. Del. Family Court Civil Procedure R. 7(a).
    d. Delaware Family Court Civil Procedure Rule 7(a).

13-A.5. Which of the following is the correct full citation to District of Columbia Superior Court Rules of the Probate Division, Rule 5.1, subsections (1) to (2)?

a. D.C. Super. Ct. R. Prob. Div. 5.1(1) & (2).
b. D.C. Super. Ct. R. Prob. Div. 5.1(1)-(2).
c. D.C. Super. Ct. R. of Prob. Div. 5.1(1)-(2).
d. D.C. Super. Ct. R. of Prob. Div. 5.1(1) & (2).

EXERCISE SET 13-A

INTERMEDIATE LEVEL: COURT RULES

Before beginning Exercise Set 13-A Intermediate Level, review the following and keep the *Manual* at hand as you work through the exercises:

• Rule 17.1, Full Citation Format for Rules Currently in Force

To complete the exercises, you may also need to refer to the following:

• Rule 2.2, Spacing for Abbreviations
• Rule 6.4, Subsections and Subparagraphs

• Rule 6.8, Citing Consecutive Subdivisions within a Single Section or Paragraph
• Appendix 3, General Abbreviations

13-A.6. Write the full citation to subsections (a) and (c) of current Rule 11 of the Federal Rules of Civil Procedure.

13-A.7. Write the full citation to the current Indiana Rules of Appellate Procedure, specifically Rule 22, subsection B, subsubsection 1.

13-A.8. Write the full citation to the current Kentucky Rules of Civil Procedure, specifically Rule 76.28, subsection 4(c).

13-A.9. Write the full citation to the current Rules of the Supreme Court of Georgia, specifically Rule 22.

13-A.10. Use the information provided below to answer the question. Write the full citation to subsection (b) of this rule from the current Connecticut Code of Evidence.

§ 4–5. **Evidence of Other Crimes, Wrongs or Acts Inadmissible to Prove Character; Admissible for Other Purposes; Specific Instance of Conduct**
(a) Evidence of other crimes, wrongs or acts inadmissible to prove character. . . .
(b) When evidence of other crimes, wrongs or acts is admissible. Evidence of other crimes, wrongs or acts of a person is admissible for purposes other than those specified in subsection (a), such as to prove intent, identity, malice, motive, common plan or scheme, absence of mistake or accident, knowledge, a system of criminal activity, or an element of the crime, or to corroborate crucial prosecution testimony.

.   .   .

EXERCISE SET 13-A

EXPERT LEVEL: COURT RULES

Before beginning Exercise Set 13-A Expert Level, review the following and keep the *Manual* at hand as you work through the exercises:

- Rule 17.1, Full Citation Format for Rules Currently in Force
- Rule 17.2, Full Citation Format for Rules No Longer in Force

To complete the exercises, you may also need to refer to the following:

- Rule 2.2, Spacing for Abbreviations
- Rule 6.4, Subsections and Subparagraphs
- Rule 6.8, Citing Consecutive Subdivisions within a Single Section or Paragraph
- Appendix 3, General Abbreviations

13-A.11. Use the following information to provide a full citation to this current rule of the United States Supreme Court.

Rule 28. Oral Argument

1. Oral argument should emphasize and clarify the written arguments in the briefs on the merits. Counsel should assume that all Justices have read the briefs before oral argument. Oral argument read from a prepared text is not favored.

13-A.12. You would like to refer to the pre-February 16, 2010, rule for historical purposes. Use the following information to write its full citation.

REVISIONS TO RULES
OF THE
SUPREME COURT OF THE UNITED STATES
ADOPTED January 12, 2010
EFFECTIVE February 16, 2010

· · ·

Current Rule 37.1. Brief for an *Amicus Curiae*
1. An *amicus curiae* brief that brings to the attention of the Court relevant matter not already brought to its attention by the parties may be of considerable help to the Court. An *amicus curiae* brief that does not serve this purpose burdens the Court, and its filing is not favored.

Revised Rule 37.1. Brief for an *Amicus Curiae*
1. An *amicus curiae* brief that brings to the attention of the Court relevant matter not already brought to its attention by the parties may be of considerable help to the Court. An *amicus curiae* brief that does not serve this purpose burdens the Court, and its filing is not favored. **An *amicus curiae* brief may be filed only by an attorney admitted to practice before this Court as provided in Rule 5.**

[CLERK'S COMMENT: The change incorporates a longstanding practice of the Court into the Rule.]

13-A.13. Write the full citation to subsections (e) and (j) of the following rule of the Federal Rules of Appellate Procedure.

Rule 28. Briefs

.   .   .

(e) References to the Record. References to the parts of the record contained in the appendix filed with the appellant's brief must be to the pages of the appendix. If the appendix is prepared after the briefs are filed, a party referring to the record must follow one of the methods detailed in Rule 30(c). If the original record is used under Rule 30(f) and is not consecutively paginated, or if the brief refers to an unreproduced part of the record, any reference must be to the page of the original document. For example:

- Answer p. 7;
- Motion for Judgment p. 2;
- Transcript p. 231.

Only clear abbreviations may be used. A party referring to evidence whose admissibility is in controversy must cite the pages of the appendix or of the transcript at which the evidence was identified, offered, and received or rejected.

.   .   .

(j) Citation of Supplemental Authorities. If pertinent and significant authorities come to a party's attention after the party's brief has been filed—or after oral argument but before decision—a party may promptly advise the circuit clerk by letter, with a copy to all other parties, setting forth the citations. The letter must state the reasons for the supplemental citations, referring either to the page of the brief or to a point argued orally. The body of the letter must not exceed 350 words. Any response must be made promptly and must be similarly limited.

13-A.14. Write the full citation to the comment following Rule 5 of the Arizona Rules of Civil Appellate Procedure, shown below.

Rule 5. Computation; Shortening or Extension of Time.

(a) Computation of Time. In computing any period of time prescribed by these rules, or by an order of court, or by any applicable statute, the provision of Ariz. Rules Civ. Proc. 6(a) and (e), or Ariz. Rules Fam. L. Proc. 4(A) and (D), shall apply.

.   .   .

Comment

Rule 5(a) incorporates by reference Ariz. Rules Civ. Proc. 6(a), and is based on FRAP 26(a). This provides one system which applies both in superior court and the appellate courts.

.   .   .

13-A.15. Write the full citation to the 2002 Court Commentary to the rule shown at right.

**FLORIDA RULES
OF
JUDICIAL
ADMINISTRATION
2010 Edition
RULE 2.215. TRIAL COURT ADMINISTRATION**

. . .

Court Commentary

1996 Court Commentary. Rule 2.050(h) [renumbered as 2.215(h) in 2006] should be read in conjunction with Florida Rule of Appellate Procedure 9.140(b)(4)(A).

. . .

2002 Court Commentary. Recognizing the inherent differences in trial and appellate court dockets, the last sentence of subdivision (g) is intended to conform to the extent practicable with appellate rule 9.146(g), which requires appellate courts to give priority to appeals in juvenile dependency and termination of parental rights cases, and in cases involving families and children in need of services.

B.   ETHICS OPINIONS

Citations to formal and informal ethics opinions have three components:

- the name of the state or entity that issued the opinion;
- the type of ethics opinion; and
- the opinion number.

Words in the first two components may be abbreviated using Appendix 3. If a pinpoint reference is available, include that information after the opinion number. If the opinion has a title, you may include it at the beginning of the citation in ordinary typeface. (This is a change from the third edition of the *Manual*.) You may also include a parenthetical telling the reader where to find the opinion (in a specific print source or in an online database). If the opinion has been superseded or withdrawn, add a parenthetical at the end of the citation that provides information about when the opinion was superseded, withdrawn, revised, etc.

The exercises below help you construct the full citations for ethics opinions.

EXERCISE SET 13-B

BASIC LEVEL: ETHICS OPINIONS

Before beginning Exercise Set 13-B Basic Level, review the following and keep the *Manual* at hand as you work through the exercises:

• Rule 17.4, Full Citation Format for Ethics Opinions

To complete the exercises, you may also need to refer to the following:

• Rule 2.2, Spacing for Abbreviations
• Rule 3.0, Spelling and Capitalization
• Rule 5.0, Page and Location Numbers
• Rule 6.0, Citing Sections and Paragraphs
• Rule 9.0, Graphical Material, Appendices, and Other Subdivisions

• Rule 17.2, Full Citation Format for Rules No Longer in Force
• Rule 46.0, Explanatory Parentheticals and Related Authority
• Appendix 3, General Abbreviations

13-B.1.   **True or False:** A date parenthetical is needed in the following citation.

ABA Formal Ethics Op. 95-391.

a. True
b. False

13-B.2.   Explain your answer to Question 13-B.1 and provide the applicable rule number.

13-B.3.   **True or False:** The following citation is formatted correctly.

Disclosure of Conflicts Information When Lawyers Move between Law Firms, ABA Formal Ethics Op. 09-455.

a. True
b. False

13-B.4.   Choose the correct full citation to an ethics advisory opinion of the South Carolina Bar Ethics Advisory Committee, Opinion 06-12, released on November 17, 2006.

a. S.C. Bar Ethics Advisory Committee Advisory Op. 06-12.
b. S.C. B. Ethics Adv. Comm. Adv. Op. 06-12.
c. S.C. B. Ethics Advisory Comm. Advisory Op. 06-12.
d. S.C. B. Ethics Advisory Comm. Advisory Op. 06-12 (2006).

13-B.5.   You would like to cite an American Bar Association formal ethics opinion and include the title in the full citation. Which of the following is the correct format for the title?

a. lawyer's obligations when outsourcing legal and nonlegal support services
b. Lawyer's Obligations When Outsourcing Legal and Nonlegal Support Services
c. *lawyer's obligations when outsourcing legal and nonlegal support services*
d. *Lawyer's Obligations When Outsourcing Legal and Nonlegal Support Services*

13-B.6. You would like to cite Alaska Ethics Opinion 92-2 for historical purposes. When you look up the opinion, you find the following reference in the pocket part. Draft the parenthetical that should appear after Alaska Ethics Op. 92-2.

ETHICS OPINION NO. 92-2

Editor's notes.— This Ethics Opinion was withdrawn by Ethics Opinion No. 2003-1. The version that appears in the main volume should be disregarded.

EXERCISE SET 13-B

INTERMEDIATE LEVEL: ETHICS OPINIONS

Before beginning Exercise Set 13-B Intermediate Level, review the following and keep the *Manual* at hand as you work through the exercises:

• Rule 17.4, Full Citation Format for Ethics Opinions

To complete the exercises, you may also need to refer to the following:

• Rule 2.2, Spacing for Abbreviations
• Rule 3.0, Spelling and Capitalization
• Rule 5.0, Page and Location Numbers
• Rule 6.0, Citing Sections and Paragraphs
• Rule 9.0, Graphical Material, Appendices, and Other Subdivisions

• Rule 17.2, Full Citation Format for Rules No Longer in Force
• Rule 46.0, Explanatory Parentheticals and Related Authority
• Appendix 3, General Abbreviations

13-B.7. You would like to refer to the ethics opinion published by the American Bar Association shown below. Write the full citation, without a title.

E-Mail

• Metadata, Formal Opinion 06-442

13-B.8. Write the full citation to the following American Bar Association ethics opinion and include the title.

INFORMAL OPINION 87-1524 JUDGE'S DISQUALIFICATION WHERE FORMER ASSOCIATE IS COUNSEL
December 14, 1987

13-B.9.   Write the full citation to the following ethics opinion, without the title.

> Board of Professional Responsibility of the Supreme Court of Tennessee
> Formal Ethics Opinion Number 2004-F-150
>
> *1 September 17, 2004
> Guidance is provided concerning the ethical obligations of attorneys who receive confidential documents
> of adverse parties which were inadvertently sent or disclosed.

13-B.10.   Write the full citation to the following ethics opinion, including the title.

> Executive Ethics Board Advisory Opinion 02-04
> Washington
> Advisory Opinion 02-04
> June 14, 2002
>
> Use Of State Facilities, Including Electronic Mail, To Distribute Newspaper Articles and Editorial
> Opinions

EXERCISE SET 13-B

EXPERT LEVEL: ETHICS OPINIONS

Before beginning Exercise Set 13-B Expert Level, review the following and keep the *Manual* at hand as you work through the exercises:

• Rule 17.4, Full Citation Format for Ethics Opinions.

To complete the exercises, you may also need to refer to the following:

• Rule 2.2, Spacing for Abbreviations
• Rule 3.0, Spelling and Capitalization
• Rule 5.0, Page and Location Numbers
• Rule 6.0, Citing Sections and Paragraphs
• Rule 7.0, Citing Footnotes and Endnotes
• Rule 9.0, Graphical Material, Appendices, and Other Subdivisions

• Rule 17.2, Full Citation Format for Rules No Longer in Force
• Rule 46.0, Explanatory Parentheticals and Related Authority
• Appendix 3, General Abbreviations

13-B.11.   The Vermont Bar Association Professional Responsibility Section released an ethics opinion, 2009-1, on October 7, 2009. Write the full citation to footnote 2 of the opinion, at page 5.

13-B.12.   Write the full citation to the following ethics opinion, without the title. You are referring to the opinion for historical purposes.

Minnesota Lawyers Professional Responsibility Board
MAINTENANCE OF BOOKS AND RECORDS

Opinion Number 9
Adopted: September 10, 1976
Amended: June 22, 1977, June 23, 1983, December 4, 1987, September 15, 1989, and September 18, 1998,
August 1, 1999

REPEALED January 26, 2006

13-B.13.   Write the full citation, including the title, to the following advisory opinion published by the Committee on Codes of Conduct of the United States Judicial Conference.

Committee on Codes of Conduct
Advisory Opinion No. 9
Testifying as a Character Witness

. . .

June 2009

13-B.14.   Write the full citation, without the title, to the following informal opinion issued by the Washington Rules of Professional Conduct Committee.

Informal Opinion: 2110
Year Issued: 2006
RPC(s): RPC 7.2
Subject: the ethical implications of a non-profit, community based organization requesting a donation from attorneys to whom cases were referred and produced financial results

---

13-B.15.   On the Louisiana State Bar Association Web page, you find an ethics opinion that you would like to cite in a document, referring to page 4 and to footnotes 12 and 14 on page 5 of the opinion. Write the full citation, with the title, for the opinion.

Louisiana State Bar Association
Rules of Professional Conduct Committee
PUBLIC Opinion 05-RPCC-001   April 4, 2005
Lawyer Retirement – Ethical Requirements to Client

C.   JURY INSTRUCTIONS

Citations to jury instructions contain the same type of information as citations to court rules and ethics opinions discussed above:

- the name of the instructions;
- the volume of the instructions, if any;

- the pinpoint reference—rule or section number; and
- a date parenthetical containing the edition number (for an edition after the first) and the date.

Words in the name of the instructions may be abbreviated using Appendix 3. Official jury instructions—standard, pattern, and approved jury instructions—are set out in ordinary typeface, whereas the name or title of unofficial jury instructions is italicized.

The exercises below help you construct the full citations for jury instructions.

EXERCISE SET 13-C

BASIC LEVEL: JURY INSTRUCTIONS

Before beginning Exercise Set 13-C Basic Level, review the following and keep the *Manual* at hand as you work through the exercises:

• Rule 17.6, Full Citation Formats for Jury Instructions

To complete the exercises, you may also need to refer to the following:

• Rule 2.2, Spacing for Abbreviations
• Appendix 3, General Abbreviations

13-C.1. You would like to cite the Hawaii Civil Jury Instruction that discusses considering only the evidence, Instruction 2.2. The instruction was approved in 1999. Use this information to answer the following four questions:

13-C.1.a. What is the correct name of the instruction?

a. Civil Jury Instruction, Hawaii
b. Haw. Civ. Jury Instr.
c. Hawaii Civil Jury Instr.
d. Haw. Civ. Jur. Instr.

13-C.1.b. **True or False:** The full citation to the instruction does not contain the title of the instruction.

a. True
b. False

13-C.1.c. What rule or section number should be included in the full citation?

a. no. 2.2
b. #2.2
c. number 2.2
d. 2.2

13-C.1.d. Write the date parenthetical for the full citation.

13-C.2.   You would like to cite the Idaho Criminal Jury Instruction that discusses the possession of a firearm by a felon, Instruction 1401. The instruction was updated on November 30, 2005. Which of the following is the correct full citation?

    a. Idaho Crim. Jury Instr. 1401 (2005).
    b. Idaho Crim. Jur. Instr. 1401 (2005).
    c. Idaho Crim. Jur. Instr. no. 1401 (2005).
    d. Idaho Crim. Jury Instr. no. 1401 (2005).

13-C.3.   You find the following citation in a law review article: *Jury Instructions in Commercial Litigation* § 10.02[1], 10-5 (LexisNexis 2009).

True or False: The jury instructions cited above are official jury instructions.

    a. True
    b. False

EXERCISE SET 13-C

INTERMEDIATE LEVEL: JURY INSTRUCTIONS

Before beginning Exercise Set 13-C Intermediate Level, review the following and keep the *Manual* at hand as you work through the exercises:

• Rule 17.6, Full Citation Formats for Jury Instructions

To complete the exercises, you may also need to refer to the following:

• Rule 2.2, Spacing for Abbreviations
• Appendix 3, General Abbreviations

13-C.4.   Write the full citation to the following unofficial Connecticut civil jury instruction, drafted by the Connecticut Civil Jury Instructions Committee.

2.1-2 Duty to Follow the Law Revised to January 1, 2008

13-C.5.   Write the full citation to the jury instruction below, which is from the Oklahoma Juvenile Jury Instructions, published in 2005.

Juvenile Instruction No. 3.7   **Failure to Contribute to Support of Child**

13-C.6. Write the full citation to the following instruction from the United States Court of Appeals for the Seventh Circuit Pattern Criminal Jury Instructions.

3.07 WEIGHING EXPERT TESTIMONY

You have heard a witness [witnesses] give opinions about matters requiring special knowledge or skill. You should judge this testimony in the same way that you judge the testimony of any other witness. The fact that such a person has given an opinion does not mean that you are required to accept it. Give the testimony whatever weight you think it deserves, considering the reasons given for the opinion, the witness' qualifications, and all of the other evidence in the case.

EXERCISE SET 13-C

EXPERT LEVEL: JURY INSTRUCTIONS

Before beginning Exercise Set 13-C Expert Level, review the following and keep the *Manual* at hand as you work through the exercises:

• Rule 17.6, Full Citation Formats for Jury Instructions

To complete the exercises, you may also need to refer to the following:

• Rule 2.2, Spacing for Abbreviations
• Appendix 3, General Abbreviations

13-C.7. Write the full citation to the following model instruction from the Michigan Supreme Court Committee on Model Civil Jury Instructions. This instruction was adopted by the Committee on Model Civil Jury Instructions and is unofficial.

MCivJI 80.05 Dog Bite Statute—Lawfully on Property of Dog Owner

A person is lawfully on the property of the owner of the dog if the person is on the owner's property in the performance of any duty imposed upon [him/her] by the laws of this state or by the laws or postal regulations of the United States.

Note on Use

This instruction should be used only if the incident occurred on the property of the dog's owner.

History

Added September 2006.

13-C.8. Write the full citation to the following jury instruction. This recent jury instruction has not yet been included in the Illinois Pattern Jury Instructions bound volumes.

155.01 The Drug or Alcohol Impaired Minor Responsibility Act – Injury to Person or Property by an Impaired Minor

There was in force in the State of Illinois at the time of the occurrence in question a statute called "The [Drug][or][Alcohol] Impaired Minor Responsibility Act," which states: Any person 18 years of age or older who [willfully supplies, sells, gives or delivers (alcoholic liquor)(illegal drugs)] [willfully permits the consumption of (alcoholic liquor)(illegal drugs) on non-residential premises owned or controlled by that person] to a person under the age of 18 and causes or contributes to cause the impairment of that person, is liable for [death][or][injury] to a [person][or] [property] caused by the impairment of such person.

Instruction, Notes on Use and Comment approved January 2010.

13-C.9. Use the information shown at right to write the full citation to jury instruction § 11:330. The source was published in 2009.

Federal Employment Jury Instructions

Volume II

Todd J. McNamara
J. Alfred Southerland

Contributing Author:
Kristina James

JAMES PUBLISHING
Incorporated

13-C.10. Use the information provided below to write the full citation to the instruction. The source was published by Matthew Bender & Company, Inc.

Jury Instructions in Commercial Litigation

Publication 63567   Release 9   March 2009

10-5   COPYRIGHT   § 10.03[1]

§ 10.02 Copyright infringement—Sound recording.

[1]   Instruction
You will find for the plaintiff if you find from the evidence that:

.   .   .

D. **SHORT-FORM CITATIONS**

The short-form citations for the three sources discussed in this chapter are straightforward. For court rules, when *id.* is not appropriate, repeat the full citation. For ethics opinions and jury instructions, when *id.* is not appropriate, repeat the full citation, minus the date parenthetical, if any.

The exercises below help you construct short citations for court rules, ethics opinions, and jury instructions.

EXERCISE SET 13-D

BASIC LEVEL: SHORT-FORM CITATIONS

Before beginning Exercise Set 13-D Basic Level, review the following and keep the *Manual* at hand as you work through the exercises:

- Rule 17.3, Short Citation Format [for Court Rules]
- Rule 17.5, Short Citation Format for Ethics Opinions
- Rule 17.7, Short Citation Formats for Jury Instructions

13-D.1.   Write the short-form citation to the following source, referring to the entire section. Do not use *id.*

Neb. Code Jud. Conduct § 5-202(B).

13-D.2.   Write the short-form citation to the following source. Do not use *id.*

ABA Formal Ethics Op. 07-449.

13-D.3.   Write the short-form citation to the following source. Do not use *id.*

Pa. B. Assn. Comm. Leg. Ethics & Prof. Resp., Ethics Op. 2009-02 (available at 2009 WL 934623).

13-D.4.   Write the short-form citation to the following source. Do not use *id.*

Okla. Civ. Jury Instr. 7.1 (2009).

EXERCISE SET 13-D

INTERMEDIATE LEVEL: SHORT-FORM CITATIONS

Before beginning Exercise Set 13-D Intermediate Level, review the following and keep the *Manual* at hand as you work through the exercises:

- Rule 17.3, Short Citation Format [for Court Rules]
- Rule 17.5, Short Citation Format for Ethics Opinions

  Rule 17.7, Short Citation Formats for Jury Instructions

13-D.5.   Use the following information from the California Court Rules to answer the two questions.

Rule 2.1032. Juror notebooks in complex civil cases

A trial judge should encourage counsel in complex civil cases to include key documents, exhibits, and other appropriate materials in notebooks for use by jurors during trial to assist them in performing their duties.

Rule 2.1032 adopted effective January 1, 2007.

Comment

While this rule is intended to apply to complex civil cases, there may be other types of civil cases in which notebooks may be appropriate or useful. Resources, including guidelines for use and recommended notebook contents, are available in *Bench Handbook: Jury Management* (CJER, rev. 2006, p. 59).

13-D.5.a.   Write the full citation to the comment to this rule.

13-D.5.b.   Write the short-form citation to the same comment (assuming *id.* is not appropriate).

13-D.6.   Use the following information about an ethics opinion to answer the following two questions.

LOS ANGELES COUNTY BAR ASSOCIATION

PROFESSIONAL RESPONSIBILITY AND ETHICS COMMITTEE

OPINION NO. 518

June 19, 2006

ETHICAL CONSIDERATIONS IN OUTSOURCING OF LEGAL SERVICES

13-D.6.a.   Write the full citation to Opinion Number 518, "Ethical Considerations in Outsourcing of Legal Services." Include the title in the full citation.

13-D.6.b.   Write the short-form citation to the opinion (assuming *id.* is not appropriate).

13-D.7.   The passage shown at right is from an Alaskan ethics opinion. It was reprinted in the *Alaska Statutes 1962: Alaska Legal Ethics Opinions and Rules Governing the Legal Profession*, published by the Alaska Legislative Council and Lexis Law Publishing in 1999. Use the information to answer the following two questions:

> **ETHICS OPINION NO. 98-2**
>
> **Communication by Electronic Mail**
>
> Electronic mail (e-mail) is fast becoming the accepted and preferred method for attorneys to communicate with their clients, and vice versa. It has the obvious advantages of speed, efficiency and cost to commend its application, and it will like follow the path of the fax machine and soon become an everyday mainstream business tool . . . .

13-D.7.a.   Write the full citation to the opinion, including the title and information about where the opinion was reprinted.

13-D.7.b.   Write the short-form citation to the opinion (assuming *id.* is not appropriate).

13-D.8.   You found a model federal civil jury instruction on the United States Court of Appeals that you would like to refer to in a paper. The title is provided below. The instruction was prepared by the Committee on Model Civil Jury Instructions within the Third Circuit and published in 2010. Use this information to answer the following two questions:

> **5.06 Willful Blindness** *[Deliberate Ignorance]*

13-D.8.a.   Write the full citation to the instruction, including the title.

13-D.8.b.   Write the short-form citation to the instruction (assuming *id.* is not appropriate)

EXERCISE SET 13-D

EXPERT LEVEL: SHORT-FORM CITATIONS

Before beginning Exercise Set 13-D Expert Level, review the following and keep the *Manual* at hand as you work through the exercises:

- Rule 17.3, Short Citation Format [for Court Rules]
- Rule 17.5, Short Citation Format for Ethics Opinions
  Rule 17.7, Short Citation Formats for Jury Instructions

13-D.9.   Write the short-form citation to the following source, referring to comments 1 and 3. Do not use *id.*

> Ga. R. Prof. Conduct 8.1.

13-D.10. In the court rules for the United States Court of Appeals for the Second Circuit, you found the following internal operating procedure under Rule 32.1. Use this information to answer the following two questions:

IOP 32.1.1 Summary Order

(a) Use of Summary Orders. When a decision in a case is unanimous and each panel judge believes that no jurisprudential purpose is served by an opinion (i.e., a ruling having precedential effect), the panel may rule by summary order.

(b) Summary Order Legend. Summary orders filed on or after January 1, 2007, must bear the following legend:

SUMMARY ORDER

Rulings by summary order do not have precedential effect. Citation to a summary order filed on or after January 1, 2007, is permitted and is governed by Federal Rule of Appellate Procedure 32.1 and this court's Local Rule 32.1.1. When citing a summary order in a document filed with this court, a party must cite either the Federal Appendix or an electronic database (with the notation "summary order"). A party citing a summary order must serve a copy of it on any party not represented by counsel.

13-D.10.a. Write the full citation to the whole internal operating procedure.

13-D.10.b. Write the short-form citation, but refer only to subsection (a). Do not use *id.*

13-D.11. The following instruction is from the United States Court of Appeals for the Seventh Circuit Pattern Criminal Jury Instructions, which were approved in 1998. Use this instruction to answer the following two questions.

1.03 TESTIMONY OF WITNESSES (DECIDING WHAT TO BELIEVE)

You are to decide whether the testimony of each of the witnesses is truthful and accurate, in part, in whole, or not at all, as well as what weight, if any, you give to the testimony of each witness.

In evaluating the testimony of any witness, you may consider, among other things:

- [— the witness's age;]
- — the witness's intelligence;
- — the ability and opportunity the witness had to see, hear, or know the things that the witness testified about;
- — the witness's memory;
- — any interest, bias, or prejudice the witness may have;
- — the manner of the witness while testifying; and
- — the reasonableness of the witness's testimony in light of all the evidence in the case.

[You should judge the defendant's testimony in the same way that you judge the testimony of any other witness.]

Committee Comment

The portion of the instruction relating to age should be given only when a very elderly or a very young witness has testified.

The bracketed final sentence should be given only when a defendant testifies.

13-D.11.a.   Write the full citation to this instruction. You would like to refer to only the committee comment.

13-D.11.b.   Write the short-form citation to this instruction and refer to only the committee comment. Do not use *id.*

13-D.12.   Use the information provided at right to answer the following three questions. The source is published in 2005, by the American Bar Association.

> SECTION OF LITIGATION
> American Bar Association
>
> ## MODEL JURY INSTRUCTIONS
>
> # Business Torts Litigation
> FOURTH EDITION
>
> Business Torts Litigation Committee
> SECTION OF LITIGATION
> AMERICAN BAR ASSOCIATION

13-D.12.a.   Write the full citation to the instruction in section 7.3.1.

13-D.12.b.   You are writing a document *without* footnotes, and you have provided a full citation to the instruction. You would like to refer to the instruction again later in the document, after citing other sources. Write the short-form citation to the instruction in section 7.3.1.

13-D.12.c.   You are writing a document *with* footnotes, and you have provided a full citation to the instruction in footnote 63. Assume that you would like to refer to the instruction again in footnote 72 and *id.* is not appropriate. Write the short-form citation to the instruction in section 7.3.1.

PRACTITIONER AND COURT

DOCUMENTS

Unlike the citations discussed thus far in the *Companion*, the citations covered in this chapter—practitioner and court documents, transcripts, and appellate records—are used primarily when you are referring to materials within a case that you are litigating. In law school, these citations are typically used in the semester in which you are writing pretrial briefs or memoranda of law, or appellate briefs. If you need citations to these types of documents in other situations, use Rule 12.19. Rule 12.19 of the current (fourth) edition of the *Manual* (which was Rule 12.20 in the third edition) has an extensive discussion of citations to these types of documents.

Also included in this chapter is a discussion of citations to letters and memoranda because these documents are typically cited as evidence in cases.

A. DOCUMENTS, TRANSCRIPTS, AND RECORDS

Documents and Transcripts

As discussed in Rule 29.1(b), there are many types of practitioner and court documents such as "pleadings, motions and responses, briefs, memoranda of law, discovery and disclosure material, affidavits, declarations, evidence, notices, stipulations, orders, and judgments."

Assuming that there are no local rules governing the citation format,[1] a full citation to a practitioner or court document has three components:

- document name;
- pinpoint reference; and
- date

Present the document name as it appears on the face of the document. Abbreviating the words in the document name is not required. Some attorneys prefer to spell out the document name in the full citation and use abbreviations in short-form citations. This is an acceptable practice, as provided in Rule 29.2(a)(2). However, you may choose to abbreviate the words in the document name using Appendix 3. If you choose to abbreviate, keep the following points in mind:

- Refer to Rule 2.2 for guidance on abbreviation spacing.
- If the document name uses the possessive form of a noun (e.g., Petitioner's), make the abbreviation possessive (e.g., Petr.'s).
- If the document name uses an ordinal number (e.g., "Second"), use the appropriate ordinal contraction, as shown in Rule 4.3(b) ("2d").
- You may omit articles and prepositions so long as the clarity of the information is not affected.

The type of pinpoint reference varies, depending on the document. Remember to be as specific as possible when providing the pinpoint reference.

- In practitioner and court documents, the pinpoint reference could be a page number or something more specific, such as a page number with a paragraph number. Refer to Rule 6.0 for specific guidance on using paragraph symbols.
- Some documents have pages with line numbers. Place the line number immediately after a colon that follows the page number. For example, the pinpoint reference to page 45, line 17 is 45:17. The pinpoint reference can include more than one line; the pinpoint reference to page 45, lines 17, 18, and 19, is 45:17–19.

The last part of the full citation is the date parenthetical, which uses the exact date of the document, the month–day–year. Check Appendix 3(A) for abbreviations for the months. The date will depend upon the document. For example,

- If the document has been filed with the court, use the filing date.
- If the document has been served on opposing counsel, but not filed with the court, use the date that the document was served.
- If the document was not filed with the court or served on opposing counsel, use the date that the document was prepared.
- If a date cannot be determined, use the abbreviation for "no date"—("n.d.").

The same components are also used in full citations to transcripts, with only two minor differences: first, the transcript abbreviation replaces the document name, and second, the pinpoint reference includes not only a page number, but also a line number. When you

---

[1] Local rules are addressed in Chapter 15.

format the transcript abbreviation, follow the same guidelines provided above for the document name.

To assist the reader in identifying citations to documents and transcripts, you may change the typeface to bold, you may put the citation in parentheses, or both, as discussed in Sidebar 29.1.

Appellate Records

The citation to an appellate record is probably the simplest of all full citation formats. The full citation has two components:

- the abbreviation for "record" ("R.") and
- a pinpoint reference.

The pinpoint reference can be simply a page, or it could also include a line number. An appellate record consists of a collection of documents from the litigation at the trial-court level. Consequently, the documents not only have their original pagination, but when they are all combined to form the appellate record, the documents receive a second pagination, representing the appellate record pagination. Use the appellate record pagination, not the pagination of the original document.

The entire appellate record citation may be enclosed in parentheses or brackets to set the citation apart from the text of the sentence. Rule 29.5(a) provides six acceptable formats for appellate record citations. Whatever format you choose, use it consistently throughout the document. You may put appellate record citations in boldface, in parentheses, or both, if desired.

The exercises below help you construct the full citations to court documents, transcripts, and appellate records.

EXERCISE SET 14-A

BASIC LEVEL: DOCUMENTS, TRANSCRIPTS, AND RECORDS

Before beginning Exercise Set 14-A Basic Level, review the following and keep the *Manual* at hand as you work through the exercises:

- Rule 29.2, Full Citation Format for Practitioner and Court Documents
- Rule 29.3, Full Citation Format for Transcripts

- Rule 29.5, Full Citation Format for Appellate Records

To complete the exercises, you may also need to refer to the following:

- Rule 2.2, Spacing for Abbreviations
- Rule 4.3, Ordinal Numbers
- Rule 6.0, Citing Sections and Paragraphs

- Sidebar 29.1, Inserting Document Names and Record Cites in Memoranda and Court Documents
- Appendix 3, General Abbreviations

14-A.1. You are working with documents whose names include the following words. Write the words as they should be used in a citation to a court document, abbreviating any words appearing in Appendix 3.

14-A.1.a. Request

14-A.1.b. Transcript

14-A.1.c. Notice

14.A.1.d. Defendant's

14-A.1.e. Response

14-A.1.f. Production

14-A.2. **True or False:** When you provide a full or short citation to practitioner and court documents and transcripts, you are permitted to put the entire citation in bold.

a. True
b. False

14-A.3. You are working with documents that display the names shown below. Write the document names as they should be used in a citation in a court document, abbreviating any words appearing in Appendix 3 and omitting articles or prepositions not needed for clarity.

14-A.3.a. Plaintiff's Motion for Reconsideration

14-A.3.b. Defendant's Motion to Vacate the Order

14-A.3.c. Plaintiff's Request for Document Production

14-A.3.d. Plaintiffs' First Amended Complaint

14-A.3.e. Joint Stipulations

14-A.3.f. Temporary Restraining Order

14-A.4. Write the pinpoint reference portion of a full citation to paragraph 15 of a motion.

14-A.5. Write the pinpoint reference portion of a full citation to paragraphs 15 and 17 of a motion.

14-A.6. If the document has been filed with the court, what is the *best* date to use in the full citation?

a. The date that the document was prepared
b. The date that the document was served on opposing counsel
c. The phrase "n.d."
d. The date the document was filed with the court

14-A.7. **True or False:** If you select [R. at 17.] as the format for your appellate record citations, a reference to page 32 of the appellate record should appear as [R. at 32.] in your document.

a. True
b. False

14-A.8. True or False: The following citation to page 15, line 11, of the appellate record is formatted correctly: (R. at 15:11).

    a. True
    b. False

EXERCISE SET 14-A

INTERMEDIATE LEVEL: DOCUMENTS, TRANSCRIPTS, AND RECORDS

Before beginning Exercise Set 14-A Intermediate Level, review the following and keep the *Manual* at hand as you work through the exercises:

- Rule 29.2, Full Citation Format for Practitioner and Court Documents
- Rule 29.3, Full Citation Format for Transcripts

- Rule 29.5, Full Citation Format for Appellate Records

To complete the exercises, you may also need to refer to the following:

- Rule 2.2, Spacing for Abbreviations
- Rule 4.3, Ordinal Numbers
- Rule 6.0, Citing Sections and Paragraphs

- Sidebar 29.1, Inserting Document Names and Record Cites in Memoranda and Court Documents
- Appendix 3, General Abbreviations

14-A.9. Write the full citation to page 48 of the appellate record, specifically lines 11 through 14.

14-A.10. Write the full citation to page 53 and to page 58 of the appellate record, specifically lines 3 through 5.

14-A.11. You would like to cite page three of the document whose title is shown below. The document was filed with the court on July 2, 1996. Write the full citation, with the pinpoint reference. Abbreviate any words appearing in Appendix 3 and omit articles or prepositions not needed for clarity.

PLAINTIFF'S REQUEST FOR PRODUCTION OF DOCUMENTS AND THINGS

14-A.12. You need to refer to paragraphs 2 and 4 of the document whose title is shown below. The document was filed with the court on July 29, 1996. Write the full citation, with the pinpoint reference. Abbreviate any words appearing in Appendix 3 and omit articles or prepositions not needed for clarity.

DEFENDANTS' RESPONSE TO REQUEST FOR PRODUCTION OF
DOCUMENTS AND THINGS

14-A.13. You would like to cite the document whose title is shown below. The document was filed with the court on July 27, 2007. You wish to refer to paragraphs 3, 4, and 7. Write the full citation, with the pinpoint reference. Abbreviate any words appearing in Appendix 3 and omit articles or prepositions not needed for clarity.

AFFIDAVIT OF JO ANDERSON

14-A.14.   You would like to cite the document whose title is shown below. You wish to refer to page 1, line 17. Write the full citation, with the pinpoint reference. Abbreviate any words appearing in Appendix 3 and omit articles or prepositions not needed for clarity.

<u>EXCERPT OF DEPOSITION OF PROFESSOR SARAH WOOD</u>
TAKEN ON DECEMBER 8, 2004

EXERCISE SET 14-A

EXPERT LEVEL: DOCUMENTS, TRANSCRIPTS, AND RECORDS

Before beginning Exercise Set 14-A Expert Level, review the following and keep the *Manual* at hand as you work through the exercises:

- Rule 29.2, Full Citation Format for Practitioner and Court Documents
- Rule 29.3, Full Citation Format for Transcripts

- Rule 29.5, Full Citation Format for Appellate Records

To complete the exercises, you may also need to refer to the following:

- Rule 2.2, Spacing for Abbreviations
- Rule 4.3, Ordinal Numbers
- Rule 6.0, Citing Sections and Paragraphs

- Sidebar 29.1, Inserting Document Names and Record Cites in Memoranda and Court Documents
- Appendix 3, General Abbreviations

14-A.15.   You would like to cite the document shown below. Specifically, you wish to refer to information starting on line 25 of page 4 and ending on line 5 of page 6. Write the full citation, with the pinpoint reference. Abbreviate any words appearing in Appendix 3 and omit articles or prepositions not needed for clarity.

```
              IN THE UNITED STATES DISTRICT COURT
            FOR THE MIDDLE DISTRICT OF NORTH CAROLINA

   EDWARD CARRINGTON, et al.,        *
                                     *
                                     *   Docket No. 1:08CV119
                                     *
            Plaintiffs,              *
                                     *
               vs.                   *   Winston-Salem, North
                                     *   Carolina
                                     *   April 15, 2008
   DUKE UNIVERSITY, et al.,          *   2 p.m.
                                     *
            Defendants.              *
   * * * * * * * * * * * * * * * * * * * * * * * * * * * *

              TRANSCRIPT OF MOTION HEARING
```

14-A.16. You would like to cite the document from Westlaw shown below. Specifically, you wish to refer to paragraphs 9, 10, 12, 13, and 18. Write the full citation, with the pinpoint reference. Abbreviate any words appearing in Appendix 3 and omit articles or prepositions not needed for clarity.

United States District Court, S.D. Florida.
RAMOS et al,
v.
TOYOTA MOTOR SALES.
No. 10CV20630.
March 2, 2010.

General Jurisdiction Division

"Class Representation Complaint"

Note: This document was obtained from the above titled case.

Court: Circuit Court of Florida.

Title: Antonio Ramos and Tahiry Ramos, on behalf of themselves and others similarly situated, Plaintiff, vs. Toyota Motor Sales U.S.A., Inc. Defendant.

Docket Number: No. 10-07117CA40.

Date: February 3, 2010.

B.   LETTERS AND MEMORANDA

Full citations to letters or memoranda have ten components, as shown in the sample citation at the beginning of Rule 32.0. The components are discussed below:

1. Description of the document

   Identify the type of document (letter or memorandum, for example). Capitalize and abbreviate words in the description according to Appendix 3. For example, if you refer to an unpublished report, the first component of the full citation is "Rep. from." Other examples of descriptions of documents are provided in Rule 32.1(a). If the letter or memorandum is not addressed to a specific recipient or group of recipients, start the full citation with the word "Open" before the description of the document, and skip to component 7.

2. Author's name

3. Author's title and affiliation

   The second and third components can be addressed together because both describe the document's author. Present the author's full name as it appears on the document, with designations such as "Sr." or "II," but omitting titles of respect such as "Hon." or degree information such as "J.D." Rule 32.1(b) cross-references Rule 22.1(a), which discusses how to present an author's name, and Rule 32.1(c) cross-references Rule 31.1(c), which states that words in an author's title and affiliation may be abbreviated if they are listed in Appendix 3. Remove articles and prepositions from the title and affiliation.

4. The word "to"

After the author's affiliation and a comma, insert the word "to" before the recipient's name.

5. Recipient's name

6. Recipient's title and affiliation

The fifth and sixth components can also be addressed together because they describe the recipient's name, title, and affiliation. Information about the recipient is presented in the same manner as information about the author. Rule 32.1(d) cross-references Rule 22.1(a), which discusses how to present the recipient's name, and Rule 32.1(e) cross-references Rule 31.1(c), which discusses how to format the recipient's title and affiliation.

7. Subject of the letter or memorandum

The subject is usually found in the subject or "Re:" line of the letter or memorandum. If the document does not have a subject or Re: line, write your own brief description of the subject of the document. Italicize, but do not abbreviate, words making up the subject, as explained in Rule 32.1(f).

8. Pinpoint reference

The pinpoint reference should be as specific as possible. Typically, the pinpoint reference is a page number. However, as Rule 6.3(a) and its example demonstrate, if the document does not have page numbers, but has indented, unnumbered paragraphs, cite the document as if the paragraphs had been numbered, by inserting bracketed paragraph symbols and numbers for the pinpoint reference.

9. Date parenthetical

Provide the exact date of the document (month-day-year) in parentheses. Abbreviate months listed in Appendix 3(A).

10. Location of the letter or memorandum

Because letters and memoranda are unpublished, in a second parenthetical following the date parenthetical, provide information about whether or how the reader may obtain a copy of the document. Abbreviate words in the name of the organization that maintains the document, using Appendix 3, and omit articles and prepositions not needed for clarity.

The exercises below help you identify the different components of and construct full citations to unpublished letters and memoranda. The exercises in this set are for all levels.

EXERCISE SET 14-B

ALL LEVELS: LETTERS AND MEMORANDA

Before beginning Exercise Set 14-B All Levels, review the following and keep the *Manual* at hand as you work through the exercises:

• Rule 32.1, Full Citation Format for Unpublished Letters and Memoranda

To complete the exercises, you may also need to refer to the following:

• Rule 2.2, Spacing for Abbreviations   • Rule 31.1(d), Date
• Rule 22.1(a), Author's name   • Appendix 3, General Abbreviations
• Rule 31.1(c), Interviewee's title and affiliation

14-B.1. Use the information in the following full citation to a letter to answer the five questions below:

> Ltr. from Kristin Gerdy, Teaching Prof. & Dir., Rex E. Lee Advoc. Program, BYU L. Sch., to Suzanne Rowe, Dir., Leg. Research & Writing, Assoc. Prof. of L., U. of Or. Sch. of L., *Journal Article and Publication* 2 (Apr. 9, 2010) (copy on file with Author).

14-B.1.a. Identify the author's name, title, and affiliation, without the abbreviations.

14-B.1.b. Identify the recipient's name, title, and affiliation, without the abbreviations.

14-B.1.c. Identify the subject of the letter.

14-B.1.d. Identify the pinpoint reference.

14-B.1.e. Identify the date of the letter.

14-B.2. Use the information in the following full citation to a memorandum to answer the five questions below:

> Open memo. from Debbie Brown, V.P. of H.R. & Leg. Affairs, Stetson U. College of L., *New Healthcare Program* 4 (Dec. 15, 2009) (memo on file with Author).

14-B.2.a. Identify the author's name, title, and affiliation, without the abbreviations.

14-B.2.b. Identify the recipient's name, title, and affiliation, without the abbreviations.

14-B.2.c. Identify the subject of the memo.

14-B.2.d. Identify the pinpoint reference.

14-B.2.e. Identify the date of the memo.

14-B.3. The full citations in Questions 14-B.1 and 14-B.2 end with the same type of explanatory parenthetical. Explain when and why you should add the explanatory parenthetical to the full citation, and identify the applicable rule(s).

14-B.4. You would like to cite the following unpublished memorandum, referring to page 3. Write the full citation to this document. Use <u>underlining</u> to indicate any components of the citation that should be *italicized*.

Tucker & Streetman
Attorneys at Law
1494 S.E. Second Avenue
Lincoln City, Oregon 97367
Memorandum

TO: Sharon Warren, Associate
FROM: Scott Tucker, Senior Partner
DATE: September 10, 2009
RE: Robert Harrison; felon in possession of firearm charge (file no. 09-142)

14-B.5. James B. Levy, Editor-in-Chief of the Legal Writing Journal, sent a memorandum to a number of different listservs. The memorandum was a call for the submission of articles for volume 13, and it was sent on July 10, 2006. The memorandum also provides authors with the guidelines for submissions. You wish to refer to pages 1 and 3 of the memorandum. Write the full citation to this document.

14-B.6. You would like to cite the following unpublished letter, referring to page 2. Write the full citation to this document.

**Stetson University
College of Law**

June 30, 2009

Paula Bentley
Student Mailbox: 155

Re: Teaching Fellow Position, Fall 2009

Dear Paula,

.   .   .

Sincerely,

Michael A. Farley
Michael A. Farley
Assistant Dean of Student Life

C. SHORT-FORM CITATIONS

As discussed in Chapter 3, you provide a full citation the first time you refer to a particular source; a short-form citation is used only after a full citation has been provided. The goal of both a full citation and a short citation remains the same—to provide sufficient information in the citation so that the reader can locate the source and the information within the source. When appropriate, use *id.*, as provided in Rule 11.3. Otherwise, use the short citation formats in Rules 29.4, 29.6, and 32.2, depending on the source. Short-form citation formats are summarized in Table 14.1.

The exercises below help you construct the short-form citations to court documents, transcripts, and appellate records.

TABLE 14.1

SHORT-FORM CITATIONS FOR PRACTITIONER AND COURT DOCUMENTS

Practitioner Documents, Court Documents, and Transcripts **Rule 29.4**	When *id.* is not appropriate, repeat the full citation and omit the date parenthetical and all parts of the individuals' names, besides the surname.
Appellate Records **Rule 29.6**	There is no short citation format for record citations because it is not customary to use *id.* with record citations. Simply repeat the full citation.
Unpublished Letters or Memoranda **Rule 32.2**	When *id.* is not appropriate, the short citation format for letters or memoranda is dependent upon whether the document you are writing has footnotes or not. Documents *without* footnotes: The short citation to a letter or memorandum has three components: (1) designation, (2) author's full name, and (3) the word "at" and the pinpoint reference. Documents *with* footnotes: The short-form citation to a letter or memorandum has the same components, but the second component is replaced with "*supra* n. *X*," in which *X* represents the footnote number in which the full citation to the letter or memorandum originally appeared.

EXERCISE SET 14-C

ALL LEVELS: SHORT-FORM CITATIONS

Before beginning Exercise Set 14-C All Levels, review the following and keep the *Manual* at hand as you work through the exercises:

- Rule 29.4, Short Citation Format for Practitioner Documents, Court Documents, and Transcripts
- Rule 29.6, Short Citation Format for Appellate Records
- Rule 32.2, Short Citation Format for Unpublished Letters and Memoranda

To complete the exercises, you may also need to refer to the following:

- Rule 11.3, *Id.* as a Short Citation

14-C.1. **True or False:** You may use *id.* to refer to a record citation.

   a. True
   b. False

14-C.2. **True or False:** You may use *id.* to refer to a court document, such as a motion or a transcript.

   a. True
   b. False

14-C.3. **True or False:** You cannot use *id.* to refer to an unpublished letter.

   a. True
   b. False

14-C.4. You have cited an appellate record earlier in your document, and you now want to refer to it again, specifically at page 15, lines 6 through 8. Write the short-form citation to this part of the record.

14-C.5. You have cited an appellate record earlier in your document, and you now want to refer to it again, specifically at page 15, lines 6 through 8; page 22; and page 23, line 23 through page 24, line 4. Write a single short-form citation that refers to all these parts of the record.

14-C.6. You have provided the following full citation in a document *without* footnotes:

> Ltr. from Kristin Gerdy, Teaching Prof. & Dir., Rex E. Lee Advoc. Program, BYU L. Sch., to Suzanne Rowe, Dir., Leg. Research & Writing, Assoc. Prof. of L., U. of Or. Sch. of L., *Journal Article and Publication* 2 (Apr. 9, 2010) (copy on file with Author).

You wish to cite the letter again but to refer to page 1. *Id.* is not appropriate. Which of the following is the correct short-form citation?

  a. Ltr. from Kristin Gerdy, Teaching Prof. & Dir., Rex E. Lee Advoc. Program, BYU L. Sch., to Suzanne Rowe, Dir., Leg. Research & Writing, Assoc. Prof. of L., U. of Or. Sch. of L., *Journal Article and Publication* 2 (Apr. 9, 2010) (copy on file with Author).
  b. Ltr., *supra* at 1.
  c. Ltr. from Gerdy at 1
  d. Ltr. from Kristin Gerdy at 1.

14-C.7. You have provided the following full citation in a document *with* footnotes, specifically in footnote 24:

> Open memo. from Debbie Brown, V.P. of H.R. & Leg. Affairs, Stetson U. College of L., *New Healthcare Program* 4 (Dec. 15, 2009) (memo on file with Author).

You wish to cite the memorandum again in footnote 41, and *id.* is not appropriate. Which of the following is the correct short-form citation to pages 2 and 4?

  a. Open memo. from Debbie Brown, V.P. of H.R. & Leg. Affairs, Stetson U. College of L., *New Healthcare Program* 4 (Dec. 15, 2009) (memo on file with Author).
  b. Open memo., *supra* n. 24, at 2, 4.
  c. Open memo. from Debbie Brown, *supra* n. 24, at 2, 4.
  d. Open memo., from Debbie Brown, *supra* n. 24.

14-C.8. Use the following information to answer two questions:

HEARING ON TEMPORARY INJUNCTION ORDER
March 10, 2010

14-C.8.a. Write the full citation to the document and refer to page 5, line 11.

14-C.8.b. Write the short-form citation to the document, referring to page 5, lines 10 to 22. Do not use *id.*

14-C.9. Use the following information from Westlaw to answer two questions.

United States District Court, S.D. Florida.
John N. ("JACK") HEARN, Christopher O. Bartlett, John Rousselle, Timothy Harkins,
and Henry P. Mallon, Plaintiffs,
v.
Michael MCKAY, Robert Mckay Thomas Bethel, Edward Kelly, Donald Nilsson, Paul Cates,
Daniel Smith, John Hafner, Donald Cree, Joseph Gremelsbacker, and Robert Keifer,
Individually and As Officers of the American Maritime Officers Union, and the American
Maritime Officers Union, Defendants.
No. 007CV60209.
February 27, 2007.

Motion for Accelerated, Pre-conference Discovery

14-C.9.a. Write the full citation to the document, referring to paragraph 4, subsections (c) and (f). Abbreviate any words appearing in Appendix 3 and omit articles or prepositions not needed for clarity.

14-C.9.b. Write the short-form citation to the document, referring to paragraph 4. Do not use *id.* Abbreviate any words appearing in Appendix 3 and omit articles or prepositions not needed for clarity.

14-C.10. Use the following information to answer two questions.

```
              IN THE UNITED STATES DISTRICT COURT
           FOR THE MIDDLE DISTRICT OF PENNSYLVANIA

TAMMY J. KITZMILLER, et al.,        :
Plaintiffs                          :
                                    :     Case Number
        vs.                         :     4:04-CV-02688
                                    :
DOVER AREA SCHOOL DISTRICT;         :
DOVER AREA SCHOOL DISTRICT          :
BOARD OF DIRECTORS,                 :
Defendants                          :


                  MORNING SESSION
             TRANSCRIPT OF PROCEEDINGS
                 OF BENCH TRIAL
        Before: HONORABLE JOHN E. JONES, III
             Date: September 26, 2005
```

14-C.10.a. Write the full citation to the document, referring to page 8, line 8. Abbreviate any words appearing in Appendix 3 and omit any articles or prepositions not needed for clarity.

14-C.10.b. Write the short-form citation to the document, referring to page 8, lines 13 to 22. Do not use *id.* Abbreviate any words appearing in Appendix 3 and omit articles or prepositions not needed for clarity.

ALTERNATE FORMATS

Because law-trained readers use citations to locate authorities, materials intended for general legal audiences are usually cited using standardized formats, such as the *ALWD Citation Manual* system you are learning. And yet, as a law-trained reader, you have likely encountered citations representing a wide variety of citation systems, originating in a broad number of locations, published at different times—even different eras. You may even have noticed the evolution of some citation styles over time, largely as a reflection of the changing nature of the materials themselves.

No system of citation is truly universal. You may encounter or be required to use different citation rules or systems in certain contexts (e.g., law review writing) or localities (e.g., jurisdictions with unique local citation formats). As you gain experience in legal writing, you may find you need to learn these alternative rules and systems, much as you might learn to understand and speak another dialect or language if you moved to a new location.

Chapters 15 and 16 are designed to introduce you to those other citation languages and to give you practice in toggling between the formats you have learned in the *ALWD Citation Manual* and other citation rules or systems, such as local rules or *The Bluebook*.

CHAPTER

LOCAL RULES AND

SPECIAL FORMATS

One common situation that calls for you to become "bilingual" in citation systems is the existence of a court rule requiring that a particular form of citation be employed in documents submitted to that court. As the *Manual* explains, "Many state and federal courts have adopted local citation rules that practitioners **must** follow when submitting documents to those courts."[1]

In some cases, the local rules call for a certain form of citation, such as a parallel citation (explained in section B below), but leave it up to you to consult one of the standard citation manuals to determine how to construct the citation. It is also true that many jurisdictions, while not mandating a particular format, nonetheless express a *preference* for certain formats. In other instances, the local rules may call for a unique format that is used only within that jurisdiction. Moreover, you may discover that local custom extends the application of these rules to citations in documents other than those submitted to a court.

A more recent phenomenon has been the development of special citation formats that do not reflect the place or form of publication. They are designed to retrieve the source no matter the medium in which it is published. Because these formats do not favor a particular publisher or medium, they are called "neutral" citations. This chapter provides exercises in working with local rules of court, parallel citations, and neutral citations.

---

[1] ALWD & Darby Dickerson, *ALWD Citation Manual* 8 (4th ed., Aspen Publishers 2010) (emphasis in original).

A. CIRCUMSTANCES REQUIRING ADHERENCE TO LOCAL RULES

Most local rules affect the citation of cases, although some jurisdictions' local rules also regulate the citation of other sources. For example, many states mandate a certain citation format for citing statutes, and some states have explicit requirements for citing court documents submitted electronically. Until you are experienced in working with the rules of a particular jurisdiction, when you are writing a document that is to be submitted to the courts of that jurisdiction, you should develop the habit of checking for local rules affecting citations.

Appendix 1 of the *Manual* indicates, for each jurisdiction, whether it had local rules at the time of the *Manual*'s publication. The local rules themselves are set out by jurisdiction in Appendix 2. Because local rules may be promulgated or amended at any time, it is also wise to check other sources, such as a state supreme court's Web site or a state's court rules publication, for the most current information. To get a feel for the extent of local rules, leaf through Appendix 2.

A few states direct you to use their own style manuals or local rule compilations, such as the *California Style Manual*; Michigan's *Uniform System of Citation*; the *Official Reports Style Manual* of New York (popularly known as *The Tanbook*); and Ohio's *Revisions to the Manual of Citation*. These lengthier works are not reproduced in Appendix 2, although you will find some explanatory materials about them and Web site links, where available.

The exercises in this section are designed to help you gain familiarity with the existence (or not) of local rules for various jurisdictions and to work with local rules to recognize and draft citations to comply with those rules.

EXERCISE SET 15-A

BASIC LEVEL: LOCAL RULES

> Before beginning Exercise Set 15-A Basic Level, review the following and keep the *Manual* at hand as you work through the exercises:
>
> - Rule 12.4(b), General rules regarding which reporter or reporters to cite
> - Rule 12.4(c), Reporter for United States Supreme Court cases
> - Rule 12.4(d), Parallel citations and court reporters
> - Rule 14.4, Full Citation, Print Format for State Statutes
> - Rule 14.6, Short Citation, Print Format for Federal and State Statutes
>
> Be prepared to consult Appendix 1, Primary Sources by Jurisdiction, and Appendix 2, Local Court Citation Rules, to answer the questions.

15-A.1. **True or false:** The State of Missouri has local citation rules requiring citation to an official reporter.

   a. True
   b. False

15-A.2. **True or false:** The State of Texas has local citation rules requiring citation to an official reporter.

   a. True
   b. False

15-A.3.   **True or false:** The State of Mississippi has local citation rules requiring that statutory citations be made to the official code.

    a. True

    b. False

15-A.4.   Which of the following full citations displays a local-rule format?

    a. *People v. Lawley*, 115 Cal. Rptr. 2d 614 (2002).

    b. *People v. Lawley*, 38 P.3d 461 (Cal. 2002).

    c. *People v. Lawley* (2002) 27 Cal.4th 102.

    d. *People v. Lawley*, 115 Cal. Rptr. 2d 614, 38 P.3d 461 (2002).

15-A.5.   Which of the following citations displays a local-rule format?

    a. *State v. Atkinson*, 774 N.W.2d 584 (Minn. 2009).

    b. *State v. O'Leary*, 153 N.H. 710 (2006).

    c. *State v. Tillman*, 289 S.W.3d 282 (Mo. App. W. Dist. 2009).

    d. *Kansas v. Marsh*, 548 U.S. 163 (2006).

15-A.6.   Which of the following short-form citations displays a local-rule format?

    a. § 731.106, Fla. Stat.

    b. Md. Agric. Code Ann. § 10-201.

    c. 10 Laws P.R. Ann. § 437.

    d. N.D. Cent. Code § 9-03-04.

15-A.7.   Which of the following short-form citations displays a local-rule format?

    a. 20 Ill. Comp. Stat. 210/11.1.

    b. Del. Code Ann. tit. 3, § 8704.

    c. 18 U.S.C.S. § 115.

    d. NMSA 1978 § 30-14-1.

15-A.8.   You are a law student in Virginia who is writing a seminar paper about the same-sex marriage issue in California. You find a case whose Westlaw caption shows the following reporters: 43 Cal.4th 757, 183 P.3d 384, 76 Cal.Rptr.3d 683, 08 Cal. Daily Op. Serv. 5820, 2008 Daily Journal D.A.R. 7079. Which of the following reporters should you use in the case citation?

    a. Cal. 4th

    b. P.3d

    c. Cal. Rptr. 3d

    d. Cal. Daily Op. Serv.

15-A.9.   You are clerking for a federal judge in the United States Court of Appeals for the First Circuit. Writing the first draft of an opinion, you wish to cite *Carroll v. Ringgold Education Association*, a 1996 Pennsylvania Supreme Court case reported in Pennsylvania Reports, the Atlantic Reporter, Second Series, and the Education Law Reporter. Which of the following citations should you use in the opinion?

    a. *Carroll v. Ringgold Educ. Assn.*, 545 Pa. 192 (1996).

    b. *Carroll v. Ringgold Educ. Assn.*, 680 A.2d 1137 (Pa. 1996).

    c. *Carroll v. Ringgold Educ. Assn.*, 545 Pa. 192, 680 A.2d 1137 (1996).

    d. *Carroll v. Ringgold Educ. Assn.*, 545 Pa. 192, 680 A.2d 1137, 111 Educ. L. Rep. 1261 (1996).

15-A.10. You are clerking for a federal judge in the United States Court of Appeals for the Seventh Circuit. Writing the first draft of an opinion, you wish to cite *Village of Skokie v. Illinois State Labor Relations Board*, a 1999 Illinois First District Appellate Court case reported in Illinois Appellate Court Reports, Third Series, the North Eastern Reporter, Second Series, and West's Illinois Decisions. Which of the following citations should you use in the opinion?

    a. *Village of Skokie v. Ill. St. Lab. Rel. Bd.*, 306 Ill. App. 3d 489 (1st Dist. 1999).

    b. *Village of Skokie v. Ill. St. Lab. Rel. Bd.*, 239 Ill. Dec. 529 (App. 1st. Dist. 1999).

    c. *Village of Skokie v. Ill. St. Lab. Rel. Bd.*, 714 N.E.2d 87 (Ill. App. 1st Dist. 1999).

    d. *Village of Skokie v. Ill. St. Lab. Rel. Bd.*, 306 Ill. App. 3d 489, 714 N.E.2d 87 (1st Dist. 1999).

EXERCISE SET 15-A

INTERMEDIATE LEVEL: LOCAL RULES

Before beginning Exercise Set 15-A Intermediate Level, review the following and keep the *Manual* at hand as you work through the exercises:

• Rule 12.4(b), General rules regarding which reporter or reporters to cite
• Rule 12.4(d), Parallel citations and court reporters

Be prepared to consult Appendix 1, Primary Sources by Jurisdiction, and Appendix 2, Local Court Citation Rules, to answer the questions.

15-A.11. Your brief to the Supreme Judicial Court of Maine cites the case whose LexisNexis caption is shown below. Which of the following citations complies with Maine's local rule?

---

226 A.2d 530, *; 1967 Me. LEXIS 191, **

Helen RHODA v. AROOSTOOK GENERAL HOSPITAL and Viola DeFalco

[NO NUMBER IN ORIGINAL]

Supreme Judicial Court of Maine

226 A.2d 530; 1967 Me. LEXIS 191

February 20, 1967

---

    a. *Rhoda v. Aroostook Gen. Hosp.*, 226 A.2d 530, 1967 Me. LEXIS 191 (1967).

    b. *Rhoda v. Aroostook Gen. Hosp.*, 1967 Me. LEXIS 191 (1967).

    c. *Rhoda v. Aroostook Gen. Hosp.*, 226 A.2d 530 (Me. 1967).

    d. *Rhoda v. Aroostook Gen. Hosp.*, 1967 Me. LEXIS 191 (Me. Feb. 20, 1967).

15-A.12. You are writing a brief to the New Hampshire Supreme Court, and you wish to cite the Ohio case whose running head and caption are displayed at right. Which of the following citations complies with New Hampshire's local rule?

> **CASEY v. REIDY**   Ohio **1139**
> Cite as 906 N.E.2d 1139 (Ohio App. 7 Dist. 2009)

> 180 Ohio App.3d 615
> 2009-Ohio-415
> **CASEY et al., Appellants
> and Cross–Appellees,**
> v.
> **REIDY et al., Appellees and
> Cross–Appellants.**
> **No. 04 MA 6.**
> Court of Appeals of Ohio,
> Seventh District, Mahoning County.
> Decided Jan. 6, 2009.

a. *Casey v. Reidy*, 906 N.E.2d 1139 (Ohio App. 7th Dist. 2009).
b. *Casey v. Reidy*, 180 Ohio App.3d 615, 906 N.E.2d 1139 (Ohio App. 7th Dist. 2009).
c. *Casey v. Reidy*, 906 N.E.2d 1139 (2009).
d. *Casey v. Reidy*, 2009-Ohio-415, 180 Ohio App. 3d 615 (7th Dist. 2009).

15-A.13. You are writing a brief to the Washington Supreme Court, and you wish to cite the case whose Westlaw caption is shown below. Which of the following reporter/initial page references should appear in a full citation to the case in Washington Appellate Reports?

> 107 Wash.App. 902, 28 P.3d 832
>
> Briefs and Other Related Documents
>
> Court of Appeals of Washington,
> Robert JOHNSON, Appellant,
> v.
> SI-COR INC., d/b/a, McDonalds of Wenatchee and Lopez Foods Inc., an Oklahoma Corporation doing business in Washington, Respondents.
> Nos. 19606-2-III, 19639-9-III.
> Aug. 14, 2001.

a. 107 Wash.App. 902
b. 107 Wash. App. 902
c. 107 Wn. App. 902
d. 107 WA APP 902

15-A.14. Your brief will be filed with the United States Court of Appeals for the Third Circuit. Research on LexisNexis retrieved a case whose caption shows the reporters set out below. In your brief, you wish to cite material that appears at star page *171 in the Federal Reporter version and at star page **12 in the online version. Which of the following reporter/page references should appear in a full citation to the case?

> *488 F.3d 163, *; 2007 U.S. App. LEXIS 12605, ***

a. 488 F.3d 163, 171
b. 488 F.3d 163, *171
c. 488 F.3d 163, 171, 2007 U.S. App. LEXIS 12605 at *12
d. 488 F.3d 163, *171, 2007 U.S. App. LEXIS 12605, *12

15-A.15. You are writing a brief to be filed with the United States District Court for the Southern District of New York. The brief cites section 203 of New York's Limited Liability Company Law, using McKinney's Consolidated Laws of New York Annotated. Which of the following citations should you use?

a. N.Y. Ltd. Liab. Co. Law § 203 (McKinney 2007).
b. N.Y. Ltd. Liab. L. § 203 (Consol. 2008).
c. NY CLS LLC § 203.
d. NY LIMIT LIAB CO § 203.

EXERCISE SET 15-A

EXPERT LEVEL: LOCAL RULES

Before beginning Exercise Set 15-A Expert Level, review the following and keep the *Manual* at hand as you work through the exercises:

- Rule 12.4(b), General rules regarding which reporter or reporters to cite
- Rule 12.4(c), Reporter for United States Supreme Court cases
- Rule 12.4(d), Parallel citations and court reporters

- Rule 14.4, Full Citation, Print Format for State Statutes
- Rule 14.6, Short Citation, Print Format for Federal and State Statutes

Be prepared to consult Appendix 1, Primary Sources by Jurisdiction, and Appendix 2, Local Court Citation Rules, to answer the questions.

15-A.16. You are reading a slip opinion from the South Carolina Supreme Court. One of the citations in the opinion refers to "Rule 204(b), SCACR." Write the full name of the source.

15-A.17. You are writing a brief to the Oklahoma Court of Criminal Appeals, in which you cite page 775, paragraph 10 of the case whose caption appears at right. Write a full citation to this case that complies with Oklahoma's local rule.

772 Okl. 204 PACIFIC REPORTER, 3d SERIES
2009 OK CR 10
John Christian BURTON, Appellant
v.
STATE of Oklahoma, Appellee.
No. F–2007–511.
Court of Criminal Appeals of Oklahoma.
March 6, 2009.

15-A.18. You are reading an Idaho trial court brief. One of the citations in the brief refers to "IDAPA 04.11.01.770." Write the full name of the source.

15-A.19. According to section 17-2-18 of the New Mexico Statutes 1978, "[t]he naming of game and fish upon any menu or bill of fare as food for patrons shall be prima facie evidence of the possession of the same by the proprietor of such hotel, restaurant, cafe or boardinghouse." This statute was enacted in 1912; it appears in the 2009 official compilation of the state's statutes. Write a full citation to this statute that complies with New Mexico's local rule.

15-A.20. In a brief to the Florida Supreme Court, you wish to cite Article IV, section 8, subsection (a) of the executive clemency provision of the current Florida Constitution. Write a full citation to this source that complies with Florida's local rule.

> (a) Except in cases of treason and in cases where impeachment results in conviction, the governor may, by executive order filed with the custodian of state records, suspend collection of fines and forfeitures, grant reprieves not exceeding sixty days and, with the approval of two members of the cabinet, grant full or conditional pardons, restore civil rights, commute punishment, and remit fines and forfeitures for offenses.

B. PARALLEL CITATIONS

The local rules of many jurisdictions require parallel citations to cases. Parallel citations offer readers the convenience of citations to two or more reporters containing the case. You will often find references to parallel reporters set out above case captions, as in these examples from the LexisNexis electronic version and Atlantic 2d print reporter version of the same case:

> *117 Conn. App. 237, *; 978 A.2d 570, **;*
> *2009 Conn. App. LEXIS 423, ****
>
> CITY OF MILFORD v. HELEN F. MAYKUT ET AL.
>
> AC 29177
>
> APPELLATE COURT OF CONNECTICUT
>
> 117 Conn. App. 237; 978 A.2d 570; 2009 Conn. App. LEXIS 423
>
> February 18, 2009, Argued
> September 22, 2009, Officially Released

> 117 Conn.App. 237
>
> **CITY OF MILFORD**
>
> v.
>
> **Helen F. MAYKUT et al.**
>
> No. 29177.
>
> Appellate Court of Connecticut.
>
> Argued Feb. 18, 2009.
> Decided Sept. 22, 2009.

Unless the local rule requiring a parallel citation prescribes a different format, follow Rule 12.4(d): after the case name, set out the volume number and abbreviation of the official reporter, the initial page and any pinpoint reference(s) from the official reporter, a comma, and then the volume, abbreviation, and initial page of the unofficial print reporter, ending the citation with a single court/date parenthetical. Do not use a semicolon to separate the parallel citations; semicolons are used only for separating citations to *different* authorities in string citations.

If the official reporter name reflects the name of the court that issued the opinion, omit any repetitive identification of the court from the court/date parenthetical, but keep information about districts or divisions. See the examples in Rules 12.4(d) and 12.6(e). Do not provide a parallel citation to a looseleaf service or the LexisNexis or Westlaw version of a case if it is available in an official or unofficial print reporter.

Connecticut's local rule is typical: "[C]itations to state cases shall be to the official reporter first, if available, followed by the regional reporter." The citation this rule produces is the same as a parallel citation created under *ALWD Citation Manual* rules. The parallel citation to the case used in the illustrations above is *City of Milford v. Maykut*, 117 Conn. App. 237, 978 A.2d 570 (2009). The official reporter abbreviation reflects the name of the court issuing the opinion, and therefore, the court name is omitted from the court/date parenthetical. The citation omits reference to the LexisNexis version.

Decisions of the United States Supreme Court are commonly shown with parallel citations. Unless a local rule requires parallel citation, however, you need only cite a Supreme Court decision to the highest ranking available reporter listed in Rule 12.4(c), typically the United States Reports.

Many local rules do not require pinpoint page references for every reporter in a parallel citation, but for your reader's convenience, provide them if you can. Online resources furnish star pagination for that very purpose. As Sidebar 12.5 explains, you may find embedded pagination references for multiple reporters in the text of the case. Online databases use patterns of asterisks to indicate specific page numbers in a reporter. In the LexisNexis example above for *City of Milford*, single asterisks refer to the page number in the official reporter, Connecticut Appellate Reports; double asterisks refer to the regional reporter, Atlantic 2d; and triple asterisks refer to the LexisNexis online version. Some print reporters indicate parallel versions' page numbers with a subscript number (e.g., $\perp_{75}$) or a bracketed superscript (e.g., $^{[466\ \text{U.S.}\ 875]}$). Be careful in matching page numbers if the version you are viewing provides star pagination for more than one reporter.

Once you have constructed a parallel citation, your subsequent references to the case may use short-form citations, but you cannot use *id.* to refer to the *entire* parallel citation. If *id.* would be appropriate with a single citation, you may use *id.* (or *id.* at [page]) to stand for the *first* reporter reference in the parallel citation, followed by the volume-reporter-pinpoint reference for each subsequent reporter version. If you have cited other intervening sources, making the use of *id.* inappropriate, the short-form citation will have to use one party name, followed by volume-reporter-pinpoint references for each reporter, if available. Compare the examples below:

- **Full citation:** *City of Milford v. Maykut*, 117 Conn. App. 237, 247, 978 A.2d 570, 577 (2009).
- **Short-form citation using *id.*:** *Id.* at 248, 978 A.2d at 578.
- **Short-form citation using party name:** *City of Milford*, 117 Conn. App. at 248, 978 A.2d at 578.

In any event, always provide the pinpoint reference for the West regional reporter. Study the examples in Rule 12.21(f) for guidance.

EXERCISE SET 15-B

BASIC LEVEL: PARALLEL CITATIONS

Before beginning Exercise Set 15-B Basic Level, review the following and keep the *Manual* at hand as you work through the exercises:

- Rule 12.4(d), Parallel citations and court reporters
- Sidebar 12.5, Locating Parallel Citations
- Rule 12.5(c), Pinpoint references and parallel citations
- Rule 12.6(e), Parallel citations and court abbreviations
- Rule 12.20(f), Short citation formats for parallel citations

Be prepared to consult Appendix 1, Primary Sources by Jurisdiction, and Appendix 2, Local Court Citation Rules, to answer some of the questions.

15-B.1. **True or false:** The State of New Jersey requires parallel citations to its courts' decisions in an official New Jersey reporter and the Atlantic Reporter.

    a. True
    b. False

15-B.2. **True or false:** The State of Nebraska requires parallel citations to its courts' decisions in an official Nebraska reporter and the North Western Reporter.

    a. True
    b. False

15-B.3. **True or false:** If you cite a Louisiana Supreme Court case *decided in 1990* in a brief to that court, you must supply parallel citations to a public domain citation form and to the Southern Reporter.

    a. True
    b. False

15-B.4. To establish factual disputes in summary judgment determinations, the evidence must be such that a "reasonable jury could return a verdict for the nonmoving party." That language comes from *Anderson v. Liberty Lobby, Inc.*, on page 248 of volume 477 of the United States Reports; on page 2510 of volume 106 of the Supreme Court Reporter; on page 212 of volume 91 of the United States Supreme Court Reports, Lawyers' Edition, Second Series; and on page 4757 of volume 54 of United States Law Week. Which of the following reporter/page references should appear in a full citation to *Anderson* in a brief to the Connecticut Appellate Court?

    a. 477 U.S. 242, 248
    b. 477 U.S. 242, 248, 106 S. Ct. 2505, 2510
    c. 477 U.S. 242, 248, 106 S. Ct. 2505, 2510, 91 L. Ed. 2d 202, 212
    d. 477 U.S. 242, 248, 106 S. Ct. 2505, 2510, 91 L. Ed. 2d 202, 212, 54 U.S.L.W. 4755, 4757

15-B.5. You are writing a brief that cites *J.T. Fargason & Sons, Inc. v. Cullander Machinery Co.*, decided by the Mississippi Supreme Court in 1955. The case is published in two reporters: volume 80 of the Southern Reporter, Second Series, beginning at page 757, and volume 224 of the official Mississippi Reports, beginning at page 620. Which of the following reporter/initial page references should appear in a full citation in your brief to the Mississippi Supreme Court?

 a. 224 Miss. 620
 b. 80 So. 2d 757
 c. 80 So.2d 757, 224 Miss. Rpts. 620
 d. 224 Miss. 620, 80 So. 2d 757

EXERCISE SET 15-B

INTERMEDIATE LEVEL: PARALLEL CITATIONS

Before beginning Exercise Set 15-B Intermediate Level, review the following and keep the *Manual* at hand as you work through the exercises:

• Rule 12.4(d), Parallel citations and court reporters
• Sidebar 12.5, Locating Parallel Citations
• Rule 12.5(c), Pinpoint references and parallel citations
• Rule 12.6(e), Parallel citations and court abbreviations
• Rule 12.20(f), Short citation formats for parallel citations

Be prepared to consult Appendix 1, Primary Sources by Jurisdiction, and Appendix 2, Local Court Citation Rules, to answer some of the questions.

15-B.6. Researching an evidence issue concerning hearsay, you found *May v. Caruso*. The case is published in volume 264 of the Virginia Reports, beginning at page 358, and in volume 568 of the South Eastern Reports, Second Series, beginning at page 690. The rule appears at star pages **692 and *362 in the Westlaw version of the case. Which of the following reporter/page references should appear in a full citation to the case in your brief to the Virginia Supreme Court?

 a. 264 Va. 358, 362
 b. 568 S.E.2d 690, 692
 c. 568 S.E.2d 690, 692, 264 Va. 358, 362
 d. 264 Va. 358, 362, 568 S.E.2d 690, 692

15-B.7. Your brief to the Hawai'i Supreme Court cites the case whose caption is shown at right. The rule you are discussing appears at page 384 of Hawai'i Reports and page 1061 of the Pacific Reporter 3d. Assume you have just cited the case in full and will immediately cite the same page(s) again. Which of the following short-form citations should you use in your brief to the Hawai'i Supreme Court?

    a. *Kato*, 118 Haw. at 384.
    b. *Kato*, 191 P.3d at 1061.
    c. *Id.*, 191 P.3d at 1061.
    d. *Id.*

> 1052 Haw.   191 PACIFIC REPORTER, 3d SERIES
>
> 118 Hawai'i 375
> **Irene KATO and Ralph Kato,**
> **Petitioners/Plaintiffs–**
> **Appellants,**
>
> v.
>
> **Frederick FUNARI,**
> **Respondent/Defendant–Appellee,**
>
> **and**
>
> **John Does 1–10; Jane Does 1–10; Doe Corporations 1–10; Doe Partnerships 1–10; Doe Non-Profit Entities 1–10; and Doe Governmental Entities 1–10, Defendants.**
> **No. 27237.**
> Supreme Court of Hawai'i.
> Aug. 25, 2008.

15-B.8. You are researching an appeal to the Connecticut Supreme Court. On Westlaw, you found the passage shown below in *Bruss v. Przybylo*, 385 Ill. App. 3d 399, 407 n. 2, 895 N.E.2d 1102, 1110 n. 2 (Ill. App. 2d Dist. 2008). You would like to cite as persuasive authority the Illinois case, quoting the passage from the historic United States Supreme Court case. Which of the following citations should you use in your brief to the Connecticut Supreme Court?

> Congregational polity exists when "a religious congregation * * *, by the nature of its organization, is strictly independent of other ecclesiastical associations, and so far as church government is concerned, owes no fealty or obligation to any higher authority." *Watson v. Jones*, 13 Wall. 679, 80 U.S. 679, 722, 20 L. Ed. 666, 674 (1871).

    a. *Bruss v. Przybylo*, 895 N.E.2d 1102, 1110 n. 2 (Ill. App. 2d Dist. 2008) (quoting *Watson v. Jones*, 80 U.S. 679, 722 (1871)).
    b. *Bruss v. Przybylo*, 385 Ill. App. 3d 399, 407 n. 2, 895 N.E.2d 1102, 1110 n. 2 (Ill. App. 2d Dist. 2008) (quoting *Watson v. Jones*, 80 U.S. 679, 722 (1871)).
    c. *Bruss v. Przybylo*, 385 Ill. App. 3d 399, 407 n. 2 (2d Dist. 2008) (quoting *Watson v. Jones*, 80 U.S. (13 Wall.) 679, 722 (1871)).
    d. *Bruss v. Przybylo*, 385 Ill. App. 3d 399, 407 n. 2, 895 N.E.2d 1102, 1110 n. 2 (Ill. App. 2d Dist. 2008) (quoting *Watson v. Jones*, 13 Wall. 679, 722, 80 U.S. 679, 722, 20 L. Ed. 666, 674 (1871)).

15-B.9. In researching an issue concerning easements, you found the case whose caption is shown at right in volume 670 of the South Eastern Reporter, Second Series, beginning at page 734. Which of the following citations should you use to cite the case in your brief to the United States District Court for the Eastern District of Tennessee?

    a. *Va. Highlands Airport Auth. v. Singleton Auto Parts, Inc.*, 670 S.E.2d 734 (Va. 2009).
    b. *Va. Highlands Airport Auth. v. Singleton Auto Parts, Inc.*, 277 Va. 158 (2009).
    c. *Va. Highlands Airport Auth. v. Singleton Auto Parts, Inc.*, 277 Va. 158, 670 S.E.2d 734 (Va. 2009).
    d. *Va. Highlands Airport Auth. v. Singleton Auto Parts, Inc.*, 277 Va. 158, 670 S.E.2d 734 (2009).

> 277 Va. 158
> **VIRGINIA HIGHLANDS AIRPORT AUTHORITY**
>
> v.
>
> **SINGLETON AUTO PARTS, INC.**
> **Record No. 080286.**
> Supreme Court of Virginia.
> Jan. 16, 2009.

15-B.10. You are briefing an issue concerning the Texas Free Enterprise and Antitrust Act, and you have found an important case whose LexisNexis caption is shown below. Which of the following citations should you use to cite the case in your brief to the Texas Court of Appeals sitting in Austin?

THE COCA-COLA COMPANY ET AL., PETITIONERS, v. HARMAR BOTTLING COMPANY ET AL., RESPONDENTS

No. 03-0737

SUPREME COURT OF TEXAS

218 S.W.3d 671; 2006 Tex. LEXIS 1038; 50 Tex. Sup. J. 21; 2006-2 Trade Cas. (CCH) P75,464

November 9, 2004, Argued
October 20, 2006, Opinion Delivered

---

    a. *Coca-Cola Co. v. Harmar Bottling Co.*, 218 S.W.3d 671; 2006 Tex. LEXIS 1038; 50 Tex. Sup. J. 21; 2006-2 Trade Cas. (CCH) P75,464 (Tex. 2006).

    b. *Coca-Cola Co. v. Harmar Bottling Co.*, 218 S.W.3d 671, 2006 Tex. LEXIS 1038, 50 Tex. Sup. J. 21, 2006-2 Trade Cas. (CCH) P75,464 (Tex. 2006).

    c. *Coca-Cola Co. v. Harmar Bottling Co.*, 2006 Tex. 1038, 218 S.W.3d 671 (2006).

    d. *Coca-Cola Co. v. Harmar Bottling Co.*, 218 S.W.3d 671 (Tex. 2006).

EXERCISE SET 15-B

EXPERT LEVEL: PARALLEL CITATIONS

Before beginning Exercise Set 15-B Expert Level, review the following and keep the *Manual* at hand as you work through the exercises:

- Rule 12.4(d), Parallel citations and court reporters
- Sidebar 12.5, Locating Parallel Citations
- Rule 12.5(c), Pinpoint references and parallel citations
- Rule 12.6(e), Parallel citations and court abbreviations
- Rule 12.20(f), Short citation formats for parallel citations

Be prepared to consult Appendix 1, Primary Sources by Jurisdiction, and Appendix 2, Local Court Citation Rules, to answer some of the questions.

15-B.11. In a brief to the Pennsylvania Superior Court, you wish to cite the case whose LexisNexis caption is shown below. Write a full citation that complies with the court's local rule, if any.

---

593 Pa. 20, *; 928 A.2d 186, **;
2007 Pa. LEXIS 1463, ***

GEORGINA TOY, Appellant/Cross-Appellee v. METROPOLITAN LIFE INSURANCE COMPANY AND BOB MARTINI, Appellees/Cross-Appellants

Nos. 33 & 34 WAP 2005

SUPREME COURT OF PENNSYLVANIA

593 Pa. 20; 928 A.2d 186; 2007 Pa. LEXIS 1463

February 28, 2006, Argued
July 18, 2007, Decided

15-B.12. Your brief to a state trial court in Albany, New York, cites the case whose Westlaw caption is shown below. Write a full citation that complies with the court's local rule, if any.

---

645 F.Supp.2d 258, 37 Media L. Rep. 2288

Motions, Pleadings and Filings

United States District Court,
S.D. New York.
Howard K. STERN, Plaintiff,
v.
Rita COSBY, Hachette Book Group USA, Inc. d/b/a Grand Central Publishing,
and John or Jane Doe, Defendants.

No. 07 Civ. 8536 (DC).
Aug. 12, 2009.
Opinion Denying Reconsideration Sept. 25, 2009.

15-B.13. Your brief to the Arkansas Court of Appeals cites the case whose caption is shown at right. Write a full citation that complies with the court's local rule, if any.

---

308   Ark.   843 SOUTH WESTERN REPORTER, 2d SERIES

311 Ark. 187
Winston BRYANT, Attorney General, Appellant,

v.

Dr. Arthur ENGLISH, the Republican Party of Arkansas, the Democratic Party of Arkansas, and Martin Borchert, Appellees and Cross-Appellees,

v.

Jim Guy TUCKER, Lieutenant Governor, Cross–Appellant.
No. 92-1284.

Supreme Court of Arkansas.

Dec. 4, 1992.

15-B.14. You are writing a brief to be submitted to the United States District Court for the Southern District of Ohio, and you wish to cite the case whose Westlaw caption is shown below. Assume that if you were performing the research today, you would retrieve the same result. Write a full citation that complies with the court's local rule, if any.

---

129 S.Ct. 2277, 2009 A.M.C. 1555, 174 L.Ed.2d 1, 77 USLW 4481, 09 Cal. Daily Op. Serv. 7339, 2009 Daily Journal D.A.R. 8543, 21 Fla. L. Weekly Fed. S 921

Briefs and Other Related Documents
Oral Argument Transcripts with Streaming Media

Supreme Court of the United States
POLAR TANKERS, INC., Petitioner,
v.
CITY OF VALDEZ, ALASKA.
No. 08-310.
Argued April 1, 2009.
Decided June 15, 2009.

15-B.15. Your brief to Florida's First District Court of Appeal cites the case whose Westlaw caption is shown below. Assume that if you were performing the research today, you would retrieve the same result. Write a full citation that complies with the court's local rule, if any.

— So.3d ——, 2010 WL 22703 (Fla.App. 4 Dist.), 35 Fla. L. Weekly D126

Briefs and Other Related Documents
Only the Westlaw citation is currently available.

NOTICE: THIS OPINION HAS NOT BEEN RELEASED FOR PUBLICATION IN THE PERMANENT LAW REPORTS. UNTIL RELEASED, IT IS SUBJECT TO REVISION OR WITHDRAWAL.

District Court of Appeal of Florida,
Fourth District.
Lionel JEANCHARLES, Appellant,
v.
STATE of Florida, Appellee.
No. 4D07-4032.
Jan. 6, 2010.

C. NEUTRAL CITATIONS

The term "neutral citation" is a catch-all label that includes citation formats for nonproprietary materials (i.e., materials in the public domain) that are "vendor neutral" (not citing the source to a particular publisher's product) or "medium neutral" (using the same format whether the source is in print, online, or on a CD-ROM, for example). In the interest of promoting free public access to primary authorities, many states have promulgated local rules requiring or permitting neutral citations.

Some states prescribe a specific format for neutral citations to be used in documents submitted to their courts. These rules are set out in Appendix 2, and as you can see by examining them, they do not follow a single standardized format. When you submit a document to a court that prescribes a certain format for neutral citations, follow the mandates of the local rule.

However, in situations in which a local rule does not prescribe a specific format for neutral citations, you may still wish to provide your readers with a parallel citation to the case in both traditional and neutral format, giving them the option to choose the source from which they will access it. Use the standardized format set out in Rule 12.16, which calls for the case name, the year of decision, the abbreviation of the court issuing the opinion, the sequential number assigned to the opinion, and a parallel citation to a print or online source. See the examples in Rule 12.16(c).

To easily discover whether a jurisdiction has neutral citation rules, check its entry in Appendix 1. If it does, then check the jurisdiction's entry in Appendix 2 for specific requirements in the local rules, if any.

EXERCISE SET 15-C

BASIC LEVEL: NEUTRAL CITATIONS

Before beginning Exercise Set 15-C Basic Level, review the following and keep the *Manual* at hand as you work through the exercises:

• Rule 12.16, Neutral Citations

Be prepared to consult Appendix 1, Primary Sources by Jurisdiction, and Appendix 2, Local Court Citation Rules, to answer some of the questions.

15-C.1. **True or false:** If a person is writing a brief to an appellate court in Arkansas, he or she should cite a case decided by the Arkansas Supreme Court on October 4, 2007, according to that state's neutral citation rules.

    a. True
    b. False

15-C.2. **True or false:** If a person is writing a brief to an appellate court in Louisiana, he or she should cite a case decided by the Louisiana Supreme Court on October 15, 2007, according to that state's neutral citation rules.

    a. True
    b. False

15-C.3. **True or false:** If a person is writing a brief to an appellate court in Maine, he or she should cite a case decided by the Maine Supreme Court on October 18, 2007, according to that state's neutral citation rules.

    a. True
    b. False

15-C.4.   You are writing a brief to the Wisconsin Supreme Court, and you wish to cite the case whose Westlaw caption is shown below. Which of the following reporter and initial page references should appear in your full citation to the case?

---

313 Wis.2d 294, 752 N.W.2d 862, 234 Ed. Law Rep. 368, 2008 WI 98

Supreme Court of Wisconsin.

Kenneth W. HORNBACK, Dennis L. Bolton, Ronald W. Kuhl, David W. Schaeffer and Glenn M. Bonn, Plaintiffs-Appellants-Petitioners,

v.

ARCHDIOCESE OF MILWAUKEE and Diocese of Madison, Defendants-Respondents, Commercial Union Insurance Company, Intervening Defendant.

No. 2006AP291.
Argued March 13, 2008.
Decided July 16, 2008.

---

    a. 313 Wis. 2d 294, 752 N.W.2d 862, 234 Ed. Law Rep. 368, 2008 WI 98
    b. 2008 WI 98, 313 Wis. 2d 294, 752 N.W.2d 862
    c. 313 Wis. 2d 294, 752 N.W.2d 862
    d. 2008 WI 98, 313 Wis. 2d 294

15-C.5.   You were recently hired by a law firm in Vermont, and you have been given the job of editing a brief that will be submitted to the Vermont Supreme Court. The Westlaw caption for one of the cited cases is shown below. The brief cites paragraph 12, the relevant portion of which appears at page 274 of the Vermont Reports version and page 487 of the Atlantic Reporter version. Which of the following citations complies with Vermont's local rule?

---

182 Vt. 267, 939 A.2d 482, 2007 VT 81

Briefs and Other Related Documents

Supreme Court of Vermont.
Joseph SALATINO and Judith Salatino
v.
David S. CHASE, Brianne E. Chase and Vermont Associates in Ophthalmology.

Nos. 05-506, 06-101.
Aug. 31, 2007.

---

    a. *Salatino v. Chase*, 939 A.2d 482, 487 (Vt. 2007).
    b. *Salatino v. Chase*, 182 Vt. 267, 274, 939 A.2d 482, 487 (2007).
    c. *Salatino v. Chase*, 2007 VT 81, ¶ 12, 182 Vt. 267, 274, 939 A.2d 482, 487.
    d. *Salatino v. Chase*, 2007 VT 81, ¶ 12, 182 Vt. 267, 939 A.2d 482.

EXERCISE SET 15-C

INTERMEDIATE LEVEL: NEUTRAL CITATIONS

Before beginning Exercise Set 15-C Intermediate Level, review the following and keep the *Manual* at hand as you work through the exercises:

• Rule 12.16, Neutral Citations

Be prepared to consult Appendix 1, Primary Sources by Jurisdiction, and Appendix 2, Local Court Citation Rules, to answer some of the questions.

15-C.6. You are writing a brief to the Wyoming Supreme Court, and you wish to cite paragraph 21 of the case whose caption in LexisNexis is shown below. Paragraph 21 appears on page 928 of the Pacific Reporter version and on page ***11 of the LexisNexis version. Which of the following citations should you use?

---

*2007 WY 76, *; 157 P.3d 923, **;*
*2007 Wyo. LEXIS 85, ****

RUSSELL JAMES MARTIN, Appellant (Defendant), v. THE STATE OF WYOMING, Appellee (Plaintiff).

No. 05-263

SUPREME COURT OF WYOMING

2007 WY 76; 157 P.3d 923; 2007 Wyo. LEXIS 85

May 10, 2007, Decided

---

a. *Martin v. State*, 2007 WY 76, ¶ 21, 157 P.3d 923, ¶ 21, 2007 Wyo. LEXIS 85, ¶ 21 (2007).
b. *Martin v. State*, 2007 WY 76, ¶ 21, 157 P.3d 923, 928 (Wyo. 2007).
c. *Martin v. State*, 2007 WY 76, ¶ 21.
d. *Martin v. State*, 157 P.3d 923, 928, ¶ 21 (Wyo. 2007).

15-C.7. In analyzing a public utility's ability to enter into a contract, you find *City of St. Marys v. Auglaize County Board of Commissioners*, a case for which Westlaw provides the following sources: 115 Ohio St. 3d 387, 875 N.E.2d 561, 2007-Ohio-5026. In a brief to Ohio's Twelfth District Court of Appeals, which of these parallel citations can you safely **omit**?

a. 115 Ohio St. 3d 387
b. 875 N.E.2d 561
c. 2007-Ohio-5026
d. None. All must be included in the citation.

15-C.8.   Researching an issue of testamentary capacity, you find the case whose caption is shown below. Which of the following citations should you use to cite a quotation from page 284, paragraph 20 in a brief to the South Dakota Supreme Court?

IN RE ESTATE OF PRINGLE   S. D. **277**
Cite as 751 N.W.2d 277 (S.D. 2008)

2008 SD 38

In the Matter of the ESTATE OF Mary Louise PRINGLE,
Deceased.

No. 24506.

Supreme Court of South Dakota.

Argued Jan. 9, 2008.
Decided May 28, 2008.

evidence, the appellate court is left with the definite and firm conviction that a mistake has been made.

See publication Words and Phrases for other judicial constructions and definitions.

4. Appeal and Error ☞931(1)

All conflicts in the evidence must be resolved by the appellate court in favor of

---

a. *In re Est. of Pringle*, 751 N.W.2d 277, 284 ¶ 20 (S.D. 2008).

b. *In re Est. of Pringle*, 2008 SD 38 ¶ 20.

c. *In re Est. of Pringle*, 2008 SD 38 ¶ 20, 751 N.W.2d 277, 284 ¶ 20.

d. *In re Est. of Pringle*, 2008 SD 38 ¶ 20, 751 N.W.2d 277.

15-C.9.   You work for a trial judge in Portland, Maine, and you are editing an opinion in which the judge cited the case whose running head and caption in an unofficial reporter are shown below. Which of the following citations should you use for the judge's quotation of language from paragraph 6, on page 68?

---

66 Me.   **852 ATLANTIC REPORTER, 2d SERIES**

2004 ME 74

Arthur REARDON

v.

LOVELY DEVELOPMENT, INC.

Supreme Judicial Court of Maine.

Submitted On Briefs: Dec. 12, 2003.
Decided: June 3, 2004.

---

a. *Reardon v. Lovely Dev., Inc.*, 2004 ME 74, ¶ 6, 852 A.2d 66, 68, ¶ 6 (Me. 2004).

b. *Reardon v. Lovely Dev., Inc.*, 852 A.2d 66, 68, ¶ 6 (Me. 2004).

c. *Reardon v. Lovely Dev., Inc.*, 2004 ME 74, ¶ 6, 852 A.2d 66, 68.

d. *Reardon v. Lovely Dev., Inc.*, 2004 ME 74, ¶ 6.

15-C.10. Researching in Westlaw, you found the case whose caption is shown below. Assume that if you were performing the research today, you would retrieve the same result. Which of the following citations should you use to cite the case in a brief to the Utah Court of Appeals?

— P.3d ——, 2009 WL 4981854 (Utah App.), 646 Utah Adv. Rep. 11, 2009 UT App 386

NOTICE: THIS OPINION HAS NOT BEEN RELEASED FOR PUBLICATION IN THE PERMANENT LAW REPORTS. UNTIL RELEASED, IT IS SUBJECT TO REVISION OR WITHDRAWAL.

Court of Appeals of Utah.

STATE of Utah, Plaintiff and Appellee,
v.
Arvin MOORE, Defendant and Appellant.
No. 20080686-CA.

Dec. 24, 2009.

---

    a. *State v. Moore*, ___ P.3d ___, 2009 WL 4981854 (Utah App.), 646 Utah Adv. Rep. 11, 2009 UT App 386.

    b. *State v. Moore*, 646 Utah Adv. Rep. 11, 2009 UT App 386.

    c. *State v. Moore*, 2009 UT App 386, 646 Utah Adv. Rep. 11.

    d. *State v. Moore*, 646 Utah Adv. Rep. 11, ___ P.3d ___.

EXERCISE SET 15-C

EXPERT LEVEL: NEUTRAL CITATIONS

Before beginning Exercise Set 15-C Expert Level, review the following and keep the *Manual* at hand as you work through the exercises:

• Rule 12.16, Neutral Citations

Be prepared to consult Appendix 1, Primary Sources by Jurisdiction, and Appendix 2, Local Court Citation Rules, to answer the questions.

15-C.11. Your brief to the New Mexico Court of Appeals cites paragraph 16 of the case whose Westlaw caption is shown below. Paragraph 16 is found on page 425 of the New Mexico Reporter and on page 286 of the Pacific Reporter. Write a full citation to the case, with pinpoint reference, that complies with the state's neutral citation rule.

---

137 N.M. 420, 112 P.3d 281, 2005 -NMCA- 061

Court of Appeals of New Mexico.

Ermelinda WILLIAMS, Nasario Lopez, Lillian Starzyk, Olivama Sandoval, and Erlinda Trujillo, on their own behalves and as Representatives of a class of similarly situated persons, Plaintiffs-Appellants,

v.

Michael W. STEWART, M.D., Defendant-Appellee.

No. 23,730.
March 22, 2005.
Certiorari Denied, No. 29,167, May 10, 2005.

15-C.12. Your brief to the District Court of Cass County, North Dakota, cites paragraphs 7 and 8 of the case whose LexisNexis caption is shown below. Paragraphs 7 and 8 are found on page 869 of the North Western Reporter, Second Series. Write a full citation to the case, with pinpoint reference, that complies with the state's neutral citation rule.

2006 ND 25, *; 708 N.W.2d 867, **;
2006 N.D. LEXIS 20, ***

State of North Dakota, Plaintiff and Appellee v. Daniel Allen Nikle, Defendant and Appellant

No. 20050172

SUPREME COURT OF NORTH DAKOTA

2006 ND 25; 708 N.W.2d 867; 2006 N.D. LEXIS 20

January 31, 2006, Filed

15-C.13. You are writing a brief to the Oklahoma Supreme Court that discusses the case whose regional reporter caption is shown at right. The case is reported in volume 174 of the Pacific Reporter, Third Series, beginning at page 996. You are using the case to describe the court's rejection of the "apex doctrine" on page 1004 of that reporter, and more specifically, in paragraph 17 on that page. Write a full citation to the case, with pinpoint reference, that complies with the state's neutral citation rule.

> 2007 OK 77
>
> **CREST INFINITI II, LP, d/b/a Crest Infiniti, Crest Infiniti/Cadillac/Olds Isuzu; Crest Auto Group, Van Enterprises, and VT, Inc., Petitioners,**
>
> v.
>
> **Honorable Barbara G. SWINTON, District Judge of the 7th Judicial District Court Oklahoma County, Respondent.**
>
> **No. 104,884.**
>
> Supreme Court of Oklahoma.
>
> Oct. 9, 2007.
> As Corrected Oct. 10 and Oct. 17, 2007.

15-C.14. In your brief to the Montana Supreme Court, you discuss paragraphs 17 and 18 of *Hauschulz v. Michael Law Firm*, a case you found using LexisNexis. Paragraphs 17 and 18 deal with the standards for a motion to dismiss for failure to prosecute, and they are found on pages 100–101 of the Montana Reports and on page 911 of the Pacific Reporter. Write a full citation to the case, including pinpoint references, that complies with the state's neutral citation rule.

> *2005 MT 189, *; 328 Mont. 95, **;*
> *117 P.3d 908, ***; 2005 Mont. LEXIS 346*
>
> TRAVIS HAUSCHULZ, Plaintiff and Appellant, v. MICHAEL LAW FIRM, Defendant and Respondent.
>
> No. 04-635
>
> SUPREME COURT OF MONTANA
>
> 2005 MT 189; 328 Mont. 95; 117 P.3d 908; 2005 Mont. LEXIS 346
>
> March 16, 2005, Submitted on Briefs
>
> August 2, 2005, Decided

CHAPTER

16

TOGGLING BETWEEN

CITATION FORMATS

In both law school and law practice, legal writers may find that they need to comply with the requirements of other citation systems. Many law reviews adhere to the citation formats prescribed by the current edition of *The Bluebook: A Uniform System of Citation.* Similarly, practicing attorneys may need to comply with state-mandated citation formats for documents filed in courts, either because the state requires *Bluebook* style or because the state has its own local citation rules that affect the format of the citations. No matter which citation system you are asked to use, the fundamental components of the citation are the same: "author, the name of the authority or source, information about where the pertinent information can be found within the source (such as a volume or a page number), the publisher, and the date," as described on page 3 of the *ALWD Citation Manual.*

The citation systems differ only in the way they present the components. For example, Appendix 3(E) of the *Manual* lists an abbreviation for the word "accounting" ("acctg."), but Table T6 in *The Bluebook* does not list an abbreviation for the same word. You can spot the differences between citation systems simply by paying attention to the details.

There are five primary differences between *Manual* and *Bluebook* citation formats:

- Typeface. This difference only occurs in the citations in law review articles. The typeface for *Bluebook* citations in court documents is identical to the typeface for *Manual* citations.
- Abbreviations.
- Citations to different forms of periodicals.
- Citations to books and treatises.
- Signals and the order of sources.

In addition, there are some other very minor differences that are discussed below in section F. All the differences, except for typeface, can be seen in citations in legal memoranda, court documents, and scholarly documents.

The exercises in this chapter are designed to give you practical experience in negotiating the transition between *ALWD Citation Manual* and *Bluebook* citation formats. Each difference will be illustrated or explained in the introductory paragraphs at the beginning of the section and exercises provided. Section G contains an exercise that involves identifying which citation format is being used by simply looking at the citation. Section H is a capstone exercise that involves converting a series of footnotes from *Manual* to *Bluebook* format.

A. BLUEBOOK TYPEFACE

The difference between typeface in the *Manual* and *The Bluebook* affects only one kind of document—a law review article. *The Bluebook* requires legal writers to distinguish the citation formats used in law review footnotes from the citation formats used in the everyday documents produced by practicing lawyers, such as office memoranda and court briefs. To see the differences between the citations used in different documents, compare the inside front covers of *The Bluebook*, which show law review footnote style, with the inside back covers of *The Bluebook*, which show the same sources in the style used in legal memoranda and court documents.

Because the typeface difference occurs only in law review footnotes, the exercises in this section focus on that style. In law review writing, text and footnotes use three kinds of typeface:

- Ordinary Roman (Plain Text)
- *Italics*
- Large and Small Capitals

Note that *The Bluebook* does not allow underlining in law review text or footnotes, although this format is acceptable for practitioner documents, as explained in *Bluebook* Rule 2.0. Law review articles use two typeface conventions: one for the text (the main text and text in footnotes) and the other for citations in footnotes.

The following tables highlight the typeface conventions of *The Bluebook*. Table 16.1 summarizes the typeface requirements for the most commonly cited sources in law review footnotes. Table 16.2 summarizes the typeface conventions for text in the body of an article or in a "textual footnote" (a footnote that contains sentence(s) of text).

The exercises in this section help you to identify the differences in the typeface conventions between the *Manual* style and *The Bluebook* style used in law review articles.

TABLE 16.1

BLUEBOOK'S TYPEFACE REQUIREMENTS FOR CITATIONS IN FOOTNOTES—RULE 2.1

Authority Classification/ *Bluebook* Rule Number(s)	Ordinary Roman (Plain Text)	*Italics*	LARGE AND SMALL CAPITALS
Cases **Rule 2.1(a), (e)** **Rule 10.2** **Rule 10.7.1**	Case name in full citation Reporter abbreviation Court/date parenthetical	*Case name* in short form Procedural phrase (*in re, ex rel.*) Explanatory phrase (*aff'd, cert. denied, overruled by, rev'd*) for subsequent history; significance of disposition; abrogated and superseded cases; multiple decisions	
Constitutions **Rule 11**	Subdivision (article, amendment, section, clause) Parenthetical fact of modification (e.g., amended 1913)	Explanatory phrase for citation to modifying authority (e.g., *amended by* U.S. Const. amend. XVII)	CONSTITUTION NAME
Statutes **Rule 12**	Popular name Subdivision (article, section) Parenthetical fact of modification (e.g., repealed 1975)	Explanatory phrase for citation to modifying authority (e.g., *repealed by* Securities Acts Amendments of 1975, Pub. L. No. 94-29, 89 Stat. 97)	FEDERAL OR STATE CODE ABBREVIATION

TABLE 16.1

(Continued)

Authority Classification/ Rule Number(s)	Ordinary Roman (Plain Text)	*Italics*	LARGE AND SMALL CAPITALS
Other Codified Materials **Rule 12.9.2** **Rule 12.9.4** **Rule 12.9.5**	Subdivision (sections, rules) Parenthetical reference to author and draft		MODEL ACT OR CODE UNIFORM ACT TITLE ORDINANCE ABBREVIATION RESTATEMENTS
Rules of Practice and Procedure **Rule 12.9.3**	Subdivision Parenthetical fact of modification (e.g., repealed 1986)		RULE NAME
Legislative Materials **Rule 13**	Bill name and number Congressional session number	*Hearing subject-matter title*	SENATE OR HOUSE REPORTS AND DOCUMENTS CONGRESSIONAL RECORD
Books **Rule 2.1(b)** **Rule 15**	Parenthetical information in full citation including editor or translator name, edition, date		AUTHOR NAME, BOOK TITLE
Periodical Materials **Rule 2.1(c)** **Rule 16**	Author name	*Title*	PERIODICAL NAME

TABLE 16.2

BLUEBOOK'S TYPEFACE REQUIREMENTS FOR CITATIONS IN MAIN OR FOOTNOTE TEXT—RULE 2.2

Authority Classification/ *Bluebook* Rule Number(s)	Ordinary Roman (Plain Text)	*Italics*
Case Names (in main text) **Rule 2.2(a)(i)**		*Case name*, including *v.* Procedural phrase (*in re, ex rel.*)
Case Names (in footnote text) **Rule 2.2(b)(i)**	Case name in citation clause	*Case name* grammatically part of the sentence
Titles of Publications, Speeches, or Articles (in main text) **Rule 2.2(a)(ii)**		*Title*
Other authorities, in footnote text **Rule 2.2(b)(ii)**	Whether the citation is grammatically part of the sentence, use the typeface conventions in Rule 2.1 when citation information is provided (e.g., author name, publisher, edition, publication date). If the reference to the authority contains no citation information (whether in a full citation or a short-form citation), italicize titles.	

EXERCISE SET 16-A

BASIC LEVEL: *BLUEBOOK* TYPEFACE

Before beginning Exercise Set 16-A Basic Level, review the following *Bluebook* rules and keep *The Bluebook* at hand as you work through the exercises:

• Rule 2.1, Typeface Conventions for Citations   • Rule 10.2, Case Names
• Rule 4.1, *"Id."*

To complete the exercise, you may also refer to examples in the following *Bluebook* rules:

• Rule 11, Constitutions   • Rule 15, Books, Reports, and Other Nonperiodic
• Rule 12, Statutes   Materials
                                            • Rule 16, Periodical Materials

16-A.1. In a footnote in a law review article, the correct citation in *Manual* style is:

> *In re U.S. Airways Group, Inc.*, 296 B.R. 734, 745 (Bankr. E.D. Va. 2003).

Which of the following full citations displays the correct *Bluebook* typeface to use in a law review footnote?

a. In re U.S. Airways Group, Inc., 296 B.R. 734, 745 (Bankr. E.D. Va. 2003).
b. *In re U.S. Airways Group, Inc.*, 296 B.R. 734, 745 (Bankr. E.D. Va. 2003).
c. *In re* U.S. Airways Group, Inc., 296 B.R. 734, 745 (Bankr. E.D. Va. 2003).
d. In re *U.S. Airways Group, Inc.*, 296 B.R. 734, 745 (Bankr. E.D. Va. 2003).

16-A.2. In a footnote in a law review article, the correct citation in *Manual* style is:

> Vt. Stat. Ann. tit. 15, § 308(4) (Supp. 1998).

Which of the following full citations displays the correct *Bluebook* typeface to use in a law review footnote?

a. Vt. Stat. Ann. tit. 15, § 308(4) (Supp. 1998).
b. *Vt. Stat. Ann.* tit. 15, § 308(4) (Supp. 1998).
c. Vᴛ. Sᴛᴀᴛ. Aɴɴ. tit. 15, § 308(4) (Supp. 1998).
d. *Vᴛ. Sᴛᴀᴛ. Aɴɴ.* tit. 15, § 308(4) (Supp. 1998).

16-A.3. In a footnote in a law review article, the correct citation in *Manual* style is:

> David L. Bacon et al., *Employee Benefits Guide* § 2.05 (LexisNexis 2008).

Which of the following full citations displays the correct *Bluebook* typeface to use in a law review footnote?

a. 1 Dᴀᴠɪᴅ L. Bᴀᴄᴏɴ ᴇᴛ ᴀʟ., Eᴍᴘʟᴏʏᴇᴇ Bᴇɴᴇꜰɪᴛs Gᴜɪᴅᴇ § 2.05 (2008).
b. 1 David L. Bacon et al., *Employee Benefits Guide* § 2.05 (2008).
c. 1 David L. Bacon et al., Eᴍᴘʟᴏʏᴇᴇ Bᴇɴᴇꜰɪᴛs Gᴜɪᴅᴇ § 2.05 (2008).
d. 1 Dᴀᴠɪᴅ L. Bᴀᴄᴏɴ *et al.*, Employee Benefits Guide § 2.05 (2008).

16-A.4. In a footnote in a law review article, the correct citation in *Manual* style is:

> Mich. Const. art. V, § 29.

Which of the following full citations displays the correct *Bluebook* typeface to use in a law review footnote?

    a. *Mich. Const. art. V, § 29.*
    b. Mich. Const. art. V, § 29.
    c. MICH. CONST. ART. V, § 29.
    d. MICH. CONST. art. V, § 29.

16-A.5. In a footnote in a law review article, the correct citation in *Manual* style is:

> Bradley G. Clary, *Thinking about Law School: The Big Picture*, 80 U. Det. Mercy
> L. Rev. 467 (2003).

Which of the following full citations displays the correct *Bluebook* typeface to use
in a law review footnote?

    a. Bradley G. Clary, *Thinking About Law School: The Big Picture*, 80 U. Det. Mercy L. Rev.
       467 (2003).
    b. BRADLEY G. CLARY, *Thinking About Law School: The Big Picture*, 80 U. DET. MERCY L. REV.
       467 (2003).
    c. Bradley G. Clary, *Thinking About Law School: The Big Picture*, 80 U. DET. MERCY L. REV.
       467 (2003).
    d. Bradley G. Clary, <u>Thinking About Law School: The Big Picture</u>, 80 U. Det. Mercy L. Rev.
       467 (2003).

16-A.6. In a footnote in a law review article, the correct citation in *Manual* style is:

> 3d Cir. App. R. 28.1(a)(2).

Which of the following full citations displays the correct *Bluebook* typeface to use in a law review
footnote?

    a. 3d CIR. APP. R. 28.1(a)(2).
    b. 3d Cir. App. R. 28.1(a)(2).
    c. 3d *Cir. App. R.* 28.1(a)(2).
    d. 3d <u>Cir. App. R.</u> 28.1(a)(2).

EXERCISE SET 16-A

INTERMEDIATE LEVEL: BLUEBOOK TYPEFACE

> Before beginning Exercise Set 16-A Intermediate Level, review the following *Bluebook* rules and keep *The Bluebook* at hand as you work through the exercises:
>
> • Rule 2.1, Typeface Conventions for Citations
> • Rule 4.2, "*Supra*" and "Hereinafter"
>
> To complete the exercise, you may also need to refer to the examples in the following *Bluebook* rules:
>
> • Rule 15, Books, Reports, and Other Nonperiodic Materials
> • Rule 16, Periodical Materials

16-A.7. In a footnote in a law review article, the correct citation in *Manual* style is:

> Molly Warner Lien, *The Cooperative and Integrative Models of International Judicial Comity: Two Illustrations Using Transnational Discovery and* Breard *Scenarios*, 50 Cath. U. L. Rev. 591 (2001).

Which of the following full citations displays the correct *Bluebook* typeface to use in a law review footnote? [Note: This article discusses *Breard v. Greene*, 523 U.S. 371 (1998).]

a. MOLLY WARNER LIEN, *The Cooperative and Integrative Models of International Judicial Comity: Two Illustrations Using Transnational Discovery and Breard Scenarios*, 50 CATH. U. L. REV. 591 (2001).

b. Molly Warner Lien, *The Cooperative and Integrative Models of International Judicial Comity: Two Illustrations Using Transnational Discovery and* Breard *Scenarios*, 50 CATH. U. L. REV. 591 (2001).

c. Molly Warner Lien, *The Cooperative and Integrative Models of International Judicial Comity: Two Illustrations Using Transnational Discovery and Breard Scenarios*, 50 CATH. U. L. REV. 591 (2001).

d. Molly Warner Lien, *The Cooperative and Integrative Models of International Judicial Comity: Two Illustrations Using Transnational Discovery and* Breard *Scenarios*, 50 Cath. U. L. Rev. 591 (2001).

16-A.8. Assume you are writing a law review article. You cite the article by Molly Warner Lien in footnote 5, and you cite it a second time in footnote 42. In footnote 42, the correct citation in *Manual* style is:

> Lien, *supra* n. 5, at 597.

Which of the following short-form citations displays the correct *Bluebook* typeface to use in footnote 42?

a. Lien, supra note 5, at 597.
b. LIEN, SUPRA note 5, at 597.
c. LIEN, *supra* note 5, at 597.
d. Lien, *supra* note 5, at 597.

16-A.9. In a footnote in a law review article, the correct citation in *Manual* style is:

> Robyn Rone, *Students as Research Subjects: The Privacy Rights of Students and Their Families*, 36 Sch. L. Bull. (Sch. of Govt., U.N.C. Chapel Hill) 8 (Winter 2005).

Which of the following full citations displays the correct *Bluebook* typeface to use in a law review footnote?

a. Robyn Rone, *Students as Research Subjects: The Privacy Rights of Students and Their Families*, 36 Sᴄʜ. L. Bᴜʟʟ. (Sch. of Gov't, U.N.C. Chapel Hill), Winter 2005, at 8.

b. Robyn Rone, *Students as Research Subjects: The Privacy Rights of Students and Their Families*, 36 Sch. L. Bull. (Sch. of Gov't, U.N.C. Chapel Hill), Winter 2005, at 8.

c. Rᴏʙʏɴ Rᴏɴᴇ, Sᴛᴜᴅᴇɴᴛs ᴀs Rᴇsᴇᴀʀᴄʜ Sᴜʙᴊᴇᴄᴛs: Tʜᴇ Pʀɪᴠᴀᴄʏ Rɪɢʜᴛs ᴏғ Sᴛᴜᴅᴇɴᴛs ᴀɴᴅ Tʜᴇɪʀ Fᴀᴍɪʟɪᴇs, 36 Sch. L. Bull. (Sch. of Gov't, U.N.C. Chapel Hill), Winter 2005, at 8.

d. Robyn Rone, Students as Research Subjects: The Privacy Rights of Students and Their Families, 36 Sch. L. Bull. (Sch. of Gov't, U.N.C. Chapel Hill), Winter 2005, at 8.

16-A.10. In a footnote in a law review article, the correct citation in *Manual* style is:

> Charles Alan Wright & Arthur R. Miller, *Federal Practice and Procedure: Civil*
> vol. 5, § 1297, 590 (2d ed., West Publg. Co. 1990).

Which of the following full citations displays the correct *Bluebook* typeface to use in a law review footnote?

a. 5 CHARLES ALAN WRIGHT & ARTHUR R. MILLER, FEDERAL PRACTICE AND PROCEDURE § 1297, at 590 (2d ed. 1990).

b. 5 Charles Alan Wright & Arthur R. Miller, Fᴇᴅᴇʀᴀʟ Pʀᴀᴄᴛɪᴄᴇ Aɴᴅ Pʀᴏᴄᴇᴅᴜʀᴇ § 1297, at 590 (2d ed. 1990).

c. 5 Cʜᴀʀʟᴇs Aʟᴀɴ Wʀɪɢʜᴛ & Aʀᴛʜᴜʀ R. Mɪʟʟᴇʀ, Fᴇᴅᴇʀᴀʟ Pʀᴀᴄᴛɪᴄᴇ ᴀɴᴅ Pʀᴏᴄᴇᴅᴜʀᴇ § 1297, at 590 (2d ed. 1990).

d. 5 Charles Alan Wright & Arthur R. Miller, *Federal Practice And Procedure* § 1297, at 590 (2d ed. 1990).

16-A.11. In a footnote in a law review article, the correct citation in *Manual* style is:

> Wright & Miller, *supra* n. 16, at § 1297, 592.

Assume that the Wright & Miller treatise was cited in full in footnote 16, and it is cited a second time in footnote 19. Which of the following short citations displays the correct *Bluebook* typeface to use in footnote 19?

a. Wʀɪɢʜᴛ & Mɪʟʟᴇʀ, sᴜᴘʀᴀ ɴᴏᴛᴇ 16, § 1297, at 592.

b. Wʀɪɢʜᴛ & Mɪʟʟᴇʀ, *supra* note 16, § 1297, at 592.

c. Wʀɪɢʜᴛ & Mɪʟʟᴇʀ, supra note 16, § 1297, at 592.

d. Wright & Miller, *supra* note 16, § 1297, at 592.

16-A.12. In a footnote in a law review article, the correct citation in *Manual* style is:

> John C. Dernbach et al., *A Practical Guide to Legal Writing & Legal Method* 239 (3d ed., Aspen Publishers 2007).

Which of the following full citations displays the correct *Bluebook* typeface to use in a law review footnote?

a. John C. Dernbach et al., A Practical Guide to Legal Writing & Legal Method 239 (3d ed. 2007).
b. John C. Dernbach et al., *A Practical Guide to Legal Writing & Legal Method* 239 (3d ed. 2007).
c. John C. Dernbach et al., A Practical Guide to Legal Writing & Legal Method 239 (3d ed. 2007).
d. John C. Dernbach et al., A Practical Guide to Legal Writing & Legal Method 239 (3d ed. 2007).

16-A.13. In a footnote in a law review article, the correct citation in *Manual* style is:

> H. Conf. Rep. 1009-203 at 837 (July 28, 2005) (reprinted in 2005 U.S.C.C.A.N. 452, 457).

Which of the following full citations displays the correct *Bluebook* typeface in a law review footnote?

a. H. Conf. Rep. 109-203, at 837 (2005), as reprinted in 2005 U.S.C.C.A.N. 452, 457.
b. H. Conf. Rep. 109-203, at 837 (2005), as reprinted in 2005 U.S.C.C.A.N. 452, 457.
c. H. Conf. Rep. 109-203, at 837 (2005), *as reprinted in* 2005 U.S.C.C.A.N. 452, 457.
d. H. *Conf. Rep.* 109-203, at 837 (2005), *as reprinted in* 2005 U.S.C.C.A.N. 452, 457.

16-A.14. In a footnote in a law review article, the correct citation in *Manual* style is:

> 131 Cong. Rec. 15,605 (1985) (statement of Sen. Proxmire).

Which of the following full citations displays the correct *Bluebook* typeface in a law review footnote?

a. 131 Cong. Rec. 15,605 (1985) (statement of Sen. Proxmire).
b. 131 *Cong. Rec.* 15,605 (1985) (statement of Sen. Proxmire).
c. 131 Cong. Rec. 15,605 (1985) (statement of Sen. Proxmire).
d. 131 Cong. Rec. 15,605 (1985) (statement of Sen. Proxmire).

EXERCISE SET 16-A

EXPERT LEVEL: *BLUEBOOK* TYPEFACE

Before beginning Exercise Set 16-A Expert Level, review the following *Bluebook* rules and keep *The Bluebook* at hand as you work through the exercises:

- Rule 2.1, Typeface Conventions for Citations
- Rule 2.2, Typeface Conventions for Textual Material
- Rule 4.2, "*Supra*" and "Hereinafter"
- Rule 10.2, Case Names

To complete the exercise, you may also need to refer to the examples in the following *Bluebook* rule:

- Rule 15, Books, Reports, and Other Nonperiodic Materials

16-A.15. Which of the following full citations displays the correct *Bluebook* typeface to use in a law review footnote?

    a. D. Ray Heisey, *Sensitivity to an Image*, in *Kent State/May 4: Echoes Through a Decade* 187, 195 (Scott L. Bills ed., 1988).

    b. D. Ray Heisey, *Sensitivity to an Image*, in Kent State/May 4: Echoes Through a Decade 187, 195 (Scott L. Bills ed., 1988).

    c. D. Ray Heisey, *Sensitivity to an Image, in* Kent State/May 4: Echoes Through a Decade 187, 195 (Scott L. Bills ed., 1988).

    d. D. Ray Heisey, *Sensitivity to an Image*, in Kent State/May 4: Echoes Through a Decade 187, 195 (Scott L. Bills ed., 1988).

16-A.16. Assume that the Heisey work from Question 16-A.15 was originally cited in footnote 18, with pinpoint reference to page 193, and it is cited a second time, at the same page, in footnote 111. Write the short-form citation for footnote 111.

16-A.17. Which of the following case names displays the correct *Bluebook* typeface to use in the following sentence from the main text of an article?

> Justice Kennedy began with an analysis of _____, acknowledging that two other justices did not support the reasoning of that opinion.

    a. Planned Parenthood of Southeastern Pennsylvania v. Casey

    b. *Planned Parenthood of Southeastern Pennsylvania v. Casey*

    c. Planned Parenthood of Southeastern Pennsylvania v. Casey

    d. *Planned Parenthood of Southeastern Pennsylvania v. Casey*

16-A.18. Which of the following case names displays the correct *Bluebook* typeface to use in the following sentence from the text of a footnote of an article?

> Justice Kennedy began with an analysis of _____, 505 U.S. 833 (1992), acknowledging that two other justices did not support the reasoning of that opinion.

    a. *Planned Parenthood of Southeastern Pennsylvania v. Casey*

    b. Planned Parenthood of Southeastern Pennsylvania v. Casey

    c. Planned Parenthood of Southeastern Pennsylvania v. Casey

    d. *Planned Parenthood of Southeastern Pennsylvania v. Casey*

16-A.19. Which of the following case names displays the correct *Bluebook* typeface to use in the following sentence from the text of a footnote of an article?

> *Bluebook* Rule 10.6.1 states that if a case does not have a "single, clear holding of a majority of the court," *e.g.*, _____, 505 U.S. 833 (1992), "indicate that fact parenthetically."

    a. *Planned Parenthood of Southeastern Pennsylvania v. Casey*

    b. *Planned Parenthood of Southeastern Pennsylvania v. Casey*

    c. Planned Parenthood of Southeastern Pennsylvania v. Casey

    d. Planned Parenthood of Southeastern Pennsylvania v. Casey

16-A.20.   The following sentence is in the text of the footnote of an article.

> The foundation for this argument can be found in Bickel and Lake, supra note 31, at 195, and the argument was further developed in Peter F. Lake, Beyond Discipline: Managing the Modern Higher Education Environment (2009).

Both sources are books. Rewrite the sentence, providing the correct *Bluebook* typeface for the book references.

B.   *BLUEBOOK ABBREVIATIONS*

Although abbreviation practice and most of the abbreviations used in the *ALWD Citation Manual* and *The Bluebook* are the same, writers and editors must carefully verify abbreviations by checking the appropriate rules, tables, and appendices. Until the fourth edition of the *Manual*, there was a minor difference in the format of abbreviations in *Manual* style and the format of abbreviations in *Bluebook* style. Beginning with the fourth edition, Appendix 3 of the *Manual* gives you the option to use contractions for certain abbreviations, similar to certain abbreviations in *The Bluebook*. Note, however, that the list of available abbreviations in Appendix 3 of the *Manual* is much longer than the list of available abbreviations in *Bluebook* Table T6.

The abbreviations in *Manual* Appendix 3 may be used not only for case names, but also for statutory abbreviations and in connection with most other rules that require or permit abbreviations, whereas some of the abbreviation tables in *The Bluebook* are restricted to use in citations to particular sources. For example, Table T6 abbreviations are solely for use in case names, and Table T9 abbreviations apply solely to legislative documents. Table 16.3 below lists many comparable *Manual* and *Bluebook* appendices, tables, as well as major charts, sidebars, or rules for various classes of abbreviations.

TABLE 16.3

LOCATING ABBREVIATIONS IN THE *MANUAL* AND *THE BLUEBOOK*

Citation Components	*Manual* Appendices/Rules	*Bluebook* Tables/Rules
Cases: Case names	• Rule 12.2, Case Name • Appendix 3(E), General Abbreviations	• Rule 10.2, Case Names • Table T6, Case Names and Institutional Authors in Citations
Cases: Court names and official and unofficial reporters	• Chart 12.1, Common Reporter Abbreviations • Sidebar 12.4, Names and Dates of Early Supreme Court Reporters • Appendix 1, Primary Sources by Jurisdiction • Appendix 4, Court Abbreviations	• Rule 10.4, Court and Jurisdiction • Table T1, United States Jurisdictions • Table T7, Court Names

TABLE 16.3

(Continued)

Citation Components	*Manual* Appendices/Rules	*Bluebook* Tables/Rules
Cases: Parenthetical information and subsequent history phrases	• Rule 12.8(a), Actions to Include	• Rule 10.6.1(b), [Meaning of "mem." and "per curiam" descriptions] • Table T8, Explanatory Phrases
Titles for judges and other officials	• Chart 12.2, Abbreviations for Titles of Judges and Other Judicial Officials	• Rule 9, Titles of Judges, Officials, and Terms of Court • Table T11, Judges and Officials
Statutory compilations	• Appendix 1, Primary Sources by Jurisdiction • Appendix 3(E), General Abbreviations	• Table T1, United States Jurisdictions
Internal Revenue Code	• Rule 14.2(b)(3), [Internal Revenue Code Abbreviation]	• Rule 12.9.1, Internal Revenue Code
Session laws and legislative documents	• Appendix 1, Primary Sources by Jurisdiction • Appendix 3(E), General Abbreviations	• Table T1, United States Jurisdictions • Table T9, Legislative Documents
Administrative compilations and registers	• Appendix 1, Primary Sources by Jurisdiction • Appendix 8, Selected Official Federal Administrative Publications	• Table T1, United States Jurisdictions
Dates	• Appendix 3(A), Calendar Divisions	• Table T12, Months
Geographic locations	• Appendix 3(B), United States and World Geography	• Table T10, Geographical Terms

TABLE 16.3

(Continued)

Citation Components	*Manual* Appendices/Rules	*Bluebook* Tables/Rules
Treaties	• Chart 21.1, Selected Bound Treaty Sources	• Table T4, Treaty Sources
Looseleafs	• Chart 28.1, Abbreviations for Looseleaf Publishers	• Table T15, Services
Periodical names	• Appendix 5, Abbreviations for Legal Periodicals	• Table T13, Periodicals

Both citation manuals ask you to delete spaces between single capital letters in abbreviations, except for geographical and institutional references in abbreviations for certain periodicals (compare *Manual* Rule 2.2 and Appendix 5 with *Bluebook* Rule 6.1 and Table T13). Both citation manuals advise readers against using abbreviations they do not list (see *Manual* Rule 2.1(a) and *Bluebook* Rule 6.1).

The exercises in this section help you differentiate the abbreviations used in *Manual*-formatted citations and *Bluebook*-formatted citations.

EXERCISE SET 16-B

BASIC LEVEL: *BLUEBOOK* ABBREVIATIONS

Before beginning Exercise Set 16-B Basic Level, have both the *Manual* and *Bluebook* citation manuals available. Review the following rules in the *Manual*:

• Rule 2.0, Abbreviations
• Appendix 1, Primary Sources by Jurisdiction

• Appendix 3, General Abbreviations
• Appendix 4, Court Abbreviations

And in *The Bluebook*, review the following rules:

• Rule 6.1, Abbreviations
• Table T1, United States Jurisdictions

• Table T6, Case Names and Institutional Authors in Citations
• Table T7, Court Names

16-B.1. You want to cite a case in the Federal Appendix. Choose the option that correctly displays the reporter abbreviation in **both** *Manual* and *Bluebook* formats.

a. *Manual:* F. App'x; *Bluebook:* F. App'x
b. *Manual:* Fed. Appx.; *Bluebook:* Fed. Appx.
c. *Manual:* F. App'x; *Bluebook:* Fed. Appx.
d. *Manual:* Fed. Appx.; *Bluebook* F. App'x.

16-B.2. You want to cite sections 4420(b)(1) to (b)(6) of the California Government Code in West's Annotated California Codes. The citation will appear in the footnote of a law review article. Choose the option that correctly displays the citation in **both** *Manual* and *Bluebook* formats.

a. *Manual:* Cal. Govt. Code Ann. § 4420(b)(1)–(b)(6) (West 2009); *Bluebook:* Cal. Gov't Code Ann. § 4420(b)(1)–(b)(6) (West 2009).
b. *Manual:* Cal. Govt. Code Ann. § 4420(b)(1)–(b)(6) (West 2009); *Bluebook:* Cal. Govt. Code Ann. § 4420(b)(1)–(b)(6) (West 2009).
c. *Manual:* Cal. Govt. Code Ann. § 4420(b)(1)–(b)(6) (West 2009); *Bluebook:* Cal. Gov't Code Ann. § 4420(b)(1)–(b)(6) (West 2009).
d. *Manual:* Cal. Govt. Code Ann. § 4420(b)(1)–(b)(6) (West 2009); *Bluebook:* Cal. Gov't Code Ann. § 4420(b)(1)–(b)(6) (West 2009).

16-B.3. You want to cite a case decided by the Iowa Supreme Court. Choose the option that correctly displays the court abbreviation in **both** *Manual* and *Bluebook* formats.

a. *Manual* and *Bluebook:* Iowa
b. *Manual:* Iowa; *Bluebook:* Iowa Sup. Ct.
c. *Manual* and *Bluebook:* Iowa Sup. Ct.
d. *Manual:* Iowa Sup. Ct.; *Bluebook:* Iowa Ct.

16-B.4. You want to cite a case with the following case name: *Outdoor Academy Incorporated versus Southeastern Subcommittee Corporation.* Choose the option that correctly abbreviates words in the case name in **both** *Manual* and *Bluebook* formats.

a. *Manual* and *Bluebook:* Outdoor Acad., Inc. v. Se. Subcomm. Corp.
b. *Manual:* Outdoor Acad., Inc. v. S.E. Subcomm. Corp.; *Bluebook:* Outdoor Acad., Inc. v. Se. Subcomm. Corp.
c. *Manual:* Outdoor Acad., Inc. v. Se. Subcomm. Corp.; *Bluebook:* Outdoor Acad., Inc. v. S.E. Subcomm. Corp.
d. *Manual* and *Bluebook:* Outdoor Acad., Inc. v. S.E. Subcomm. Corp.

16-B.5. You want to cite a case decided by the Alaska Court of Appeals. Choose the option that correctly displays the court abbreviation in **both** *Manual* and *Bluebook* formats.

a. *Manual* and *Bluebook:* Alaska Ct. App.
b. *Manual* and *Bluebook:* Alaska App.
c. *Manual:* Alaska App.; *Bluebook:* Alaska Ct. App.
d. *Manual:* Alaska Ct. App.; *Bluebook:* Alaska App.

16-B.6. You want to cite a case decided by the Third District of the Illinois Appellate Court. Choose the option that correctly displays the court abbreviation in **both** *Manual* and *Bluebook* formats.

     a. *Manual* and *Bluebook*: Ill. App.
     b. *Manual*: Ill. App. 3d Dist.; *Bluebook*: Ill. App. Dist.
     c. *Manual*: Ill. App.; *Bluebook*: Ill. App. Ct.
     d. *Manual*: Ill. App. 3d Dist.; *Bluebook*: Ill. App. Ct.

EXERCISE SET 16-B

INTERMEDIATE LEVEL: *BLUEBOOK* ABBREVIATIONS

Before beginning Exercise Set 16-B Intermediate Level, have both the *Manual* and *Bluebook* citation manuals available. Review the following rules in the *Manual*:

- Rule 23.0, Legal and Other Periodicals
- Appendix 5, Abbreviations for Legal Periodicals

And in *The Bluebook*, review the following rules:

- Rule 16, Periodical Materials
- Table T13, Periodicals

16-B.7. You want to cite an article published in the June 2008 issue of the American Bar Association Journal. Choose the option that correctly displays the journal abbreviation in **both** *Manual* and *Bluebook* formats.

     a. *Manual* and *Bluebook*: ABA J.
     b. *Manual* and *Bluebook*: A.B.A. J.
     c. *Manual*: A.B.A. J.; *Bluebook*: ABA J.
     d. *Manual*: ABA J.; *Bluebook*: A.B.A. J.

16-B.8. You want to cite an article published in volume 1 of the Asian-Pacific Law and Policy Journal. Choose the option that correctly displays the journal abbreviation in **both** *Manual* and *Bluebook* formats.

     a. *Manual*: Asian-P. L. & Policy J.; *Bluebook*: ASIAN-PAC. L. & POL'Y J.
     b. *Manual*: Asian-P. L. & Policy J.; *Bluebook*: Asian-Pac. L. & Pol'y J.
     c. *Manual* and *Bluebook*: Asian-Pac. L. & Pol'y J.
     d. *Manual*: ASIAN-P. L. & POLICY J.; *Bluebook*: ASIAN-PAC. L. & POL'Y J.

16-B.9. You would like to cite a 1985 article published in volume 35 of the Journal of Legal Education. Choose the option that correctly displays the journal abbreviation in **both** *Manual* and *Bluebook* formats.

     a. *Manual* and *Bluebook*: J. Leg. Educ.
     b. *Manual*: J. Leg. Educ.; *Bluebook*: J. LEGAL EDUC.
     c. *Manual*: J. Legal Educ.; *Bluebook*: J. LEGAL EDUC.
     d. *Manual*: J. Leg. Educ.; *Bluebook*: J. LEG. EDUC.

16-B.10. You would like to cite an article published in volume 27 of the American Journal of Trial Advocacy. Choose the option that correctly displays the journal abbreviation in **both** *Manual* and *Bluebook* formats.

     a. *Manual* and *Bluebook*: Am. J. Trial Advoc.
     b. *Manual*: Am. J. Trial Advoc.; *Bluebook*: AM. J. TRIAL ADVOC.
     c. *Manual*: Am. J. Tr. Advoc.; *Bluebook*: AM. J. TR. ADVOC.
     d. *Manual*: Am. J. Tr. Advoc.; *Bluebook*: AM. J. TRIAL ADVOC.

EXERCISE SET 16-B

EXPERT LEVEL: *BLUEBOOK* ABBREVIATIONS

Before beginning Exercise Set 16-B Expert Level, have both the *Manual* and *Bluebook* citation manuals available. Review the following rules in the *Manual*:

- Rule 2.0, Abbreviations
- Rule 23.1(d), Periodical abbreviation
- Appendix 5, Abbreviations for Legal Periodicals

And in *The Bluebook*, review the following rules:

- Rule 6.1, Abbreviations
- Table T13, Periodicals

16-B.11. Provide the journal abbreviations—from **both** the *Manual* and *The Bluebook*—for each of the following journals.

     16-B.11.a.   Teaching and Teacher Education

     16-B.11.b.   Publishing Research Quarterly

     16-B.11.c.   Contemporary Clinical Trials

16-B.12. Abbreviate the following case names according to Appendix 3 in the *Manual* **and** Table T6 in *The Bluebook*. (If both an abbreviation and a contraction are listed in Appendix 3, provide the abbreviation.)

     16-B.12.a.   Connection Coalition for Justice in Education Funding, Incorporated v. Rell

     16-B.12.b.   Burlington County College Faculty Association v. Burlington County College

     16-B.12.c.   Central Regional Employees Benefit Fund v. Cephalon, Incorporated

     16-B.12.d.   Piasa Commercial Interiors, Incorporated v. J.P. Murray Company

     16-B.12.e.   Embry v. Pierce County Detention Corrections Center

     16-B.12.f.   Dupre v. Healthcare Integrity and Protection Data Bank

     16-B.12.g.   Medic Ambulance Service v. National Emergency Medical Services Association

C.	**BLUEBOOK FORMAT FOR LEGAL PERIODICALS**

The difference between the formatting of legal periodical citations in the *ALWD Citation Manual* and *The Bluebook* appears in all legal documents. It does not matter if the document is a legal memorandum or a law review article.

Consecutively Paginated Journals versus Non-Consecutively Paginated Journals

In *The Bluebook*, there are two differences between citations to consecutively paginated journals and citations to non-consecutively paginated journals: (1) the order of the components within the citation; and (2) the presentation of the date of publication. For a consecutively paginated journal, the full citation contains the following components in order: author(s), title, volume number, journal abbreviation, initial page, pinpoint reference, and parenthetical containing the date of publication. The date of publication for a consecutively paginated journal is typically the date assigned to the volume.

For a non-consecutively paginated journal, the full citation contains the following components in order: author(s), title, volume number (if available), journal abbreviation, publication date, initial page, and pinpoint reference. The date of publication for a non-consecutively paginated journal is still the date assigned to the issue, but there is more information needed than just the year—a day, a month, or a season, for example. Without specific information regarding the date, a reader will not be able to tell whether the article is found in the January issue or the February issue, for example.

How do you determine whether the article you are citing is in a consecutively or non-consecutively paginated journal? Most law reviews or law journals are consecutively paginated, but Appendix 5 of the *Manual* indicates the non-consecutively paginated journals with a green star.

Student-Authored Journal Articles

In both the *Manual* and *Bluebook* citation formats, you can identify whether a law review article was written by a student or by a professional (an attorney, professor, or judge). The only difference is that in *Bluebook*-formatted citations, the student-authored work is identified by its classification (e.g., Note, Comment, Recent Development—see Rule 16.7.1), instead of the phrase "Student Author." Follow these hints to determine the classification of a student-authored article: (1) look at the title of the article; or (2) look at the journal's table of contents to see in what section the article appears.

Abbreviations for Periodical Names in Table T13

The abbreviations used in the *Manual* and the abbreviations used in *The Bluebook* are not always the same. Sometimes the difference is the format of the abbreviation; other times it is the number of abbreviations available. Periodical abbreviations in the *Manual* are in Appendix 5. Periodical abbreviations in *The Bluebook* are in Table T13. If a journal is not on the list, you can create an abbreviation using the information found in Appendix 3 of the *Manual* or Tables T10 and T13 of *The Bluebook*.

The exercises in this section help you negotiate the differences between *Manual*-formatted legal periodical citations and *Bluebook*-formatted legal periodical citations. The exercises in this section are for all levels.

EXERCISE SET 16-C

ALL LEVELS: *BLUEBOOK* FORMAT FOR LEGAL PERIODICALS

Before beginning Exercise Set 16-C All Levels, review the following *Bluebook* rules and keep *The Bluebook* at hand as you work through the exercises:

- Rule 16.5, Nonconsecutively Paginated Journals and Magazines
- Rule 16.7.1, Student-Written Law Review Materials
- Table T13, Periodicals

16-C.1. Identify whether the following journals are consecutively paginated or non-consecutively paginated.

16-C.1.a. *The Student Lawyer*

a. consecutively paginated
b. non-consecutively paginated

16-C.1.b. *Antitrust Bulletin*

a. consecutively paginated
b. non-consecutively paginated

16-C.1.c. *Current Issues in Criminal Justice*

a. consecutively paginated
b. non-consecutively paginated

16-C.1.d. *Litigation*

a. consecutively paginated
b. non-consecutively paginated

16-C.1.e. *Law & Psychology Review*

a. consecutively paginated
b. non-consecutively paginated

16-C.1.f. *The Bar Examiner*

a. consecutively paginated
b. non-consecutively paginated

16-C.2. You would like to cite a newspaper article in the *New York Times* by Noam Cohen, titled *Courts Turn to Wikipedia, but Selectively*. The article begins on page C3, and the newspaper was published on January 29, 2007. The newspaper has no volume number. The correct citation in *Manual* style is:

> Noam Cohen, *Courts Turn to Wikipedia, but Selectively*, N.Y. Times C3 (Jan. 29, 2007).

Which of the following is the correct full citation according to *The Bluebook*?

a. Cohen, Noam, *Courts Turn to Wikipedia, but Selectively*, N.Y. Times, Jan. 29, 2007, at C3.
b. Noam Cohen, *Courts Turn to Wikipedia, but Selectively*, N.Y. Times C3 (Jan. 29, 2007).
c. Noam Cohen, *Courts Turn To Wikipedia, but Selectively*, N.Y. TIMES (Jan. 29, 2007), at C3.
d. Noam Cohen, *Courts Turn to Wikipedia, but Selectively*, N.Y. TIMES, Jan. 29, 2007, at C3.

16-C.3. You would like to cite an article in the *ABA Journal* by Jason Krause, titled *Law Hacks: 101 Tips, Tricks and Tools to Make You a More Productive, Less Stressed-Out Lawyer*. The article begins at page 36, and the journal was published in July 2007. The volume number is 93. The correct citation in *Manual* style is:

> Jason Krause, *Law Hacks: 101 Tips, Tricks and Tools to Make You a More Productive, Less Stressed-out Lawyer*, 93 ABA J. 36 (July 2007).

Which of the following is the correct full citation according to *The Bluebook*?

a. Jason Krause, *Law Hacks: 101 Tips, Tricks and Tools to Make You a More Productive, Less Stressed-Out Lawyer*, 93 A.B.A. J., July 2007, at 36.
b. Jason Krause, *Law Hacks: 101 Tips, Tricks and Tools to Make You a More Productive, Less Stressed-Out Lawyer*, 93 ABA J. 36, July 2007.
c. Jason Krause, *Law Hacks: 101 Tips, Tricks and Tools to Make You a More Productive, Less Stressed-Out Lawyer*, 93 ABA J. 36 (July 2007).
d. Jason Krause, *Law Hacks: 101 Tips, Tricks and Tools to Make You a More Productive, Less Stressed-Out Lawyer*, 93 ABA J., July 2007, at 36.

16-C.4. You would like to cite Marc Parry's article titled *Online Educators Won't Be Forced to Spy on Students, New Rules Say*, which begins at page A19 of volume LV of the *Chronicle of Higher Education*, published on June 12, 2009. The correct citation in *Manual* style is:

> Marc Parry, *Online Educator Won't Be Forced to Spy on Students, New Rules Say*, 55 Chron. Higher Educ. A19 (June 12, 2009).

Which of the following is the correct full citation according to *The Bluebook*?

a. MARC PARRY, *Online Educators Won't Be Forced to Spy on Students, New Rules Say*, LV CHRON. OF HIGHER EDUC. A19 (June 12, 2009).
b. *Marc Parry, Online Educators Won't Be Forced to Spy on Students, New Rules Say, 55 CHRON. OF HIGHER EDUC., June 12, 2009, at A19.*
c. Marc Parry, *Online Educators Won't Be Forced to Spy on Students, New Rules Say*, LV CHRON. OF HIGHER EDUC., June 12, 2009, at A19.
d. Marc Parry, *Online Educators Won't Be Forced to Spy on Students, New Rules Say*, 55 CHRON. OF HIGHER EDUC. A19 (June 12, 2009).

16-C.5. The following citation is in correct *Manual* format. Write the citation as it should appear in *Bluebook* format in a law review article's footnotes. [Note: This article is published in a non-consecutively paginated journal.]

> Brooke J. Bowman, *Writing Tips: Learning the Art of Rewriting and Editing*, 15 Persps. 54, 55 (Fall 2006).

16-C.6. The following citation is in correct *Manual* format. Write the citation as it should appear in *Bluebook* format in a law review article's footnotes. [Note: This student-written article appeared in a section of the law review under the heading *Comments*.]

> Alison S. Aaronson, Student Author, *Changing with the Times: Why Rampant School Violence Warrants Legalization of Parental Wiretapping to Monitor Children's Activities*, 9 J.L. & Policy 785, 790 (2001).

16-C.7. Use the information shown below to write full citations in **both** *Manual* format and *Bluebook* format, referring specifically to pages 1514 through 1533. The article was published in volume 88 of the Yale Law Journal, in 1979.

From the top of the first page, page 1511

> Essay
>
> Efficiency and Competition in the Electric-Power Industry

From the bottom of the first page

> † This essay was selected for publication from among a number submitted by non-editor members of the Yale Law School third-year class.
> * The author gratefully acknowledges the valuable assistance and comments of Daniel I. Davidson, James F. Fairman, Paul W. MacAvoy, Phillip Nicholson, and Gordon T.C. Taylor.

From the end of the article

> dinated management of production and transmission facilities. For this reason the structural reform proposed in this paper deserves consideration. It would inject a welcome dose of competition into the national energy plan.
>
> *Matthew Cohen*

16-C.8.   Use the information provided below to write full citations in both *Manual* and *Bluebook* formats, referring specifically to footnote 71, at page 310. The article was published in volume 46 of the Harvard Journal on Legislation, in 2009.

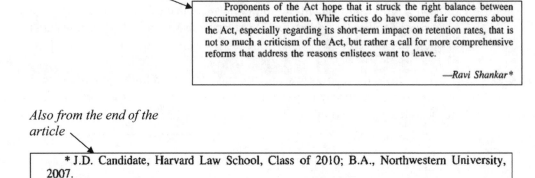

From the top of the first page, page 303 →

RECENT DEVELOPMENT

POST-9/11 VETERANS EDUCATIONAL ASSISTANCE ACT OF 2008

From the end of the article

> Proponents of the Act hope that it struck the right balance between recruitment and retention. While critics do have some fair concerns about the Act, especially regarding its short-term impact on retention rates, that is not so much a criticism of the Act, but rather a call for more comprehensive reforms that address the reasons enlistees want to leave.
>
> —*Ravi Shankar**

Also from the end of the article

> * J.D. Candidate, Harvard Law School, Class of 2010; B.A., Northwestern University, 2007.

D. *BLUEBOOK* FORMAT FOR BOOK OR TREATISE CITATIONS

The differences between the formatting of book or treatise citations in the *Manual* and *The Bluebook* appear in all legal documents. Besides the typeface differences discussed in section A above and the capitalization differences discussed in section E below, *Bluebook* citations to books and treatises differ in three minor ways from *Manual* citations:

- location of the volume number, as shown in the second example in *Bluebook* Rule 15.1(b);
- omission of the publisher's name from the date parenthetical, as shown in *Bluebook* Rule 15.4; and
- the addition of the designation "Annotation" after the author's name in citations to *American Law Reports*, as shown in *Bluebook* Rule 16.7.6.

The exercises in this section help you identify the differences in the formatting of *Manual* citations for books or treatises and *Bluebook* citations for books or treatises. The exercises in this section are for all levels.

EXERCISE SET 16-D

ALL LEVELS: *BLUEBOOK* FORMAT FOR BOOK OR TREATISE CITATIONS

Before beginning Exercise Set 16-D All Levels, review the following *Bluebook* rules and keep *The Bluebook* at hand as you work through the exercises:

- Rule 15, Books, Reports, and Other Nonperiodic Materials
- Rule 16.7.6, Annotations

16-D.1. You would like to cite the definition of the word "citation" on page 260 of the 8th edition of *Black's Law Dictionary*, published by Thomson in 2004. Which of the following full citations is in correct *Bluebook* format for a footnote in a law review article?

  a. *Black's Law Dictionary* 260 (8th ed., Thomson 2004).
  b. *Black's Law Dictionary* 260 (8th ed., 2004).
  c. BLACK'S LAW DICTIONARY 260 (8th ed., Thomson 2004).
  d. BLACK'S LAW DICTIONARY 260 (8th ed. 2004).

16-D.2. The following citation to an encyclopedia entry is in correct *Manual* format. Which of the following full citations is in correct *Bluebook* format for a footnote in a law review article?

  16 C.J.S. *Constitution* § 65 (2005).

  a. 16 C.J.S. *Constitution* § 65 (2005).
  b. 16 C.J.S. CONSTITUTION § 65 (2005).
  c. C.J.S. *Constitution* vol. 16, § 65 (2005).
  d. C.J.S. CONSTITUTION vol. 16, § 65 (2005).

16-D.3. The following citation to an encyclopedia entry is in correct *Manual* format. Which of the following full citations is in correct *Bluebook* format for a footnote in a law review article?

  4 Am. Jur. 2d *Appellate Review* § 35 (2007).

  a. 4 Am. Jur. 2d *Appellate Review* § 35 (2007).
  b. 4 Am. Jur. 2d Appellate Review § 35 (2007).
  c. 4 AM. JUR. 2D APPELLATE REVIEW § 35 (2007).
  d. 4 AM. JUR. 2D *Appellate Review* § 35 (2007).

16-D.4. A footnote cites pages 676 to 679 of volume II of a multi-volume treatise by Louis Loss, Joel Seligman, and Troy Paredes, titled *Securities Regulations*. The set was published by Aspen Publishers in 2007. Which of the following full citations is in correct *Bluebook* format for a footnote in a law review article?

  a. II LOUIS LOSS ET AL., SECURITIES REGULATIONS 676–79 (2007).
  b. II LOUIS LOSS, JOEL SELIGMAN & TROY PAREDES, SECURITIES REGULATIONS 676–79 (Aspen Publishers 2007).
  c. II Louis Loss et al., SECURITIES REGULATIONS 676–79 (Aspen Publishers 2007).
  d. Louis Loss et al., SECURITIES REGULATIONS VOL. II, 676–79 (2007).

16-D.5.   A footnote cites section 12A.02, page 244, volume II of a multi-volume treatise by Stephen W. Schlissel, Elena Karabatos, and Ronald F. Poepplein. The title of the treatise is *Separation Agreements and Marital Contracts*, which was published by Michie in 1997. Which of the following full citations is in correct *Bluebook* format for a law review article?

    a. II Stephen W. Schlissel et al., Separation Agreements and Marital Contracts § 12A.02, at 244 (1997).

    b. Stephen W. Schlissel et al., Separation Agreements and Marital Contracts vol. II, § 12A.02, at 244 (1997).

    c. II Stephen W. Schlissel, Elena Karabatos & Ronald F. Poepplein, Separation Agreements and Marital Contracts § 12A.02, at 244 (Michie 1997).

    d. II Stephen W. Schlissel et al., Separation Agreements and Marital Contracts § 12A.02, at 244 (1997).

16-D.6.   You want to cite a shorter work contained in a book titled *Looking Back at Law's Century,* published by Cornell University Press in 2002 and edited by Austin Sarat, Bryant Garth, and Robert A. Kagan. The author of the shorter work is Robert W. Gordon, and the title of his work is *The Legal Profession.* The shorter work starts at page 287. You wish to cite page 292. Which of the following full citations is in correct *Bluebook* format for a law review article?

    a. Robert W. Gordon, *The Legal Profession, in* Looking Back at Law's Century 287, 292 (Austin Sarat et al. eds., Cornell U. Press 2002).

    b. Robert W. Gordon, *The Legal Profession, in* Looking Back at Law's Century 287, 292 (Austin Sarat et al. eds., Cornell U. Press 2002).

    c. Robert W. Gordon, *The Legal Profession, in* Looking Back at Law's Century 287, 292 (Austin Sarat et al. eds., 2002).

    d. Robert W. Gordon, *The Legal Profession, in* Looking Back at Law's Century 287, 292 (Austin Sarat et al. eds. 2002).

16-D.7.   The following citation to a book is in correct *Manual* format. Write the citation as it should appear in *Bluebook* format in a law review article's footnotes.

    William A. Kaplin & Barbara A. Lee, *The Law of Higher Education* vol. 2, 927 (4th ed., Jossey-Bass 2006).

16-D.8.   The following citation to a book is in correct *Manual* format. Write the citation as it should appear in *Bluebook* format in a law review article's footnotes.

    R.J. Sharpe, *The Law of Habeas Corpus* 51 (2d ed., Clarendon Press 1989).

16-D.9.   The following citation to a book is in correct *Manual* format. The book has five authors. Besides Mr. Greene, the other authors are Edward J. Rosen, Leslie N. Silverman, Daniel A. Braverman, and Sebastian R. Sperber. Write the citation as it should appear in *Bluebook* format in a law review article's footnotes.

    Edward F. Greene et al., *U.S. Regulation of the International Securities and Derivatives Market* vol. II, § 14.08[1], 14-80 to 14-82 (Aspen Publishers 2006) (defining "commodity").

16-D.10.   The following citation to a book is in correct *Manual* format. There are four authors for the shorter work; besides Ms. Blankenship, the other authors are Beth Rushing, Suzanne A. Onorato, and Renee White. Write the citation as it should appear in *Bluebook* format in a law review article's footnotes.

> Kim M. Blankenship et al., *Reproductive Technologies and the U.S. Courts*, in *Reproduction, Sexuality, and the Family* 150, 154–157 tbl. 1 (Karen J. Maschke ed., Garland Publg., Inc., 1997).

E.   *BLUEBOOK* FOOTNOTES, SIGNALS, AND ORDER OF AUTHORITIES

The differences between the formatting of signals and the order of authorities in a string citation in the *ALWD Manual* and *The Bluebook* appear in all legal documents. Keep the following two differences in mind when you are formatting citations in string citations:

- the order of sources, which may also depend upon the signals used, if any; and
- the punctuation between sources.

   Review *Bluebook* Rules 1.2 and 1.3 when using signals; these rules discuss not only the definitions of the different signals, but also the punctuation and order of the signals. Read the signal definitions closely; there are variations between the definitions of *Manual* signals and the same signals in *Bluebook*. For example, according to *Bluebook* Rule 1.2, the signal "*see*" is used when the citation "clearly supports the proposition." In contrast, *ALWD Citation Manual* Rule 44.3 explains that the signal "*see*" is used when the authority "supports the stated proposition implicitly or . . . contains dicta that support the proposition."

   Also review *Bluebook* Rule 1.4, which discusses the order of authority. In both formats, citations that have no signal come first in a string citation. But the order of signals is somewhat different, as shown below in Table 16.4. Citations possessing signals within the same category are separated by semi-colons. Citations possessing signals in different categories are separated into different citation sentences. See the example in *Bluebook* Rule 1.3. Note also that the punctuation of the signal "*e.g.*" is different in the two formats. *The Bluebook* inserts a comma after the signal "*e.g.*"; if another signal precedes the "*e.g.*," it should be set off with a comma. There are no commas in any signals in *Manual* format.

TABLE 16.4

ORDER OF SIGNALS IN STRING CITATIONS

ALWD Citation Manual	*The Bluebook*
no signal	no signal
See	*E.g.,*

TABLE 16.4

(Continued)

ALWD Citation Manual	The Bluebook
Accord	Accord
See also	See
Cf.	See also
Compare . . . with	Cf.
Contra	Compare . . . with
But see	Contra
But cf.	But see
See generally	But cf.
E.g.	See generally

The two primary differences between the order of authorities in string citations in *The Bluebook* and the *Manual* are reflected in citations to statutes and to cases. In *The Bluebook*, citations to federal statutes and rules of evidence and procedure precede citations to state statutes and rules of evidence and procedure. In contrast, in the *Manual*, citations to federal statutes precede citations to state statutes; both types of statutes precede citations to rules of evidence and procedure (federal first, followed by state).

The Bluebook treats federal courts *on the same level* as a single court. If a string citation contains multiple cases from that court, they are presented in a group in reverse chronological order. In contrast, the *Manual* groups numerically (or alphabetically) by the court name, and only if there are multiple cases within a single group, presents them in reverse chronological order. For example, consider the following five cases:

- Case from the Fifth Circuit, decided in 1981
- Case from the Southern District of New York, decided in 1988
- Case from the Ninth Circuit, decided in 2001

- Case from the Northern District of Illinois, decided in 2002
- Case from the Federal Circuit, decided in 2004

In *Bluebook* style, the cases should be ordered as follows: Fed. Cir. 2004; 9th Cir. 2001; 5th Cir. 1981; N.D. Ill. 2002; S.D.N.Y. 1988. The same group of cases, however, should be ordered as follows in *Manual* style: 5th Cir. 1981; 9th Cir. 2001; Fed. Cir. 2004; N.D. Ill. 2002; S.D.N.Y. 1988.

A minor punctuation difference between *Manual* style and *Bluebook* style concerns separation of the title of the title of a law review article from the rest of the citation when the title ends in a question mark. In *Manual* style, do not insert a comma after the question mark to separate the title from the rest of the citation. In *Bluebook* style, insert a comma after the question mark; see the examples in Rules 16.3 and 16.4.

The exercises in this section are for all levels.

EXERCISE SET 16-E

ALL LEVELS: *BLUEBOOK* FOOTNOTES, SIGNALS, AND ORDER OF AUTHORITIES

> Before beginning Exercise Set 16-E All Levels, review the following *Bluebook* rules and keep *The Bluebook* at hand as you work through the exercises:
>
> - Rule 1.2, Introductory Signals
> - Rule 1.3, Order of Signals
> - Rule 1.4, Order of Authorities Within Each Signal

16-E.1. Determine the correct order of the following four citations according to *The Bluebook*, assuming that the citations appear in a single string citation in a law-review footnote. Write the number "1" beside the authority that should come first, "2" beside the second, and so on.

Levan v. Capital Cities/ABC, Inc., 190 F.3d 1230 (11th Cir. 1999).
Zeiler v. Deitsch, 500 F.3d 157, 162 (2d Cir. 2007).
Project Hope v. M/V Ibn Sina, 250 F.3d 67, 70 (2d Cir. 2001).
Jenkins v. Missouri, 216 F.3d 720, 725 (8th Cir. 2000).

16-E.2. Determine the correct order of the following eight citations according to *The Bluebook*, assuming that the citations appear in a single string citation in a law-review footnote. Write the number "1" beside the authority that should come first, "2" beside the second, and so on.

Pavese v. Gen. Motors Corp., 1998 WL 57761 (E.D. Pa. 1998).
Levan v. Capital Cities/ABC, Inc., 190 F.3d 1230 (11th Cir. 1999).
Zeiler v. Deitsch, 500 F.3d 157, 162 (2d Cir. 2007).
Tandia v. Gonzales, 236 Fed. Appx. 455, 457 n.4 (10th Cir. 2007).
Bd. of Curators of Univ. of Mo. v. Horowitz, 435 U.S. 78, 85 (1978).
Project Hope v. M/V Ibn Sina, 250 F.3d 67, 70 (2d Cir. 2001).
Smith v. TMC Acquisitions, LLC, No. 2:05CV3237-HRH, 2006 WL 2613426 (D. Ariz. June 22, 2006).
Bd. of Regents of State Colls. v. Roth, 408 U.S. 564, 573 (1972).

16-E.3. Determine the correct order of the following ten citations according to *The Bluebook*, assuming that the citations appear in a single string citation in a law-review footnote. Write the number "1" beside the authority that should come first, "2" beside the second, and so on.

Carter v. Chrysler Corp., 743 So. 2d 456 (Ala. Civ. App. 1998).

Zeiler v. Deitsch, 500 F.3d 157, 162 (2d Cir. 2007).

United States v. Progressive, Inc., 467 F. Supp. 990, 992 (W.D. Wis. 1979).

People *ex rel.* Bluett v. Bd. of Trs. of Univ. of Ill., 134 N.E.2d 635, 670 (Ill. App. Ct. 1956).

Johnson v. Ford Motor Co., 113 P.3d 82 (Cal. 2005).

Novak v. C.M.S. Builders & Developers, 404 N.E.2d 918, 921 (Ill. App. Ct. 1980).

Med. & Surgical Soc'y of Montgomery County v. Weatherly, 75 Ala. 248 (1883).

UWM Post, Inc. v. Bd. of Regents of Univ. of Wis. Sys., 774 F. Supp. 1163 (E.D. Wis. 1991).

Rabel v. Ill. Wesleyan Univ., 514 N.E.2d 552, 554 (Ill. App. Ct. 1987).

Gallagher v. Delaney, 139 F.3d 338, 343 (2d Cir. 1998).

16-E.4. Determine the correct order of the following fifteen citations according to *The Bluebook*, assuming that the citations appear in a single string citation in a law-review footnote. Write the number "1" beside the citation that should come first, "2" beside the second, and so on.

Haw. Const. art. I, § 5.

Darby Dickerson, *Background Checks in the University Admissions Process: An Overview of Legal and Policy Considerations*, 34 J.U. & C.L. 419, 423 (2008).

Carter v. Chrysler Corp., 743 So. 2d 456 (Ala. Civ. App. 1998).

Zeiler v. Deitsch, 500 F.3d 157, 162 (2d Cir. 2007).

Ronald Dworkin, Taking Rights Seriously 75 (1978).

34 C.F.R. pt. 99 (2009).

U.S. Const. amend. XIV.

Shannon L. Noder, Comment, Morse v. Frederick: *Students' First Amendment Rights Restricted Again*, 43 Val. U. L. Rev. 859, 863 (2009).

42 U.S.C. §§ 12101–12213 (2006).

Novak v. C.M.S. Builders & Developers, 404 N.E.2d 918, 921 (Ill. App. Ct. 1980).

Bd. of Regents of State Colls. v. Roth, 408 U.S. 564, 573 (1972).

Civil Rights Act of 1968, Pub. L. No. 90-284, 82 Stat. 73 (1968).

Karen Arenson, *Worried Colleges Step Up Efforts over Suicide*, N.Y. Times, Dec. 3, 2004, at A20.

Immanuel Kant, *Universal Principles of Law and Morality: The Theory of Right, in* Law & Philosophy (Thomas W. Simon ed., 2001).

Edward Castronova, *On Virtual Economies* 15 (CESifo Working Paper No. 752, July 2002).

16-E.5. Determine the correct order of the following eight citations according to *The Bluebook*, assuming that the citations appear in a single string citation in a law-review footnote. Write the number "1" beside the citation that should come first, "2" beside the second, and so on. (Note: *The Bluebook* strongly recommends that when you use certain signals such as "*see also*" or "*compare with*," you append explanatory parentheticals to the citations that discuss the nature of the support or contradiction. To save space, the explanatory parentheticals are omitted from the citations below.)

E.g., Pavese v. Gen. Motors Corp., 1998 WL 57761 (E.D. Pa. 1998).
Compare Levan v. Capital Cities/ABC, Inc., 190 F.3d 1230, 1235 (11th Cir. 1999), *with* Zeiler v. Deitsch, 500 F.3d 157, 162 (2d Cir. 2007).
But see Tandia v. Gonzales, 236 Fed. Appx. 455, 457 n.4 (10th Cir. 2007).
Contra Bd. of Curators of Univ. of Mo. v. Horowitz, 435 U.S. 78, 85 (1978).
See generally Project Hope v. M/V Ibn Sina, 250 F.3d 67 (2d Cir. 2001).
Jenkins v. Missouri, 216 F.3d 720, 725 (8th Cir. 2000).
E.g., Smith v. TMC Acquisitions, LLC, No. 2:05CV3237-HRH, 2006 WL 2613426 (D. Ariz. June 22, 2006).
Accord Bd. of Regents of State Colls. v. Roth, 408 U.S. 564, 573 (1972).

16-E.6. The following citation is in correct *Manual* format. Write the citation in correct *Bluebook* format for the footnote of a law review article.

See e.g. Semrad v. Edina Realty, Inc., 493 N.W.2d 528, 533 (Minn. 1992).

16-E.7. The following string citation is in correct *Manual* format. Write the string citation in correct *Bluebook* format for the footnote of a law review article.

See e.g. William H. Rehnquist, *The Supreme Court* 243 (Knopf 2001); *see generally* Warren D. Wolfson, *Oral Argument: Does It Matter?* 35 Ind. L. Rev. 451 (2002); Tony Mauro, *What's Wrong with Oral Arguments?* 12 Leg. Times 9 (Apr. 16, 1990); Robert R. Salman, *Oral Argument: Improving Appellate Advocacy,* 12 Natl. L.J. 15 (Mar. 12, 1990).

16-E.8. Combine the two citations into a string citation according to *The Bluebook*.

See REHNQUIST, *supra* note 1, at 242.
See Nancy Winkelman, *Just a Brief Writer?*, 29 LITIG. 50, Summer 2003, at 50–51.

16-E.9. Combine the two citations into a string citation according to *The Bluebook*.

See Posner, *supra* note 11, at 4.
See REHNQUIST, *supra* note 1, at 235.

16-E.10. Combine the two citations into a string citation according to *The Bluebook*.

Wolfson, *supra* note 1, at 454.
But see Posner, *supra* note 11, at 3.

F. OTHER MINOR DIFFERENCES IN FORMATTING

The other minor differences in the formatting of *Manual* citations and *Bluebook* citations appear in all legal documents. These differences include the following:

- capitalization, as shown in *Bluebook* Rule 8;
- page spans, as shown in *Bluebook* Rule 3.2(a); and
- citations to cases available only on Westlaw or LexisNexis, as shown in *Bluebook* Rule 10.9(a)(ii).

The capitalization differences affect articles, conjunctions, and prepositions. Both *The Bluebook* and the *Manual* capitalize an article, conjunction, or preposition when it is the first word of a title or the first word following a colon. However, if a conjunction or preposition appears elsewhere in a title, the *Manual* does not capitalize it. *The Bluebook*, in contrast, capitalizes conjunctions and prepositions that are five letters or more in length no matter where they appear in a title.

When the pinpoint reference is a page span, *The Bluebook* requires removal of repetitious digits, yet retaining the last two digits; see Rule 3.2(a). The *Manual* gives you the choice of retaining all the digits in the span or retaining only the last two digits, as explained in Rule 5.3(b).

Bluebook citations to cases available only on Westlaw or LexisNexis must include the docket number; see Rule 10.8.1(a). This is optional in *Manual* style, as of the fourth edition; see *Manual* Rule 12.12(d).

This series of exercises helps you learn the minor differences in the citation formats. The exercises in this section are for all levels.

EXERCISE SET 16-F

ALL LEVELS: OTHER MINOR DIFFERENCES IN FORMATTING

Before beginning Exercise Set 16-F All Levels, review the following *Bluebook* rules and keep *The Bluebook* at hand as you work through the exercises:

- Rule 3.2(a), Pages
- Rule 8, Capitalization
- Rule 10.8.1(a), Cases available on electronic media

16-F.1. The following citation is in correct *Manual* format. Write the citation as it should appear in *Bluebook* format in a law review article's footnotes.

Lawton v. Tarr, 327 F. Supp. 670, 672–674 (E.D.N.C. 1971).

16-F.2. Your case note discusses a recent Iowa case whose LexisNexis caption is shown below. Write the citation as it should appear in *Bluebook* format in your case note's first footnote.

2001 U.S. Dist. LEXIS 1349, *

LIESLELOTTE SUSKIND, TRAVELERS INSURANCE COMPANY OF AMERICA, Plaintiffs, v. HOME DEPOT CORPORATION, TEST RITE PRODUCTS CORPORATION, Defendants.

CIVIL ACTION NO. 99-10575-NG

UNITED STATES DISTRICT COURT FOR THE DISTRICT OF MASSACHUSETTS

2001 U.S. Dist. LEXIS 1349

January 2, 2001, Decided

16-F.3. Your case note discusses a recent Alabama case whose Westlaw caption is shown below. Write the citation as it should appear in *Bluebook* format in your case note's first footnote.

— So.2d ——, 2008 WL 5195040 (Ala.Civ.App.)

Only the Westlaw citation is currently available.
NOT YET RELEASED FOR PUBLICATION.

Court of Civil Appeals of Alabama.

Alvin JOHNSON and The Johnson Realty Company, Inc.
v.
Darryl HALL, Sr., and Sondra D. Hall.

2070927.

16-F.4. Rewrite the following titles, capitalizing them according to Rule 3 in the *ALWD Citation Manual* **and** Rule 8 in *The Bluebook*.

16-F.4.a. Civil liability arising from the use of cell phone while driving

16-F.4.b. Employers' control or ownership of corporation as precluding receipt of benefits under state unemployment compensation provisions

16-F.4.c. Who is "executive officer" of insured within liability insurance policies

16-F.4.d. Getting beyond religion as science: "unstifling" worldview formation in American public education

16-F.4.e. Are you in or are you out? The effect of a prior criminal conviction on bar admission & a proposed national uniform standard

16-F.5. The following short-form citation to a book is in proper *Manual* format. Write the citation in proper *Bluebook* format for a footnote in a law review article.

Adams, *supra* n. 56, at 355.

16-F.6.   The following full citation is in proper *Manual* format. Write the citation in proper *Bluebook* format for a footnote in a law review article.

> Jane Massey Draper, *Retirement of Husband as Change of Circumstances Warranting Modification of Divorce Decree—Early Retirement*, 36 A.L.R.6th 1 (2008).

G.   NAME THAT FORMAT! EXERCISE: DIFFERENCES IN CITATION FORMAT IN COURT DOCUMENTS

As discussed above, the *Manual* and *Bluebook* styles are more similar than different. This is especially true for citations in documents submitted to a court. In fact, the differences between *Manual* and *Bluebook* citation formats in documents submitted to courts are very minor—the typeface differences discussed above in section A only apply to citations in law review articles.

But as was mentioned in the Introduction, prospective employers make judgments about your abilities from the citations you construct. Precision is important. The goal of the next exercise is to help you spot these minor differences between citation styles used in court documents.

Each question contains a citation correctly formatted for a **court document**. Identify whether the format is *Manual* style, *Bluebook* style, both *Manual* and *Bluebook* style, or neither *Manual* nor *Bluebook* style.

EXERCISE SET 16-G

ALL LEVELS: NAME THAT FORMAT! EXERCISE

> While working on Exercise Set 16-G All Levels, keep the *Manual* and *The Bluebook* at hand as you work through the exercises.

16-G.1.   *Meritor Sav. Bank v. Vinson*, 477 U.S. 57, 60 (U.S. 1986).

   a. *Manual* format
   b. *Bluebook* format
   c. Both *Manual* and *Bluebook* formats
   d. Neither *Manual* nor *Bluebook* format

16-G.2.   *J.M. v. Webster County Bd. of Educ.*, 534 S.E.2d 50, 55 (W. Va. 2000).

   a. *Manual* format
   b. *Bluebook* format
   c. Both *Manual* and *Bluebook* formats
   d. Neither *Manual* nor *Bluebook* format

16-G.3.   *Am. Nat'l Fire Ins. Co. v. L Constr. Co.*, 920 P.2d 192, 194 (Wash. Ct. App. 1996).

   a. *Manual* format
   b. *Bluebook* format
   c. Both *Manual* and *Bluebook* formats
   d. Neither *Manual* nor *Bluebook* format

16-G.4.   Richard Michael Fischl & Jeremy Paul, *Getting to Maybe: How to Excel on Law School Exams* (1999).

   a. *Manual* format
   b. *Bluebook* format
   c. Both *Manual* and *Bluebook* formats
   d. Neither *Manual* nor *Bluebook* format

16-G.5.   Catharine A. MacKinnon, *Vindication and Resistance: A Response to the Carnegie Mellon Study of Pornography in Cyberspace*, 83 Geo. Wash. L. Rev. 1959, 1963 (1995).

   a. *Manual* format
   b. *Bluebook* format
   c. Both *Manual* and *Bluebook* formats
   d. Neither *Manual* nor *Bluebook* format

16-G.6.   Sarah A. Klein, *Protection or Persecution?*, Am. Med. News, Feb. 15, 1999, at 20.

   a. *Manual* format
   b. *Bluebook* format
   c. Both *Manual* and *Bluebook* formats
   d. Neither *Manual* nor *Bluebook* format

16-G.7.   Ryan Gill, Case Note, *State Immunity and the Americans with Disabilities Act After* Board of the University of Alabama v. Garrett, 74 U. Colo. L. Rev. 1239 (2003).

   a. *Manual* format
   b. *Bluebook* format
   c. Both *Manual* and *Bluebook* formats
   d. Neither *Manual* nor *Bluebook* format

16-G.8.   *Gregory*, 597 F.2d at 1089–90.

   a. *Manual* format
   b. *Bluebook* format
   c. Both *Manual* and *Bluebook* formats
   d. Neither *Manual* nor *Bluebook* format

16-G.9.   § 350.34, Fla. Stat. (2008).

   a. *Manual* format
   b. *Bluebook* format
   c. Both *Manual* and *Bluebook* formats
   d. Neither *Manual* nor *Bluebook* format

16-G.10. 28 C.F.R. § 35.130(b)(7) (2009).

    a. *Manual* format
    b. *Bluebook* format
    c. Both *Manual* and *Bluebook* formats
    d. Neither *Manual* nor *Bluebook* format

16-G.11. *Sotolongo v. State*, 530 So. 2d 514, 515 (Fla. 2d DCA 1988).

    a. *Manual* format
    b. *Bluebook* format
    c. Both *Manual* and *Bluebook* formats
    d. Neither *Manual* nor *Bluebook* format

16-G.12. S. Rep. No. 95-797, at 4 (1978), *reported in* 1978 U.S.C.C.A.N. 9260, 9263.

    a. *Manual* format
    b. *Bluebook* format
    c. Both *Manual* and *Bluebook* formats
    d. Neither *Manual* nor *Bluebook* format

H. CAPSTONE CONVERSION EXERCISE

The citations in the following twelve footnotes are in correct *Manual* format. On your answer sheet, convert the footnotes to correct *Bluebook* format for law review footnotes. *Hint*: Think about the differences discussed above and make a checklist of the differences. In the conversion process, take one step at a time. For example, start with typeface, and then move to order of authorities, and so forth.

EXERCISE SET 16-H

ALL LEVELS: CAPSTONE CONVERSION EXERCISE

While working on Exercise Set 16-H All Levels, keep *The Bluebook* at hand as you work through the exercises.

1. Michael J. Lynch, *An Impossible Task but Everybody Has to Do It—Teaching Legal Research in Law Schools*, 89 L. Libr. J. 415, 415 (1997). But at its simplest, "legal research is nothing more than locating the relevant law." Jasper L. Cummings, Jr., *Legal Research in Federal Taxation*, in *Tax Planning for Domestic & Foreign Partnerships, LLCs, Joint Ventures & Other Strategic Alliances* 739, 745 (Practising L. Inst. 2007).

2. *Research Skills for Lawyers and Law Students* 3 (Thomson/West, white paper 2007) [hereinafter *Research Skills*]; Byron D. Cooper, *The Integration of Theory, Doctrine, and Practice in Legal Education*, 1 J. ALWD 50, 50 (2002) (mentioning over five years ago "the effort to integrate theory and practice in American law schools has been

gathering momentum"); *see* Matthew C. Cordon, *Beyond Mere Competency: Advanced Legal Research in a Practice-Oriented Curriculum*, 55 Baylor L. Rev. 1, 3 (2003) ("Improvement in legal research instruction has coincided with a rather spirited debate regarding the role of law schools as training grounds for training lawyers, not merely as graduate schools teaching about the theory of law."). The integration of skills-and-values-across-the-curriculum discussion resulted in two books: Roy Stuckey et al., *Best Practices for Legal Education: A Vision and a Road Map* (Clin. Leg. Educ. Assn. 2007), and William M. Sullivan et al., *Educating Lawyers: Preparation for the Profession of Law* (Jossey-Bass 2007). The topic of integrating skills and values into the law school curriculum has resulted in discussions at the institutional, state, regional, and national levels.

3. In his recent article discussing the book *Educating Lawyers*, Richard A. Leiter, Law Library Director at the University of Nebraska-Lincoln, argued that "[l]egal research is rarely mentioned as a lawyering skill." Richard A. Leiter, *The Missing Lawyering Skill*, AALL Spectrum 22, 22 (July 2008) (discussing Sullivan et al., *supra* n. 2). Leiter explained why legal research was not part of the discussion in *Educating Lawyers*—the authors give the impression "that the simple act of reading cases and analyzing them imparts legal research skills." *Id.* (discussing Sullivan et al., *supra* n. 2). Learning and developing research skills requires much more than reading and analyzing cases; the law student or attorney must know how to find the cases first.

4. *See* Ellie Margolis, *Surfin' Safari—Why Competent Lawyers Should Research on the Web*, 10 Yale J.L. & Tech. 82, 84–85 (2007).

5. *See* Robert C. Berring & Elizabeth A. Edinger, *Finding the Law* 4 (12th ed., Thomson/West 2005) (stating that "[r]arely does a casebook require the student to read external materials, and when the students in a first year law school class are assigned 'outside' reading, it is usually put on reserve in the law library," which means that the students do not need to do any research to obtain the "outside" reading); Davalene Cooper, *Adopting the "Stepchild" into the Legal Academic Community: Creating a Program for Learning Legal Research Skills*, in *Expert Views on Improving the Quality of Legal Research Education in the United States* 11, 13 (West Publg. Co. 1992) [hereinafter *Expert Views*] (discussing how historically, skills training was not part of legal education, but acknowledging that the shift towards incorporating skills-based education was beginning); Robert C. Berring, *Collapse of the Structure of the Legal Research Universe: The Imperative of Digital Information*, 69 Wash. L. Rev. 9, 32 (1994) (remarking that fifteen years ago, Professor Berring was amazed that "law students still read casebooks, desiccated to collections of appellate opinions"); Thomas A. Woxland, *Why Can't Johnny Research? Or It All Started with Christopher Columbus Langdell*, 81 L. Libr. J. 451, 456–457 (1989) (stating that "the case method, in concert with its bibliographical offspring—the casebook—has made library research (and thus the learning of research skills) largely *irrelevant* in modern legal education" (emphasis added), and discussing how the casebooks gather all the necessary material into one book).

   The "substantive" courses in law school "train[ ] the student[s] to recognize the legal issues confronted in practice on a day-to-day basis." Bonita K. Roberts & Linda L. Schlueter, *Legal Research Guide: Patterns and Practice* 1 (3d ed., Michie Co. 1996). However, "[a]n equally important task . . . is to locate the sources of that substantive law." *Id.*

6. Robin K. Mills, *Legal Research Instruction in Law Schools, The State of the Art or, Why Law School Graduates Do Not Know How to Find the Law*, 70 L. Libr. J. 343,

343 (1977); Sandra Sadow & Benjamin R. Beede, *Library Instruction in American Law Schools*, 68 L. Libr. J. 27, 30 (1975). And when a student starts clerking at a law firm, there is not a casebook available that provides the background of the law, the fact patterns, and the applicable cases for a specific client. *Partnership and Solutions for Preparing Job-Ready Attorneys* 10 (Thomson/West, white paper July 2008); *see* Carol L. Golden, *Teaching Legal Research as an Integral Step in Legal Problem Solving*, in *Expert Views*, *supra* n. 5, at 37, 39 (mentioning that some students and first-year associates will consult their old casebooks as "a starting point for conducting legal research." This is not always a wise thing to do.).

7. Mary Whisner, *On Not Doing Research*, 97 L. Libr. J. 391, 393 (2005) (explaining that during closed-book law school exams, students are simply drawing on what they already know). If attorneys did not conduct legal research and only relied on what they remembered about the law, this would not be a good situation. *Society of American Law Teachers Statement on the Bar Exam*, 52 J. Leg. Educ. 446, 447 (2002).

8. Whisner, *supra* n. 7, at 393 (discussing how students prepare by using resources and materials required for the course; very limited research skills are used or required).

9. Steven M. Barkan, *Should Legal Research Be Included on the Bar Exam? An Exploration of the Question*, 99 L. Libr. J. 403, 410 (2007); *see* Terrence R. White, *National Bar Exam for Idaho???* 51 Advoc. (Idaho) 6, 6 (Mar.–Apr. 2008) (stating that the MPT tests "fundamental skills in a realistic situation," but in the real world, an attorney is not given a "Library"); *see generally* ABA Sec. Leg. Educ. & Admis. to B., *Legal Education and Professional Development—An Educational Continuum, Report of the Task Force on the Law Schools and the Profession: Narrowing the Gap* 281–282 (ABA 1992) (discussing the pros and cons of the MPT; one of the cons discussed is how the MPT does not test other lawyering skills, like research, that are identified in the *MacCrate Report*); Andrea A. Curcio, *A Better Bar: Why and How the Existing Bar Exam Should Change*, 81 Neb. L. Rev. 363, 378–379 (2002) (discussing the problems with the MPT and how the MPT may be testing the same skills that are tested in the essay portion of the bar exam).

10. Helene S. Shapo & Christina L. Kunz, *Teaching Research as Part of an Integrated LR & W Course*, 4 Persps. 78, 78 (1996) (quoting Robert C. Berring & Elizabeth A. Edinger, *Finding the Law* 2 (10th ed., West Publg. Co. 1995)); *see* Golden, *supra* n. 6, at 39 ("Beginning law students often do not understand the relationship between the casebooks they use in their substantive courses and the case reporters they learn about in their legal research class.").

11. Mills, *supra* n. 6, at 343. Professor Woxland mentioned,

> It is the casebook itself that has kept many students ignorant of the laboratory; it is the casebook that has obviated the need for library research for most law students. The casebook, by gathering all cases and materials necessary for a course into one volume, has become a substitute for the library. It has condensed and recompiled sources that are scattered throughout dozens of reporters, codes, periodicals, and secondary literature into a portable law library and has freed the student from the need to master even the most basic research skills.

Woxland, *supra* n. 5, at 457 (noting that the cases are heavily edited). A survey of law firm librarians from across the United States reported the following response, "Students seemed to be force-fed in law schools—they are given '*canned*' materials in law school and then they are upset with the real world when it doesn't provide them with the same service." Joan S. Howland & Nancy J. Lewis, *The Effectiveness of Law School Legal Research Training Programs*, 40 J. Leg. Educ. 381, 389 (1990) (emphasis added). Professor Woxland said it well when he wrote, "[T]he research skills—such as they are—of the vast majority of students (except those who participate in such extracurricular activities as the law review or moot court) are left to atrophy until the new lawyers begin professional practice." Woxland, *supra* n. 5, at 455.

12. *E.g.* Berring & Edinger, *supra* n. 5, at 4; Pamela Lysaght, *Opening Remarks*, 1 J. ALWD 1, 1 (2002); Sadow & Beede, *supra* n. 6, at 30. Unlike the substantive courses, in which the rules are provided in the cases that the students read, in legal research and writing classes, the students must conduct research and find the sources that provide the applicable rules. Amy E. Sloan, *Erasing Lines: Integrating the Law School Curriculum*, 1 J. ALWD 3, 5 (2002). Also, the edited cases in the casebooks do not contain West headnotes and other annotations that students will find when conducting research. John D. Edwards, *Teaching Legal Research: Evaluating Options*, in *Expert Views*, *supra* n. 5, at 29, 39; *see* Berring & Edinger, *supra* n. 5, at 4 (discussing how casebooks are organized in certain ways in order to make certain points).